VATICAN SECRET DIPLOMACY

CHARLES R. GALLAGHER, S.J.

Vatican
Secret Diplomacy

JOSEPH P. HURLEY AND POPE PIUS XII

YALE UNIVERSITY PRESS   NEW HAVEN & LONDON

Set in Scala and Scala Sans by Duke & Company, Devon, Pennsylvania.
Printed in the United States of America by Sheridan Books, Ann Arbor, Michigan.

Library of Congress Cataloging-in-Publication Data

Gallagher, Charles R., 1965–
Vatican secret diplomacy : Joseph P. Hurley and Pope Pius XII / Charles R. Gallagher.
p. cm.
Includes bibliographical references and index.
ISBN 978-0-300-12134-6 (cloth : alk. paper)

1. Hurley, Joseph P. 2. Pius XII, Pope, 1876–1958. 3. World War, 1939–1945—
Religious aspects—Catholic Church. 4. Catholic Church—Foreign relations. I. Title.
BX4705.H873G35 2008
282.092—dc22
[B]

2007043743

A catalogue record for this book is available from the British Library.

The paper in this book meets the guidelines for permanence and durability of the Committee on Production Guidelines for Book Longevity of the Council on Library Resources.

10 9 8 7 6 5 4 3 2 1

To my father and in loving memory of my mother

CONTENTS

ACKNOWLEDGMENTS

I OWE A DEEP DEBT of personal gratitude to a number of people who inspired, encouraged, and cheerfully assisted in bringing this biography to press. Dr. Steven M. Avella suggested the subject for my dissertation at Marquette University and has continued to be a source of inspiration. His astute counsel and passion for the craft of history have influenced me greatly.

This study of Vatican diplomacy could not have been undertaken without the consent and permission of a number of Roman Catholic clerics. First, I am deeply indebted to the Most Reverend John J. Snyder, D.D., who graciously allowed access to Archbishop Hurley's extensive archive. Without Bishop Snyder's esteem for freedom of research, this project could not have been conceived. I am indebted to Rev. Keith R. Brennan, former Chancellor of the Diocese of St. Augustine, and Rev. Michael Morgan, the current Chancellor of the Diocese of St. Augustine, for their many kindnesses.

There are many Jesuits to thank. My Provincial, the Very Reverend Thomas J. Regan, S.J., has been supportive and helpful in so many ways. In 2006 it was my good fortune to be assigned to the Jesuit community at the College of the Holy Cross, where this project was finalized. The constant support of so many fine and lively scholars, and especially Rectors Anthony J. Kuzniewski, S.J., and James M. Hayes, S.J., was crucial to its completion.

I am indebted to many who provided interviews and practical advice, especially James Martin, S.J., of *America* magazine; Ms. Kathleen Bagg-Morgan, of the Diocese of St. Augustine; Monsignor Frank M. Mouch; and the late Raymond E. Brown, S.S. The late Monsignor John P. McNulty, Archbishop Hurley's valiant secretary at the Belgrade nunciature, provided many helpful insights. Mrs. Anne Bryant very kindly allowed access to the diaries of her mother, Caroline D. Phillips. Professor David J. O'Brien, of the College of the Holy Cross, supplied pivotal advice. I am truly grateful to the anonymous reviewers of the manuscript for Yale University Press. This is a much better book as a result of their generosity, encouragement, and critical guidance.

I wish to acknowledge the help of a number of scholars who have assisted me in various stages of the writing of this book, especially Rev. Gerald P. Fogarty, S.J., of the University of Virginia; Michael Gannon, of the University of Florida; Michael Phayer and Patrick Carey, of Marquette University; and Dianne Kirby, of the University of Ulster. Athan Theoharis of Marquette University read the entire manuscript, made copious suggestions, and assisted in the analysis of various intelligence-related documents. His early enthusiasm for the project gave me a real boost in confidence.

Many archivists and librarians kindly lent their expert assistance. I am especially grateful to W. John Shepherd, of the American Catholic History Research Center at the Catholic University of America; William Kevin Cawley, of the University of Notre Dame Archives; Diana Antul, of the College of the Holy Cross Dinand Library; Phil Runkel, at Marquette University Archives; John Fox, of the Federal Bureau of Investigation; Nicholas Scheetz, at Georgetown University Special Collections; Ms. Carol A. Leadenham, at the Hoover Institution Archives; Leslie A. Morris, of Harvard University's Houghton Library; and Milton O. Gustafson, Senior Specialist for Diplomatic Records at the U.S. National Archives.

The support of Mrs. Mercedes Hughes, Archbishop Hurley's loving niece, was invaluable in the completion of this project. Her benefaction was both deeply generous and entirely unconditional. A Cyril E. Smith Fellowship at Marquette University was instrumental in the development from thesis to book. Last but not least, I wish to express my gratitude to my editor at Yale University Press, Chris Rogers, and his assistant, Laura

Davulis. Special thanks go to Ann Hawthorne, who edited the manuscript with a keen eye and offered immensely valuable advice. I cannot thank her enough for her brilliant work. All have shown immense patience and kindness and have helped me to become a better writer and a better historian.

Introduction

THIS BOOK is a political biography of a religious person. It is the story of one man's struggle to clarify patriotic loyalty to his country in light of his commitments as a Roman Catholic leader in time of war, both hot and cold. Joseph Patrick Hurley was a man of prayer, patriotism, and sacrifice for his church. He engaged at high levels in the diplomacy of war and peace, both for his church and at the behest of his government. Much of his diplomatic work was carried out in secret and was deliberately hidden from his close friends and colleagues. Such was the style of Vatican diplomacy during the era of World War II. From the nineteenth century through the onset of the Cold War, the diplomatic negotiations of most countries were conducted behind closed doors, in accordance with strict notions of protocol, and treaties were finalized by a select handful of accredited principals. By the 1960s secrecy had given way to openness in negotiation. The success of diplomacy was measured less by the substance of undisclosed consultations and more by the "spirit" generated in public conferences. Although Hurley would live to see this revolution in diplomacy, his own endeavors took place in a very different environment.

The first reason to investigate Hurley's diplomatic work connects precisely to the unpublicized nature of his dealings. Since the Vatican's Secret Archives for most of the period in which he worked are currently closed to researchers, Hurley's reminiscences and attitudes provide a unique real-time glimpse into the debates surrounding the Holy See's position on Nazism, wartime neutrality, antisemitism, and the Holocaust. They are important, as well, because they reflect an American perspective on Vatican procedure, posture, and policy. Hurley's attitudes and experiences also embody the struggles of a first-generation American cleric to reconcile his assimilation into American culture with his loyalty to his church. In many ways his life highlights various areas of conflict and stress encountered by many twentieth-century Catholics as they struggled to acculturate to the larger American society.

Through much of his political and diplomatic career, Hurley served as the Roman Catholic bishop of the Diocese of St. Augustine, presiding over the expansion and consolidation of Catholicism in Florida during a period of extraordinary ecclesiastical growth. As one of the first modern Sunbelt bishops, he moved his diocese into the new religious landscape with prescience, aplomb, and vigor.[1]

Until now Hurley's diplomatic career has been unexplored. Given the length and breadth of his career, and the fact that he was the first American to be raised to the equivalent rank of nuncio, or Vatican ambassador, the omission seems surprising. A major reason for this silence is that his official archive was held under seal for many years, but other factors also played a part. With few notable exceptions—as many Florida priests recall—Hurley remained tight-lipped about his work for the Vatican. He refused to speak about it with his priests unless they had been hand-picked to join him in diplomacy. When the *St. Petersburg Times* chose its top twenty-five Floridians of the twentieth century, Archbishop Hurley was included on the basis of his spiritual leadership in the Diocese of St. Augustine. No mention was made of his diplomatic career.[2]

To the American Catholic public of his era, Hurley was almost invisible, even though he held a Vatican position previously occupied by one of the most media-conscious American prelates of the twentieth century—Francis Cardinal Spellman of New York. By 1950, lost or more likely unknown was that Hurley had conversed privately with an emperor, a prince, two popes, and a prime minister and had stared down a communist dictator. He corresponded confidentially with three U.S. presidents. Characteristically, Hurley would have wanted his diplomacy to remain invisible. Unless moral duty called him to speak out, he preferred to act behind the scenes. But much as he would have wished otherwise, Hurley's public life begs for examination for many reasons, not the least of which is that he was the first American to practice diplomacy under the two most studied popes in Roman Catholic church history—Pius XI and XII.

In 2000 papal historian Frank J. Coppa claimed that more has been written about the papacy of Pius XII than about all previous popes combined.[3] Yet in the voluminous scholarship that has grown up around the pontiff, there is very little evidence of firsthand criticism of papal policy from within the Vatican. The record on Pope Pius XII has been constructed largely from the notes of Vatican dignitaries who either set or agreed with papal policy or of accredited diplomats who may have attempted to color the reports to their foreign ministries. A large part of the debate about Pope Pius XII has been constructed from moral arguments generated at least five years after the pope's death and from carefully selected documentation released many years afterward.

Joseph Patrick Hurley worked under and with Cardinal Eugenio Pacelli for nearly twenty years, and he kept informative Vatican diaries that are explored here for the first time. He is a little-known personality within the ranks and history of Vatican diplomacy. With one or two notable exceptions, he stayed in the background and allowed others to claim headlines. For this reason, he does not have the name recognition of American contemporaries such as the photogenic Francis Cardinal Spellman, the telegenic Rev. Fulton Sheen, or the politically admired Edward Cardinal Mooney.

As an official diplomat of the Holy See, Hurley worked behind the scenes during the pivotal years from 1927 to 1940. He was privy to the leanings, deliberations, and pressures that enveloped the Vatican in the run-up to World War II. He was at the center of a controversial shift in papal policy and commented copiously on this in his diaries. The Hurley diaries offer a firsthand assessment of the controversies, anxieties, and demands that beset Vatican decision-makers as they struggled to maintain neutrality in a war that increasingly thrust aside moral voices. Over time, Hurley came to see the Holy See's wartime program as essentially flawed: he was convinced that Pope Pius XII was overly fearful about communism, and not fearful enough about Nazism. The pontiff's attitude and actions (or lack of them) have been abundantly discussed by historians for more than four decades, with no clear resolution. When Hurley spoke up on such issues within the Vatican's walls, Pius XII responded with what amounted to an ecclesiastical banishment. This study aims to discover what drove Hurley to voice opposing views, even to the detriment of his own ecclesiastical career.[4]

No single issue precipitated Hurley's behind-the-scenes resistance to Pope Pius XII's larger diplomatic programs. Rather, his unfriendliness to the wartime papal policy drew its impetus from a combination of his own "Americanized" political views, an adherence to the tenets of the new Catholic "muscular Christianity" of his day, and the lionization of his benevolent papal mentor, Pope Pius XI. The triple threads of Americanism, muscular Christianity, and unshakable esteem for Pope Pius XI formed part of the texture of Hurley's complex and heady diplomatic career. As we shall see in the following chapters, Hurley's enculturation as a Roman Catholic into American life intensified the political stress points between Vatican wartime strategy and American interests.

The process of Americanization that Hurley embraced as a young man played a significant role in shaping his later views on Vatican policy and the policies of Pope Pius XII. At an early age he was inculcated with strong beliefs in the value of democracy, freedom, and the projection of military power in the service of democracy. For Hurley, both World War I and World War II became tests of patriotism and allegiance. More importantly, they provided cases of how Catholics might justly approve of the use of military force. His wartime work as a churchman helped him to assimilate into American culture and reveal his attitude on the role Americans should play in the nation. As American Catholic historian Philip Gleason has pointed out, "the *intensity* of public life is heightened in wartime," and such intensification forced Catholics to come to terms with exactly how they fitted into the larger American project.[5]

Since there was no antiwar or pacifist wing of American Catholicism in 1914 to influence him otherwise, Hurley had no problem accommodating the belief that Catholic participation in the U.S. armed forces was both commendable and fitting. Indeed the military offered a speedy path to assimilation and exhibited Catholic patriotism to a still suspicious Protestant American majority. Philip Gleason notes that many Catholics "were also moved by a deep and genuine patriotism that was linked to the idealistic goals so eloquently set forth by Woodrow Wilson." Hurley imbibed the "deep and genuine patriotism" of the war, and indeed even as a student of divinity he longed to be on the front lines in France with his school chums.

As historian William A. Halsey has observed, World War I served as "a mechanism of collective awakening" to American ideals for a generation of Catholics one step removed from immigration. Joseph Patrick Hurley received his theological education as a Roman Catholic priest at precisely the time of this awakening.[6]

In 1921 U.S. Catholic bishops declared their approval of America's emergence as a world power. "The very Marrow" of Catholicism in America, they argued in the report titled *American Catholics in the War*, was "the blessed harmony that has always existed, and which now exists, and which, please God, shall always exist, between the spirit of the Catholic church and the spirit of the United States of America."[7] The "blessed harmony" thesis was one that Joseph Hurley appropriated as a young man, stayed with him through his entry into the Holy See's diplomatic corps, and ultimately swayed him to clash with Pope Pius XII as Vatican wartime policy diverged from U.S. global strategy. Later Hurley's "blessed harmony" would be shattered a second time amid American Cold War political realities.

Hurley's ecclesiastical career provides an important glimpse into how papal wartime policy was formed from the perspective of a Vatican insider who was able to observe and influence events as they unfolded. As diplomatic historian T. Michael Ruddy has pointed out, "one cannot clearly grasp how policy develops without delving beyond top-level policymakers and examining the thinking of those in the second echelon who also contributed to policy formation."[8] Joseph Patrick Hurley attained positions of influence during World War II and the Cold War that were recognized by both the United States and the Holy See. During the 1930s he crucially influenced how the Vatican reacted to the antisemitic Detroit priest Rev. Charles Coughlin. By late 1940 he became convinced that the wartime policy of the U.S. government was right and that of the Holy See wrong. The decision of Pope Pius XII to move him abruptly out of the Vatican to the Diocese of St. Augustine shows that Hurley's clandestine prodemocracy propaganda efforts made him a liability to the Vatican's new guiding principle of nonaligned neutrality.

During World War II, Hurley began to work independently of the Holy See and other American bishops. Dissatisfied with papal foot-dragging and the neutrality of the American bishops, he aligned himself with the U.S. Department of State and began to act under the direction of American government officials. In this respect, his activities bordered on those of a renegade or rogue bishop within the American Catholic hierarchy. Many of Hurley's wartime activities with the Roosevelt administration, the U.S. Office of War Information, and the lower echelons of British intelligence were kept secret at the time. Reviewed here for the first time, they were efforts of "black" propaganda, or the use of false source attributions in the media and in public discourse. Hurley's black propaganda work with the Roosevelt administration during World War II defied the prevailing anticatholicism of the day. As is clear from the furor that erupted in 1939 when President Roosevelt sent a personal representative to the pope, most mainline and evangelical Protestants in the United States were still wary of the Vatican and vehemently opposed the creation of formal links to the Holy See's diplomatic apparatus. Operating out of public view, Hurley's propaganda activity reflected a strong belief that he was working from a position of moral righteousness. Had it come to light that a former Vatican official was working secretly with the U.S. Department of State and was in some degree of contact with President Roosevelt for secret missions abroad, the fallout could have been ecumenically disastrous for Catholics and politically embarrassing for the administration. Despite these risks, between 1940 and 1945, from his see in Florida, he dedicated all his political energy and ecclesiastical leadership to assisting the U.S. government in prosecuting a war that was aimed squarely at defeating evil. His robust secret activity during the war reflected his disdain for the Vatican's equivocal wartime diplomacy.

In 1943 Hurley became the only Roman Catholic bishop to issue a moral clarion call to Catholics to speak out against the extermination of the Jews taking place in the Nazi death camps. In an April 1943 editorial in his diocesan newspaper, Hurley claimed that "the very basis of the Roman Catholic faith" compelled Catholics to challenge the "orgies of extermination" being perpetrated against the Jewish people. It should be "an honor," he echoed for Roman Catholics, to take up the "defense of the Jews" being sent to the death camps of occupied Europe.[9]

In a twist of irony, after World War II Hurley's fierce antinazism suddenly restored him to the good graces of Vatican policymakers. Searching for candidates acceptable to both communist leaders and American diplomats, the Vatican sent Hurley to Cold War Yugoslavia, where for five years he faced up to the communist dictator Marshal Josip Broz Tito, won diplomatic battles, and worked ever more closely with U.S. officials. During this time his relationship with Pope Pius XII again became fractious as he confronted the pontiff on the issue of Archbishop Aloysius Stepinac's removal from Croatia and his perception that the pope was not taking a hard enough line toward Tito. In 1945 he vigorously resisted a summons from Pius to vacate his post in the Balkans. Hurley's personality and political philosophy were as complex as the diplomacy he was commissioned to undertake. He was an antisemite conditioned by the culture of his times who, under the force of inner moral compulsion, issued one of the most gripping philosemitic statements uttered by a Roman Catholic leader during World War II. He was an outspoken antinazi who offered political absolution to a group of Croatian Catholics who had sided with Croatia's Nazi puppet state during World War II. He was an ardent anticommunist who by and large dismissed communism as a threat to Catholicism during World War II. He was known to many diocesan priests under his care as an eminent man of the church, a stately prelate who always fit the role of churchman to the highest degree. Yet when Vatican policy diverged from aggressively attacking Nazism, aiding the Allies, or combating communism, he undertook clandestine activity that essentially undermined the prevailing policy of Vatican neutrality.

This study is not intended to be a survey of the debates and competing interests that embroiled the Vatican during World War II and the Cold War. It is a political biography of an ecclesiastical diplomat. Larger thematic surveys have yet to be written, and any comprehensive study of papal diplomacy during the period surely will require the opening of the Vatican Secret Archives. At the same time, an examination of Joseph Patrick Hurley's career touches on many issues connected to current debates surrounding the Holy See's diplomatic strategy during World War II and the Cold War. In 1940, while Hurley was practicing secret diplomacy, the diplomatic correspondent for the London *Times* unknowingly described a Hurley speech as representing "the voice of the Vatican."[10] It is hoped that adding this heretofore hidden voice to the diplomatic and religious historiography of the era will further illuminate our understanding of Vatican and U.S. diplomacy.

CHAPTER ONE

A Priest in the Family

THE LATE SPRING OF 1940 was a period of hot diplomatic action in Rome. As the Luftwaffe dropped bombs on Britain, German foreign minister Joachim von Ribbentrop sat down with Benito Mussolini and gleefully recounted the recent successes of the Nazi war machine. Poland, Denmark, Sweden, and Norway were under German control. On June 22 France fell to humiliating defeat, signing an armistice with Nazi officials at Rethondes, where in 1918 the French had played the role of victors at the armistice ending World War I. "The press hints that the 'final phase' of war has been decided," broadcaster William Shirer wrote from Berlin; "the military situation is so rosy for the Axis that Ribbentrop and the Duce actually spent most of their time planning the 'new order' in Europe and Africa." The Roman consultations between Mussolini and Ribbentrop were being watched carefully just paces away on the Vatican hill.[1]

Pope Pius XII had met privately with Ribbentrop at the Vatican on March 11, 1940. "No one feels, however, that that the pope will stand up to him," Caroline Phillips, wife of U.S. ambassador William Phillips, wrote in her diary at the time. "The pope's reputation is of a saintly man, but a very diplomatic one, not a courageous fighter like Julius II or Gregory VIII. . . . I believe that this is a war of spiritual forces," Phillips assured herself, counting more on the intercession of saints "on the other side" than on the earthly diplomacy of men.[2]

8

For his part, Pope Pius XII attempted to be as firm as diplomatic protocol allowed. Ribbentrop was warned not to wear the Nazi swastika to his audience, nor was his limousine allowed to fly the Nazi flag. An announcement was placed in the Vatican's official newspaper, *Osservatore Romano*, making clear that the request for the meeting had come from the Germans. Such measures were designed to show that the pope was meeting with the Nazi foreign minister reluctantly. But diplomatic pricks held no terrors for the erratic Ribbentrop. "Everybody seems afraid of the Devil in Germany," Phillips despondently confided to her diary, "even Christ's vicar on earth."[3]

Reportedly, it was at that meeting in March 1940 that the newly elected pope gently leaned over to Ribbentrop and asked his monumental question: "Do you believe in God?" "I do believe in God," replied Ribbentrop. "Then," the pope responded, "your conscience should tell you what is right and what is wrong." This brief invitation to rally Ribbentrop's grotesquely malformed conscience was as straightforward a challenge as Pope Pius XII could muster on that occasion. Commenting on these events, a despondent friend writing Caroline Phillips from Vienna announced of the newly elected Pope Pius XII that she could not "help thinking if another had been on that throne, the dove would not have perched upon it."[4]

Perhaps the pope believed that the new relationship developing between the Vatican and the United States would offer a stronger arm with which to sow the seeds of justice and peace. In 1940 U.S. representation at the Vatican was embodied in President Roosevelt's newly appointed envoy, Myron C. Taylor. The former chief financial officer of United States Steel, Taylor also directed the American Telephone & Telegraph Company, the First National Bank of New York, and the New York Central Railroad. The move from captain of industry to envoy to the barque of Peter was carried off with "supreme tact," in the eyes of one observer, belying his cumbersome title of "The President's Personal Representative to His Holiness Pope Pius XII." Regardless of titles, it was in Myron Taylor that the Vatican may have glimpsed its own future. Symbolically at least, Taylor epitomized the melding of all things that the United States would mean to the Catholic church over the next fifty years: wealth, global expansion, strength, and religious pluralism.[5]

Though commissioned to seek a "parallel endeavor for peace" with Pope Pius XII, the "businessman of action" was finding it difficult to meet even the basic goals of his mission. Roosevelt had appointed Taylor with great haste on December 23, 1939. The panzers had already overrun Poland, and German forces were preparing to attack France and the Benelux countries when Taylor arrived in Rome. Before Taylor, who offered direct representation between the two heads of state, U.S. diplomatic communications with the Vatican had been sporadic, cumbersome, and fraught with difficulties. Most contact was either low-level or secret. The reasons for this were political, constitutional, and above all cultural. "In these days of tranquil politeness between Catholic and Protestant," historian John S. Conway has written, "it is hard to credit, let alone recapture, the virulence of feelings of earlier years." Traditional American Protestant anti-romanism made wartime Vatican contacts extremely sensitive. One U.S. ambassador, Joseph P. Kennedy, was reluctant to communicate officially with the pope within weeks of the German invasion of Poland, "because whether I wished it or not, it would put a political aspect on it."[6]

Generally speaking, it was "the common objective of preservation of peace [that] drew the United States and the Vatican together" on the eve of World War II. The Roosevelt White House believed that "two of the world's greatest moral voices" speaking together might have some effect in maintaining peace in Europe. But on June 10, 1940, Italy joined the Axis and declared war on France and England. One month later, five squadrons of British fighters met sixty-four German bombers as the Battle of Britain began.[7]

Taylor's peace initiative disintegrated into failure with each dropping bomb, and it was decided that he would return to the United States claiming health reasons. As he took leave of the Vatican, he had an unprecedented seventy-minute audience with Pope Pius XII on August 22. Little is known of what transpired during that meeting. Since the official Vatican archives are currently closed to researchers, all that is known of the meeting comes from the notes of an obscure but astute American cleric serving in the Vatican's diplomatic corps, Monsignor Joseph Patrick Hurley. In his personal notes on the meeting, Hurley recorded that Taylor "asked a thousand questions" and that Pius answered "as well as possible." As Hurley put it down, Taylor's first leave-taking of Pope Pius XII ended on an awkward note when the gaunt and sallow Pius abruptly "kissed [Taylor] as he accompanied him to the door." The ill-chosen papal osculation caught the burly financier off guard and "left him speechless."[8]

"Few thought the ailing Envoy Taylor would ever return [to the United States]," *Time* magazine announced in a brief column titled "Diplomats on the Move." "But the Holy See's diplomacy, canniest in the world, has already taken a step to neutralize the effects of Taylor's departure." In a remarkable bit of speculation, *Time* posited that the altogether unknown Monsignor Hurley would be made the next apostolic delegate—or Vatican representative—to the United States. This information must have astounded the incumbent apostolic delegate, the powerful Italian archbishop Amleto Giovanni Cicognani, who had been working in Washington since 1933. Nevertheless, *Time* lobbied convincingly for the Cleveland priest who had stumbled into diplomacy nearly fourteen years earlier, insisting that "Hurley's six-year tenure at the Vatican, plus the diplomatic posts he capably filled in India and Japan, makes him a logical choice" for the Holy See's Washington station.[9]

Joseph Patrick Hurley's family origins were tied to the sweeping patterns of nineteenth-century Irish immigration to the United States and in particular to Cleveland, Ohio. While many immigration historians are quick to point out that the infamous Great Famine of 1845–1849 did not initiate the mass exodus from Ireland, it did accelerate emigration as a permanent aspect of both Irish and American life. By the second half of the nineteenth century, immigration was a prime feature of Irish demographics. The "push" of Irish distress was, on balance, stronger than the "pull" of the tenuous gamble for prosperity in America. In the United States, midwestern cities such as Cleveland offered new advantages to the immigrant classes. As a result of labor shortages, by 1880 steelworkers in Cleveland were being paid almost twice as much as their counterparts in New York.[10]

Most likely these apparent opportunities motivated Joseph Patrick's father, Michael Hurley, to emigrate to Cleveland at age twenty-one. In 1885 "the handsome red-haired man from County Mayo" married eighteen-year-old Anna Durkin of Sligo, Ireland. In 1886 they emigrated to England so that Michael could book passage on a ship to the United States. Anna gave birth to the couple's first child in Liverpool but returned to her family in Ireland once Michael left for America. After six months in the United States Michael sent the fare for his wife and son to join him in Cleveland.[11]

In 1888 Michael Hurley finally secured full-time employment at a

Cleveland steel mill fitting together pressed steel plates sixteen hours a day six days a week. "All he did was work hard," daughter Loretta later recalled; "he came home, read the *Penny Press* by the light of a kerosene lamp, and then went to bed." Eventually the family took rooms at a boardinghouse on Elmo Street, in the heart of the Irish enclave of Newburgh.[12]

The township of Newburgh, located about six miles from Cleveland's business district, was annexed to Cleveland in 1873 and by the 1880s was inhabited mainly by Irish from County Mayo. Kinship, social ties, and common bonds of immigrant experience held the people together. In 1892 Michael Hurley moved out of the steel trade and took a job as an inspector for the Buffalo-based Iroquois Gas Company. He would hold this job for the next forty years. The next year the family moved to a permanent home, where the middle child of nine, Joseph Patrick, was born on January 21, 1894.[13]

The Hurley household was a gritty place. The wood-framed house was located just one block east of the Pennsylvania Railroad tracks. Directly behind the house was a livery stable. The "iron ward," as Newburgh came to be known, was a dingy industrial community. "Roads were rutted, and modest homes were grimy with smoke from the mills and the railroad that ran through the heart of the village," one Cleveland historian has noted. "But to the Irish families, Newburgh was home. There was a spirit that bound them together, born, perhaps, of sweat, toil, and clannish fellowship." And Newburgh, though an uninspiring industrial pocket, offered the Hurley family opportunity for social mobility.[14]

In 1910 Michael Hurley was promoted to foreman at Iroquois Gas. Within two years the Hurleys moved two blocks south to a larger house at 8807 Harvard Avenue. Throughout these years, everyone in the family pitched in to help pay the rent. Anna Hurley took a job as a laundress at the Cleveland State Hospital, two sons were employed by the local trolley company, and another worked at a local grocery. Even daughter Anna brought in a wage as a "light bulb inspector." Curiously, Joseph Patrick, at sixteen, was the only employable family member not earning a wage. Instead he was listed in the 1910 census as simply "attending school." In fact he was the only child in the family to continue his education past age sixteen. Thus he came into contact with intellectual and social currents that would not have affected his siblings.[15]

In Cleveland, Roman Catholic schoolchildren were encouraged to

be part of a program of "Americanization." During the nineteenth and early twentieth centuries, Americanization frequently meant the eager adoption of the core values of American society coupled with an effort to integrate seamlessly with the prevailing culture. It also meant shedding Old World languages, habits, and political allegiances—prospects that many non-English-speaking Catholic immigrant groups struggled to reconcile. "Americanizing" bishops decided that Catholicism had a role to play in defining the national identity of the next generation. The notion that the United States had been singled out by God to serve as an exemplar of freedom to the world was a common theme of the Catholic Americanizers. Loyalty to the nation was paramount. Only by such loyalty could the attacks of the nativists be repelled and the entrenched suspicions of the American Protestant elite expunged.

"Next to God," James Cardinal Gibbons declared, "country should have the strongest place in man's affections." In many ways, Americanization was aimed at dispelling the lingering question directed at Catholics from the American Protestant establishment: "Can any Catholic be more than a 'provisional patriot?'" The insecurity involved in this one question would help fuel Hurley's later work on behalf of U.S. government officials, most of whom were Protestant and from the upper class. The same question would also be instrumental in forming his low-grade battles with Pope Pius XII during World War II and the Cold War.[16]

The spirit of Americanization took hold in the family's Catholic parish and the parish school. From 1901 to 1911 young Joseph Hurley attended Holy Name School in Newburgh. As historian Jay P. Dolan has pointed out, "Catholic parochial schools were a major force in the shaping of Catholic culture." For American Catholics of Irish birth and descent, the nationalist climate of the schools also "fanned the flames of their patriotism." Parish schools combined religion, intellect, and patriotism with the aim of forging a new American Catholic middle class.[17]

Although there are no extant records documenting Hurley's academic record at Holy Name School, he must have done well academically simply because he was encouraged to apply to college. The move into the collegiate ranks was an option only for the brightest and the most intelligent students, and was a defining moment for any young man of the era. And it was during this college application process that he was forced to come to terms with his future.

"Military prowess has, in all ages, commanded the admiration of mankind," read a small storybook that Hurley kept in his boyhood library. "From the earliest dawn of history, down through the ages, display of martial valor, whether in conquest or defense, has formed the theme of song and story." In Joseph Hurley's life, the theme of martial valor was quickly taking shape. "The United States Marines," he later remarked, "are the heroes of American youth." At age eighteen Hurley decided that he would be happiest serving his country as an officer in the U.S. Army. Setting his sights on a military career, he attempted to gain entry to his dream school, the United States Military Academy at West Point.[18]

For Hurley to apply to West Point in 1912, two years before the outbreak of World War I and five years before American entry, was a profound testament to his patriotism. Before the war, the position of the American Catholic church toward patriotism and military combat was somewhat ambivalent. In 1893, in his sweeping social encyclical *Rerum Novarum,* Pope Leo XIII had "expressed a new attitude toward peace. His central concern was for a new international order in which peace was based on justice and love rather than on military defense. He called for a reevaluation of the justice of defensive wars in a technological world." Consequently, lay Catholics such as Hurley were left to their own devices to decide how state militarism, patriotism, and faithful Catholicism could be morally reconciled.[19]

Any lingering theological complications for Joseph Patrick Hurley were overridden by his demonstration of Americanized patriotism in applying to West Point. Besides expressing patriotic fervor, the move reflected a desire to escape the grimy parameters of Newburgh. West Point offered both an opportunity for the ultimate in Americanization and a wide avenue for upward social mobility.

In November 1912 Hurley approached the Twenty-first District's Democratic congressman, Robert Johns Bulkley, seeking an appointment for the coveted position. A scion of the Cleveland social elite, Bulkley was a graduate of Harvard College and had recently established himself as a brilliant young attorney. Bulkley included Hurley among his five cadet nominations to West Point. Hurley eagerly began writing his application.[20]

Hurley made a fine impression at his interview, and all seemed to be going smoothly. Then, on November 20, 1912, Bulkley informed Hurley that his office had made a horrible mistake. "I regret to inform you,"

he wrote, "that I have just discovered that your residence is not in the twenty-first Congressional District, and I am unable to consider your application for appointment to the United States Military Academy." To make matters worse, the margin of error was infinitesimally small: the district's boundary on Harvard Avenue ran right down the middle of the street. "Your residence being on the north side of the street leaves you just beyond the line."[21]

On November 25 Hurley wrote to Bulkley asking for a review of the residency requirement for prospective cadets. To his credit, and in what may be considered a mark of personal esteem for the young Hurley, Bulkley assured him that he had privately "asked the Adjutant General of the United States Army for an interpretation of the actual residence restriction in the regulations governing appointments to the Military Academy."[22]

But Bulkley could not overcome the fact that Hurley was not an "actual resident" of his district. He could do little more than offer an oblique recommendation that the Hurley family move its residence across the street before December 20—something far beyond the capacity of a poor immigrant family. Thus Hurley's efforts ultimately proved fruitless.[23]

Hurley was profoundly disappointed. Both then and later, even his relationship with God was defined in military terms. In one of the few written descriptions of his spiritual life, in a later sermon note he described Christian prayer in bare military terms: "Prayer is the line of communications with God. It must be kept open by constant effort and use. How easily it becomes blocked by the drift of material life. And once blocked, in time of need, it is very difficult to get victuals and reinforcements through."[24]

Thus Hurley just missed attending West Point in the immediate footsteps of the famed class of 1915, later known as "the class the stars fell on." That class included future generals Dwight D. Eisenhower, Omar Bradley, and James A. Van Fleet. Later in life Hurley looked back on these events with a romantic eye. When recounting the evolution of his priestly vocation he altered the facts to suggest that he "turned down an appointment to West Point" in order to pursue priestly studies.[25]

The aftermath of the West Point fiasco left Hurley in a vocational quagmire. College applications were imminently due. If West Point was not waiting for him on the other side of Harvard Avenue, Holy Name parish was. As Hurley ruminated about his future, it became clear that his distinguished academic record at Holy Name School would allow him to be considered for admission to Cleveland's St. Ignatius College. The pastor of Holy Name Church, Father John T. Carroll, recognized the piety of the altar boy who lived down the street. Father Carroll must have alerted the Jesuit fathers at St. Ignatius (later renamed John Carroll University) that Joseph Hurley should be considered for admission.

The Society of Jesus, a Roman Catholic religious order commonly known as the Jesuits, had established St. Ignatius College in 1886. Hurley entered St. Ignatius College as a freshman in the late fall of 1912. The Jesuits were obsessed with the social advancement of their students. The stated aim of St. Ignatius's president, Father George J. Pickel, S.J., was to "educate a thoroughly Catholic laity, who in every walk of life, professional and business, who will be the equal of their non-Catholic fellow citizens." Along these lines, the college privately published a multitude of motivational pamphlets that were meant to inspire immigrant children to dream big. These pamphlets, handed out to students as required reading, bore titles such as *The Self-Made Man, The Best Course,* and *Why Catholics Do Not Lead.*[26]

Another pamphlet designed to provide a leg-up on Hurley's "non-Catholic fellow citizens" was titled *Piles of Money.* "It is a fact that cannot be questioned that the great money-makers of the world are the Jews," the first sentence asserted. "As a class, they succeed in this beyond all others." This outright antisemitism was symptomatic not only of a Catholic inferiority complex but also of Jesuit education. Since the late sixteenth century the Society of Jesus had become incrementally exclusionist and antisemitic. Jesuit historian James Bernauer quotes the philosopher Hannah Arendt on this Jesuit proclivity in her epochal study *The Origins of Totalitarianism:* "It was the Jesuits who had always best represented, both in the written and spoken word, the anti-Semitic school of Catholic theology." A perhaps more balanced view acknowledges that there were "both non-anti-Semitic Jesuits and anti-Semitic Jesuits" at various times and places in the history of the order. Whatever the case, at the time of Joseph Hurley's move into early adulthood, the Jesuits in Cleveland harbored some decidedly antisemitic opinions.[27]

"We find them out of all proportion in the high schools of New York, in the College of the City of New York, in Columbia University," *Piles of Money* continued. "The fact is indisputable." The Jewish people, from the

Jesuit perspective in Cleveland, had "greater earning capacity, advance more rapidly, and reach heights and stations impossible for them without a finished education." St. Ignatius College students, on the other hand, were described as "unworldly" and as Christian "children of the light." They were given the go-ahead to aspire to "culture and money power" but with an adjuration to use such blessings with rectitude as "children of light." The notion of Catholics and Jews as being in steady social competition stayed with Hurley throughout his career. But these unfortunate intellectual strains at St. Ignatius College were not all that the Jesuits offered. More wholesome pursuits were also encouraged.[28]

Hurley thrived at St. Ignatius College. In his first year he was placed in all the top courses and distinguished himself academically. As a sophomore he took top honors in philosophy. By his third year he was president of the College Debating Society, the highest-profile of all clubs in the Jesuit educational system. Competitive by nature, Hurley considered a great orator to be "a man of good moral virtue and patriotism." In 1915 Hurley's peers at St. Ignatius voted him to be the speaker at the commencement ceremony. A classmate recalled that his address, titled "The Dawn of a New Era," was rendered with a "beautiful and expressive delivery."[29]

Academic and cultural pursuits were not the only intramural endeavors at St. Ignatius. For years college officials emphasized the role of athletics. As early as 1904 the athletic coaches were forging an effort to "turn out athletic teams that will be able to compete with any college in the country." This enthusiastic effort in many ways paralleled the expanding movement known as "muscular Christianity." Proceeding from the basic principle that schoolboys, seminarians, and priests should be "real men," muscular Christianity extolled the aggressive, athletic, and even pugilistic nature of youth. By and large a Protestant phenomenon, the idea was that achievement in sport counteracted the perception of "religious young fellows" as "milksops." Although mainstream institutions of Catholic higher education in the United States did not subscribe to the ethos of muscular Christianity, there is evidence that American Jesuits did.

Historian Clifford Putney uses the research of historian Krista Klein to show that by 1890 the American Jesuit colleges were beginning to ape the Protestant program. "The trained man surpasses the less well-trained in all fields," announced the St. Ignatius College motivational pamphlet *Why Catholics Do Not Lead*. "It is so in baseball, football, running, boxing—

all the sports. What chance has an untrained man without skill and with flabby muscles in these contests?" To ward off the shame of flabby muscles, Hurley participated in athletic activities at St. Ignatius.[30]

The sport that epitomized the creed of the true athlete was football. Although St. Ignatius College did not field a football team until the 1930s, the Jesuits arranged for the students to play in the Cleveland city leagues. In 1915 Hurley joined the Geiger Clothes Company football team, composed of players from Holy Name and St. Ignatius College. Catholic athletic camaraderie was key, as the nicknames suggest. Hurley joined "Packey" McCafferty, "Lefty" Eland, and the brothers "Bananas" and "Doughnuts" Gallagher for a remarkable season. Described as a "healthy young gridder," Hurley joined a team that went undefeated in sixteen games and won the Cleveland Class B city championship in 1916. As a running back, Hurley became immortalized in Cleveland Catholic sports lore as "The Breezer," since all his opponents could do was feel the breeze generated as he dashed past them down the sideline.[31]

More muscular still, "Breezer" Hurley's favorite sport was "the sweet science," boxing. During his summer vacations Hurley attended an Ohio Knights of Columbus youth camp where he took boxing lessons. The "Saturday night fights" became the social high point of the week for the campers. As a teenager, he put together two whole scrapbooks of clippings of his favorite fighters. Much later in life, when confronted by what he viewed as increasing "softness" within the American Catholic church, he mused that it was "too bad the youth have given up boxing." "Fistfights were good," he concluded.[32]

Under the impulse of muscular Christianity, leadership—and specifically Catholic leadership—was to be exemplified by Catholics who "fought" and were not "soft." Athletic combat and spiritual combat were kin. To Hurley, only Catholics who were "fighters" were best equipped to lead the church. Confrontation, power, and projection of Catholic power showed true authority. The impact of these virtues on Joseph Hurley's personal formation cannot be understated. Dominating concepts of Catholic militarism, Americanism, patriotism, and athleticism would all be transferred to his religious outlook and his later diplomatic career. Given the features underlying his early religious training, to compromise, dither, walk away from a fight, or "not face up to facts" placed one in the detestable category of "the Catholic milksop."

After graduating from St. Ignatius College in May 1915, Hurley confronted more agonizing vocational choices. Although a military commission now seemed out of the picture, Hurley and Robert J. Bulkley maintained a correspondence throughout 1915, with Bulkley eventually becoming something of a mentor to "My dear Hurley," as he addressed his letters. In the spring of 1915 Bulkley recommended him for a summer job as a law clerk in Cleveland. By the end of the summer Hurley expressed an interest in attending Bulkley's alma mater, Harvard Law School. Still somewhat remorseful about the West Point foul-up, Bulkley was poised to push hard for Hurley's entrance to Harvard—a crowning achievement for a working-class immigrant's son.[33]

Then, just as Hurley was thinking over his next move, tragedy struck. Hurley's mother, Anna, was returning from a day of shopping when the trolley car she was riding stopped suddenly, throwing her forward. Anna suffered serious internal injuries and died at the Harvard Avenue home on September 15, 1915. Her death devastated the entire family. The large Hurley clan was at a crossroads in dealing with the emotional impact. Most likely for economic reasons, Michael Hurley left the house on Harvard Avenue and moved to Buffalo, New York, where the Iroquois Gas Company was headquartered and was expanding its natural gas pipelines. After his departure, the Hurley children basically were left to raise themselves.

Under these changed circumstances, Joseph Hurley knew now more than ever that he needed to view the future with a strategic eye. The idea of attending Harvard Law School receded into a pipe dream. The shattered family was surviving on only the barest of pooled incomes. In the midst of loss and emotional turmoil, Hurley consulted about his future with Monsignor Patrick J. O'Connell, the admired pastor of Holy Name Church. O'Connell was a kindly, prayerful man who helped the Hurley family deal with Anna's untimely death. Later O'Connell related that it had been his "happy privilege to lead Joseph Hurley to the altar." In the fall of 1915 O'Connell convinced Hurley to petition Bishop John P. Farrelly to adopt him as a seminarian for the Diocese of Cleveland. The vocational shift was abrupt and unusual, perhaps impelled by the family's financial straits. Yet his bookishness and solid faith made Hurley a potentially excellent candidate for the priestly life.[34]

At age twenty-one, Hurley entered St. Bernard's Seminary in Rochester, New York. Though staffed and governed by the Diocese of Rochester, by the time Hurley arrived it was in fact a thoroughly interdiocesan seminary. In 1915 St. Bernard's was an imposing fortress of Catholic pride. Built on a vast tract of land on Lake Avenue, the Victorian Gothic facade was constructed of gray mottled fossilized rock resembling cemetery stone. Later graduates of the institution referred to it offhandedly as "the rock," not only because the structure looked like a penitentiary, but because its graduates tended to be unswervingly loyal to the church hierarchy and to "the rock" of the Roman Catholic church, the pope.

The daily regimen for the seminarians was rigorous, and discipline was meted out with little mercy. "As a sanction for breaking the rule against smoking," the student handbook threatened, "even outside seminary buildings . . . it is decided that a second reproof by the rector should entail postponement of Orders [ordination to priesthood], and the third offense should merit expulsion from the seminary. Pool-playing should be punished by dismissal." Two students from Chicago were expelled for honking the horn of the car in which senior seminarians drove to the cathedral for Sunday Mass. Tom Hogan, a friend of Hurley's who entered another seminary, wrote of St. Bernard's: "from the experiences of some I know who have done time there, I am glad I escaped!"[35]

Hurley thrived under such discipline, and attended to his studies with great diligence. By the spring of 1916 the rector of the seminary regarded his work as "highly creditable" and included him among the eleven Cleveland students "on the honor list." Hurley the seminarian was rising to the challenge and using his talents to progress academically. Unfortunately, his scholastic progress could not be counted on to assist him in shedding some of his darker inclinations. When Hurley arrived at St. Bernard's he carried with him his own cultural baggage. His outlook was conditioned by his upbringing in an Irish Catholic community in turn-of-the-century Cleveland. Inevitably he harbored ambivalence toward Jews.[36]

Between 1904 and 1914, the formative years of Hurley's grade and high schooling, thousands of Orthodox Ashkenazi Jews immigrated to Cleveland. In the United States, unlike in Europe, 70 percent of Jewish immigrants worked as industrial laborers—a social circumstance that must necessarily have interfered with Irish-Americans' own upward trajectory from the factory floor. More significantly for Hurley, an isolated Orthodox Jewish community, or *shtetl*, was beginning to take shape on the borders of Irish Newburgh. Hurley saw the strangely clad aliens there every day as he traveled by trolley to St. Ignatius College. Some believed that that these eastern European Jews were simply inassimilable. Their Old World habits and their "foreignness" were an affront to the Americanizing concepts that Hurley had readily absorbed at his Newburgh parish school.[37]

Hurley's uncritical antisemitism surfaced at St. Bernard's Seminary, where some of the faculty also revealed animosity toward Jews. Teachers such as the feisty Frederick J. "Fritz" Zwierlein were ready to lay down the gauntlet in defense of Roman Catholicism, even if it meant going toe-to-toe with Jewish critics of Catholic policies. Zwierlein, who taught church history for more than thirty years at St. Bernard's, was a towering academic figure when Hurley arrived at the seminary. He demonstrated his siege-oriented attitude by scouring the newspapers for what he considered to be anticatholic material and then boisterously responding to any and all critics.

Antisemitic and fearful, Zwierlein devised tortuous religious constructions that resulted in a distorted view of Judaism. For example, in a 1920 speech he measured patriotism during World War I by the amount of blood spilled in battle. Insinuating Jewish cowardice, he proclaimed that whereas 138 of Rochester's Catholic men had died in battle, only 12 Jewish men had lost their lives. Zwierlein also created a category that he called "practical Jews in religion." These Jews were faithful to their religious practices and more palatable than Jews who were not. He described one Jewish war veteran enigmatically as "a Jew like most Protestants are Protestant." Intriguingly, these same delineations would be outlined again fifteen years later by another Catholic priest with whom Hurley would come into contact, Father Charles E. Coughlin of Detroit. He, like Zwierlein, believed that "secular international Jews" deserved less respect from Catholics than "religious Jews."[38]

Antisemitism was thriving at St. Bernard's in 1916. In Hurley's notebooks from Zwierlein's history class, he consistently referred to the Jewish people as "kikes." The Christian Old Testament was simply a chronicling of "kike history." Emulating Zwierlein's proclivity for simple categories, Hurley referred to the Keraikas, a group of Jews who disagreed theologically with the Talmudists, as "kike Protestants." "The Halakah" (the entire body of Jewish law and tradition), Hurley inscribed in his notes, "is altogether arbitrary and has no value; a large part of the Halakah is useless, and parts of it are ridiculous." It is unclear whether Hurley was transcribing his notes verbatim from Zwierlein's lecture or was penning his own thoughts. Whatever the case, this was the intellectual formation that he carried with him for many years, even into the Vatican on the eve of World War II.[39]

Throughout his career, Hurley exhibited a mercurial attitude toward Jews and things Jewish. He privately spoke of an "international Jewish conspiracy" with its "tentacles" spread throughout the world. During the 1950s he subscribed to the virulently antisemitic Catholic underground newsletter *Alerte!,* with its references to the Jewish "brotherhood" and the Jewish plot to control world finance. Even in friendly correspondence, the Jew was the object of derision and stereotype. "The Heeb in you that your nose betrays," Hurley wrote to classmate Bud Walsh concerning their correspondence, "prohibits you from debiting me with another letter until I have chalked one up on the credit side."[40]

Catholic "Americanization," with its emphasis on the shedding of European customs, may have played a role in boosting Hurley's antisemitism. Father Zwierlein's descriptions of Jews branded them as unpatriotic and as cowardly in battle. In contrast, patriotism, Americanism, and even jingoism would provide the seminarians with a common bond of assured citizenship as America leaned into World War I.[41]

"Our answer to '*Kultur,*'" Hurley's self-designed Liberty Bond poster proclaimed; "This is the spirit we want!" That spirit, captured in crisp color, was of a smoking cannon barrel, with a cannonball blowing Kaiser Wilhelm's head to bits. In the background a smiling cassocked priest hugged the American flag while brandishing a Liberty Bond. The image, designed by Hurley for distribution at the seminary, caught his martial spirit, the cult of the flag that was emerging at the seminary, and his heartfelt embrace of American war aims. Excluded from the front lines by his cassock, Hurley was determined to help the cause as much as his limitations allowed. "I hear you are getting to be some liberty bond salesman," brother Ray Hurley wrote from his Navy station, congratulating his brother for "doing his bit." The spirit of West Point was undiminished in his heart.[42]

In May 1917 Hurley was approved for ordination to priesthood and was assigned to upper-level theological studies at St. Mary's Seminary in Cleveland. Among other things, Hurley's advanced training at St. Mary's was meant to instill in him a lifelong loyalty to his home diocese. The pervading standards of duty to God and country found at St. Bernard's were unbroken. Although he was exempted from military service because of his status as a student of divinity, his remarkable patriotism went unsuppressed. During his summer vacations at St. Mary's he took a quasi-military civil service job as a naval observer in Sandusky, Ohio.[43]

The regimen and strict ecclesiastical atmosphere of St. Mary's were much like those at St. Bernard's. The seminary's greatest advantage to Hurley was the presence there of a professor who would serve him as a lifelong father figure. The relationship would become the single most significant one in his life. It was at St. Mary's in 1917 that Hurley first met Edward Mooney, the future cardinal-archbishop of Detroit.

At age twenty-three, Mooney was acknowledged as one of the best and brightest of the Cleveland Diocese. Sent to Rome for further studies, in 1909, at age twenty-seven, Mooney took a doctorate "with highest honors" from the Pontifical Urban College of the Propaganda. In 1910 he was assigned to a professorship in dogmatic theology at St. Mary's Seminary. Mooney's grace, style, and erudite sophistication struck a chord with Hurley. For the bookish young seminarian, "Doc" Mooney, as Hurley later called him, became his "leader, companion, counselor, and friend."[44]

Hurley was ordained to the priesthood with thirteen other classmates on May 29, 1919, in Cleveland's Cathedral of St. John the Evangelist by Bishop John Patrick Farrelly. His first Mass was celebrated back in Newburgh at Holy Name Church. In a note of personal friendship, the Reverend Doctor Mooney preached a stirring tribute to the young ordinand. Cleveland's diocesan newspaper, the *Catholic Universe Bulletin,* lavishly covered the ordination. A handsome photograph of a chisel-faced and clean-cut Joseph Hurley graced the front page.

As it turned out, the newspaper unwittingly offered a glimpse into the young priest's future. In the column beside Hurley's photo, a brief entry discussed the plight of an obscure papal nuncio in Bavaria, a Monsignor Pacelli, who had been forced to leave Munich on account of "actual danger to his life" at the hands of the Bolsheviks. According to historian Ronald J. Rychlak, that year Pacelli's residence was strafed by machine-gun fire in a drive-by shooting. On another occasion, a small band of Bolsheviks broke into the Munich nunciature and held Pacelli at gunpoint. Joseph Hurley, with the oils of ordination still wet on his hands, had no way of knowing that twenty-six years later that same embattled papal diplomat, as Pope

Pius XII, would ask him to enter the police state of communist Yugoslavia and brave many of the same actual dangers to his own life.[45]

Hurley's first assignment as a priest took him to an assistant pastorate at St. Columba's Church in Youngstown, Ohio. On October 17, 1919, Hurley was able to take leave from his daily assignments and travel to Cleveland, which was honoring an emerging Catholic patriot. Désiré Cardinal Mercier, the primate of Belgium, arrived in Cleveland amid "bells, singing children and cheers." Mercier was on a speaking tour of the United States and had just received honorary degrees at Harvard, Princeton, and Yale—the first Catholic to be so honored. A motorcade "of several hundred automobiles escorted the distinguished visitor through a lane of thousands of cheering persons" to City Hall. Mercier represented on an international scale all that the American Catholic church, and young Joseph Patrick Hurley, were striving to achieve: a complementary mixture of faith, determination, and patriotism.[46]

During World War I Mercier had called on all Belgians to resist the German occupying regime. In December 1914 he secretly wrote and circulated a pastoral letter titled *Patriotism and Endurance.* "Patriotism is an internal principle of unity and order, an organic bond of the members of a nation," Mercier proclaimed. "The religion of Christ made patriotism a law. There can be no perfect Christian who is not a perfect patriot." For the twenty-five-year-old Hurley, the notion that "the religion of Christ made patriotism a law" resonated strongly. Here was a modern-day Catholic leader, a fighter, who theologically integrated patriotism as an essential good of Roman Catholicism. In his reading of *Patriotism and Endurance,* Hurley was impressed with Mercier's naming the Germans as the aggressors in Belgium, his endurance in standing up to the German attack, and his furtive political resistance to the German armies. For Hurley, Mercier offered the antithesis of the dreaded "milksop Catholic."[47]

In the wake of Cardinal Mercier's visit, Hurley stayed busy with routine parish duties at St. Columba's. His rounds included daily Mass, rosary with the parish sodality, and preaching every Sunday. This regimen was interrupted in February 1921, when Bishop Farrelly died of pneumonia while on a family visit to Tennessee. The young priest grieved at the loss of his ordaining bishop. Farrelly's death, however, ushered in a set of circumstances that eventually started Hurley on a public career. On September 8, 1921, Joseph Schrembs was installed as the fifth bishop of

Cleveland. Schrembs immediately undertook a massive reorganization of the diocesan staff. But this was no easy transition. Under Schrembs's reorganization, chancery staff positions were slashed along ethnic lines.

Clerical ethnic tension was nothing new in the Cleveland Diocese. Since its creation in 1847, the diocese had been "beset by two factions, one composed of ethnically self-conscious Irish clerics and the other of Germans." Over the years each faction attempted to control the diocese by "ensuring that as many representatives of their own ethnic group as possible should fill important positions."[48]

Schrembs's appointment caused the clerical ethnic divisions to erupt anew. German pride had been bruised for twelve years under Farrelly; now the time had come to put the feisty Irish in their place. As if to counteract Farrelly's purge of Germans from the chancery in 1909, Schrembs set out to restore the diocese to German lines. Very quickly Irish-American priests in the chancery found themselves outside the episcopal loop. The symbolic peak of this German-Irish tension came in 1922, when Bishop Schrembs utilized his episcopal authority to ban the public celebration of St. Patrick's Day—a quintessential way to infuriate any Irishman. Irish Catholics grumbled as Schrembs pronounced that since the holiday fell within the season of Lent, it should be celebrated "in accordance with the church's penitential season of sober thought."[49]

Mooney, who had been moved from St. Mary's Seminary to take over as headmaster at Cleveland's prestigious Cathedral Latin School, quickly got the sack from Schrembs. The new Cleveland bishop assigned him to St. Patrick's parish in far-flung Youngstown, a declining parish in considerable debt. "With certain propriety on the feast of the beheading of John the Baptist, I have been cut off as the head of this scholastic body," he wrote to a friend. "It seems that I should get another job." The job that Mooney aspired to was back in Rome, at the North American College, the hall for American seminarians where he had resided while pursuing his doctorate. Mooney, who still had powerful friends in Rome, played some ecclesiastical power politics of his own and petitioned his Roman friends to get him moved back.[50]

While waiting for his plan to materialize, Mooney began adjusting to life as pastor of St. Patrick's. The assignment gave him the opportunity to renew his acquaintance with Hurley, the assistant at Youngstown's St. Columba's parish. Removed from the swirl of events in Cleveland, the two neighboring priests could dine together and discuss topics of inter-est. Hurley undoubtedly sympathized with his former professor in his "feud with Schrembs" and wished him to improve his circumstances. But though sympathizing with Mooney, Hurley was too young a priest to engage in a personal quarrel with his bishop and remained merely an observer. Indeed, Schrembs later played a major role in advancing Hurley's diplomatic career.[51]

On December 23, 1922, Mooney's machinations to secure a position at the North American College paid off: he was appointed the college's spiri-tual director. As Mooney packed his bags to leave a dead-end appointment for the Eternal City, Hurley was among the first to tender encouragement and congratulations. Mooney would not forget Hurley as he took his new position overseas.

Hurley soon faced changes himself. On March 23, 1923, he was moved from St. Columba's in Youngstown on an interim assignment to St. Philomena's parish in Cleveland. In September he was transferred to Cleveland's Immaculate Conception parish. His pastoral service at Im-maculate Conception continued undisturbed until 1926, when an un-foreseen set of circumstances ultimately placed him in the service of the Vatican. On July 14 Hurley was placed on sick leave from the Diocese of Cleveland. Extant records fail to indicate the diagnosis, severity, or ex-tent of his ailment; on one occasion Mooney described Hurley's illness as rheumatism. Yet despite his mysterious illness, Hurley applied for a passport in the fall of 1926.[52]

Hurley's "illness" may have been a "diplomatic" one, literally. By secur-ing medical permission, Hurley realized that he could get out of Cleve-land for the winter, and he obtained permission from Bishop Schrembs to do just that. In the fall of 1926 he traveled to France and enrolled at the University of Toulouse. Seemingly without prior encouragement, through 1926 and 1927 he studied diplomacy and diplomatic history at Toulouse, concentrating in nineteenth-century diplomatic relations. While this major move was taking place, Hurley's friend Edward Mooney was experiencing his own large life event.[53]

In January 1926 Mooney concluded his tenure as spiritual director of the North American College. In a vote of confidence by Pope Pius XI, he was appointed apostolic delegate to India. This promotion marked the first time in history that the Holy See appointed an American as a permanent representative. As apostolic delegate, Mooney would represent the Holy See to the episcopacy of India. He was stationed in the city of Bangalore, an important British administrative capital. Mooney's latest assignment also changed Hurley's life.[54]

"I was greatly surprised when I opened a letter under French postmark and found that it came from your own good self," Mooney wrote to Hurley. "I had heard, indeed, that you were in the hospital, but did not know that you had capitalized [on] it for European travel and the acquisition of a new language." Mooney then came to the point of his letter: "I have a proposition to make." Probably a little homesick and in need of cheerful company, Mooney called upon the goodwill of his former student: instead of spending the summer months in France, would Hurley buy a steamship ticket and "come over here for a few months with me"? He reminded Hurley that "the climate is recommended for just such a convalescence as yours."[55]

Hurley did not immediately accept the offer, and Mooney was plainly disappointed, writing that he was "sorry to hear . . . you do not feel in shape to say 'yes' right off to my proposal." He reiterated his invitation: the offer was "wide open, and the door of our bungalow even wider. . . . this place seems to me to be warm enough to boil the rheumatism out of anyone." But Hurley spent the summer of 1927 traveling back to Cleveland to prepare to officiate at his sister's wedding. Later he traveled to Tucson, Arizona, to spend the winter.

"Los Angeles—Friday, 9 December 1927—Awaiting me at the station was Father Hurley in the pink of condition," Cleveland's Father John M. Powers recorded in his travel diary. Powers was beginning his 1927 "around the world tour," financed by the parishioners of St. Anne's Church in Cleveland Heights. The trip was a gift in celebration of his twenty-five years of priesthood. Powers, a founding member of the Cleveland Symphony Orchestra as well as the founding pastor of St. Anne's, was a redoubtable figure. He was also a close friend of Mooney's, and during his troubled times with Schrembs he had opened up St. Anne's rectory to the distressed headmaster.[56]

In January 1928 Powers embarked on the S.S. *Belgenland*'s "world cruise" and invited Joseph P. Hurley to be his traveling companion. The elder priest and his younger assistant would sail to Honolulu, Yokohama, Shanghai, Manila, and Singapore on the way to India, where they would meet with Mooney. Both priests enjoyed mingling with the other passengers, shopping, and visiting tourist sights.

By mid-March the two priests were touring India. On March 15 the duo arrived in Bangalore and "were driven to the Delegation where Doc was awaiting our arrival." During the next week the three Cleveland priests enjoyed themselves and got reacquainted in the cool climate of the Bangalore mission. Powers left no record of their conversations or activities, but a week later Mooney left with Hurley and Powers to accompany them back to Europe. Arriving in Jerusalem on Holy Thursday, the trio "drove to the Garden of Gethsemane where Doc said a private Mass." After arriving in Naples in mid-April, Hurley and Powers proceeded through Germany, Switzerland, and Belgium, where they "prayed at Cardinal Mercier's cathedral in Malines."[57]

Hurley returned to Cleveland with Powers, but sometime in May 1929 Mooney convinced him to join him back in India as his secretary. The Powers tour had cemented a bond between the former student and teacher. During his weeklong visit at the Bangalore apostolic delegation, Mooney assessed Hurley as a young man suitable for diplomatic life. On a home visit to Cleveland in May 1930, Hurley finalized plans to accompany his former seminary professor back to India. It would be years before Hurley would see Cleveland again. He recalled his sister Loretta "putting on the Irish cry as usual," while adding that it "hurt more than the last time." Indeed, in making this second transpacific trip within one year, he was leaving all that was important to him—family, friends, and the diocese he loved. But the influences fostered in Cleveland accompanied him to his new post.[58]

The poignancy of the moment struck full force as the S.S. *President McKinley* pulled out of Honolulu, the last U.S. port Hurley would see for another seven years. "A lump in the throat as they played the 'Star Spangled Banner'—stood a little more erect than usual," he penned in his travel diary. "A memorable day." Cleveland's own Joseph P. Hurley, loyal American and loyal Roman Catholic, was about to commence a new and exciting phase of his life.[59]

CHAPTER TWO

Diplomatic Observer

INDIA AND JAPAN, 1927–1934

THE SECOND TIME AROUND, Hurley began to recognize the signifi-cance of Mooney's invitation to Bangalore. Accepting Mooney's offer meant forgoing the traditional path to a prestigious Cleveland pastor-ate. Even so, he probably realized that the long-standing seniority system meant that many of the pastorates were already "sewn up" by senior clerics and so-called irremovable rectors. In addition, any jockeying for a pastor-ate could have been riddled with difficulties, both potential and actual, given the ethnic tensions that afflicted the Cleveland Diocese. Mooney's offer of a post in India would allow Hurley to abandon the mundane world of diocesan politics and enter the urbane world of international society, travel, study, and diplomacy.

Hurley arrived in India in early 1930 to begin his secretarial assign-ment and unofficial apprenticeship to Mooney. From his patron he re-ceived both crucial training in diplomatic tact and hands-on experience. Mooney also proved to be a superb role model for Hurley in his later work. Hurley's admiration for Mooney grew as Mooney's work in India met with historic success.

Mooney's first diplomatic success involved settling the historically vex-ing problem of the *padroado* (Portuguese for "patronage"), a seventeenth-century holdover whereby the king of Portugal, under patronage bestowed on him by the pope, claimed the exclusive right to nominate bishops and

29

pastors in India. By the time of Mooney's appointment, the Vatican wanted to take control of episcopal appointments and looked to the missionary branch of the Vatican, the Sacred Congregation of the Propaganda Fide, to get the problem worked out. Great Britain, the colonial overlord of India, also had an interest in the nullification of the *padroado*.[1]

To resolve the *padroado* issue, Mooney was expected to bridge the gap between the ecclesiastical and governmental spheres. In its official capacity, the post of apostolic delegate was an internal ecclesiastical designation. An apostolic delegate is not accredited to the government, and his relations are restricted to the hierarchy and faithful of the country—a "purely ecclesiastical" position in the eyes of some. "In practice, however," Vatican diplomatic historian David J. Alvarez points out, "the Apostolic Delegate maintains contacts with the government and acts like a diplomat." Without a doubt, Mooney's appointment as apostolic delegate to India in 1926 was as much political as pastoral.[2]

In 1928 Mooney solved the *padroado* question when he successfully negotiated a treaty with the local churches. In the Mylapore Agreement, the system of double jurisdiction was abolished, and the Portuguese colonial government agreed to hand control of ecclesiastical matters over to the Vatican and Propaganda. The sticking point of the entire Mylapore negotiation was article 3 of the Vatican proposal. Encouraged by the British, article 3 stipulated that the Vatican's appointment of a Portuguese archbishop would be accompanied by the appointment of a British coadjutor "with right of succession." The point-by-point negotiations were long and contentious. In the end, it was only through hardened and inflexible posturing that the Vatican was able to achieve its goal. "It appears," Alec Randall wrote to Sir Austin Chamberlain in 1928, "that the assent of the Portuguese Government to article three was only obtained by an ultimatum on the part of the Holy See."[3]

The Mylapore Agreement was undoubtedly Hurley's first experience of high-level church-state negotiation. Here he saw his mentor Mooney stand fast and advance the cause of the Vatican through courageous and principled diplomacy. Moreover, he saw that there was no room for compromise when it came to defending Catholic interests. The Mylapore Agreement became a reality only through a forceful ultimatum. This lesson in the diplomacy of the ultimatum was one that Hurley would carry with him for the rest of his diplomatic career. For Hurley, even during the harshest negotiations it was the diplomacy of inflexibility that prevailed. Further diplomacy in India would reinforce this attitude.

Within months Mooney achieved another diplomatic success, this time resolving a problem that had existed since the mid-seventeenth century. In 1599 the Portuguese archbishop of Goa decided to Latinize the Syrian-rite bishops of the north. A number of Catholics rebelled, forcing a schism and the creation of two "Jacobite" churches in 1653. In 1930 Mooney decided that the Vatican should accept two Jacobite bishops, whose churches had been schismatized since 1653, as converts to Catholicism and thereby allow the churches to become fully united with Rome. "Through the Apostolic Delegate Mgr. Mooney," one of the Jacobite bishops later wrote, "we held regular correspondence with Rome." Delicate points of religion, culture, and papal authority were gently but firmly resolved in favor of the Vatican. "Monsignor Mooney's correspondence brought us great consolation and encouragement," one Jacobite bishop wrote. On September 20, 1930, in what was designated an "epoch-making document," Bishops Mar Ivanios and Mar Theophilos voluntarily resubmitted to Roman Catholicism and formed the Syrian-Rite Malankara church. Here too, Mooney's diplomacy was based on persuasion and forceful tact. There was no wavering on the final goal, and while the negotiations went smoothly, they were undertaken by the Vatican from a position of religious superiority. While Mooney's subtle negotiation forced the hand of the Jacobite bishops, they were nonetheless accepting. "His Excellency and Your Reverence continue to have a warm place in the hearts and prayers of so many in this country," Mar Ivanios thankfully wrote to Hurley, noting that Hurley performed well as "His Excellency's loyal secretary and guardian angel."[4]

Hurley's role of "loyal secretary and guardian angel" was a full-time job. Throughout Mooney's stay in India, he was constantly by the archbishop's side offering encouragement and managing daily affairs. Hurley's official position at the Vatican's Indian mission was a mixture of secretary, liturgical coordinator, valet, and operations supervisor. Records indicate that Hurley was in charge of everything from purchasing food to maintaining the delegation's automobile. These duties provided a firsthand introduction to life in the Vatican diplomatic corps. Yet the pace of work at the apostolic delegation was professional and gentlemanly, never harried or rushed. "I pound out my six to eight letters per day," Hurley wrote to an old Cleveland friend, "and take my walks and baths in the approved English fashion."[5]

His first impressions of India and its culture were positive. He generally liked his new circumstances, never mentioned homesickness, and was happy to be in an exotic and faraway land. "To the one who comes fresh to India from the Occident of sky-scrapers and sanitary plumbing and public schools," he romanticized, "India is a home, a rebirth, an apocalyptic experience." But though captivated by the wonder and scenic beauty of India, he formed a low opinion of the Indian people. He still tended to pigeonhole broad sections of humanity into narrowly defined stereotypical categories. The cultural experience of India did little to broaden his personal understanding of the contributions of foreign peoples and cultures. Perhaps it is unreasonable to expect that Hurley would transcend the cultural biases of his time, but his imposition of colonial stereotypes onto the Catholic faithful reveals a psychology that allowed him to categorize religions according to race and culture.

His descriptions of the Indian people were consistently grounded in physical characteristics. Indians possessed "dark faces, flashing eyes, and gleaming white teeth"; in conversation the Indian would "smile his smile of red gums and flashing white teeth." His travel diary constantly deplores the character of the Indian people. "Unreliable as a sand foundation. Tricky, treacherous, devoid of gratitude. . . . They are vain as peacocks and on less grounds," he wrote after a trip to an Indian bazaar. "Bloated with vanity. . . . They are parasites looking for an attachment. Even the smartest of them are dishonest cadgers, liars, disloyal cheats." He once described his cadre of Catholic altar servers as "eight little Telugu pickaninies [sic]."[6]

The Indian social construct of caste reinforced Hurley's notion of class distinction. As it happened, Indian society itself contained sociological and racial constructs designed to solidify and accentuate the barriers between the social classes. Caste has been universally recognized as one of the most problematic concepts for modern Indian Catholicism to overcome. To Hurley's mind, this construct of class segregation and inequality was all for the good. "Personally, I'm for caste," he noted; "I would prefer that the untouchables should not come within two miles of me."[7]

Fortunately, by late 1930 Hurley no longer needed to worry about mingling with the poorest of the poor. After five absorbing years, Edward Mooney had planted the apostolic vision of Propaganda on Indian soil. Others would follow and cultivate that seed. Mooney's work in India has been described by one historian as "simply remarkable," and Vatican authorities must have had the same view. The settlement of the *padroado* issue and the establishment of the Malankara church won him deep respect in Rome. With these feats to his credit, the hierarchs at Propaganda decided to move Edward Mooney to another area of missionary growth.[8]

On February 22, 1931, Mooney received "an official communication from Rome" stating that he was to be transferred to the post of apostolic delegate to Japan. "When the word came that he was going to leave for Japan," Hurley later recalled, "one salty old archbishop used a four letter word to explain what he thought about the departure—they really loved him over there." Mooney took up his new assignment "with cheerful and ready obedience" to Pope Pius XI, and he asked Hurley to accompany him to Japan. As Hurley cruised through the Indian Ocean toward the Sea of Japan, the sun rose on new opportunities, new responsibilities, and new encounters.[9]

Mooney and Hurley arrived at Kobe, Japan, on March 25, about four weeks after leaving Madras. "The reason for being so long about it is to be found in the leisurely habits of the Messageries boats," Mooney wrote to a friend, "and the fine opportunity they give for sightseeing in various ports. We spent four days at Singapore and five at Saigon—and literally stewed in both places." The next day Mooney and Hurley set up their offices in the Tokyo legation. Mooney's predecessor, Archbishop Mario Giardini, stayed on for ten days. This arrangement allowed Mooney to "size up the situation under experienced guidance and thus ensure that continuity of attitude and action, which is the rule in clerical circles."[10]

The mission to Japan was a historic one. While Giardini and Mooney were technically apostolic delegates—representatives only to the Catholic hierarchy in the country—their posting held great political influence, since the apostolic delegate moved freely in diplomatic circles. The Vatican had been covetously weighing the establishment of diplomatic ties with Japan since the early twentieth century. But the treading was cautious.

It was not until after World War I, when the Japanese realized that "the Vatican was an excellent source of information," that the first step was taken on the road to formal diplomatic relations, with the designation of an apostolic delegate. For the Vatican, there were other elements that made a Japanese mission desirable. Diplomatically, since Japan was a sovereign island nation, it could set its own foreign policy. Unlike India, where British and Portuguese colonial domination presented myriad problems, Japan offered a relatively streamlined situation. In addition, for various reasons, both Japan and the Holy See were extremely wary of the new Soviet system emerging in Russia after World War I.[11]

The Japanese still harbored memories of their own war with Russia fifteen years earlier. And the Vatican viewed Japan as an anti-Soviet outpost in Asia—a barricade against the encroachment of godless communism on the Pacific Rim. Some years later, in 1933, Hurley wrote from Tokyo to Mooney that he had committed "a horrible diplomatic faux-pas"—one that could have upset the balance of Vatican-Japanese relations—by chatting cordially with Soviet ambassador Constantin Yurenev and his wife at a diplomatic reception. Yurenev, who had previously served as the Soviet ambassador in Rome, had been appointed to Tokyo personally by Stalin in 1924. The symbolism of a Vatican representative socializing amiably with a communist apparently was not a part of the Holy See's Japan program. "You needn't mention it to your friends over there," Hurley penned cautiously, stating plainly that in reviewing the delegation's files he noticed that Mooney's predecessor, Archbishop Giardini, had been "censured" in "a mean letter from the Secretary of State" for "having an interview with an attaché of the same embassy."[12]

Hurley's letter indicates that various levels of tension already existed as the two prelates made their way to Japan in 1930. In his 1931 audience with Emperor Michinomiya Hirohito, Mooney noted "the good and cordial rapport which exists between the Imperial Family and the Sovereign Pontiff." But his words of cordiality may have come too soon. As Hurley later recalled, Mooney's reception in Japan "was not a warm one." Emperor Hirohito's uneasy welcome to Mooney signaled that his appointment as apostolic delegate to Japan was occurring during a time of transition. Propaganda wisely chose Mooney to fulfill the post in Japan because of his diplomatic talents and spiritual understanding. History, however, slowly intervened to obstruct any initiatives Mooney might put forth.[13]

On September 18, 1931, at Mukden, in the Chinese province of Manchuria, a small group of Japanese army officers staged an explosion and exchanged gunfire with Chinese troops. Japan invaded Manchuria. The "Manchurian incident," which gave the Japanese Kwantung Army a pretense to occupy the city of Mukden, dashed Western hopes of post–World War I cooperation and collective security in Asia. The United States, in concert with the League of Nations, vigorously condemned the Japanese invasion of Manchuria and its subsequent establishment of the puppet state Manchukuo. In May 1932, after a round of political assassinations, the Japanese military took control of the cabinet. According to one Japanese observer, the new militarists "existed on anti-foreign feelings, reverence for the Emperor, expulsion of the foreigner, and patriotism." The objective of the militarists was to place Japan on a comprehensive footing for war.[14]

At the same time, the role of Catholicism in Japan was undergoing re-evaluation as the militarists revealed their new policy of "state Shinto"—a nationalist sacralization of the public sphere. State Shinto was a non-sectarian form of Shinto that fostered veneration of the emperor and an orderly society. Concurrent with the move to state Shinto, the government initiated a campaign of *tenko,* or social conversion "under the pressure of state power," signaling a social shift that would become "one of the gravest questions confronting the Christian churches from 1931 to 1945."[15]

Mooney and Hurley experienced the ravages of *tenko* early on in their mission. Their first public diplomatic crisis, a dramatic confrontation between the tenets of Roman Catholicism and the imperial governance of the Japanese state, came on May 5, 1932, in Yasukuni. Briefly described by George Minamiki, S.J., the "Yasukuni Shrine Incident" occurred when "some Catholic students from the Jesuit university in Tokyo allegedly refused to bow in front of a Shinto shrine." Sophia University president Father Herman Hoffman, S.J., considered such an act to be sacrilegious. Catholic catechesis of the day buttressed Hoffman's view.[16]

The Japanese militarists in the government were incensed. The government suspended military training at the school, pulled out its assigned military officer, and stated that the university did not "conform to the principles of Japanese education." Bereft of a military officer, the university could no longer claim to be an authentic Japanese institution. In late May 1932 the Japanese newspapers published the story and aroused public turmoil and debate. The situation simmered throughout the summer, and by the fall it reached an impasse.[17]

During this period of tension, a new American ambassador, Joseph C. Grew, arrived in Tokyo. As the ambassador settled into his office, he was confronted with deciphering the delicate interactions of church, state, and society. Grew wished to get to the bottom of the matter early. Ever the courtly diplomat, he invited Archbishop Mooney to play a round of golf.

"I took on the Vatican today and sallied forth to Asaka with Monsignor Mooney, who plays a very credible game and easily defeated me." On the drive back and forth from the links, Grew "learned much of Vatican politics and their problems in Japan. They are having the same trouble that our missionary schools are encountering," Grew recorded from his Protestant perspective, "because the military people want the school children on national holidays to bow before the spirits of the departed Emperors at the Shinto shrines which the Western churches consider to be religious worship, while the military hold that it is only patriotic. . . . Thus far the missionaries have stood their ground," Grew noted, "but trouble is apparently brewing."[18]

With trouble brewing, Mooney again showed his diplomatic skill. In a deft move, he obtained a written statement from the Japanese Ministry of Education that defined bowing at Shinto shrines as a purely patriotic act, bereft of religious significance. "In effect," Richard Drummond noted, "the Catholic Church took at face value the contention of the government that state Shinto and its ceremonies were not religious." A relieved Joseph Grew marveled at Mooney's diplomatic maneuver. "Thus a mere letter seems to have cut the Gordian knot," Grew recorded, appreciating that Mooney had "smoothed out all the trouble" not only for Catholic schools but for Protestant missionary schools as well.[19]

Not long after these events, Mooney conveniently decided to take "an extended vacation" and sailed for the United States in late February 1933 to visit family and friends. On the heels of all the Japanese-American turmoil, Mooney surmised that his status at the Foreign Office in Tokyo was on shaky ground and that his days were numbered. In January President-elect Roosevelt had met with Secretary of State Henry L. Stimson and announced his determination to "make clear that American foreign policies must uphold the sanctity of international treaties" and to refuse American recognition of Manchukuo. With Washington standing firm, Mooney undoubtedly expected to be replaced in Tokyo. Sailing for America, he knew that his diplomatic career hung in the balance.[20]

As the summer of 1933 drew to a close, so did Mooney's vacation, and he made preliminary arrangements to return to Japan. On August 28, the very day he arrived in Seattle to sail for Yokohama, Mooney received an urgent telegram from the apostolic delegation in Washington, D.C., notifying him that he had been appointed the fourth bishop of Rochester,

New York. Mooney's episcopal schedule had apparently been accelerated by the course of international events. With the arrival of Joseph Grew, the Japanese militarists hardly wanted two Americans as heads of missions in Tokyo. Mooney's departure left Hurley officially in charge of the Tokyo apostolic delegation and opened the next phase of his career.[21]

Shortly after Mooney's Rochester appointment, Hurley was given all the diplomatic responsibilities that would fall to a chargé d'affaires, but he was left on the diplomatic rolls simply as the "secretary" of the apostolic delegation in Tokyo. Until 1969 the Vatican did not even have an official classification for Hurley's position. In 1933 he was accredited neither to the foreign minister nor to the emperor. Yet his role acquired a much wider scope than the familiar "six to eight letters a day" routine. He was now in one of the great capital cities of the world, alone, and thrust into managing a Vatican diplomatic mission.[22]

If Mooney's appointment to Rochester caught everyone off guard, Hurley's bump up to "chargé of mission" was equally surprising. In his new capacity, he was responsible for carrying out all the official functions of the mission, including negotiations, reporting, and protocol. Obviously, Hurley had not expected to be put into a position of authority so rapidly. He probably expected he would follow Mooney as a traveling companion and secretary; the thought of replacing his mentor in such a crucial administrative position never occurred to him. His year of studying diplomatic history at Toulouse had hardly prepared him for such a position. In fact, according to ecclesiastical tradition, Hurley was barely equipped to head an overseas mission at all. He had not attended the Academy of Noble Ecclesiastics, the Vatican's rigorous diplomatic training academy, nor did he possess the requisite training in canon law.[23]

The Holy See did not necessarily care about Hurley's suitability. It was playing a larger game. To retaliate for the humiliating ouster of Mooney, the Vatican took its time replacing Hurley with a minister of suitable rank. "When it is desired to manifest displeasure with a foreign government," British diplomatic historian Harold Nicolson has pointed out, "the chargé d'affaires is maintained for a long period of time and no successor to the departed ambassador or minister is appointed." This Vatican strategy made Hurley's new position all the more challenging.[24]

Pursuing this drawn-out course, Pietro Fumasoni-Biondi, the cardinal prefect of Propaganda, wrote Hurley to "hold on until the new Apostolic

Delegate arrives." In asking Hurley to "hold on" in Japan, Fumasoni-Biondi was taking a huge gamble that an untried and unheralded priest who did not even turn up on the Vatican's diplomatic list could carry out a plan of delicate retaliation against a new government filled with radical antichristian ultranationalists. Moreover, Fumasoni-Biondi planned to leave Hurley "holding on" for over a year.[25]

Fumasoni-Biondi, who privately understood the diplomatic situation in both Japan and the United States, was fully aware of the tension surrounding Mooney's Japanese tour. As the Vatican snubbed the new Japanese government, Hurley was left in charge of a crucial mission at arguably one of the most critical times in Japanese Catholic history. "Short, studious, and bespectacled" was how one Japanese observer described Hurley. "He was probably the first American priest ever given a position in the Secretariat of State who had not had some previous Roman experience," wrote Thomas B. Morgan, head of United Press International's Rome Bureau. Tokyo was a difficult assignment, not only because of the Vatican's delicate diplomatic dance, but because Hurley was just as "American" as Mooney—"As American as baseball" was how Morgan described Hurley. How the Japanese would respond to this new pinch hitter was anybody's guess.[26]

Complicated talks came early, and the Vatican probably never guessed that the next twelve months in Japan would be a time of immense change and strategic importance. The issue of greatest concern to Hurley was the Catholic school question. In 1933 the Japanese military cabinet assigned a training officer to each school. As a result of the Yasukuni shrine incident, government hard-liners successfully lobbied for the withdrawal of all military training officers from Catholic schools. At the same time the Japanese press initiated a campaign intended to send the signal that since no officers were present, parents who sent their children to Catholic schools should be considered unpatriotic. This tactic had the effect of drastically reducing enrollments at Catholic universities and secondary schools.

On February 18, 1933, Father Hoffman of Sophia University had an unsuccessful conference with the vice minister of war in hopes of getting the military officer reinstated. While these talks were going on, an "internal storm" was brewing at the Jesuit-run university. According to Hurley, nationalist members of the student body "engaged in recriminations against Catholic boys who were loyal to the university."[27]

The military officer at the Christian Brothers School in Nagasaki was also being withdrawn. In addition, the local department of education issued an order barring students' access to the chapel. In his effort to address the situation at Nagasaki, Hurley had his first direct contact with an authoritarian regime attempting to impose its will on the Catholic church. This was a defining moment of conflict between state sovereignty and religious freedom. And it was Hurley's first negotiation in the Japanese Catholic conflict between church and state. He would have to make a decision alone and on the spot. The lesson learned in India was not to back down to government pressure, particularly where questions of the spiritual rights of Catholics were concerned. "Of course they will ignore the order," he informed Mooney.[28]

Hurley authorized the students to enter the chapel at Nagasaki—a daring move given the new militarist composition of the government. Fortunately, when the students defied the order, the government backed down. His first diplomatic decision reinforced his conviction that steadfastness in the face of state encroachment would pay off. The diplomacy of inflexibility was the diplomacy of success.

Yet the question of religious rights continued to simmer in Japan throughout the 1930s. In the fall of 1933 a new political problem erupted at the Catholic Mission School in Kagoshima. This latest crisis, arguably the most international in scope during the entire history of the fledgling Japanese apostolic delegation, pitched the Japanese militarists against both Canada and the Vatican. To complicate matters, Hurley, an American, was left to smooth out the situation. Since 1925 Canadian Franciscans had run the mission and school in southern Kyushu. In October 1933 the Kagoshima newspapers launched an attack on the missionaries claiming that they were conducting spying operations on the fortified islands off Kagoshima Bay. Canadian ambassador Herbert Marler was "highly incensed and insisted that Canadian prestige was involved and that he would take strong measures," including lodging formal representations with the Japanese government. Marler, an admirer of Hurley, believed that the whole affair was a matter of Canadian national diplomacy and pride. Canadian citizens had been maligned in the Japanese press, and it was imperative that Canada redress the situation.[29]

Jesuit historian John Meehan offers three reasons why the situation of the missionaries emerged as a high-level diplomatic issue in 1933

and 1934. First, Americans and Canadians accounted for the two largest Christian missionary groups in Japan. Secondly, in many cases the
missionaries were better known among the people than either Western
diplomats or businessmen. (Many missionaries had been in Japan for
several decades, had learned the Japanese language, and had achieved a
high level of enculturation.) Finally, as ultranationalism rose, Catholics
became primary targets of state repression—with police raids occurring
on Catholic premises, and culminating in the unresolved murder case of
the politically outspoken priest Émile Charest in February 1934.[30]

As the campaign against the missionaries heated up in 1933, Hurley
recognized the intricate questions in play and called on both Marler and
Father Pierre Charbonneau, the Franciscan superior at Kagoshima, for
a calm and circumspect reply. By 1933 Kagoshima was a heavily fortified
Japanese naval port. Socially, the city was an antiwestern tinderbox and
was the hometown of one of Japan's most aggressive militarists, General
Hideki Tojo. Much as he sympathized with Marler, Hurley knew that
this was not necessarily a question of Canadian nationalism, but rather a
question of church and state—a question that could affect future Vatican
relations with the Japanese government. With this in mind, Hurley immediately arranged an interview with Marler and skillfully persuaded him
to postpone representations to the Japanese until the Holy See's opinion
could be obtained.

The Kagoshima mission question was Hurley's first experience of
face-to-face persuasive diplomacy. The last thing that the Vatican wanted
was an international incident centering on Catholic missionaries. A show
of force, though it might have met Canadian interests, was certain to pro-
voke even more enmity toward Japanese Catholics. Hurley was on the spot,
and his position was not made any easier given that the missionaries at
Kagoshima were actively soliciting the Canadian embassy to step forward.
"Marler still held to his idea of raising hell because the men were Canadian
citizens," Hurley reported about his second interview with the Canadian
ambassador. Then, in a show of diplomatic realism, Hurley adamantly
hammered home his position.[31]

"Foreign intervention would be disastrous," the young Vatican chargé
cautioned Marler. Hurley argued that the Canadians were in Kagoshima
primarily for religious purposes, and that far from earning the gratitude of
the Canadians involved, Marler would only make himself responsible for

"the increase in persecution which was sure to result from a protest by the [Canadian] Legation." Marler backed off. Hurley held the Canadians at bay and calmed the storm of nationalistic agitation. In the end, his first brush with persuasive diplomacy was brash, unstinting, and uncompromising. Of his explosive final interview with Marler he wrote to Mooney: "I had to get a little rough with him before he saw the light."[32]

Essentially no more than a secretary, Hurley was playing diplomatic hardball and "getting a little rough" with the Canadians and Marler—a personal political appointee of Mackenzie King. Kagoshima required not only inflexible diplomacy but even combative diplomacy. The Vatican was pleased because by scuffling with Marler, Hurley kept all information about Canadian Catholic hostility toward the Japanese out of the press. In this way he staved off Japanese counteractions against Catholics, and may have saved the Vatican mission in Japan. The Japanese were looking for any excuse to expel foreigners, and Hurley's determined diplomacy at the Canadian embassy forestalled any Japanese pretense for shutting down the Vatican's treasured Tokyo delegation. It also left Hurley with a lingering impression that "getting a little rough" with diplomats was a sure strategy for ultimate success.

During the Kagoshima crisis, Hurley won a crucial diplomatic battle with the Canadians. Using the only style of diplomacy he knew, he changed the attitude of the Canadian ambassador, maintained discretion, and guaranteed that Vatican interests ultimately triumphed. Mooney and the pope's men at the Vatican were bowled over by Hurley's success.

The Kagoshima Mission incident also helped shape Hurley's outlook on church-state relations within a totalitarian system. For the first time, Hurley used the term "persecution" to describe the fate of Catholics worshipping in the shadow of an unfriendly regime. On one hand, the Japanese experience accentuated Hurley's understanding of abuses that totalitarian or military states could inflict upon Catholics. These were the serious matters of diplomatic negotiation. On the other hand, though abandoned in Japan, he could now engage in the more delightful aspects of the "silver spoon" diplomatic culture. None of the lofty social circles that he had dreamed of entering by applying to West Point or Harvard Law School could ever match the levels of society in which he was now moving.[33]

Hurley's position as chargé d'affaires of the Tokyo apostolic delegation proved to be his first opportunity to experience life as a full-fledged diplomat. Japanese diplomatic life in the early 1930s was, in the words of W. Cameron Forbes, "a promenade of silk hats, cutaways, spats, frock coats, and white gloves." For Hurley, grand social activities now became official duties. In February 1933 Rumania's Prince Ghyka was due to visit Japan and drop in at the apostolic delegation. "It looks like a lion for my social season," Hurley wrote to Mooney, while gently chiding, "even you never entertained a Prince." That November he played host to the Marchese Guglielmo Marconi, father of modern radio and founder of Vatican Radio. He gave Marconi a tour of the apostolic delegation, took his autograph, and offered a private Mass. Hurley thoroughly enjoyed the social aspect of his mission. High conversation, receptions, parties, and being chauffeur-driven in the delegation's Marmon touring car were all new and exciting experiences for the steelworker's son from Newburgh.[34]

In the end, Hurley was not made apostolic delegate, and plans had to be laid concerning his future career. In January 1934 Archbishop Paolo Marella arrived in Tokyo to assume his office as the new apostolic delegate to Japan. Marella's appointment left Hurley in a quandary about his role at the delegation. Marella indicated via telegram from Rome that Hurley "should be in no hurry to leave Japan" and was to make no future plans until he talked with him. Hurley speculated that Marella might ask him to stay on indefinitely—a thoroughly unappealing idea. "I am afraid that the position of Secretary," he explained to the new bishop of Rochester, "where no particular sentiment of personal devotion is involved, would not tempt me."[35]

In a spirit of friendship and gratitude, Mooney offered his help in obtaining Hurley a chancery position in Rochester or Cleveland. Having tasted diplomatic culture, however, Hurley was not about to go back to the subservient position of an Ohio Valley curate. "I can work fairly well with Superiors if they are half-decent," he revealed to his mentor, "and I think I can work with subordinates, although I have not had much experience so far. But I'm no good with equals or quasi-equals and a good deal of self-examination and self-criticism has not been able to exorcise this particular demon." Marella may have been relieved that he did not have to contend with the upwardly mobile Hurley. As Hurley moved on in his ecclesiastical career, he would work admirably with superiors whom he regarded as "half-decent" and who fitted his personal view of Christian manliness and leadership. Superiors who did not approach these standards would meet with quick dismissal, disenchantment, or even contempt.[36]

Now anxious to move on, Hurley generously oriented Paolo Marella to his new post. By the time he left Yokohama on March 19, 1934, the departing chargé d'affaires was able to comment upon Marella's "wonderful character." Marella reciprocated Hurley's sentiments, writing to superiors that Hurley was "sincere, faithful, and genuine in every way." In due course Marella would see intangible qualities that set Hurley apart from other priests.[37]

Hurley had acted skillfully in Japan and enabled the Vatican to win its diplomatic contest with the Japanese militarists. A review of his writings from the period indicates that he probably did not grasp the significance of his own achievements. But Paolo Marella did understand, and his handling of Hurley's career bears this out. Although Hurley had no posting, Marella urged him to go to Rome and stay there for "a rest and a short visit." Then Marella wrote to Pietro Fumasoni-Biondi, cardinal prefect at Propaganda, informing him that Hurley would be taking the "slow boat to New York" and then a short trip to Rome, giving the cardinal ample time to find a new position for the young priest. Before he sailed for Rome aboard the *Asama Maru*, the apostolic delegation's amanuensis, Harry Akkido, hastily scribbled a friendly note on the back of a farewell snapshot. "Prophecy," the inscription read; "one to two years—Monsignor—Wonderful host—excellent linguist—In ten years—Bishop." For Hurley, the logical place to begin fulfilling that prophecy was Rome.[38]

In Rome, Hurley's two biggest backers turned out to be Archbishops Paolo Marella and Edward Mooney. The two joined hands to ensure that Hurley was promoted to the next level of diplomatic responsibility. While Hurley steamed toward the United States en route to Europe, back-channel plans regarding his future were being made. In October 1933 Mooney petitioned Propaganda to appoint Hurley a papal chamberlain in recognition of his service in India and Japan. Marella not only gave his hearty approval to the plan, but one-upped Mooney by personally lobbying Propaganda to grant Hurley the even more prestigious title of domestic prelate.[39]

Cleveland's Bishop Schrembs joined Mooney and Marella, pointing out the "genuine good qualities of Father Hurley, his real priestly character as well as his intellectual ability and his 'savoir-faire.'" "Not only am I willing to give my *Nihil Obstat* to Father Hurley's promotion to a Papal

Prelacy," Schrembs wrote to Mooney, "but, on the contrary, I am most happy to give my own personal recommendation to that effect. As his Ordinary, I am proud of his record." Hurley received news of his having been named a "Domestic Prelate of His Holiness with the title of Monsignor" while he was steaming toward Hawaii for a six-week vacation. "Marella just radioed me that I had been named a Domestic Prelate," he wired Mooney from aboard the *Asama Maru;* "it looks like I sort of suffered a 'sea change.'"[40]

By May 1934 Hurley was in New York and was able to have a friendly chat with Mooney. There is no indication what the two prelates talked about, but shortly after their visit Hurley headed for Rome. His Roman trip met with Bishop Schrembs's approval. Now deferential to Hurley, Schrembs seconded Marella's sentiments that Hurley was tired and "needed a rest." Mooney secretly broached the question of Hurley's health to Schrembs. "As you know," Mooney reminded Schrembs, "for the past two years Father Hurley has been a patient sufferer from arthritis, and I fear that the extremely damp climate of Tokyo has aggravated the condition." If the damp climate of Tokyo was an aggravation to arthritis, the prospects of a winter in Cleveland were even more daunting. The mysterious condition of Hurley's health, the reason he was sent abroad in the first place, thus might have played a role in his being sent to Rome in 1934. Yet, given that warmer climes existed in the United States, it is clear that there were other reasons for the trip.[41]

Hurley headed for Rome, ostensibly to follow Marella's suggestion of a visit, but in reality to allow others to press for a position with the Vatican's Secretariat of State, the foreign ministry of the Holy See. Hurley arrived in Rome during the latter part of the summer of 1934 and took up residence at the North American College, the residence hall for American seminarians studying in Rome. He made contact with Alfredo Ottaviani, the Vatican's substitute secretary of state. Since 1928 Ottaviani had been Marella's superior in the Congregation of Extraordinary Ecclesiastical Affairs. One of the most powerful men at the Vatican, Ottaviani now took on the role of Hurley's promoter and protector.[42]

Ottaviani acted, as one modern observer has put it, "as the pope's chief of staff." In the Vatican bureaucratic system, the papal secretary of state designated one person to be a *sostituto,* or substitute, secretary of state. In 1929 Ottaviani was promoted to that position and named substitute secretary of state for extraordinary ecclesiastical affairs. "Extraordinary affairs" meant that he headed the branch of the Secretariat of State concerned with the church's dealings with states.[43]

In addition to Alfredo Ottaviani, others at the Vatican were soon involved in support of Hurley's career. "Fumasoni [Biondi] has been wonderful to me, treating me almost as a *protetto* [protégé]," he informed Mooney. "I must have made a great hit with Paolo [Marella] and he has been touting me as a world-beater." Still, he was getting restless waiting for others to move the wheels of fate.[44]

He chafed at the waiting game. "I have been dangling here at the Villa," he reported to Mooney, "as Ottaviani insisted that I wait." The sticking point was the negotiation of a salary. "Unfortunately, the wind is still indefinite," he informed Mooney in the fall of 1934; "the Holy Father has refused to sanction another salary in the Secretariat of State and Ottaviani has been trying to 'systematize' another fellow there to make room for me." In 1934 such salary concerns were real, and not a superficial way of scuttling Ottaviani's efforts to assist Hurley. Pope Pius XI's massive building and restoration campaign of the 1920s had put a huge strain on the Vatican treasury. Just five years earlier, according to historian John Pollard, "the Vatican was virtually down to its last dollar."[45]

Eventually, it was not a Roman connection that provided Hurley's entrée into the Vatican's diplomatic corps. In the final analysis, Bishop Joseph Schrembs lubricated the gears of Vatican bureaucracy by resolving the vexatious monetary issue. When Ottaviani met with Schrembs during a 1934 Rome visit, he indicated to Schrembs that if the Diocese of Cleveland could help underwrite Hurley's salary, the new monsignor could officially enter the Holy See's Secretariat of State. Schrembs immediately agreed to grant money for Hurley's salary. "The old boy sure has mellowed a lot," Hurley reflected upon hearing the news.[46]

Ironically, the bishop whom Hurley had once referred to as "the mighty bellower in bad English" played the primary role in furthering his career. "Indeed it is too true," he chronicled to Mooney. "Schrembs came to Rome in time to give me a very warm and cordial recommendation, and the thing was decided the next day." Hurley's future in Vatican diplomacy was now assured. As the *Cleveland Plain Dealer* reported, "Monsignor Hurley will remain in Vatican City indefinitely."[47]

Within the month Hurley reported to Mooney that in an audience with Pope Pius XI, he had been nominated as an *addetto,* or assigned expert, in the Secretariat of State. Historically, the position of *addetto* was used to provide an apprenticeship for aspirants in the papal diplomatic service. The candidate would serve two or three years while superiors assessed the qualities of the entrant. "You are now in correspondence with an authentic diplomat," Hurley proudly wrote to Mooney after his audience with the pope, "and not a mere shove-tail of the unofficial variety." Hurley gleefully referred to his appointment as "the ambition of a lifetime reached."[48]

Hurley's nomination was even more impressive considering that in 1934 Italians controlled all the middle and upper levels of the Secretariat. More striking, Hurley gained the position of *addetto* without ever having graduated from the Academy of Noble Ecclesiastics, the Holy See's school for diplomats. His new assignment was particularly important since he was the only American attached to the Vatican's Secretariat of State during the period of the dictators. In a sense, Hurley replaced the only other American to serve in the Secretariat, Francis J. Spellman, soon to be named the cardinal-archbishop of New York. Spellman had served as an *addetto* in the First Section of the Secretariat of State for seven years. In that capacity, he had monitored "external" church affairs, that is, relations between the church and civil governments. But after his departure in 1932 there was no American presence in the Secretariat of State—a situation Ottaviani was eager to remedy. During the 1930s, numerous American Catholics were moving into the world financial elite, and President Franklin Roosevelt was beginning to pepper his administration with Catholics. Hurley's arrival filled the American void at the Vatican and signaled the growing prominence of the United States in Vatican international affairs.[49]

Ottaviani had Hurley placed in the Second Section of the Secretariat of State for Ordinary Ecclesiastical Affairs. This was the branch of the Secretariat of State that reviewed issues concerning the church's own internal policies and important cases within the church. In the Second Section, tasks and correspondence were delineated along the lines of particular languages and regions. More importantly, any declaration issued by the pope had to pass through the Second Section for review.

The Secretariat of State's Second Section was arguably the most important branch of the papal diplomatic service. It was the part of the foreign ministry of the Holy See that monitored the internal church relations of a particular country. Whereas the First Section dealt mainly with assessing how civil governments related jurisdictionally to the Holy See, especially in terms of signed concordats, the Second Section tracked the influence of cultural, political, and sociological trends. It monitored and dealt with the behavior of bishops and priests and larger national theological trends. Its reporting aimed to keep the pope up to date on the impulses and social conditions that affected the church in a specific region. Its diplomats were particularly watchful of areas where the spiritual and political life of a country intermingled.

Since the Second Section represented the direct lines of communication between the nunciatures and the Secretariat of State, Hurley's new position gave him a bird's-eye view of the American Catholic scene. Officially the Second Section was responsible for "the preparation of instructions and the analysis of reports sent in from the various Nunciatures and inter-Nunciatures"—information that formed the backbone of Vatican policy for a specific region. In November 1934 the *New York Times* accurately reported that Hurley would "act as liaison officer [in the Vatican] to the clergy in the United States," inasmuch as his position called for him to be in constant contact with the apostolic delegation in Washington.[50]

Characteristically, Hurley passed his probationary period as *addetto* and performed his duties well. In late 1936 he was raised to the rank of *minutante* in the Secretariat of State. The *minutante* acted as a gatekeeper of information for the pope. The *minutante* is the first line of analysis regarding the information received from the nunciatures, and is generally considered to be an "expert" on a region or subject. Essentially, the *minutante* analyzes incoming dispatches, prepares summaries, and adds commentary reflecting previous correspondence or policy on a particular subject. The commentary and recommendation of the *minutante* is then passed to the office of secretary or substitute secretary of state for review and action.[51]

Hurley's position, then, was one of great responsibility and influence. He would be the filter through which any initial assessment of United States–Vatican relations would flow. Unless dismissed outright by his superiors, at least a distilled version of Hurley's thinking would be contained in reports reaching the pope. In a very real way, Hurley could either subtly or overtly influence the Vatican's policy toward the United States. Ideally, the process of news analysis and report preparation was to be an impartial one. Hurley, however, found it difficult to leave his cultural baggage behind. His Cleveland upbringing would influence how he wrestled with one of the most important Catholic issues in American church-state relations during the twentieth century: the antisemitic rhetoric of the Reverend Charles Edward Coughlin.

CHAPTER THREE

Silencing Charlie

THE REV. CHARLES E. COUGHLIN AND THE VATICAN

THE EXPLOSION happened at three in the morning. A bookish Franciscan monk, sleeping on the second floor of Father Charles E. Coughlin's residence in Royal Oak, Michigan, was "awakened by a terrific noise and the sudden shaking of the house." In March 1933, as Father Coughlin, America's "radio priest," was ascending to the acme of his fame, someone allegedly broke the basement window, lowered a small wooden box filled with gunpowder into his basement, and lit a fuse. Coughlin immediately claimed that the "bombing" was the work of thugs allied to "certain local bankers," at odds with his recent preaching on monetary subjects. "Shaken, but uninjured," the priest repaired to the massive stone tower then being constructed adjacent to his new church for a safe night's sleep. The damage from the explosion, however, was minor—"some broken window glass, a steam pipe, and the wrecking of considerable canned goods."[1]

Given the turbulent life of Father Charles E. Coughlin, it is not outside the realm of possibility that the Detroit priest concocted his own "gunpowder plot." His pattern of "crowd-forming"—local police set up a barricade at four in the morning to keep the crowds at bay—was just beginning. The cycle would continue for nearly the next ten years. Publicity about his "persecution" was crucial. Coughlin's early-morning fright was covered on the front pages of both the *Detroit Free Press* and the *New York Times*. If the "bombing" was a stunt, it certainly worked. Within the year Father

Coughlin was the recipient of more mail than any other single person in the United States, including President Franklin D. Roosevelt.

PREVENTIVE DIPLOMACY

In the era before television, when Americans tuned in for news and entertainment on a simple, crackling AM band, Father Charles E. Coughlin was arguably "the biggest thing that ever happened to radio." The lives of Father Coughlin and the Holy See's new resident American, Joseph P. Hurley, intersected at the time when Coughlin's career as the "radio priest" was becoming antisemitic in tone. In 1937 Edward Mooney was named the Catholic archbishop of Detroit. Newly discovered letters and a diary written by Hurley at the Vatican reveal the important role that he played in shaping Vatican policy on Father Coughlin. According to this correspondence, Hurley was placed in charge of "handling" the Coughlin affair for the Vatican as early as 1934. Consequently, Catholic policy toward Coughlin can be fully understood only when Hurley is taken into account as a behind-the-scenes policy advisor.[2]

Hurley's hitherto-unexamined role documents two distinct phases of the Coughlin drama. The first, lasting from about 1934 until November 1938, was the patriotic phase. During this period the Vatican tried in vain to squelch Coughlin's political and personal attacks on President Roosevelt, using clandestine efforts by Hurley, the authority of the local bishop, and even intervention by the apostolic delegate in Washington to tame the truculent priest. Since many of these efforts were secret, and all of them went unreported in the press, Coughlin was able to test the limits of an evolving Vatican policy.

The second, antisemitic phase began in 1938 and continued until Coughlin's final silencing by the U.S. government in 1942. By 1938 Coughlin ranked as the leading antisemite in America. Hurley was tied to both phases of Father Coughlin's career, both as an observer and as a formulator of policy.

After 1938 Coughlin's utterances assumed an international dimension when both Fascist and Nazi antisemites began to extol his unsavory philosophy. Remarkably, historians who have studied Father Coughlin seem to have overlooked the degree to which Nazi and Fascist propaganda spinners used Coughlin's rhetoric in Detroit to paralyze U.S. government efforts to have the priest silenced by the Vatican for his antisemitic outrages. While many historians have studied how the U.S. hierarchy dealt with Father Coughlin, none have examined how the Nazis and Fascists used Coughlin. Hurley's Roman notes chronicle the Fascist and Nazi pressure, and his letters to Mooney in Detroit reveal that the force of the Axis propaganda campaign was being felt in the halls of the Vatican.[3]

During the early years of his priesthood, however, the use of Coughlin by Fascist propagandists would have seemed out of place. Coughlin was in fact an obedient priest and a firm supporter of President Roosevelt from 1932 until 1935. During his early period of fame, Father Coughlin described the New Deal as "Christ's Deal," and he pumped slogans such as "Roosevelt or ruin!" over his airwaves. After using his radio influence to help Roosevelt gain the White House in 1932, Coughlin hoped to become an "important advisor" to the President. After the election, however, Roosevelt distanced himself from the Detroit priest, making clear that Coughlin never was to become "Roosevelt's Richelieu." Coughlin never forgot the slight. Feeling used and betrayed, he spent the rest of his radio days brazenly criticizing Roosevelt and his policies.

Simultaneously, as the Vatican began to see the value of keeping the U.S. government friendly to Rome, Coughlin's anti-FDR rhetoric started to be viewed as problematic in Vatican circles. On November 11, 1934, the Detroit priest entered the secular political arena by founding his own political party—the National Union for Social Justice (NUSJ), otherwise known as the Union Party. Without batting an eye, Coughlin had established a podium for himself outside the sanctuary—a pulpit for popular consumption of his political oratory. By 1936 his party would be granted permission to run a candidate for the presidency. Earlier that year the priest began publishing a weekly newspaper called *Social Justice*. As the fiery priest morphed into a secular politician, no one—either in the American hierarchy or at the Vatican—seemed to notice. Lost was the fact that by founding his own political party, Coughlin became the first Roman Catholic priest since Italian Don Luigi Sturzo, ousted by Benito Mussolini from the Partito Popolare in 1922, to found a major political party. Four years after Coughlin's foray into politics, Monsignor Jozef Tiso would become head of the Slovak People's Party and later prime minister in Bratislava, linking Slovakia with Hitler in a deadly arrangement that would eventually lead to the monsignor's hanging shortly after war's end.[4]

Apparently, Coughlin's political stirrings in Detroit failed to raise the suspicions of Vatican insiders, including Hurley. "In the past," Hurley wrote sometime around early 1940, "much patience [was] shown by the ecclesiastical authorities toward Father Coughlin because of the Church's respect for the American principle of free expression." The importance of Coughlin's new turn to American party politics seems to have been missed or underestimated by both Hurley and his superiors in the Secretariat of State.[5]

In 1936, as Coughlin began to flex his political muscles, one further obstacle to reining him in was his ecclesiastical superior, Detroit's Bishop Michael J. Gallagher. Gallagher "supported him to the hilt, sharing his social commitment," and also sharing the radio priest's vision of political conspiracy. "Gallagher was quite willing to allow his priest full rein," historian Earl Boyea has written, "because he mirrored his own mind." More difficult for the Roosevelt administration, Gallagher hoped that Coughlin's fame would extend beyond national borders. "I do not term him a national leader," Gallagher declared, "but I prefer to regard him as a world leader."[6]

No one was more perplexed about Father Coughlin than President Roosevelt. He asked his advisors if the Catholic hierarchy could be persuaded to silence him, or if sympathetic cardinals such as Chicago's George Cardinal Mundelein could apply pressure. The answer came back no. By church law, the relationship between a priest and his bishop was sacrosanct. No other bishop could intervene, regardless of the fact that the Detroit priest was preaching across the boundaries of his designated diocese, into other dioceses, and indeed to the entire nation. Fifteen years removed from his stint as assistant secretary to the navy, FDR tried to understand how a strict hierarchical institution could find it so hard to use the chain of command to deliver a simple order.[7]

Unbeknownst to the president, the Vatican did decide to act. Since it could not publicly undercut Bishop Gallagher's authority, Vatican officials decided to work behind the scenes. In his first of many official acts of secret diplomacy, Hurley was sent to Royal Oak in the spring of 1936 to conduct a face-to-face conference with the controversial priest. Officially, Hurley's mission was to meet with Coughlin and explain to him the mind of the pope. To this end, he carried with him a personal communiqué from Pope Pius XI. In his confidential meeting with Coughlin, Hurley indicated that he "tried to send a message to Charlie telling him that the

Pope desired that he keep in mind always that he was a priest and that prudence and charity should guide his utterances." Although Hurley was merely a messenger for the pope, his Americanism surely accorded with the pope's opinion that a Catholic priest should be "prudent" and refrain from railing against the nation's president.[8]

Later Hurley outlined the specific points of his meeting with Coughlin, recording that he told him "that he [Coughlin] should always remember that he is a priest, that he should be prudent and that he should say nothing which might diminish respect for constituted authority." Hurley's summation of his papal mission to Coughlin in early 1936 gave a brief glimpse into the restless personality of the proud radio priest. "Charlie received this message very well," he wrote to Edward Mooney, but then "protested that the desires of the Pope were orders for him—and then went out and forgot what manner of message he had received." Because his meeting with Hurley was secret, Coughlin was able to carry on publicly as though the pope had never expressed any disciplinary interest in his case. Although the strategy of private pressure showed direct papal interest, it had no influence on Coughlin.[9]

As a politician, Coughlin was not going to let the pope step in the way. During the 1936 presidential campaign cycle, the NUSJ provided him with a media-centered pulpit outside the sanctuary. Coughlin soon used the secular stage to hurl further insults at his political nemesis. On July 16, 1936, during an election convention in Hurley's hometown of Cleveland, Coughlin's explosive rhetoric hit new heights. In a speech before 10,000 cheering onlookers, Coughlin threw off his coat, ripped out his clerical collar, and accused Franklin Roosevelt of being "a liar and a betrayer"—wildly irresponsible political rhetoric in the 1930s. "F.D.R.," Coughlin bellowed, stood for "Franklin Double-crossing Roosevelt!" Major press outlets immediately highlighted the priest-politician's characterization of the president as "a liar" in front of thousands of Americans. Most major newspapers carried the story as front-page news.

"Many Americans," historian Charles Tull has written, "felt that the priest had overreached himself and would finally be curbed by his church." Yet to the contrary, Bishop Gallagher, while distancing himself from Coughlin's Cleveland remarks, stated in an interview that, "he [Coughlin] is working along the right path and has my support." Meanwhile the national media reported that Coughlin's acerbic epithets created a "painful impression" at the Vatican—pointing up a substantial rift between the local ecclesiastical and international assessments. On July 23, 1936, one day after receiving "a transatlantic phone call from the Vatican," Coughlin publicly apologized for his "liar" comment, Bishop Gallagher was summoned to Rome, and the apostolic delegate to the United States, Amleto G. Cicognani, surreptitiously hastened to the Eternal City.[10]

By August 1936, Bishop Gallagher and Apostolic Delegate Cicognani were in Rome for what was clearly a "Coughlin summit." While Leslie Woodcock Tentler has written that "what transpired in Rome is still not known," the Hurley-Mooney correspondence confirms that Bishop Gallagher was in Rome for a verbal reprimand and that Joseph Hurley was once again the one whom the pope commissioned to do the talking.[11]

Indeed, as Coughlin became a deeper concern in Rome, Hurley was placed in charge of "handling the case" for the Vatican. In late July 1936 he was again called into action. This time the problem was the loquacious Bishop Michael J. Gallagher of Detroit. While Vatican officials waited patiently for Gallagher to arrive in Italy, the Detroit bishop decided to provide extended comments to the international press corps as soon as his ship, the Italian luxury liner *Rex*, docked in Naples. This action exasperated Vatican officials. "Coughlin Defended Warmly by Bishop on Reaching Rome," were the front-page headlines of the *New York Times* Sunday edition of July 26. Gallagher, having just set foot in Italy, held a mini press conference for waiting reporters. "I cannot speak against Father Coughlin," he told the *New York Times*, which also reported that Gallagher "personally endorsed the priest's views." If any observations were to be made on the matter, he continued, "It must . . . be for myself to make them and not the Vatican."

Distressed by this outburst, rather than waiting for Gallagher's scheduled meeting with the pope the Secretariat of State commissioned Hurley to speak with Gallagher that very evening. As Hurley put it, he was commissioned to "go to him and tell him that, whatever he did in Detroit, the Holy See would thank him to keep his mouth shut while sojourning in the Eternal City." Hurley's intercession worked. When reporters hounded Gallagher the next day, the Detroit bishop astoundingly commented to the *New York Times* that "he did not intend to bring up the [Coughlin] matter" during his upcoming audience with the pope. Possibly alluding to Hurley's work on the issue, Gallagher commented that "he [the pope] is thoroughly informed on the case, however."[12]

The press was eager to question Gallagher further during his Italian visit. Gallagher, unused to handling any sort of press attention, gave in to the pressure. Flouting Hurley's personal warning to keep mum while in Rome, on September 2 he granted the *New York Times* a final Italian interview. The avuncular bishop apparently believed that since he was leaving Italy, the Vatican interdict had been lifted and he was free to express his views. Before leaving Naples, Gallagher blurted out to an anxious correspondent that "the Holy See fully approved of Father Coughlin's activities." After this parting shot, which effectively undercut the fundamental aim of the entire "Coughlin summit," the Detroit bishop boarded the *Rex* and sailed for New York. Gallagher's comments, once again splashed across the front page of the *New York Times,* must have irked Vatican officials considerably. Some form of damage control was necessary, and once again Hurley went into action.[13]

Unable to upbraid Gallagher personally or in private, Hurley and the Vatican released a scathing editorial in the Vatican news organ *Osservatore Romano.* The two-paragraph piece contradicted Gallagher's Roman statements and reproached the now seaborne bishop. Though unsigned, the editorial was most likely written by Joseph P. Hurley. It was not uncommon for Hurley, as the highest-ranking American in the Secretariat of State, to use the editorial pages of *Osservatore Romano* to express an official Vatican opinion. Moreover, close textual analysis underscores that the prose, diction, and tone of the editorial bear Joseph Hurley's imprint.[14]

"News Report Unfounded" read the caption of the anti-Coughlin editorial. Bishop Gallagher's report that the Holy See approved of the activities of Father Coughlin did "not correspond to the truth," the editorial stated. "An orator who inveighs against persons who represent the supreme social authorities, with evident danger of shaking the respect that the people owe to those authorities, sins against elementary proprieties." "The Holy See wants respect . . . for all proprieties." The warning concluded with a twist of personal communication most uncommon for the Vatican newspaper: "Bishop Gallagher knows quite well what he was told on the subject."[15]

The American press correctly construed the *Osservatore Romano* editorial as an official censure of Coughlin. Hurley's editorial efforts made the front page of the *New York Times* on September 3, unleashing a torrent of criticism from Bishop Gallagher, Coughlin himself, and his loyal supporters. When he arrived in Detroit, Gallagher once more categorically denied that the Vatican had ordered him to discipline Coughlin, "but admitted for the first time that someone in Rome had discussed Coughlin."

Having by now figured out that Hurley was the author of the editorial, Bishop Gallagher lashed back personally in a quote to the *New York Times* on September 6. "There was an inconsequential individual in Rome," he recalled, "who tried to find a flyspeck in the beautiful picture I painted of Father Coughlin's activities." Interestingly, Gallagher used the same "flyspeck" imagery to retell his conversation with the anonymous Vatican official—certainly Hurley—in *Time* magazine. "There is a spot on your picture," Hurley apparently told Bishop Gallagher. "He [Coughlin] called the President a 'liar.'" Hurley impressed on Gallagher that Coughlin was out of bounds in calling the president a liar, "because it failed to show respect for an office which deserves utmost respect." Here, Hurley's Americanism was setting the limits on Father Coughlin.[16]

Although they only met once, Coughlin sensed that Hurley's position at the Vatican was far from inconsequential. Unfortunately, the privacy of the Hurley-Gallagher exchange allowed Coughlin to publicly gain the upper hand and trump Hurley's deference to the president. "False propaganda from Rome or anywhere else," Father Coughlin later warned a crowd of 80,000 Chicagoans the next Sunday, "should not be listened to. . . . If the Vatican had cracked down, I wouldn't be here today." But Coughlin's triumph was short-lived. In January 1937 the supportive Bishop Gallagher, Coughlin's shield, died quietly in Detroit.[17]

Coughlin biographer Charles Tull has described Gallagher's death as "a staggering blow" to the radio priest. In the summer of 1937 Hurley's mentor, Edward Mooney, was moved from Rochester, New York, and became the new archbishop of Detroit. Upon his arrival he realized that his number-one concern would be the combative priest from Royal Oak. Tull's characterization of the Mooney appointment as "a staggering blow" may have been premature, given that Coughlin would operate largely unobstructed for the next five years. Lost in the move was that Mooney's arrival in Detroit meant Hurley's position in the Coughlin case took on even greater importance. As he informed Vatican officials on the Coughlin issue, he was at the same time able to forewarn Mooney about conditions at the Vatican—conditions that seemed to be worsening as the dictators embraced political antisemitism.[18]

Historian Mary Christine Athans has noted that by early 1938 Coughlin was moving toward "a build-up of anti-Jewish material" in his speeches and publications. In July 1938 *Social Justice* began publishing excerpts from the antisemitic *Protocols of the Elders of Zion,* a 1905 fabrication that purported to be the chronicle of a Jewish conspiracy to take over the world. With the publication of the *Protocols,* Coughlin formally joined the 1930s cacophony of Jew-baiting in the United States. He would become the leading antisemitic demagogue of that turbulent decade. Coughlin's domestic counterparts, William Dudley Pelley and Gerald L. K. Smith, were effective religious Jew-baiters, but they functioned on the mystical and Protestant fringes and possessed no formal institutional affiliation to their denominations. Pelley's Silvershirts and Smith's Christian National-ists were exclusively domestic in origin and secular in operation. Father Coughlin was a different matter. His Roman Catholic collar connected him with a transnational organization at the same time that radio was beginning to be broadcast on international frequencies. By 1938 this phe-nomenon would generate global problems for Vatican policy.[19]

VATICAN BACKLASH

To date, the most exhaustive and thoroughly researched biography of Father Charles Coughlin is Donald Warren's 1996 *Radio Priest: Charles Coughlin, the Father of Hate Radio.* In this masterly treatment of the com-plex priest, Warren uncovers and examines Coughlin's contacts with Nazi agents in the United States, particularly in the area of financing; his col-lusion with Nazi-sponsored groups in the United States; and the propa-ganda placement of Nazi material in Coughlin's newspaper, *Social Justice.* Much of this new information is the product of Warren's extensive use of Federal Bureau of Investigation files on Coughlin. What emerges from Warren's treatment is the story of German development of Coughlin as a spokesman for Nazi and Fascist propaganda in the United States. One of Warren's major objectives is to uncover "the use of Nazi propaganda in *Social Justice.*"[20] What remains unaddressed in all the treatments of Coughlin so far is the Nazi and Fascist use of Coughlin as a propaganda tool in Germany and Italy.

Through his antisemitic and anti-British rants, Coughlin gave excel-lent copy to the chief Nazi and Fascist propagandists. Except for a small group of liberal activists who followed such trends, very few Americans understood that the priest from Royal Oak was being used, packaged, and praised across Europe by some of the highest-ranking Axis propaganda ministers. Hurley's diaries indicate that Axis moves to adopt and praise Coughlin in the European press created new ramifications for the Holy See's approach to the Coughlin question in Detroit. This new development created a shift in policy for U.S. Catholic church officials. No longer would they be permitted to attack Coughlin from the patriotic or "Americanized" Catholic position.

On November 20, 1938, Coughlin delivered the most controversial and fantastic radio speech of his career—one that would reveal him as a demagogue with a worldwide reach. By now reaching nearly thirty million listeners in the United States, Coughlin offered his account of the Kristallnacht pogrom of November 10, 1938. The "night of the broken glass" saw 400 synagogues set ablaze in Germany, Austria, Danzig, and the Sudetenland. More than 7,000 Jewish-owned shops were wrecked and looted, and nearly 30,000 Jewish men were sent to concentration camps at Dachau and Buchenwald. With these events still gripping the American consciousness, Coughlin took to his microphone.

"Thousands of people must have been jolted out of their chairs," Charles Tull wrote, "as the Detroit priest actually proceeded to explain the Nazi persecution of the Jews as a defense mechanism against communism." Coughlin berated the "Jewish gentlemen" who "controlled the radio and press" for not adequately reporting the concurrent persecution of Catholics in Russia, Spain, and Mexico. Coughlin further expressed his full agreement with the Nazi theory that the Jews were responsible for the Russian Revolution and dominated the Lenin government of 1917. He went on to warn of the "international Jewish conspiracy." In broad and demented terms, Coughlin diminished the gravity of Kristallnacht by offering a comparative recitation of Christian persecution. With a bizarre back flip of logic, he serenely implied, through a pretentious examination of the Russian Revolution, that the real persecutors of Roman Catholics were the Jews, the recent *victims* of the Kristallnacht.[21]

Public reaction to the November speech was far-reaching. Jewish groups protested vigorously. Radio stations that broadcast Coughlin's speeches were deluged with complaints. ABC, NBC, and CBS struck him from the air. In New York City, radio station WMCA aptly summarized the view of the American broadcast community by describing the speech as "calculated to incite religious and racial strife in America." As the secular radio community in America anathematized Coughlin for broadcasting "the most un-American speech ever delivered," the Catholic church remained virtually silent.[22]

Perhaps the leadership was dumbstruck. Three days earlier, in an unprecedented move of media cooperation, the CBS and NBC radio networks simultaneously broadcast an hour of Catholic condemnations of Kristallnacht by three powerful Catholic bishops. But in the wake of Coughlin's implausible speech, there was no equal rejoinder. Firm Roosevelt supporter George Cardinal Mundelein of Chicago was the lone voice among the episcopacy who gathered enough courage to condemn Coughlin for his remarks.[23]

Archbishop Mooney declined to intervene in the affair even though his own chancery censors were prereading Coughlin's antisemitic speeches. Historian Charles Tull has observed the hypocrisy of Mooney's public condemnation of Coughlin for his name-calling of President Roosevelt while "there was no . . . direct attempt to restrain Coughlin when he was inciting race hatred on a vast scale." Donald Warren's investigations of U.S. national security files on Coughlin failed to turn up any hint explaining Mooney's now more permissive attitude on Father Coughlin. In late 1938 Mooney "seemed withdrawn and detached," Warren asserts, even as the controversy was "swirling around the news media" and "bishops around the country felt pressure to respond." With Mooney mute in time of crisis, the historian of the Archdiocese of Detroit, Leslie Woodcock Tentler, has been led to ask: "What, then, explains Mooney's apparent tolerance of Coughlin's increasingly extremist rhetoric?"[24]

Writing from the Vatican, Hurley warned his mentor against an unambiguous salvo. "The Jews are in full cry against him," he wrote to Mooney, but "after reading the speech, my opinion is that you can't touch it. . . . Mundelein is a shining example of bad tactics in handling Charlie. George [Cardinal Mundelein] must still be nursing the jaw he stuck out. . . . Your own best bet is to play a waiting game, regardless of the criticisms." Coughlin, however, used the waiting period to his own advantage. Perhaps sensing the outcry to come, Coughlin made sure that his November 20 speech was recorded on an acetate disc by studio sound engineers. On December 11 he rebroadcast the November 20 speech. Radio rebroadcasts were rare in 1938, but the new recording technology allowed Coughlin to air his rant to an even larger audience and an edgier American public. Thus, Coughlin's controversial speech was really broadcast twice, doubling its effect, a fact missed by Coughlin biographers.[25]

In the face of Coughlin's double whammy, Mooney longed to hit back. But as he would come to learn, there were concerns at the Vatican that a public denunciation of Coughlin in America could elicit a vehement attack on the Vatican by both the Italian Fascist and German Nazi regimes. Fearful of a counterattack on Catholic interests, the Vatican urged Mooney to make no public comment that might be interpreted in Europe as favoring the Jews. The first evidence of a "backlash thesis" was contained in a December 1938 confidential report written by Mooney in Detroit and delivered to Hurley at the Vatican.

In this report, Mooney offered an analysis of "the latest furor which our problem child No. 1 has stirred up." In the introduction to the document, Mooney ambiguously cautioned Hurley: "Let there be no doubt about the fact that he is at heart 'anti-Semitic,'" but he qualified this judgment by adding, "whatever that is." "I am taking it for present purposes," Mooney clarified to Hurley, "to designate [as antisemitic] one who is against the Jews as such and is obsessed with the conviction that all the evil in the world is traceable to them. . . . The Lord knows they have enough to their credit without bothering about piling it up."[26]

In a tragic maneuver, Mooney proposed a plan that failed to depart from his previous path of public nonconfrontation. The only difference this time was that he tried to move the decision-making process back into the hands of the Vatican. "If we can get—and very quickly," Mooney implored, "a bland pronouncement on the broadcasts of 20 November and 11 December just for private use with the orator, I am sure that it will help to make him more amenable both directly and also through the intimation it will carry of a possible public repudiation by the Holy See—which is, as I see the case, about the only thing he really fears."[27]

The strategy of private Vatican pressure had failed to work since the spring of 1936. Puzzlingly, while knowing that Coughlin consistently flouted private pressure, Mooney continued to believe that his only hope was more secret negotiation. "I would not blame anyone for considering the request [for a private papal reprimand], at first sight, a bit silly," he rationalized, "but we are dealing with an unbalanced individual in a crazy age and a crazy country where brass counts for more than anything else—and where a good many people are secretly glad to see that the Jews have not an absolute monopoly on the brass. This feeling is so strong that the many bishops with whom I have talked the matter over have in every case counseled against any further statement on my part than the one I have made." Nearly in desperation, Mooney signaled to Hurley that Coughlin was no longer a matter for "local handling." "Something must be done," he wrote, trying to throw the Coughlin problem into the hands of the Holy See's diplomats, "and this quiet Papal pressure strikes me as the most practical idea."[28]

On December 26, 1938, well before he could have received Mooney's December 22 appeal for the "bland Papal pronouncement," Hurley took it upon himself to brief Mooney on the status quo at the Vatican. This letter was meant to downplay and defuse the antisemitic nature of the situation, and most likely to reaffirm the Vatican position that local handling was best. In direct reference to Coughlin's antisemitic content, Hurley remarked that "nobody seems bothered about it here." The only protest registered at the Vatican came from "some irate Jews of the gonnif [a Yiddish variant of *ganef*, 'thief, scoundrel'] variety." Not yet having received Mooney's plea for papal intervention, Hurley stated plainly: "it is felt to be a local problem which you can handle." Hurley opined that international Jewish organizations had "made too much of an outcry about the speech."[29]

Hurley was jolted out of his complacency in January when he received Mooney's desperate cry for the "bland" Vatican intervention. In mid-January he responded, apprising Mooney of the situation at the Vatican. According to Hurley, there was no "definite news" on the matter of Father Coughlin's speech. Hurley let on that he had "kept the bosses informed" of the Coughlin affair, but that the question had not come up as a matter of policy. "Nor has the Pope brought up the question on the several occasions on which I have been with him lately." This statement is crucial because it shows a deliberate breakdown in Vatican bureaucratic communication. By the very nature of his position in the Secretariat of State, it was precisely Hurley's job to bring the crisis to the attention of Pope Pius XI, not the other way around. There seemed to be other forces at work, forces that would become clear as Mooney continued to press the Holy See.

Finally, Hurley began to explain the real reason for Vatican foot-dragging—the relation of Coughlin to new diplomatic conditions. A papal intervention on behalf of the Jewish people in Detroit was being conditioned by larger exigencies directly affecting the Vatican. As religious and racial prejudice grew in Europe, the Vatican dared not inflame the wrath of the surrounding totalitarian regimes by officially speaking on behalf of a persecuted minority in a far-off land. Hurley urged Mooney to "go very slowly" for fear of Nazi and Fascist repercussions against Vatican interests in Europe.[30]

"We are under severe attack here for our alleged attitude of coddling the Semites," Hurley informed Mooney. "There have been discordant voices even among the Catholic churchmen in Italy on the subject," he revealed. One of those voices belonged to Father Agostino Gemelli, a Franciscan who became one of the main proponents of showing common points of intersection between Fascist and Catholic values. In 1936 Gemelli was appointed president of the Pontifical Academy of Sciences, an illustrious body of scientific scholars that traced its lineage back to Galileo. Hurley described Gemelli as "an important figure" who had recently "out-Coughlined Coughlin" in a speech, "much to the delight of those who are promoting the new racism." In another case, "an Italian bishop had some severe things to say about the Jews in a sermon preached recently," and the sermon was widely quoted in the Italian Fascist press. More importantly, Hurley continued to the kernel of his argument: "The S. of S. [Secretariat of State] has been violently attacked by [Roberto] Farinacci, minister without portfolio and editor of the anti-clerical *Il Regime Fascista*."[31]

The "severe attack" to which Hurley alluded had definite repercussions for Mooney. Any indication that the Holy See was "coddling the Semites" would bring down Farinacci's wrath in Italy. Hurley was making plain to his friend that the Holy See could not meet his wishes and step in to curb Coughlin. Mooney would have to go it alone in Detroit.

Roberto Farinacci was a Fascist editor and politician who wielded great power in both Fascist and Nazi circles and was taken with utmost seriousness at the Vatican in 1938. Farinacci was born in 1892 in Isernia, Italy, and was for many years a political wanderer. In 1914 he became a news reporter for the socialist paper *Popola d' Italia* and met Mussolini. In 1919 he was appointed head of the Cremona *fascio,* and in 1925 he was promoted to general secretary of the Partito Nazionale Fascista (PNF). During the 1930s Farinacci emerged as a leader of both the antisemitic and anticlerical factions within the PNF. By 1938 he was using his editorial position at Mussolini's newspaper *Il Regime Fascista* to meld the two, much to the distress of the Vatican. Mussolini encouraged this dance between clericofascism and antisemitic statesmanship.

Politically speaking, biographer Harry Fornari has argued that Farinacci was "more Fascist than the Duce" and "most completely exemplified the Fascist drive to power through any and all violent means." In what was most likely a planned policy move, Farinacci unleashed a virulent anticlerical/antisemitic campaign against the Vatican at the same time that Father Coughlin was broadcasting his antisemitic speeches in Detroit. On September 15, 1938, Farinacci ridiculed Pope Pius XI's criticism of the recently adopted antisemitic *Manifesto of Italian Racism*. "The Germans are mistaken in assuming that the Catholic Church agrees with the Pope on each and every issue," Farinacci told the German newspaper *Das Schwarze Korps*. "We know that on the racial issue the clergy are split into two camps and that the Pope is powerless to do anything about it."[32]

On November 7, 1938, less than two weeks before Coughlin delivered his controversial Kristallnacht speech, Farinacci spoke to the Fascist Cultural Institute in Milan on the topic "The Church and the Jews." In this widely publicized speech, Farinacci lamented that the Catholic church, "the original source of anti-Semitism," was subduing its antisemitism just when it should be ramping it up. "What has happened to make the official Church become today so philo-Semitic rather than anti-Semitic?" he asked wistfully. "Why do communists, freemasons, democrats, and all the avowed enemies of the Church, praise her today and offer to help her?" For Farinacci, the Catholic church was allowing itself to be "used against Fascism."

Farinacci then moved to a direct threat. "We would hate to see the Church abandon its basic educational mission, in order to interfere in political questions which are the exclusive province of Fascism." The Vatican viewed this allusion to the "basic educational mission" of the church as a direct threat to the Catholic educational system in Italy. Since 1929, Catholic religious instruction in the elementary and secondary public schools had been protected by the state. Under article 36 of the Lateran Treaty, Catholic doctrine was considered to be the "foundation and crown of public instruction." Article 36 was particularly important to Pope Pius XI, who believed that Christian education of the young was a means of safeguarding the faith. Certainly, Farinacci's threat concerning the school question had to be treated seriously.[33]

In the background, Farinacci continued to hammer home his opposition to the Vatican in *Il Regime Fascista*. A "continuous barrage" was leveled against the "Judaeophile Vatican, the ally of Communists, Masons, Jews, and Protestants." Farinacci was dauntless in his quest to harass the church. "The vigilant eye of Farinacci raked the [Catholic] parochial and diocesan bulletins in search of 'treasonable' exhortations to show [Catholic] charity toward the Jews, and the results of his investigation were featured daily in the columns of his newspaper."[34]

Although some historians have concluded that Farinacci's brand of anticlerical antisemitism never gained full support from Mussolini, new research by political historian Roger Griffin indicates that Italian clerical fascism "expanded dramatically" after 1938 and that Il Duce began to encourage Farinacci's propaganda efforts. As Hurley indicated to Mooney in Detroit, Farinacci would view a thumping of Coughlin for his antisemitism as "coddling the Semites."[35]

On January 16, 1939—the same day that Hurley warned Mooney not to speak out against Coughlin—Farinacci publicly praised Father Coughlin and *Social Justice* in *Il Regime Fascista*. According to Farinacci, Coughlin was "a man who appreciates our line of conduct." The Fascist editor then heaped praise upon Coughlin, declaring that "Italians cannot fail to express their sympathy to this apostle of Christianity." Now it became clear that the "vigilant eyes" of Roberto Farinacci squarely met Father Coughlin's. To make matters worse, American Catholic leaders were dismayed when the popular glossy magazine *Look* ran a twelve-frame pictorial titled "Coughlin and the Nazi Bund." The piece argued, on the basis of several sources, that Father Coughlin had direct ties to Fritz Kuhn and his German-American Bund, an arm of German secret intelligence.[36]

Over the next six months, the international aspects of Coughlin's range continued to dog the Catholic hierarchy as various American religious leaders urged Pope Pius XII to step in and silence Coughlin once and for all. C. Everett Clinchy, leader of the National Conference of Christians and Jews, called on Pope Pius XII "to assume the leadership of the religious forces of the Western World, including the harassed ranks of Judaism." Later, Clinchy and Professor Carlton J. H. Hayes, a Catholic convert and well-known historian at Columbia University, urged Catholics to mount a "war on anti-Semitism" for the collective safety of both Catholics and Jews.[37]

In June 1939 a direct plea by Rabbi Louis Gross to Pope Pius XII urging the pontiff "to rebuke Reverend Coughlin in unequivocal terms" was met with silence in Rome and ridicule in Royal Oak. Hurley's increasingly conservative cultural bent did not help American Jewish attempts to obtain a papal censure of Coughlin. Liberals such as Clinchy and Hayes, though Catholic, were suspect for moving too quickly on behalf of Jews. "If you want to find a tyrant," Hurley commented to Luigi Cardinal Maglione in the midst of the Coughlin crisis, "scratch a liberal." "He smiled," Hurley recorded.[38]

With liberal and philosemitic Catholic voices from the United States silenced, Vatican censure of Coughlin proved difficult so long as Farinacci kept up his threats. In late January 1939 he lashed out directly at the Holy See's diplomatic corps while attending high-level meetings in Berlin. "Signor Farinacci, who arrived by train from Italy this morning," the *New York Times* reported in headlines bold enough for Archbishop Mooney to read in Detroit, "was a luncheon guest of Propaganda Minister Joseph Goebbels and this afternoon was received by Chancellor Adolf Hitler." More importantly, during a nighttime speech at the Berlin Sportspalast, Farinacci once again craftily commingled his antisemitism with Catholic anticlericalism. "What we cannot understand today," Farinacci told his Nazi admirers, "is the attitude of the Catholic Church toward this question [i.e., the Jews]. . . . Today the church has more sympathy for Jew-friendly nations than for us." Hitler and Goebbels stood shoulder to shoulder with their Berlin claque and joined in the stormy applause.[39]

U.S. diplomatic officials were both irritated and perplexed by Hitler's uses of Coughlin. In Warsaw, Ambassador Anthony Joseph Drexel Biddle Jr. wrote that for three full days the Berlin *Deutschland Zenda* radio broadcasts featured "a number of quotations" from speeches by Father Coughlin. Assistant Secretary of State George Messersmith was receiving information that verbatim Nazi propaganda was showing up in pro-Coughlin Catholic newspapers in the United States. "Unless the Catholic Church acts to silence Father Coughlin," radio commentator Lewis Browne told a town hall meeting in New York, "they may wake up one morning here in America with a very dark brown-shirt taste in their mouths." President Roosevelt was as trenchant as he was worried. Six months before Coughlin's Kristallnacht speech he told Joseph P. Kennedy, then ambassador to Britain, that he was greatly worried about a demagogue taking up the cause of antisemitism. Roosevelt told Kennedy that if that happened, "there would be more blood running in the streets of New York than in Berlin."[40]

The Nazi use of Coughlin as an anti-American propaganda tool mystified FDR. In March 1939 Julius Streicher, a nominal Catholic and editor-in-chief of the antisemitic newspaper *Der Stürmer,* declared Father Coughlin a model Fascist. "Father Coughlin, in Royal Oak, in the state of Michigan," he informed his readers, "has the courage to speak his conviction. And his conviction is that National Socialism is right." Anticlerical and antisemitic, in 1939 Streicher was reaching his peak as an editor. Hitler was reputed to have said that *Der Stürmer* "was the only paper he ever read from cover to cover." Like Farinacci in Italy, Streicher was manufacturing a view that the religious tenets of Catholicism were inherently antisemitic. With both Streicher and Farinacci praising Coughlin, the Holy See's silence became more conspicuous.[41]

Historian Earl Boyea has hinted that the Vatican was considering a stronger line on Coughlin and wished Mooney to become more vigorous in his disapproval. But Boyea's examinations focus primarily on the period of Bishop Gallagher's tenure and allude only briefly to the "strong stand" that Mooney was encouraged to take, presumably by the Vatican. Boyea's reflections do not address the greater portion of Coughlin's antisemitic phase. Hurley's diaries suggest that the Nazi propaganda tactic of portraying Coughlin as the ideal Catholic leader seemed to be succeeding in panicking high-level Vatican policymakers.[42]

Amazingly, and in diametric opposition to Boyea's suggestions, according to an undated entry in Hurley's Vatican diary there was a brief discussion at the Vatican about *supporting* Coughlin's antisemitic rants. The man who proposed such a plan was Monsignor Domenico Tardini. In 1935 he succeeded Hurley's benefactor, Alfredo Ottaviani, as secretary for the Congregation for Extraordinary Ecclesiastical Affairs. Jesuit historian and confidant of Pope Pius XII Robert Leiber wrote enigmatically in 1967 that "in some instances, as in the Jewish question, he lacked dispassionate judgment."[43]

In a striking revelation, Hurley noted in his Vatican diary that instead of squelching Coughlin out of concern for worldwide Jewish sensitivities, "Tardini thought for a moment to back up Coughlin," because "he [Coughlin] was favored by the Fascists." The disclosure provides a concrete element that may help to answer the vexing question of why neither two popes nor Archbishop Mooney ever disciplined Coughlin during his anti-semitic phase. The ramifications were international and the pressure Vatican-centered. To clamp down on Coughlin in Detroit could launch a backlash against Vatican interests in Europe by Goebbels, Streicher, Farinacci, and perhaps even Mussolini or Hitler.[44]

Looking beyond Tardini, Hurley hoped that the papal secretary of state Luigi Cardinal Maglione might help handcuff Coughlin, but "he had no intention of doing anything against Coughlin." Hurley's diary also suggests that Monsignor Enrico Pucci, the Roman press correspondent for the American bishops' conference, known then as the National Catholic Welfare Conference, also played a role. According to Hurley, Pucci had "attacked Americans." Pucci's involvement in the Coughlin matter has never been reviewed, but historian Peter R. D'Agostino's serious claim that Pucci—though employed by the American bishops—was a full-fledged Fascist spy has to be placed into the equation. Since Pucci was shaping the content of all Catholic press accounts flowing to the United States, he surely would have filtered out Fascist encomiums of the radio priest.[45]

By late 1940, Roberto Farinacci shrewdly surmised the level of his influence regarding the Vatican's position on Coughlin. And he of course used the situation to his advantage. "Father Coughlin takes a firm stand against Jewish democratic propaganda in the United States," he stated publicly in September 1940. Seizing on Mooney's Vatican-imposed help-lessness, he railed further: "High prelates in the United States have at-tempted to muzzle him, but Coughlin has not surrendered!" Hurley's final words to Mooney conveyed the confused position of the Holy See. "It is felt to be more prudent," he summarized from his vantage point at the Secretariat of State, "to wait until passions cool and issues become clarified. . . . It would be well," Hurley made plain, "to give him a little more rope until he gets particularly nasty."[46]

ROOSEVELT TURNS TO ROME
Giving Coughlin "a little more rope" was how Hurley approached the issue of Coughlin's antisemitism a year later when he met at the Vatican with Myron C. Taylor, Roosevelt's personal representative to Pope Pius XII. By 1940 both Roosevelt and Taylor considered Coughlin "particularly nasty," and since the U.S. hierarchy remained mute on the issue, FDR decided

to approach the papal curia directly to get something done regarding Coughlin. Signaling that Coughlin had now become a high-level concern for the Roosevelt administration, Taylor met with Luigi Cardinal Maglione and Hurley on March 8 to discuss the Coughlin case.[47]

Quickening the conversation was the fact that the Coughlin-inspired Christian Front terrorist organization had just been spectacularly captured by the FBI "in a series of simultaneous raids" and put on trial. "Arms, ammunition, and bombs were seized by G-men when they swooped down," the United Press reported. For more than two months, Hoover's FBI publicized this peculiar yet avowedly Catholic group's desire to terrorize Jews, assassinate fourteen members of Congress, seize the New York City Post Office, appropriate New York's Federal Reserve gold, and blow up New York's major bridges and the New York customs building to boot. Playing hardball, FDR agreed to have the Christian Front prosecuted for sedition.[48]

In what was perhaps the nation's first case of modern religious terrorism, FBI director J. Edgar Hoover described the raids as "vitally important to the Bureau," and the conspiracy as a "vast plot to overthrow the government and establish a dictatorship." While the government's case later fizzled for evidentiary reasons, in the final two weeks of January 1940 the "Front" case twisted its way through the national psyche, prewar security consciousness, and major news headlines. The Christian Front trial and accompanying media blitz were just wrapping up as the Maglione-Taylor conversations on Coughlin began.[49]

Hurley was designated to be the secretary for the talks. According to the Vatican White Book, a selectively released compilation of official Vatican documents dealing with World War II, the essence of Taylor's conversation with Maglione "revolved around the racial movement in the United States," that is, the treatment of American Jews. FDR's envoy Taylor stressed to the cardinal that before his departure from Washington, "President Roosevelt gave him a memorandum concerning an anti-Jewish movement in the towns of Brooklyn, Baltimore, and Detroit. The President is informed that this movement is supported by Catholics in those cities and he is afraid that, as a result, anti-Catholic feelings may be re-awakened in the nation." According to the Vatican-published volume under the heading "Notes of Monsignor Hurley of the Secretariat of State," Taylor went on to mention "the activity of Father Coughlin and his violent broadcasts and the misgivings caused by the excitable radio priest."[50]

In his unpublished Vatican diary, however, Hurley made plain that Taylor's conversation with Maglione was much more specific regarding the "activities of the excitable radio priest." "I gather," Hurley wrote, "that the ambassador is still concerned with the Coughlin question and related matters in the American church, e.g., the 'Christian Front' trial, [and] attitudes of certain papers such as *Social Justice* and *The Brooklyn Tablet*." These notes indicate that Roosevelt—through Taylor—was attempting to persuade the Holy See to make a statement either against Coughlin or his rhetorically inspired Christian Front terrorist band. They also prove that the Christian Front plot was a grave concern for the White House.[51]

Maglione listened intently to Taylor and replied that he "was ready to study the question and to examine a note on the matter." He made no commitments. After waiting for more than a month with no response, Roosevelt began to tire of Maglione's studious behavior. "The point to make," he cabled Taylor in frustrated tone, "is that if anti-Jewish behavior is stirred-up, it automatically stirs up anti-*Catholic* feeling, and that makes a general mess."[52]

It took over three months for FDR's concern about Father Coughlin and his "anti-Jewish movement" to register officially with the Vatican Secretariat of State. In early July 1940 the Vatican's resident Americanist Joseph P. Hurley was called in to compose a report on Taylor's concerns and make a recommendation for Vatican policy. Here he played a pivotal role.

On July 2 Hurley sent to Giovanni B. Montini, the Vatican's new substitute secretary of state, his "Opinion Written for His Excellency Mons. *Sostituto*." Until the official Vatican Secret Archives are opened, we must assume that this note written by Hurley was the "note" that Maglione offered to "study" on the matter. In this document, essentially a policy recommendation on Coughlin, Hurley's Americanism trumped any humanitarian response to Coughlin's antisemitism. Persecution of Jews was strictly a Jewish problem, not a Catholic one. Coughlin's part in that persecution was diminished, since his rhetoric fitted the categories that Hurley had imbibed at St. Bernard's under Father Zwierlein.

Consequently, Hurley fell back on the Catholic Americanism that had rankled him about Coughlin in 1936. In his note to Montini, Hurley argued that the Vatican should reprimand Father Coughlin for his "bitter criticism of American internal and external policy," and not for his continued castigation of the Jewish people. But the "patriotic" angle would not work in 1940. With Europe at war, the idea of the Vatican silencing a priest for criticizing American policy would set a poor precedent for other priests who would wish to criticize Axis policies. Only casually did Hurley point out to Montini "the intemperate activities of Father Coughlin," possibly an ambiguous reference to Coughlin's antisemitism.[53]

Unfortunately, Hurley made no mention to his superiors of Roosevelt's insistence on quelling Coughlin's "anti-Jewish" campaign. Why the Holy See did not include Hurley's sanitized memo in its White Book is also perplexing, since it leaves the impression that the published document was the final word on the matter. Taylor's emphatic philosemitic queries come across as part of the official Vatican line, while Hurley's official and sanitized observations are excluded. Hurley's control of the American desk seemed to kill Roosevelt's hopes that the Vatican might robustly silence Coughlin for his antisemitism.

In the end, Coughlin was silenced. His silencing, however, was based on a "secret agreement" made between Archbishop Mooney and Coughlin, under pressure from the U.S. government. By the spring of 1942 the U.S. Justice Department was threatening to have Coughlin jailed and prosecuted under wartime sedition laws. From Rome, Hurley saw the silencing as nothing more than a cobbled fix. Coughlin had been boxed in, not driven out. "He [Coughlin] was not forced," Hurley recorded; "Coughlin quit."[54]

These were the complexities—the multitiered levels of cause and effect—that Hurley was beginning to learn as a junior Vatican diplomat and a national of an emerging democratic superpower. Tact, balance, and keen observation were the necessities of diplomatic life in Rome in the 1930s. As the United States moved away from isolationism, U.S. foreign policy would force Hurley to reevaluate the Vatican culture of discretion. As war threatened to bring down the democracies, Hurley was forced to declare his true moral convictions on matters of war and peace.

CHAPTER FOUR

An American Monsignor in Mussolini's Italy

"THE VITTORIO EMMANUEL MONUMENT was faintly illuminated with rows of flaming torches up to the Coliseum which was red with flames against the night." As the wife of the U.S. ambassador to Italy, Caroline Phillips was provided a front-row view as Hitler, Goebbels, and deputy Nazi chief Rudolf Hess made their dazzling nighttime entry into Rome in early May 1938. "Down the street as he came were the red, white, and green bandera, the black Fascist banner and the German flag with its black swastika. The Square and streets were filled with people behind wooden barriers, soldiers were lined in double file facing the crowd," Phillips recorded in her diary. "As I was escorted from the embassy," she penned in a final recollection of the event, "I glanced and saw Father Hurley with at least thirty American priests."[1]

The period 1938–1940 was a time of heady diplomatic exchange between the United States, Italy, and the Vatican. Historian Davis Schmitz has pointed out that "from September of 1938 to June of 1940, Italy occupied a central position in the thinking of Roosevelt and the United States State Department." The planners in Washington were trying to use Italy as a moderating influence on Hitler.[2]

Mussolini, President Roosevelt reflected, was the key to peace in the Mediterranean. As the Italian dictator pondered the road to war, U.S. diplomats came to the conclusion that the Vatican should be enlisted in

the American mission to keep Italy neutral. Joseph P. Kennedy, U.S. ambassador to the Court of St. James and occasional Catholic troubleshooter,
stated in a confidential letter to Under Secretary of State Sumner Welles
that he was "definitely of the opinion that the influence of the Pope could
be utilized for the cause of peace." Welles sent a copy of Kennedy's letter
to FDR, who was becoming convinced that the United States and the Vatican could work together toward peace in Europe. Hurley, as the resident
American on the Vatican's diplomatic staff, played an important role in
shaping and carrying out America's plan for peace.[3]

Hurley's initial contact with the U.S. government was as liaison to
the office of William A. Phillips, FDR's ambassador in Rome since 1936.
A native of Beverly Farms, Massachusetts, he was a graduate of Harvard
College and had attended Hurley's dream law school, Harvard. Although
he was a lifelong Republican, his reputation for "not rocking the boat"
earned him the esteem of President Roosevelt. In his mission to Italy,
Roosevelt commissioned Phillips primarily to try to keep Mussolini out
of an alliance with Germany and Japan.

The Roosevelt administration believed that Phillips could not only
help cement favorable relations with the Italian government but also unofficially improve U.S.-Vatican relations. An integral part of Phillips's
mission to Rome from 1937 to 1940 was to informally manage Vatican
affairs with the United States. His Vatican work was conducted with utmost secrecy, since the United States had no official mission to the Vatican
and any direct involvement with Catholic diplomacy was sure to cause
considerable political problems in a predominantly Protestant America.
The State Department recognized this predicament. Jay Pierrepont Moffat,
head of the European Division, remarked in 1938 that "various groups"
had for many years been "vocal against the 'Pope of Rome.'" This tricky
church-state situation made public contacts between the United States
and the Holy See politically perilous.[4]

Undaunted, FDR forged ahead with his new diplomatic plan. Roosevelt and his advisors "recognized that the Vatican wielded significant spiritual and moral authority over millions of Catholics around the world, and
they coveted papal support for their domestic and foreign policies." As
William Phillips worked in Rome to gain the support of the papacy and
keep Italy out of the Axis, he increasingly relied on Hurley to lobby for
American interests within the Holy See's Secretariat of State.[5]

Hurley appropriately first met William Phillips on July 4, 1937, when the ambassador claimed a place of honor at the Independence Day banquet at the North American College in Rome. Hurley's contacts with Phillips increased substantially after that meeting. Indeed, Phillips's published memoirs attest to the vitality of the new relationship and to Hurley's pivotal role. "I had informal contacts with the Vatican through Monsignor Joseph P. Hurley, the American member of the Vatican Secretariat who called upon me frequently and with whom I had the pleasantest of relations," Phillips recalled. There was however, more to this "informal contact" than pleasantries. Hurley was becoming enmeshed in a vibrant and substantial secret diplomatic arrangement between the United States and the Vatican.[6]

During this period Hurley's attitudes concerning world events underwent notable revision. As contact with Phillips increased, Hurley's political leanings became more pronounced. While the Fascist tide rose in Italy, Phillips's influence gently prodded Hurley, already a proud American, into a small but active prodemocratic wing at the Vatican. In 1937 Hurley was placed on the editorial board of *Illustrazione Vaticana,* a short-lived glossy journal of opinion and culture with a decidedly democratic tone. Hurley's decision to work closely with the democrats and Americans was a remarkable one, considering, in the words of Vatican wartime observer Vincent A. McCormick, S.J., "the strong Fascist sentiments of so many of the 'smaller monsignori' in Vatican employ." Joseph P. Kennedy went even higher up the ecclesiastical ladder, asking Hurley point blank what he knew "about the Fascist Cardinals in Italy," a reality that Hurley confirmed among "the Cardinals who had direct contact with the people and were . . . naturally patriotic Italians."[7]

Through 1938 and 1939, Hurley became more and more convinced of the righteousness of the Allied cause and the despicable implications of Fascism. Beginning in 1938, William Phillips met intermittently with Hurley to discuss world events and gather Vatican intelligence. Phillips's unpublished manuscripts confirm the depth and vigor of this new alliance. A sampling of topics that the two discussed in 1938 included the Czechoslovakian crisis, Italo-Vatican relations, Fascist anti-Jewish measures, and the Anschluss. Aware of the ambassador's high-level contacts, Hurley gave serious attention to every question. For example, in September 1938 Phillips hinted that the Roosevelt administration would look favorably upon a papal denunciation of war and a statement in favor of world peace. In order to oblige, "Hurley said that he would give the matter serious thought and would talk to some of his colleagues in the Vatican." When Hurley gave "serious thought" to an American proposal, it usually meant that results followed.[8]

As Phillips's relationship with Hurley slowly became known in the Roman diplomatic community, some foreign diplomats began to feel jealous. Others assumed that Phillips had cracked the pope's inner circle. Even foreign ambassadors with official ties to the Vatican were showing up on the doorstep of the American embassy interceding with Phillips to have his "man at the Vatican" approach the papal powers. An early démarche was made by François Charles-Roux, the French ambassador to the Vatican, who "hoped that he [Phillips] could ask Hurley to speak with Cardinal Pacelli without bringing him into it, and impress upon Pacelli the importance of the pope speaking out again once more at this time for the cause of peace." Joseph P. Kennedy acknowledged Pope Pius XI's fondness for the young American. "Monsignor Hurley, who is in Cardinal Maglione's office . . . is a very good friend of the Holy Father." Indeed, Hurley enjoyed such a good relationship with the pontiff that Phillips wasted no time in sounding him out about rumors that Pius XI soon would meet with Hitler.[9]

In the first week of May 1938, as Hitler was preparing for his spectacular Roman visit, questions raged in the press about whether he would have an audience with Pope Pius XI. Surprisingly, as the Nazis continued to maltreat Catholics in Germany and Austria, Hurley relayed to Phillips that the Vatican was desperately trying to get Hitler to sit down with Pius. "William has been seeing Monsignor Hurley this afternoon," Caroline Phillips recorded, "who told him that the Pope is quite ready to see Hitler as the temporal head of one state to another, but Hitler has shown no signs of visiting him." For the feisty Pius, a sit-down with Hitler was not destined to be a friendly chat. This was to be a showdown between the pontiff and the chief persecutor of the Roman Catholic church. "Hurley says that although in weak physical health, the Pope has great moral and intellectual vigor and would undoubtedly speak his mind freely to Hitler on the latter's persecution of the Church." For Hurley, Pius XI's plan for icy confrontation made perfect sense. True ecclesiastical leadership demanded a muscular Christianity that spoke up for the rights of the church, even when it was dangerous to do so. As Mussolini prepared his nighttime extravaganza of urban illumination to welcome Hitler to Rome in "a show staged to impress the world," Hurley began to adopt Pius XI's tactics as his own.[10]

Days before his meeting with Phillips, Hurley was given permission to confront Hitler head-on by writing an anonymous editorial for *Osservatore Romano.* In Vatican circles, the piece would become known as "the Crooked Cross editorial." With swastikas unfurled over Rome's Olympic stadium, "there were now two crosses side-by-side in Rome," the Vatican paper lamented, "the cross of Christianity and crooked cross of neo-paganism." Caroline Phillips noted that the highest levels of the State Department noticed Hurley's anonymous writing. It was Secretary of State Cordell Hull who cabled William Phillips to tell him, "The *Osservatore Romano* has published an article which says that there are now two crosses in Rome[, one] representing Christianity and one paganism." If Hull was impressed with Hurley's prose, Hitler was not. The Führer was incensed by the editorial. Caroline Phillips recorded that all later editions containing Hurley's metaphorical musings were confiscated and suppressed during Hitler's visit.[11]

Even though Hitler bypassed Pope Pius XI during his Roman summit, within the year two British visitors arrived who were eager to have discussions with Vatican officials. Their meetings would have a profound influence on Hurley's thinking, convincing him that Nazism was the main threat to Roman Catholicism. It was during these meetings that Hurley learned that his revered but now ailing Pope Pius XI, who had previously believed that communism and Nazism were equally contemptible, had likewise changed his mind.

In January 1939 British prime minister Neville Chamberlain was accompanied to Rome by his foreign secretary and former viceroy of India, Viscount Halifax. For two days the pair undertook fruitless and sometimes heated conversations with Mussolini and Italian foreign minister Ciano. On January 13 Chamberlain and Halifax met in private audience with the ailing Pope Pius XI. "Much ceremony on arrival," Halifax noted; "Swiss Guards, Chamberlains, and the like. . . . We were taken straight to the Pope, who invited us to sit down." Finally, a familiar face appeared: "Monsignor Hurley, whom I had met in Bangalore, acted as interpreter." Situated midway between the leader of the Catholic spiritual empire and the leaders of the vast British empire, Hurley became privy to the thoughts of three of the world's great anti-Axis leaders.[12]

Both the British government and the Vatican kept the theme of the discussions secret, but Hurley's notes indicate that Chamberlain's objective was to convince Pius XI that Nazism posed a greater threat to the Catholic church than Bolshevik communism. Of course, this would be a tough sell, given the Holy See's long-standing formulations on theological anticommunism. But after Munich, Chamberlain and Halifax became convinced of Hitler's ruthless ambitions. In their talks in January 1939, the pontiff and the prime minister came to a firm agreement on their common "aversion" to the "brutal and totalitarian ideology of Hitlerism." Pius XI opined to Chamberlain and Halifax that Hitler was "a sick man." And Halifax wrote that it was during this conference that Pope Pius XI came to see the communist threat as secondary and "in the end realized that the more immediate menace to the Christian order of Europe was from the Nazis themselves."[13]

The conversion of Pius XI to the notion that the Nazis posed the primary threat to world Catholicism was a pivotal experience for Hurley. At first hand he witnessed a philosophical shift that directly affected papal history. For the next five years, in veiled broadcasts and public pronouncements, Hurley echoed verbatim the sentiments of the Chamberlain-Halifax meeting with Pius XI. For Hurley, it was not that the communist threat was less ideologically repugnant; it was simply that the Nazis posed the foremost *immediate* threat to Catholic interests at the time. "If you have two enemies, and one of them is holding a dagger to your throat," he confided privately, "you have to take care of the enemy holding the knife before you try to defeat the other."[14]

For Hurley, the papal switch was complete. Communism had ceded its primacy as a peril to Nazism. The complication was that within a matter of weeks, his revered Pope Pius XI would be dead. Because of his condition, Pius XI had very little time to pronounce publicly on his shift of view. Like Pius XI's emerging thoughts on Hitler's race theory, this new papal perspective would lie dormant and now faced the risk of being lost. Hurley, who had been present at the meeting at which this political recalibration was achieved, adopted Pius XI's perspective as his own. As with the "Crooked Cross" editorial, he loyally stood ready to broadcast the views of the pope. It was unclear whether Pope Pius XI's eventual successor, whoever that might be, would do the same. And all the time, rumors of war lurked in the background.

"[The] political scene [is] much confused in Europe at the moment," he wrote to Mooney, "but there is no change in the direction of the drift; it is still bad." On September 1, 1939, the drift became a breach when Hitler plunged his Panzer divisions into Poland and brought Europe to arms. "It is too early yet to say what will be the outcome of the purported [Vatican] peace proposals," Hurley wrote a month after the Polish invasion; "if they fail, I think we shall see war in the grand manner."[15]

During this crucial period of war preparation in the United States, Hurley became more active in U.S.-Vatican diplomacy. His work was secret and heretofore has gone undetected. Arguably, if Hurley's closeness to American officials had been found out, it would have caused a clamor back in a still largely anticatholic United States. Hurley's secret moves were taking place between a home front still uneasy with Catholic power and a Fascist state rapidly moving into an ambit influenced by Hitler's anticatholicism. Remarkably, Hurley managed to conduct sophisticated behind-the-scenes diplomacy through correspondence with U.S. embassy officials, through work with Vatican Radio, and in particular through the Vatican's official news organ, *Osservatore Romano*.

CASSOCK AND DAGGER, 1938–1940

"For the first time that I can recall," Jay Pierrepont Moffat of the State Department's European division reflected, "We have a curious paradox of the very groups which used to be most vocal against the 'Pope of Rome,' now being strong adherents of the Vatican because of its stand against Nazism." When Pius XI's philosophical turn against fascism became known in diplomatic circles, U.S. diplomats raced to use the new papal prerogative to their advantage. William Phillips quickly began to develop Hurley as a like-minded asset inside the Vatican. If New York's Archbishop Francis J. Spellman was "clearly the Vatican's man in the American hierarchy" by 1939, Hurley was secretly becoming FDR's "man at the Vatican" during the same time and in a more perilous place.[16]

As world circumstances slowly pulled America into the unfolding events in Europe, William Phillips increasingly counted on Hurley to help shape public opinion in Italy and at the Vatican. The mechanism by which Phillips hoped to influence public and world opinion was the editorial page of *Osservatore Romano*. "This newspaper," one observer wrote in 1937, "is really more than a newspaper. It is the organ of the Holy See, the organ of the Catholic Church, and speaks for the church to the five continents."[17]

On September 2, 1938, Phillips called Hurley to the American embassy for a private consultation. After making some preliminary observations about the general world situation, Phillips came around to the crux of his interview. "I went over with him," Phillips recalled, "several of the recent speeches by the President and Secretary Hull and pointed out to him in copies of the *Osservatore Romano* that all but one had been very poorly mentioned, and that the Secretary's statement made on the anniversary of the signature of the Briand-Kellogg Pact, which was remarkably appropriate to the present moment, had not been mentioned at all." Gently, Phillips tried to lure Hurley into representing the interests of U.S. foreign policy. "Hurley seemed interested and took away the copies which I had handed him, and I hope that they will be included in the Vatican organ," Phillips concluded. "Of course, none of them have been alluded to in the Italian press."[18]

Ten days later Hurley called again at the American embassy. Apparently he had been given the go-ahead by his superiors to gather information from the Americans for use in the Vatican paper. It is difficult to say if the permission was granted by Pius XI, Cardinal Maglione, or the *Osservatore Romano* editors. Nevertheless, he asked "that any Presidential or Secretarial speeches which had bearing on international affairs might be sent to him as soon as they were received by the embassy." The speeches, Hurley informed Phillips, "were to be transcribed literally in the *Osservatore Romano*." This was a crucial coup for Phillips, since the Vatican paper rarely published speeches of politicians. At the same time, Vatican officials gave approval for Hurley's secret work with the American embassy to continue. "I can communicate with the Embassy," he scribbled in his notebook later that day.[19]

This brief exchange between Hurley and Ambassador Phillips initiated a chain of events that drew the Vatican newspaper into a web of Fascist intrigue and suspicion. Hurley's influence upon the editorial board of *Osservatore Romano*, particularly his working friendship with its editor, Count Giuseppe Dalla Torre, allowed him to present American aims as ready fare for news comment. Dalla Torre, who was increasingly open to Allied opinions, was becoming viewed as a "Francophile editor" by the Italian Fascists and German Nazis for his openness to news from democratic quarters. Truly, Dalla Torre's free editorializing was astounding given that the Fascists had suspended freedom of the press and by 1938 were cracking down vigorously on antiregime activity. Undeterred, Dalla Torre used the neutrality of the Vatican State to ward off Fascist attempts at intimidation. The circulation of *Osservatore Romano* increased considerably during the Fascist era because it was considered to be the "only reliable source of news" in Italy.[20]

From 1938 to 1940 Hurley presented William Phillips's material to Dalla Torre for publication in *Osservatore Romano*. Phillips revealed to Hurley that the *Osservatore* would need to print the American material over a period of time. "I reminded Hurley," Phillips wrote in his unpublished memoirs, "that in America both the President and the Secretary of State had to keep saying the same thing over and over again . . . in order to make an impression on the public. . . . I said that in these days when news passed so easily in and out of men's minds, repetition seemed essential." Phillips was deftly cultivating the young monsignor to present American political opinion as synonymous with the Vatican's religious perspective.[21]

Hurley's appropriation of the "blessed harmony" equation between U.S. principles and Vatican interests allowed for little reflection. In fact, Phillips provided Hurley with direct radio bulletins that were edited and published by the State Department in Washington. Out of view, and most likely out of fear of the Italian secret police, the cassocked Cleveland monsignor shuffled to and from the U.S. embassy with William Phillips's Washington radio bulletins discreetly tucked under his black robes. In a revealing notation, Hurley hand-marked the head of one State Department radiogram "Di Notario dall O.R."—"for publication in *Osservatore Romano*." Through Hurley, Phillips had finally cracked the Italian censors. State Department material was being published verbatim in the Vatican paper. But although this was a diplomatic success for Phillips, the risks for Hurley were tremendously high.[22]

"The espionage is terrific," Caroline Phillips recorded in her diary; "no members of the government are allowed . . . [intimate conversation] with any foreigners, and dare not talk of anything dangerous—except if out in open spaces or alone in a large room in whispers." Many Vatican bureaucrats were "shadowed day and night" by the Fascist police, while "Italian Secret Service men checked on the activities of the foreign envoys to the Holy See." "Everything is watched and recorded," Hurley signaled in an undated letter to Mooney. That he was able to evade the constant eavesdropping and surveillance of the Fascists was a credit to his ingenuity and courage.[23]

A period of vehement press attack and counterattack between the Fascists and the democratic circle within the Vatican now commenced. This period came to be known, according to historian MacGregor Knox, as the time of the *"Osservatore Romano* Struggle." Hurley was quick to pick up on Phillips's admonition that "repetition seemed essential," regardless of the dangers. Soon *Osservatore Romano* began publishing news from Britain, France, and America, much to the annoyance of the Fascist regime. In the summer of 1938 the Vatican organ reported the Czechoslovak crisis with its usual objectivity, but "did not attempt to conceal its deep sympathy with the Czechs in their hour of trial." Once more Roberto Farinacci fulminated that the Vatican was undertaking a "demagogic policy" aimed at "capturing the sympathy of the democratic nations."[24]

In January 1939 the Hurley-Phillips relationship moved into high gear. On January 27, U.S. Under Secretary of State Sumner Welles delivered a strong rebuke to the dictators in a speech at the annual meeting of the New York State Bar Association in New York City. Welles's speech condemned "any country which engaged in cruel and inhuman treatment of human beings," a clear rap at the Reich's anti-Jewish and antichristian policies. "The people of the United States and their government," Welles continued, "have always maintained, and in practice have made clear, that they assert the right to protest and to condemn the cruel and inhuman treatment of human beings wherever such brutality occurs." The next day the speech received front-page coverage in the *New York Times*. Welles, eager to trumpet his message to Hitler and Mussolini, encrypted the entire speech and sent it to William Phillips in Rome.[25]

"You have presented the whole picture of our international relations in as perfect a manner as could be done," Phillips wrote to Welles, understanding that it was his job to place Welles's message behind Fascist lines. Phillips outlined his plan to Welles: "In the hope that your speech will filter into the minds of the Italian public through the Vatican press organ, the OSSERVATORE ROMANO, I have immediately sent a copy of it to a certain

Monsignor who is a member of the Vatican Secretariat. That "certain Monsignor" immediately sent the speech to Count Dalla Torre for publication in *Osservatore Romano*. With the publication of Welles's New York speech, the partnership for democracy was cemented. For covert propaganda purposes, Hurley's connection with *Osservatore Romano* proved to be an important and highly effective means by which Phillips could "filter into the minds of the Italian public" the U.S. position on world affairs. By mid-July 1939, Hurley's tactics generated a repetition of Allied news and counterfascist opinion in *Osservatore Romano* that was so noticeable that it discomfited the highest levels of Mussolini's regime.[26]

"By order of the Duce," Italian foreign minister Count Galeazzo Ciano recounted in his diary on July 20, "I have presented an ultimatum to the Nuncio for *Osservatore Romano*. Either it will cease its subtle propaganda against the Axis or we shall prohibit its circulation in Italy. . . . It has become the official organ of the anti-Fascists." Ciano's representations, however, were not enough to quell the dwindling yet vigorous forces of democracy within the Vatican. In late September 1939 the bothersome Vatican paper became the center of another international incident, an incident which marked a crisis in Italo-Vatican relations and one engineered by Monsignor Joseph Patrick Hurley.[27]

"Roosevelt Asks for Lifting of Embargo" were the headlines of *Osservatore Romano* on September 23, 1939. On September 21 President Roosevelt had called a special session of Congress to consider revision of existing U.S. neutrality laws, which prohibited Britain and France, now belligerents, from purchasing war materials from a neutral United States. Roosevelt's proposal, in what came to be known as the Neutrality Act of 1939, encompassed legislative changes that would allow Britain and France to purchase war materials on a "cash and carry" basis. "The revision of the neutrality legislation," one historian has stated, "was the first major attempt by the Roosevelt Administration to provide meaningful assistance to the British against Hitler." Roosevelt's speech to Congress spelled out the threat of the dictators, and it was widely believed that the Italian press would refuse to cover the speech.[28]

Brazenly defying the Fascist censors, *Osservatore Romano* carried the full text of Roosevelt's speech, supplied by Hurley, in four columns running the length of the front page. A sympathetic editorial written by second editor Dr. Guido Gonella characterized the new American Neutrality

Act as a legitimate instrument "to protect the neutral integrity and security of the United States." Although they could not know it at the time, the editors at *Ossservatore Romano* were entering into war with the Italian government by declaring America's neutrality.[29]

Mussolini and Ciano considered the showy publication of Roosevelt's Neutrality Act speech to be a direct affront to their official representations of July 20. The Vatican newspaper now became the object of the nastiest Fascist reprisals. No longer would Mussolini employ the angels' game of diplomacy to protest Vatican impetuosity. Now he resorted to common thuggery to get his point across. On October 5 Guido Gonella was arrested and violently thrown in jail on charges of "working against the regime." Farinacci castigated Gonella in the pages of *Il Regime Fascista* and suggested that Gonella, Count Dalla Torre, and Monsignor Giovani B. Montini (the future Pope Paul VI) were involved in a plot to place the perennial antifascist Alcide de Gasperi on the editorial staff of *Osservatore Romano*. Although it did not come to fruition, a plot was hatched to kidnap Montini, then a substitute at the Secretariat of State, in an effort to stifle his influence at the *Osservatore*. Through all the madness, Farinacci continued railing against the "Jews, Masons, and hack writers of *Osservatore Romano*."[30]

Unaware of the arrests and intrigue inside the Vatican, the American embassy in Rome reveled in the aftermath of its latest antifascist coup. Phillips sensed the extent to which the publication of FDR's neutrality speech vexed the Duce. Without delay he wired Washington that he had succeeded brilliantly in placing FDR's neutrality message before the Italian Fascist world. "Ambassador Phillips in Rome cabled me on September 25 that the Vatican newspaper *Osservatore Romano* had carried a full and objective report of the President's neutrality message to Congress," Secretary of State Hull proudly penned in his memoirs. The news went right up the line. As soon as he received Phillips's cable, Hull sent a copy "to the President for his information." Enthusiastic, but nonetheless leaving Hurley out of the equation entirely, Phillips followed up Hull's memo with a direct communication to FDR informing him that *Osservatore Romano* had been roundly condemned by Mussolini's *Regime Fascista* for printing his neutrality speech.[31]

Within ten days of Hurley's placement of the neutrality speech on the front page of *Osservatore Romano*, like a shot out of the blue, Hull received a "long memorandum" from FDR discussing the feasibility of establishing some sort of special representation at the Vatican. "This is a wholly original thought with me, and I have discussed it with no one else," Roosevelt confided. In fact various high-ranking Catholics in the United States, including New York's Archbishop Francis Spellman, had been pressing Roosevelt since the summer of 1936 to establish diplomatic relations with the Vatican. Now, with Hurley's work yielding tangible political results in Rome, FDR had a practical reason to cement such a relationship.[32]

Following publication of Roosevelt's neutrality speech, Phillips believed that he needed to offer Hurley some sort of thanks, and President Roosevelt concurred. In October 1939 Ambassador Phillips "had the pleasure of delivering to Monsignor Hurley . . . a message from the President expressing his pleasure at the attitude of the *Osservatore Romano*, which has been the only Italian paper to quote and refer generously to the president's and secretary's statements." Phillips noted that "Hurley seemed rather gratified" at receiving the personal communication from the president. This was a profound experience for the patriotic priest. He could never have imagined, while growing up in the grimy sandlots of Newburgh, that one day he would command the gratitude of so powerful a figure as Franklin Delano Roosevelt. For a young Irish-American priest whose Americanization in Catholic schools stressed the dignity of the presidency, it was a climactic experience.[33]

TWO POPES, TWO LEADERS

"I left the Vatican a few minutes before six with Monsignor Joseph Patrick Hurley," *New York Times* correspondent Camille Cianfarra jotted in his notes. It was early February 1939, and Hurley's beloved Achille Ratti, Pope Pius XI, had recently died at the Vatican. "We stood in St. Peter's Square watching the lights appear through the windows in the Cardinals' bedrooms." "Who will be the next Pope?" Cianfarra turned and asked Hurley. "You shall know fairly soon, I think." "I should not be surprised if you have the answer tomorrow." Hurley was absolutely correct.[34]

On March 2 Eugenio Cardinal Pacelli was elected Pope Pius XII in the shortest electoral conclave on record—all of one day. Described by one observer as a "gentle, almost mystical" pope, Pius XII contrasted sharply with the former "tough, practical and intransigent" Pius XI. Although he suspected Pacelli would be elected pope, Hurley was still grieving the loss of Pius XI. Cianfarra claimed that over time Hurley had become known in the English-speaking press corps as always being at Pope Pius XI's side during interviews. The American press had even tabbed Hurley "the pope's personal interpreter."[35]

Joseph P. Hurley idolized Pope Pius XI, Achille Ratti. The relationship had its roots in parallel personal histories. Whereas Hurley had virtually nothing in common with the aristocratic and elegant Eugenio Cardinal Pacelli, his background was strikingly similar to that of the pope they both served. Perhaps most important, both Hurley's and Ratti's early lives were set amid poor neighborhoods of working-class industrial cities. Like Michael Hurley, Ratti's father had been a factory manager. These origins fostered perseverance and stamina. Hurley's muscular Christianity was played out on the gridiron and in the boxing ring, Ratti's in mountain climbing. As young men, both had been tagged as equally athletic and bookish.

Their early educational trajectories were similar, with both attending local Catholic schools and the local seminary. Both quietly labored for the church in their early careers, and expected no more from their vocations than what they had first desired. For Ratti, this meant a life as librarian and a curator of ancient manuscripts at Milan's prestigious Ambrosian Library. For Hurley, it meant the life of a simple parish priest in Cleveland, Ohio. Though not on the same scale, their first ventures into papal diplomacy had come about unexpectedly—Ratti's with his selection by Pope Benedict XV to serve as apostolic visitator to Poland in 1918, Hurley's with Mooney's request to join him in Bangalore. Thereafter these two men from relatively humble backgrounds were thrust into the world of elite diplomacy. All the circumstances were ripe for a father-son or at least a mentoring relationship between the aging pope and the young priest.

In contrast to Ratti, Eugenio Cardinal Pacelli was descended from the so-called black nobility of Rome—families who had been granted their titles by the pope rather than by the king of Italy. The Pacellis were illustrious papal civil servants. Although in any larger, secular government their work might have been viewed as routine, within the minute and fiercely loyal lay civil service of the Vatican the family's prestige was second to none. Pacelli's grandfather, Marcantonio Pacelli, had served Pope Pius XI as deputy minister of the interior of the Papal States and had collaborated in founding *Osservatore Romano* in 1861. Francesco Pacelli, Eugenio's brother, had been Pius XI's personal representative at the negotiation of the 1929 Lateran Treaty; their father, the elder Francesco, had served the papal tribunals as an expert on canon law.

Such exalted lineage stood in stark contrast to the backgrounds of all the American clerics who had influenced Hurley's life up to that point—Mooney, Powers, and even the bishops of Cleveland. His experience and theirs was of an immigrant American church, of a clergy drafted from the dirt-poor Catholic ghettos of the East Coast and Midwest. Although a priestly vocation allowed entrance into the American middle class, the starting point had always been deprivation. Hurley's experience was of high-level clerics who had toiled up from the ranks through intelligence, tact, and the ability to overcome the obstacles erected by religious discrimination. His relationship with Achille Ratti had reinforced his assumptions about clerical leadership.

Eugenio Giovanni Pacelli represented something totally other. A diplomatic and smoothly urbane descendant of one of the old Roman princely families, more ascetic than athletic, he presented a frail and somber figure amid the clouds of war. Over time, as their conceptions of papal foreign policy diverged, a low-grade tension emerged between Hurley and Pacelli.

There were important personal circumstances that allowed Hurley to frame Pacelli in contrast to Papa Ratti. The primary element of Hurley's allegiance to Ratti was a face-to-face relationship that developed between the older pope and younger priest. In addition, Pacelli, who toiled in the Secretariat's First Section, may have been unconvinced of the talents of the recently arrived American in the Second Section. Moreover, it was Hurley who, through toil and merit, became a court favorite of Pope Pius XI so soon after his arrival.[36]

Within a year of landing in the curia, Hurley was requested by Pope Pius XI to act as his personal translator for all radio broadcasts and interviews conducted in English. This was a high honor and one that put him in a dialogic relationship with the pope. One of his first radio broadcasts was of the pope's words to the Seventh National Eucharistic Congress, held in Cleveland in October 1935. In 1936 he translated a long meeting between Pius XI and Martin Quigley, the Catholic movie-studio contact who was instrumental in drafting the first Hollywood Production Code. In discussing ideas for what would later become the encyclical *Vigilanti Cura* (With

Vigilant Care; June 29, 1936), the first papal treatise on motion pictures, Hurley could hardly keep up with the inquisitive pope. Since Pius spoke English poorly, he kept leaning on Hurley during the interview—at points nearly shouting "demanda lui, demanda lui!"—"ask him, ask him!" Hurley had trouble keeping up with Pius XI during the interview, but the fact that the pope kept him on as his translator until his death was a remarkable statement of trust, ability, allegiance, and personal affection.[37]

The high point of this relationship was Hurley's translation of the talks with Neville Chamberlain and Lord Halifax in January 1939. Hurley sat attentively while Pius XI attached Vatican policy to the concept that Nazism now presented a deeper threat to the church than atheistic communism, a monumental change to which Cardinal Pacelli was not privy. All of this meant that Hurley's papal relationship was personal. He possessed an entrée into the papal circle that no other American, even the former Roman curial assistant Francis Spellman, then the auxiliary bishop of Boston, was able to claim. Hurley's point of contact with Pope Pius XI was eye-to-eye, both individually and philosophically.

Consequently, the death of Pope Pius XI was a great blow to Hurley. The election of Cardinal Pacelli as his successor made the Clevelander's career path much more precarious. Hurley's extensive personal and episcopal archive is conspicuous for its absence of personal letters, testimonies, or accolades from and for Pacelli. While Hurley praised G. B. Montini at length, there was little declamation on his parallel boss, Cardinal Pacelli.

Almost from the moment Pacelli arrived at the Vatican, the two diplomats began to drift apart. The split may have occurred as early as 1936, over what Hurley perceived as Pacelli's inability to dampen his fears of communism and see Nazism as the primary threat to world Catholicism. Pacelli demonstrated his dread of communism early in his tenure as secretary of state of the Holy See, and in Hurley's own region of study for the Vatican—America.[38]

In late September 1936 the Holy See hastily announced to the world that Cardinal Pacelli would visit the United States of America. The cardinal "had intended to go to Switzerland for his usual annual vacation, but decided to at the last minute to go to the United States instead." In an era when aviators were wildly celebrated, the press dubbed Pacelli "The Flying Cardinal" as he embarked on a cross-country tour of the United States in a

Boeing airliner. During his trip Pacelli received several honorary degrees, toured hundreds of Catholic sites, and met with numerous business and civic leaders. In October, during a brief stopover in Cleveland, Pacelli invited two of Hurley's sisters onto his ceremonial platform and publicly blessed them in front of the local media and gathered dignitaries. Hurley was grateful to Pacelli for blessing his sisters, but the family blessing was probably more at the behest of Pope Pius XI than of Pacelli himself. In November, two days after the presidential election, Pacelli met privately with President Franklin Roosevelt at his mother's home in Hyde Park, New York.[39]

At the time of this writing, historians have only speculated on the substance of the talks, since formal documentation has never been published. Suggestions have ranged from a silencing of Father Coughlin, to the U.S. position on the Catholic church's struggle in Mexico, to the establishment of full diplomatic relations between the United States and the Vatican. Historian Gerald P. Fogarty, S.J., has indicated that the silencing of Coughlin "did not seem to be a major reason for the tour," and historian John Cornwell has argued that the talks were aimed at establishing U.S.-Vatican diplomatic relations, although this move did not take place until late 1939. The only eyewitness commentary on the discussions, an oral-history interview recorded in 1963, provides an inkling of the substance of these talks. In this interview there is an affirmation that in late 1936 Cardinal Pacelli was neurotically obsessed with the worldwide communist threat.[40]

In early May 1943 President Roosevelt was entertaining some dinner companions at his family home in Hyde Park. Later the guests retired to the library for some postprandial chat. At the time, Archbishop Spellman was touring Spain on a highly publicized quasi-diplomatic mission. With Spellman's trip as a backdrop, someone asked what Roosevelt thought of Pope Pius XII. One of the dinner guests, Florence Kerr, a regional supervisor of the New Deal Works Progress Administration, recalled FDR's remarkable characterization of his 1936 encounter with Cardinal Pacelli at Hyde Park. "Apparently enjoying himself greatly," Kerr said, FDR told his guests the gist of what he described as a "mental sparring contest" with Cardinal Pacelli. The first jab was thrown by Pacelli, who, sounding more like Father Coughlin than the Holy See's cardinal secretary of state, posited the far-fetched assumption that the United States was ripe for a communist takeover. "Pachelli [sic] kept saying, 'The great danger in America is that it will go communist.'" Kerr went on to describe with great verve what emerged as a confrontation between the president and the future pope. Because of the importance of the exchange, it is worth quoting at length: "FDR said, the great danger in America is that it will go Fascist. No, says Pachelli. Yes, said FDR." Kerr quoted FDR as saying: "So we chewed on that for three days. He went back to Rome saying that the great danger in America is that it will go communist. I told him it wouldn't. . . . I said, I think they are just as apt to go Fascist as they are to go communist." "No! says Pachelli, they would go communist! Mr. President, you simply do not understand the terrible importance of the communist movement." "You just don't understand the American people," the President reportedly told the Italian Cardinal during his first-ever trip to the United States.[41]

Through 1937 and 1938, as Nazi persecution of Catholics in Germany intensified, Pacelli became more critical of Hitler and his regime. In one transcribed memo—arguably the only time Pacelli personally expressed his disdain for Hitler—the cardinal described the Nazi dictator as "not only an untrustworthy scoundrel but as a fundamentally wicked person."[42] But while Pacelli uttered his distaste for Hitler behind closed doors, the looming threat of communism still prevailed. The cardinal's visceral suspicions of communism were difficult to shake.

Astonishingly, Pacelli saw Hitler's Nazism as merely a political ruse. Aware that Hitler's earliest ostensible political alliance was with the social-ist German Workers' Party in 1919, he remained suspicious of Hitler as a politician of the left. On the basis of a face-to-face conversation with Pacelli in 1937, Alfred Klieforth, then the U.S. consul in Cologne, transmitted these thoughts to the State Department in early 1939. Klieforth concluded that Pacelli believed Hitler's adoption of rightist National Socialism was a put-up job. According to Pacelli, Hitler was not a true Nazi and "in spite of appearances would end up in the camp of the left-wing Nazi extremists where he began his career." Pacelli of course had no idea that Hitler's earliest political attachment to the anticapitalist and antisemitic German Workers' Party was a trick in the first place. Hitler's first foray into politics was wholly orchestrated by the German army, which paid him to act as an infiltrator and political informant. In early 1939, State Department officials decided to reserve comment on Pacelli's flawed judgment of the Führer's political allegiances.[43]

For Hurley, Pacelli's private views on Hitler meant nothing unless they were voiced publicly. If Pacelli indeed considered Hitler a "scoundrel" and a "fundamentally wicked person," he should say so in public or at least conduct business with Hitler on that basis. A large part of what would emerge as Hurley's antagonism with Pacelli was the latter's failure to consistently and openly condemn Catholic enemies regardless of the costs. Hurley's growing Americanism, and his co-optation by Phillips into Roosevelt's camp, heightened and underscored his personal disagreements with Eugenio Pacelli.[44]

What was also certain in 1939 was that with the election of Cardinal Pacelli as Pope Pius XII, a new shift occurred in Vatican policy—a shift away from the public antinazi policy of Pope Pius XI. Diplomatic confrontation gave way to conciliation. In the words of historian Owen Chadwick, "Vatican policy changed overnight." The best and most recent chronicle of this change is papal historian Frank J. Coppa's *The Papacy, the Jews, and the Holocaust*, which chronicles the diplomatic disagreements between Cardinal Pacelli and Pope Pius XI over several years. In his treatment of contrasting viewpoints, Coppa picks up on a nuance that many at the time—and some even today—seem to overlook. Following the diplomatic style of Pope Benedict XV, who held the papacy during World War I, Pope Pius XII's new plan "insisted that the papal position was not one of neutrality—which implied indifference—but impartiality." Pius XII refused to have the Holy See officially tied to either side of the conflict. Coppa rightly describes the switch as "a nicety and distinction understood by few." Some experts who did understand the new stance, however, found it unsuitable. Hurley did understand the change, but he was also unable to accept the new strategy.[45]

To Hurley, this was a school of diplomatic procedure that was devised to fight the previous war. What Hurley would begin to iterate in his public speeches and shielded broadcasts over the next six years was that even this cautious position of impartiality could not be countenanced. Times had changed. New and more lethal political philosophies had entered the sweep of history. For Hurley, a new facet of battle had been introduced that spelled doom for the church if not resisted vocally and publicly—ideology. As Hurley would point out, the war now developing in Europe was no longer fueled by the state-to-state nationalism of World War I. Impartiality, while perhaps still amenable within the halls of some foreign ministries, became dubious when the larger conflict was an ideological one—"a war for Christian Civilization." For Hurley there could be no impartiality on Nazism. As "war in the grand manner" erupted, all of Hurley's positions would be based not on his perceptions of which "state" ought to be preferred, or how dexterously the church remained nonaligned, but precisely on which "ism" ought to be annihilated. In this sense, he differed viscerally with Pope Pius XII.

As soon as Cardinal Pacelli became Pope Pius XII, his new swing to impartiality began to take shape. "The change in the Vatican was reflected in its relationship with Germany," Peter Kent has written, "and the anti-Nazi pronouncements of Pius XI were not repeated. . . . Instead, the new pope expressed his 'burning desire' for peace between Church and State, and his love for Germany." This marked reversion to a statist view of diplomacy would make Hurley's continued presence at the Vatican precarious. And in addition to the outward policy change, an inward change was occurring.[46]

Pacelli's decision-making style also was decidedly different from his predecessor's. Reflecting on the decision-making patterns of Pope Pius XII in 1961, two years before the historiographical controversy surrounding Pius's wartime pronouncements was stirred up, Domenico Tardini revealed that as pope, Pacelli would "pray over decisions, weigh the possible consequences, both favorable and unfavorable, and then make a pronouncement." But "controversial" decisions often drove Pacelli to indecisiveness. When Pacelli was about to make a controversial decision, he wandered into a "delicate phase," in Tardini's words, and liked to "sugar the pill" for those who would have to swallow it. "Taking the document that had been prepared, he would eliminate one or another clause that he found too strong, insert some more pleasing expressions, add a few words of praise. The aim was to so skillfully sugar-coat the distasteful admonition that 'the patient . . . would sometimes absorb the sugar with relish and not even notice he had taken a pill.'"[47]

Pius XII's penchant for sugar-coating posed a growing conflict for Hurley. To the Cleveland monsignor, it was axiomatic that any diplomatic complaint register squarely with the opposing party. It was the diplomacy of intransigence that had won the Mylapore Agreement for the Vatican in 1928. In Japan, Hurley had squared off with the formidable Japanese militarists as well as the Canadians and "played rough" to bring home a diplomatic win. Now, on the eve of war, was no time to cave in to obsolete diplomatic norms. Hurley's aim in diplomacy had always been to project power, persistence, and moral inflexibility.

Since Hurley's attitudes concerning papal diplomacy had been formed under the personal aegis of Pope Pius XI, he held allegiance unswervingly to the author of the forthright antifascist encyclicals *Non Abbiamo Bisogno* (On Catholic Action in Italy; June 1931) and *Mit brennender Sorge* (With Deep Anxiety; March 1937). The castigation of Nazism was to be done publicly. "The church seems to be caught in a position of guilt," he wrote in 1965 while the Vatican grappled with allegations of wartime silence during the Holocaust in connection with the writing of *Nostrae Aetate* (In Our Time)—the first church decree on the Jews. "They [non-Catholics] blame the church for the acts of anti-God governments." But Hurley knew that forceful and public antinazism ruled the day for much of the 1930s. "Ratti said it in March 1937," a frustrated Hurley penned in reference to *Mit brennender Sorge,* the first papal encyclical to publicly criticize Nazism, "even if Pacelli missed the point later."[48]

Pacelli's "missing the point" on publicly condemning Nazism may have been situated in a point of his personality—one that also conflicted with Hurley's Americanist view of muscular Christianity. Remarking on Pacelli's temperament, Tardini later explained that "he was not made to be a fighter," and was distinct in outward personality from Pope Pius XI, "who relished a fight." In 1939 the antifascist journalist Dorothy Thompson wrote that when a friend asked Cardinal Pacelli about the emerging European "stateolatry" during his 1936 visit to America, he reportedly spoke from the "long view of things," thinking "in terms of cycles and epochs." "The Church is bound to win," Pacelli intimated, "It always has. All these movements run their course. I do not believe in fighting against them." But pacifism and sugar-coating were not in Hurley's genes. For Hurley, if the opponent did "not even notice he had taken a pill," then the entire object of diplomatic battle was moot. Hurley, like his papal mentor, also "relished a fight." Avoiding such a fight would have repercussions, as well, on the personal level.[49]

Pacelli and Hurley seemed to retain a "cool relationship," according to one former Hurley associate. The coolness was so pronounced that even many years later, whenever Hurley heard priests extolling Pope Pius XII in conversation, he would immediately break in, dominate the conversation, and begin to explain the many wonderful qualities of Pope Pius XI.

All this personal aversion emerged in spite of the fact that Eugenio Pacelli was the Vatican secretary of state for six years, and technically Hurley's boss during that time. As Pacelli assumed leadership of the church as Pope Pius XII, Hurley refused to relinquish his allegiance to Pope Pius XI, especially when it came to the public presentation of Vatican aims. A nuanced Vatican foreign policy deemphasized critical moral claims at a time when the world was searching for moral clarity and leadership. For Hurley, Christian realpolitik, especially when dealing with the Nazi threat, could not endure sugar-coating of any kind and remain morally viable.[50]

At precisely the same time as Hurley was drawing these conclusions about Vatican foreign policy, FDR and his global strategists were becoming more confrontational in their approach to Nazism. Consequently, after the election of Cardinal Pacelli as pope, Hurley became more and more attracted to the resolute anti-Axis position surfacing in U.S. foreign policy circles than the nonconfrontational style taking shape within the new pontificate. Throughout the papal transition of early 1939 and into late 1940 Hurley would refine his commitment to public antinazism and warm to the American attitude.

Like Pope Pius XI, Hurley had determined that Nazism was the primary threat to Christian civilization, a threat with which no compromises could be made. Later in his career Hurley referred to Pope Pius XI as "my revered superior for five years," who "did not shrink from a public castigation of Cardinal Innitzer and the weak-kneed Austrian Bishops in 1938." No such estimations survive for Pacelli. As Pius XII moved into his papacy, Hurley's Americanism, coupled with his brand of muscular Christianity, allowed him to become more deeply critical of the new pope's diplomatic choices. It would only be a matter of time before Monsignor Joseph P. Hurley, the former boxer, Cleveland football star, muscular Christian, and diplomat of steely determination, would fall away from the new papal program.[51]

CHAPTER FIVE

"Spies Everywhere"

HURLEY AT VATICAN CITY, 1940

SOON AFTER Cardinal Pacelli's coronation as Pope Pius XII, a flurry of diplomatic activity took place between the Vatican and the United States. This new activity meant that Hurley's role as the resident American at the Vatican would become more valuable. It also meant that his emergent Americanism would be put to a test of allegiance. If Hurley fully aligned himself with Pope Pius XII's new and nuanced diplomacy, chances were that a prestigious east coast or large midwestern bishopric awaited him. The new American diplomatic moves culminated on December 23, 1939, when Pius XII and Franklin Roosevelt finally reached an accord establishing an official U.S. presence at the Vatican. Myron C. Taylor was named President Roosevelt's personal representative to His Holiness Pope Pius XII. In this capacity, Taylor saw himself as an emissary for peace. From the start, he attempted to pressure Italy toward nonbelligerency. In this cause, he stepped up his contacts with the Vatican diplomatic corps, the key contact of which was Monsignor Hurley.

The arrival of Myron C. Taylor in Rome meant that Hurley would no longer be in contact with William Phillips and the American embassy. On February 2, 1940, Hurley presented Phillips with a commemorative papal coronation medal. He remarked to Phillips "that the only regret he had with regard to the coming of Myron Taylor was the fact that hereafter he would have to make his contacts with Taylor rather than with the embassy." "I cordially reciprocated his feelings," Phillips noted, "for I am very much attached to Hurley." Hurley spent the next six months becoming even more "attached" to Myron Taylor and his office. In one sense, the Taylor appointment gave Hurley the possibility of greater influence than that of any bishop residing in the United States. Taylor's new position cut through an entire State Department bureaucracy and gave Hurley hitherto unthinkable access to a government representative reporting directly to the president of the United States. Through Taylor, Hurley was one step away from presidential decision-making. For Catholics of Hurley's generation, this was a remarkable situation.[1]

Taylor began his mission by traveling from New York aboard the S.S. *Rex,* arriving in Naples on February 25, 1940. The new dynamic of presidential access started early, since aboard the same ship was President Roosevelt's under secretary of state, Sumner Welles. Welles was traveling to Italy at the direction of Roosevelt to undertake his greatly publicized peace talks with Mussolini, Hitler, and top-ranking European diplomats. Taylor's and Welles's simultaneous arrival at Naples afforded Hurley the opportunity to gain an introduction to Welles and converse with him at length. Hurley's connection with Welles would mature into a steadfast friendship of mutual admiration—and mutual diplomatic usefulness.[2]

Ostensibly, Hurley traveled to Naples to receive Myron Taylor and to accompany him to his destination in Rome. Since Taylor had not yet presented his diplomatic credentials to the pope, Hurley extended his welcoming courtesies in the capacity of "a private American citizen." Welles continued on to Rome by train with Count Galeazzo Ciano, Mussolini's minister of foreign affairs and an ardent foe of Hurley's clandestine work with *Osservatore Romano.* Hurley, Taylor, and his wife, Anabelle, were chauffeured by limousine to Rome. This outwardly formal meeting at Naples cemented a cordial and personal relationship between Hurley and Taylor. Throughout his stay in Rome, Taylor counted upon Hurley as his "friend, philosopher, and guide." "One thing has already been made clear," opined the *New York Times* as Taylor arrived in Rome, "and that is the important role Msgr. Joseph P. Hurley is going to play in this new diplomatic development."[3]

Hurley accompanied Taylor to his meeting with Papal Secretary of State Luigi Cardinal Maglione on February 26. Afterward Hurley prepared Taylor in the ceremonial aspects of his audience with Pope Pius XII, scheduled for February 28. On March 18 the first real substantial meetings took place as both Taylor and Welles met with Pius XII to "assess chances both for keeping the *Duce*, Benito Mussolini, out of the war and for bringing the war to an end." After the meeting both Welles and Taylor decided that Hurley was the man in the Vatican with whom they carried on the most comfortable working relationship. Later in March Taylor wrote to Montini, then the substitute for ordinary affairs, asking that his "counselor and friend" Monsignor Hurley be "counted on for contact with the Vatican Executive Organization and for such assistance as he has been rendering." That a U.S. diplomat was seeking close assistance from an American national in the employ of a foreign state blurred the church-state nexus, and the new arrangement was kept hidden from the press. The Holy See readily complied with Taylor's request, but not without a price. The Vatican began to rely on Hurley's tight relationship with Taylor to effect a diplomatic initiative of its own. The issue was one close to the pope's heart, refugee relief for the Catholics of Poland.[4]

LAWYERS, FUNDS, AND MONEY

The predominance of the Catholic religion in Poland, coupled with the violence of the German invasion of September 1939, prompted Vatican concern for Polish suffering. Following the tradition set by Pope Benedict XV during World War I, the Holy See aimed to trigger its impressive new system of charitable humanitarian relief for the victims of war.

The Vatican's effort was hampered, since the Nazis had cut off all reliable forms of communication to Catholic sources. On September 5, 1939, its nuncio posted to Warsaw, Archbishop Filippo Cortesi, fled the country and eventually ended up in Bucharest. An attempt was made to place Cortesi in Poland as an apostolic visitor, but these attempts were rebuffed by the Nazis. In the end, Cortesi stayed in Rumania and organized a relief network aimed at getting material aid to the suffering Poles. During the occupation, the Nazis effectively cut off the papal sphere of influence, both spiritual and temporal.[5]

At the same time, the Italian government suddenly forbade the Vatican to send money out of Italy to its missions in German-occupied areas. Within Italy, Mussolini's government declared that only U.S. dollars would be accepted in payment for imported raw materials. Since such materials were used in the construction of churches, the new law was a slick way of cutting off Roman Catholic institutional expansion. With its missionary mandate stymied by the Fascists both at home and abroad, the Vatican anxiously searched for alternative means to succor the Poles. Desperate, the Holy See turned to the United States. In April 1940, after exhausting all other efforts, Maglione enlisted Hurley to write a letter to President Roosevelt seeking the assistance of the United States in funneling money to the Poles. What ensued was the first Vatican-sponsored high-level diplomatic exchange of Myron Taylor's assignment, and one that has gone unrecorded by historians.[6]

On April 26 the Secretariat of State submitted a verbal note to Myron Taylor for the president. Composed by Hurley, the note aimed at channeling Vatican money for Polish refugees through the American Red Cross's Commission for Polish Relief. This recently established body was the only humanitarian organization Hitler allowed to operate in Poland. "Beginning in October of 1939," the Vatican note explained, "official representations were made to the government of the Reich with a view to securing passage into Poland of the relief at the disposition of the Holy See. The replies of the German government to these and repeated subsequent representations were dilatory, evasive, and inconclusive." In the face of German intransigence, the Holy See asked the State Department to allow the apostolic delegate to the United States, Amleto Cicognani, to donate 50,000 dollars to the American Commission for Polish Relief and allow him to place "other sums on deposit in American banks for further contributions." The Vatican asked Roosevelt for two things in response to its generous donations and promises to the commission: it sought the president's assurance that "the widest possible publicity be given, both in America and in Poland, to the fact that the Holy See is contributing largely to the Commission's labors of relief" and that "two of the representatives in Poland of the said Commission be Catholic citizens of the United States of America." On June 18 the Vatican received a reply to its first major diplomatic thrust of the new American-Vatican relationship. It was not encouraging.[7]

Secretary of State Cordell Hull formulated the United States' response to the Vatican note. Hull had never been enthusiastic about promoting Catholic affairs or papal diplomatic efforts. In fact he may have harbored some anticatholic prejudice. "The Secretary of State's Tennessee Protestantism," Jay Pierrepont Moffat quipped in early 1939, "savors of that old-time 'anti-Pope of Rome' type." Suspicious of the pope, Hull prepared a rejection letter for the president to dispatch through Myron Taylor. "The Government has no connection with any of these private organizations," Hull explained, "and the Government is not a participant in any of their respective activities. . . . It is beyond the power of the President to name the members of the commission as suggested as this power rests exclusively in the Commission for Polish Relief."[8]

Pius XII and Cardinal Maglione were evidently overconfident and out of touch with the U.S. government. In addition, Hurley's cordial relationship with Phillips and Taylor made him too optimistic and unappreciative of Hull's objection to having the president pressured to appoint Catholics to a secular commission. The Vatican's insistence that administrative appointments be based on religious affiliation was controversial if not indefensible in America. In addition, that a Protestant power structure should publicize papal humanitarian efforts ran counter to Hull's sensibilities. A functional diplomatic quid pro quo regarding Polish relief was out of the question. More convincingly, Michael Marrus has argued that the Vatican had fallen out of political favor with democracies, and in particular the United States, because "the pope refused to denounce the Reich as the aggressor in Poland, and would not explicitly protest the Nazi occupation." Was the rebuff over Polish relief a way of registering disapproval of Pius XII's new policy?[9]

The Vatican's reluctance to explicitly condemn Nazi Germany for the Polish invasion seems to have irked Hurley as well. On October 20, 1939, the reserved policy of Pius XII was made plain in his first encyclical, *Summi Pontificatus,* known by its English title as *The Function of the State in the Modern World.* As Michael Harrigan observed, "in the encyclical Pius XII carefully refrained from mentioning any country other than Poland by name, or directly linking any condemnation with a particular Party or Government." The text was revised three times at the last minute and was the subject of much international speculation before its release. Lacking a firm public condemnation of the Nazi onslaught, the document was translated into English by a disappointed Monsignor Hurley.[10]

Having translated the encyclical, Hurley penned his true thoughts. He unequivocally laid the blame for Europe's wartime misery on Adolf Hitler. "The world enemy is the criminal who has brutally bombed Warsaw, Rotterdam, and London," he wrote in the spring of 1940. "Any man who is not moved by a profound moral indignation is thereby disqualified as a moral force." Thus by early 1940 he seems to have dismissed Pius XII as a moral force on the world scene. "Old World sensibilities," he wrote in possible comment on Pacelli's aristocratic Roman background, "predominate over the new realities." Pius XII did not recognize the "new reality" that Nazism was the foremost threat to Catholicism. For Pacelli, communism moved back to the top of the list, and Hurley could not understand why.[11]

Hurley was dreadfully fearful of Nazism and had seen its ravages at first hand. In 1938, on the eve of the Anschluss, Pope Pius XI had commissioned him to go secretly to Vienna. His object was to observe the behavior of the Catholic hierarchy as the Nazis massed at the border. According to one report, it was Monsignor Hurley who stood and watched Theodor Cardinal Innitzer's controversial raise of the arm in Nazi salute to Hitler. "His description of the Nazi invasion of Austria," Sumner Welles was later informed, "sickened listeners."[12]

Pacelli's new prioritization of communism over Nazism continued to rankle Hurley. "I remember Kirk," Hurley wrote approvingly in 1940 of Alexander C. Kirk, then American chargé at the Rome embassy, "and his horror at the frequent repetition at the Vatican of anti-Communist fears. He called it weak. Panic-button pushing. It magnified Marx."[13]

Hurley began to break with the noninterventionist policy of Pope Pius XII in early 1940. While Pius XII ushered in a new policy of speaking in generalities and sugar-coating tough discussion, Hurley consciously went in the opposite direction. His plan of frank antinazism represents the first recorded instance of internal ideological dissent within the ranks of the wartime Vatican. It also marks Hurley's conversion to American foreign policy goals over those of the church he had vowed to serve.

"WHEN THE STATE IS RIGHT"

On July 1, 1940, Arnold Lunn, a Catholic commentator and correspondent for *The Tablet* of London, was stunned to hear an American voice delivering a prodemocratic and interventionist speech over Vatican Radio. Lunn investigated and uncovered the "unnamed American voice" at the Vatican to be Monsignor Joseph P. Hurley's. Meeting with Lunn shortly after the speech, Hurley "expressed his detestation of the Nazis." Lunn considered Hurley to be "a remarkable chap," and made sure that *The Tablet* published Hurley's unsigned speech in its entirety.[14]

The *Times* of London was also alerted to Hurley's speech and deemed it newsworthy, particularly since it was delivered three weeks *after* Italy declared war on the Allies. Headlined "Voice of the Vatican: Duty to Fight for the Right," Hurley's speech received dramatic front-page billing in the *Times*'s July 5 edition. "Although the *Osservatore Romano* prints no war comments nowadays," the *Times* prefaced its coverage of Hurley's speech, "the Vatican still allows strongly worded broadcasts. . . . To America goes the message that mere pacifism is wrong when there is a struggle between right and wrong." Still troubled by Pius XII's reluctance to name Nazi Germany as the aggressor in Poland, Hurley did not want the world's Catholics to underestimate the perils of National Socialism.

In this, his first public speech on foreign policy issues, Hurley exhibited the trademarks of all his future public discourses. In stark contrast to Pius XII, he was blunt, no-holds-barred, and passionate. Unabashedly contradicting Pius's broad statements on world peace, Hurley urged Americans to see the war as a necessary fight. Amazing for its opposition to the prevailing papal policy, Hurley urged Catholics around the globe not to get the wrong impression. "We shall speak tonight of the Christian attitude towards military service. We have sympathy with the pacifists, but they are wrong." In a "Cardinal Mercier moment" prompted by his patriotism and urging endurance, he let loose: "No word in the Gospel or in Papal teaching suggests that justice should go undefended, that it is not worth dying for." In a significant statement, Hurley made clear that he believed the new papal policy reflected not impartiality, but conscientious objection to war. "Conscientious objectors can be respected for their opinions, but their error does not excuse them from the responsibilities of patriotism." With the same spirit that pushed him to apply to West Point, he cried out clearly, "The Church is no conscientious objector."

"Our Lord," he continued, "lived among soldiers and never placed them in the same class as the Pharisees, publicans, money-changers, or avaricious rich men." By process of elimination, Hurley sanctified the military vocation. And in an astounding Christian justification of martial action, he concluded bluntly: "There is no suggestion in the Gospel that Our Lord could not admit the hypothesis that two nations could be at war and one of them be in the right." The Allies, of course, were "defending justice." Hurley left little doubt about which side in the new world war was "in the right."

Given the new tempered approach of Pope Pius XII, such words from an official Vatican source were considered extraordinary. But in this case they also could be considered stunningly radical. What commentators did not realize at the time was that Hurley's anonymous "Duty to Fight for the Right" speech wholeheartedly contradicted the position that Eugenio Pacelli had mapped out just nine months earlier in his first encyclical.

When Pacelli constructed *Summi Pontificatus,* he divided it into eight parts. Throwing off balance observers who were expecting a quick Vatican condemnation of Nazi wartime intentions, the first three parts of the encyclical ranged from the ostensibly pious to the sublime. The first section was a long reflection on the devotion to the Sacred Heart of Jesus —a popular devotion that focused on the physical heart of Jesus as the symbol of redemptive love. While press hounds failed to see it at the time, Pius's extended discussion of the Sacred Heart devotion had an immediate effect, among knowing listeners, of spiritually binding them to aggressive antiradicalism and anticommunism. For many European Catholics who recognized its symbolism, the Sacred Heart spoke to the worldwide Catholic antiradical crusade. The Sacred Heart had been adopted as the "badge" of Catholic antiradicalism ever since it was worn on the uniforms of Catholic anticommunard troops in 1870.[15]

The next six parts of the encyclical were lengthy and seemingly unconnected. Reflections on "the growth of secularism" and a cheery section on "the brotherhood of man" worked to subsume Pius's later controversial references to wartime Poland, "exacerbated nationalism," racism, and the "cult of brute force." It was only in the eighth and final section of *Summi Pontificatus* that Pius XII finally made a statement about the war in particular, and here he conflicted with Hurley. The section spelled out precisely how Catholics were to conduct themselves in wartime. Monsignor Ronald Knox, the Oxford scholar who worked with Hurley's original English copy of the encyclical, headed this section "Duties of Catholics in War Time"—the unspoken title of Hurley's July 1, 1940, war-hawk speech.[16]

For Pius XII, Catholics needed strict instruction on how to relate to "the storms of violence and discord, poured out as from a chalice of blood." Far from Hurley's later call for robust defense, Pius cried out for only two things from Catholics during the war: prayer and mortification. "To God, be your prayers addressed . . . your continual prayer, your prayer most of all." Secondly, Catholics were to endure the war by making "prudent use of the mortification of appetites . . . and works of penance . . . in the hope that our most merciful redeemer will put a speedy end to these tribulations." The overriding duty for Catholics at war was to pray, "pray without ceasing." Hurley's call to action over Vatican Radio in his anonymous "Duty to Fight for the Right" speech was diametrically opposed to what Pius was laying down as Catholic wartime doctrine.

It was either frustration with Pius or moral courage that led Hurley to deliver such hawkish words to a world at war. Surely, since he translated *Summi Pontificatus* from Pius XII's own hand, he had to realize that his July 1 speech flew in the face of the pope's program. And just as surely, with the international attention Hurley's speech received, his warmongering was noted by the pontiff.

There is also the strong possibility that Hurley's warlike speech was secretly encouraged by the U.S. embassy in Rome. At the very time that Hurley broadcast his bellicose address, the Roosevelt administration was stepping up its efforts to promote a pro-Allied outlook at the Vatican. Support for Hurley's opinion was in line with a new track for Myron Taylor and the American diplomats in Rome as they tried to use "Vatican influence to blunt American Catholic isolationism and obstructionism." The idea was to use the authority of official and semiofficial Vatican pronouncements to alter the entrenched isolationism of the American Catholic bishops, the lower clergy, and the ever-stubborn Coughlinites. Such isolationism was considered "obstructionist" to U.S. foreign policy goals. And if U.S. diplomats in Rome could not persuade the pope to straightforwardly condemn Nazism, the next order of business was to get an American bishop to do the job.[17]

Such an endeavor was not easy. Most of the American bishops, particularly those in the "biretta belt" of the large midwestern industrial cities, were of either German or Irish descent and were reluctant to make political statements. The Coughlin phenomenon also loomed large in their thinking. In addition, for Coughlin and much of the Catholic hierarchy, communism continued to play a large role in shaping their public positions. As one historian has put it, "isolationist sentiment was strong among American Catholics . . . and Catholic champions of neutrality were arguing that even limited material aid to the Soviet Union violated the papal ban on Catholic cooperation with Communists." In 1940 Hurley watched helplessly from his desk in Rome as "every returning bishop lauded Mussolini in the news. Haven't any of you one word for America, your country?" he asked himself. A country "which is right, and they are wrong?" In words that foretold his clash with the new Vatican policy, he recorded that this was "no time to be devious, subtle, or diplomatic." The church, he noted as the bishops remained silent about the war, should be "seething about this lack of manhood, Americanism, and leadership in the weakest episcopate outside of Austria."[18]

Hurley's anti-isolationist views were graphically spelled out in a four-page letter to Edward Mooney on July 25, 1940. This letter apparently was written to persuade Mooney to take the lead in vocally condemning Nazism as anticatholic and antireligious. Such a statement by Mooney would set a new path for the American bishops and also allow U.S. government officials to publicize Mooney's view. In the letter, Hurley bemoaned the silence of the American episcopacy in the face of a world crisis. "Anything may happen," he confided from Rome. "America is now beginning to realize what some people here have known for a long time: that Christian Civilization is in a savage battle for survival." If Pius XII failed to realize this and fight publicly, he hoped Mooney would not be as guarded. For Hurley, the choice was black and white. The American episcopacy must break its silence and choose sides. Political concerns begged the attention of the American bishops because "the Catholic press and the Bishops are preserving a suspicious silence on American foreign policy. The net result in public opinion tends to be that the Catholics in America are unpatriotic or at the best disinterested at a moment of grave crisis in American and world history." For Hurley, the sin of unpatriotism was more grave than any sin of omission.

"The stage appears set for a tragedy," he confided to Mooney, "which will portray us [Catholics] as possible enemies within the gates; a minority who respond, in times of crisis, to interests which are not American, and whose loyalty is of a questionable nature." "I know the U.S. Bishops had this 'stay out of war' fetish, and I warned you that conditions might arise which would change that," he wrote in composing notes for his letter. "Let's all be neutral," he scratched of the American bishops, thinking such an attitude "a fool's paradise." "No hope from here," he confided in a probable reference to the new policies of Pope Pius XII; "the weakness we suspected is now manifest." In a possible reference to Pius's new impartiality toward the dictators, he advised Mooney to make "no fine distinctions too subtle for the crowd." Such distinctions "strangle action."[19]

For Hurley, the European war was a cosmic battle, a struggle between ideologies of good and evil that should be clearly recognized by both the Holy See and the U.S. hierarchy. "I can well conceive that the opposition between the Kingdom of God and this world will at times bring the Church and state to grips. But I hate seeing this conflict provoked by the Church when the state [the United States] is *right*." By early 1940, Hurley had cast his lot with Roosevelt. He, too, was convinced that the state was right.[20]

DIPLOMAT ON THE MOVE: A STINGING CRITIQUE AND A HASTY EXIT

"Many Americans, both Catholic and Protestant," historian Anthony Rhodes has commented about the weeks immediately after the invasion of Poland, "considered that the Pope had not protested sufficiently against the German aggressions and atrocities in occupied lands." Harold Tittman, secretary to Myron Taylor, formally complained to the Secretariat of State that "the Vatican was too lenient with the Dictators." Jesuit historian Pierre Blet takes note that there was considerable discussion about this issue at the Vatican in September 1939. In Blet's account most of the agitation for condemnation of the Nazi aggression came from the diplomatic representatives of defeated countries. But Blet does not mention any discussion or dissension on the issue *within* the Vatican's diplomatic corps.[21]

Hurley, though holding a heartfelt attachment to the papacy and to Rome, was deeply critical of papal policy. Privately, he lamented that *Osservatore Romano* had succumbed to internal pressure to ease its criticism of the Fascists, and began carrying long articles giving "the Axis points of view." "Editorials against England and America" were now the order of the day while there were "none against the despoiler of Poland, Belgium, etc." To Hurley, the Roman cardinals were anything but fighters, hardly reflecting the pugnacious style of Pope Pius XI. "Old men in dresses," he called them. The pro-Axis defeatism even infected America, to the point that Hurley considered that the Vatican's own representative to the United States, the powerful Archbishop Amleto G. Cicognani, who served in Washington from 1933 to 1958, might be of Fascist bent. Hurley probably believed that Cicognani was behind his failed effort to get a high-level bishop to speak out against the Nazis. "Chick of the soft-pedal," he scribbled in his notes in frustration, "may want no trouble with Tot[alitarian] governments, esp[ecially] Italy. . . . Speak up, and the Fascist auditor will report you."[22]

In a second, handwritten draft of a letter to Mooney, he summarized the nuances of papal diplomacy. "So far, we have had the advantage in America of high prestige accruing to the Holy See because of its attitude in the face of the new totalitarian corruptions"—an insinuation about the fortitude of Pius XI's policy. "But the Holy See is now in eclipse," he began in code about the new papacy; "it is retreating as fast as the British at Dunkirk. And with less dignity. From now on, you in America will have to live on your own resources of prestige, to be won by a decent firmness against the encroachments of the dictators." Hurley closed by indicating his differences with Pope Pius XII. "Here the weakness which many of us feared has come to light with the first appearance of danger." "Why are the good so often weak, or dumb, or wrong minded?" he asked himself in his notes.[23]

Inside the Vatican, tensions continued to run high as morale plummeted. "As France fell," Hurley reported of conversation with the substitute secretary of state, "Montini tells me that nothing can stop a German victory. In despair—the apparent plan is to temporize on accessories, but not to yield in principle. The Pope is at times distraught." Hurley also noticed that "Twelve," his shorthand name for Pope Pius XII, was not up for the fight. Pius was experiencing many "sleepless nights" and struck him as being "mentally depressed."[24]

Personnel also came under review. "The anti-Axis men in the Vatican seem to live in waiting for the axe," Hurley recorded in his notes. Count Giuseppe Dalla Torre, the director of *Osservatore Romano*, was "beside himself and wanted to escape to America." "Spies everywhere," was his last Roman note. A depressed pope, a Catholic editor who had snapped, and Rome in firm control of the Fascists were all that Hurley could see around him. He had little hope that Pius XII would make a change and speak out strongly against the Fascists. "At a time like this," he lamented, "his only advisers are Dutch and Wop."[25]

Political tensions between Mussolini and the Vatican were entering a critical phase in 1940. "Look at those thugs," Montini remarked to Hurley as the two prelates drove through Rome; "now even Vatican diplomats are no longer safe," he commented. While the pope called for peace, the world headed toward war. As an American surrounded by Fascists, Hurley knew that it was only a matter of time before his own future became uncertain. Since he counted himself as one of "the anti-Axis men at the Vatican," he may have surmised that someone at the Vatican was sharpening an ax with his name on it.[26]

On August 13, 1940, the gentle and revered Patrick F. Barry, bishop of the Diocese of St. Augustine, Florida, died in Jacksonville. This event across the Atlantic offered an opportunity for the Vatican to move Hurley out. With astounding alacrity and unprecedented swiftness—a span of three days in a process that normally takes at least six months to a year—Hurley was nominated, approved, and appointed as the next bishop of St. Augustine. The swiftness of the appointment, bypassing the curia and forgoing a "short list" of candidates from America, indicates that the fingerprints of Pope Pius XII were on Hurley's ax handle. Only a pope could ramrod through such an appointment. "His Holiness Pope Pius XII," Carlo Cardinal Rossi, the pope's secretary, informed Hurley on August 16, "has kindly nominated and appointed you Most Reverend to the Church Cathedral of St. Augustine." *Promoveatur ut removeatur*—to promote in order to remove—was the age-old unwritten Vatican tactic for eliminating undesirables.[27]

The appointment blindsided Hurley. Since 1938 the Vatican rumor mill had been grinding out that Hurley would cut his teeth as an Ohio bishop and then remain within striking distance to someday become the bishop of Cleveland. But Florida? Others at the Vatican tried to smooth over the situation. Perhaps stretching the facts, Domenico Tardini indicated to Hurley "that all along" he had been "slated for an auxiliary or coadjutor of Florida." Montini commented that Cardinal Rossi, secretary for the Consistorial Congregation, noted the *providentia* of Hurley's nomination. Hurley wondered to himself, "What was the real reason for the haste?"[28]

Only superficial and abstract reasons were offered for the appointment. *Time* magazine surmised that because of Hurley's role as "U.S. contact man for the Holy See," he would soon be appointed apostolic delegate to the United States—chatter that was certain to irritate the unflappable Amleto Cicognani. "All the rumors say that Roosevelt won't deal with Cicognani," one nosy priest opined, "deals with Spellman and wants Hurley as Delegate." But Pius XII had no intention of appointing Hurley as anything more than a backwater bishop. The pope's quick action confused uninformed observers.[29]

"Pope Pius XII may officiate at the consecration of Monsignor Joseph P. Hurley," the *Cleveland Plain Dealer* proudly announced in August 1940.

The clerical buzz back in Cleveland was that Hurley would certainly be consecrated by Pius—speculation that, under any other circumstance, would have been well within protocol. With rumors swirling in the background, Hurley had a personal audience of congratulations with Pius on August 21. It did not go well. Hurley chronicled that "Twelve" was "anxious about Am[erican] loyalty to the Holy See," most likely an oblique reference to Hurley's own loyalty to the new papal policy. Their final embrace, according to Hurley, was "cordial but impersonal." "Each of us [read] in || [between the] lines." Hurley summed up his final audience as a member of Pius XII's Secretariat of State with two words: "No warmth."[30]

With Pius wary of Hurley's staunch Americanism and loyalty to the church's strategic neutrality, the pope declined to consecrate Hurley, even though the bishop-elect had worked with him for six years. Pius made no public comment on either Hurley's elevation or his consecration. Instead, Hurley was consecrated bishop of St. Augustine on October 6, 1940, in the chapel of the College of the Propaganda Fide by Luigi Cardinal Maglione, the papal secretary of state. *Osservatore Romano*'s announcement of Hurley's appointment mentioned his "valuable activity . . . at the curia" but dedicated the greater part of its brief announcement to extolling Hurley's work as a missionary in Japan and India. This may have been an oblique way for Pius to deemphasize Hurley's diplomatic work before his consecration. Pius did not want to give the impression that Hurley was a Vatican political insider as he headed for the United States. The plan worked. The Associated Press announced Hurley's episcopal consecration as a throwaway one-liner in a story reporting Pope Pius XII's discourse to Italian women concerning cosmetic makeup and modern fashion as risks to chastity.[31]

The consecration ceremony, which in many ways resembled a coronation, was a lavish affair filled with ritual and incense. Hurley, bedecked in gold vestments, white gloves, white shoes, and fine lace albs, accepted the miter and crozier from Maglione. The choice of Maglione as consecrator was symbolic. Throughout his ecclesiastical career, Maglione had been "closely identified with the anti-Fascist policies of the late Pope Pius XI." In another tribute, Hurley's episcopal ring, a symbol of church leadership, was inscribed with a blessing by G. B. Montini, an antifascist collaborator with Hurley during the *Osservatore Romano* struggle.[32]

As a new bishop, Hurley was expected to choose an episcopal motto,

an expression important for its symbolic value. In Roman Catholic her-
aldry, this personal motto is meant to represent one's "spirituality and
theologically-based philosophy of life." For his episcopal motto, Hurley
selected the Latin phrase *Virtus in arduis,* commonly translated "Virtue
in the midst of difficulty." This was a noble ascetic Christian claim. But
all was not as it seemed. There was a sub-rosa meaning to Hurley's new
motto. Hurley was a Latinist of the first rank who enjoyed playing with
second and third definitions of words. *Virtus,* as well as meaning ethical "virtue," also carries a distinct military translation as "resolution or
steadfastness in time of war." *Arduis* also has a separate Roman military
definition: "difficulty in following another's example." In cipher, Hurley's
episcopal motto came down as "martial steadfastness in the midst of
poor leadership." This was a cunning reference to Hurley's own Pius XI–
inspired "steadfastness" in the face of Pius XII's reluctance to call out the
Nazis by name.[33]

In the end, Hurley's consecration was not soured by the absence of
the pope. It evolved into a celebration populated by nearly all of Rome's
dwindling democrats. Conspicuous in the chapel were the Vatican ambassadors from occupied France and vanquished Poland. Alcide de Gasperi,
François Charles-Roux, Sumner Welles, Joseph Grew, William Phillips,
Breckinridge Long, Alexander Kirk, and of course Myron C. Taylor were
all invited to join Hurley on the Janiculum Hill for his consecration. FDR,
having withdrawn William Phillips from Rome, ordered U.S. Counselor
of Embassy Edward L. Reed to attend the consecration along with the
embassy's military and commercial attachés. There they saw Cardinal
Secretary of State Maglione and Archbishop Clemente Micara, former
nuncio to Belgium—the twice-violated land of Cardinal Mercier—raise
Hurley to the episcopacy.[34]

On October 7, 1940, Hurley had his farewell audience with Pius XII.
It lasted twenty minutes, the highlight of which was the pontiff's presentation of a golden pectoral cross adorned with topazes. In keeping with
the lack of warmth the pope had previously shown his American under-
ling, the only public aspect of the meeting was Pius's confirmation that
"Monsignor Hurley will leave for the United States as soon as he can
arrange transportation." After this papal shove out the door, Hurley left
Rome by train and traveled to Switzerland. Arriving in Geneva, he at once
camped out with the Americans. For two weeks he vacationed with the

career U.S. Foreign Service officer Harold H. Tittman Jr. and his family. "We can feed you up and give you plenty of rest so that you will be prepared for the hardships of travel," Tittman wrote cordially. Of course, the interlude was meant to probe and prepare Hurley for further intrigues in foreign policy.[35]

On October 24 Hurley ended his European sojourn. His prodemocratic activities went unacknowledged as he left the Vatican behind. As far as he could tell, the reason for his hasty release from diplomatic service was still unclear. Leaving from Lisbon aboard the luxury liner *Excambion,* he was surprised to see Ambassador Joseph P. Kennedy—just flown in from London amid a whirl of gossip that he, too, was about to be sacked. The two men had not seen each other since March 1939, when Hurley acted as a guide to the Kennedy family during the papal coronation ceremonies. After exchanging pleasantries aboard ship, Kennedy asked Hurley to explain why there seemed to be so many Fascist sympathizers in the Italian hierarchy.

Kennedy's notes on the conversation come across as rather abstract. Hurley reportedly answered that "Fascist Cardinals" who had "direct contact with the people" through their dioceses "were naturally patriotic Italians" and consequently "it was not surprising that they were with their country." In closing their conversation, Hurley seemed to discount the idea that Fascism was infecting the Vatican, stating that only Italians "who did not have churches or were not at the Vatican any more believed it was necessary to work with the Fascists." As Kennedy recalled, however, Hurley's summation added one final ambiguity that "others felt that the Church's position [in Italian society] made it necessary for them to be on that [the Fascist] side." Perhaps as he sped toward the United States, he finally figured out that such widespread Fascist sympathy in the Italian hierarchy may have played a part in pushing him out of Rome. Now he set his mind on preventing the American bishops from succumbing to Fascist pressure. His goal was to keep the isolationists from dominating the Roman Catholic hierarchy in his home country.[36]

Joseph P. Hurley graduation photo from St. Ignatius College,
Cleveland, Ohio, May 1915. His ambitions at the time leaned
toward either West Point or Harvard Law School. (Courtesy
Mrs. Mercedes Hurley Hughes)

hen Bishop Hurley Played Amateur Football Here

"Breezer" Hurley played running back on an undefeated 1915 Geiger Clothes Company Cleveland City football team. Athletics played a role in shaping his conceptions of Catholic leadership. (Courtesy *Catholic Universe Bulletin*)

French connections. Father Hurley while studying diplomatic history at the University of Toulouse, circa 1926. He is seen here with the visiting Cleveland priest "Red" O'Donnell. The circumstances leading to Hurley's French diplomatic sojourn are obscure, but he seems around this time to have settled on the idea of diplomatic service for the Holy See. (Courtesy Archives of the Diocese of St. Augustine, Jacksonville, Florida)

On the mission trail, circa 1930. In Mylapore, India, Hurley sits with his mentor from seminary days, Archbishop Edward Mooney, later cardinal-archbishop of Detroit. (Courtesy Archives of the Diocese of St. Augustine, Jacksonville, Florida)

The fiery Father Coughlin delivers a speech in Hurley's hometown of Cleveland on May 10, 1936, attacking President Roosevelt. Coughlin's intemperance in the spring of 1936 would trigger a Hurley secret mission from Rome to Royal Oak. In Europe the Fascist and Nazi regimes would warm to his anti-Semitic rhetoric for propaganda purposes. (Corbis)

Roberto Farinacci, editor of *Il Regime Fascista* and a member of the Fascist Grand Council, in 1939. Farinaci waged an intensive press campaign against the Vatican, which he accused of being philosemitic. (Corbis)

Vatican Secretary of State Luigi Cardinal Maglione (center) pictured next to Myron C. Taylor, President Roosevelt's newly arrived personal representative to Pope Pius XII, on February 26, 1940. Hurley, who had driven from Naples to Rome with Taylor and his wife the day before, is standing second from right. (Courtesy Archives of the Diocese of St. Augustine, Jacksonville, Florida)

On October 6, 1940, Hurley was consecrated the sixth bishop of the Diocese of St. Augustine, Florida, by Vatican Secretary of State Luigi Cardinal Maglione in the chapel of the College of the Propaganda Fide in Rome. The consecration turned into a show of force for the dwindling prodemocratic ranks in Rome. "Present were nearly all of the United States Embassy and Consular staff," the *New York Times* reported. (AP Images)

U.S. Under Secretary of State Sumner Welles, 1943. One of the most influential American diplomats of the twentieth century, Welles recruited Hurley after their first meeting in Naples on February 25, 1940. The Welles-Hurley relationship was one of the most delicate, secret, and effective diplomatic associations of World War II. (Photo by Yousuf Karsh; courtesy Camerapress, London)

Hurley's speech over the CBS radio network on July 6, 1941, split both the Catholic hierarchy and laity on the eve of war. When Hurley attempted to reconcile Vatican diplomatic practice with American interventionism, both ordinary Catholics and Coughlinites lashed out at the Florida bishop. (AP Images; used with the permission of Philadelphia Newspapers; courtesy Archives of the Diocese of St. Augustine, Jacksonville, Florida)

Pope Pius XII stares detachedly beside Hurley during a meeting in the Consistory Hall of the papal summer palace, Castel Gandolfo, circa 1948. Hurley's secretary at the Belgrade nunciature, Monsignor John P. McNulty, is second from right. (AP Images)

Marshal Josip Broz Tito, February 1945. Almost exactly a year after this photo was taken, Hurley met with Tito and urged the dictator to cease his persecution of Catholics in Yugoslavia. (John Phillips/Time & Life Pictures/Getty Images)

Hurley attended the trial of Archbishop Aloysius Stepinac during the fall of 1946. Every day of the trial, he rose from his front-row seat and bowed deeply as the archbishop was escorted past him into the courtroom under guard. The gesture, calculated to irritate Tito and his communist regime, was captured by a photojournalist, and the image was flashed across wire services worldwide. (AP Images)

Hurley shown in Zagreb, Yugoslavia, on October 11, 1946, after Tito's kangaroo war-crimes tribunal pronounced its verdict on Archbishop Aloysius Stepinac. Hurley immediately took steps to launch a worldwide Catholic media campaign to defend Stepinac and to tie the Stepinac issue to U.S. foreign policy. The United States remained mute. (*New York Times*/Redux)

Portrait (oil on canvas) of Archbishop-Bishop Joseph P. Hurley, by Guido Greganti. Hurley stood for the portrait in Rome in 1953. (Courtesy Archives of the Diocese of St. Augustine, Jacksonville, Florida)

CHAPTER SIX

An American Bishop
in President Roosevelt's Court

IN 1940 the Roman Catholic Diocese of St. Augustine, Florida, was largely undeveloped. Its territory was vast, lines of communication were slow, and its Catholic population was dispersed throughout a predominantly Protestant southern state. Though a United States diocese, it was almost as if Pius had sent Hurley back to the missionary trail. Forty percent of all churches in the diocese were undeveloped mission churches, and a large part of Catholic outreach was conducted in 150 impermanent and shacklike wooden church structures known as mission stations. But although it was impoverished, one thing his diocese did have on its side was history. On the day of Hurley's consecration, diocesan historian Jane Quinn described St. Augustine as "the oldest outpost of faith in the United States."[1]

Formally established in 1870, the diocese's Catholic history dated from Spanish colonial times, when the see city was founded as a military settlement in 1565. On September 8, 1565, the expedition of Pedro Menéndez de Avilés landed at St. Augustine. Father Francisco Lopéz de Mendoza Grajalas offered the first Catholic Mass on that day and established a Catholic parish at St. Augustine.[2]

After 1565 the lands that would become the Diocese of St. Augustine underwent seven dizzying shifts of ecclesiastical jurisdiction. Unable to gain traction amid colonial clashes, the Catholic faith reflected the ebb and flow of French, Spanish, and British imperial designs. When finally raised to a diocese in 1870, the diocesan boundaries included all of the current state of Florida except for a small portion east of the Apalachicola River. In total, the diocese spanned 47,000 square miles.[3]

On November 26, 1940, Bishop Emmet M. Walsh of Charleston, South Carolina, installed Bishop-elect Hurley as the sixth bishop of the Diocese of St. Augustine. That evening a reception was held at the Ponce de León Hotel, where Mayor Walter B. Fraser and Governor-elect Spessard Holland welcomed Bishop Hurley to St. Augustine. Hurley deeply appreciated the local fanfare and graciously accepted all good wishes that came his way. The evening concluded with a spirited speech of welcome from Florida's incumbent governor, Fred P. Cone. Perhaps having already got wind of Hurley's antinazism, Cone commended Hurley as "a great leader among his people . . . standing for religious principles against infidelity and alien 'isms.'" But then the local flavor of the appointment took over. "I want to give you a good old Florida welcome," the governor concluded with a cheery blast aimed to whisk off the cosmopolitanism of Hurley's European stay. "Bishop Hurley, I want you to become a cracker!"[4]

St. Augustine, Florida, was a far cry from the international glamor of Bangalore, Tokyo, and Rome. For a man of international experience, classical tastes, and diplomatic culture, the new assignment in Florida must have been a difficult adjustment. Once described as "a moss-grown corner of Europe, asleep for two hundred years," the town of St. Augustine was bereft of economic vitality and dotted with "sickly turf and sandy paths." Describing northern Florida in 1940, travel writer Nina Oliver Dean captured the images that Bishop Hurley soaked in for the first time, calling it a place "where cattle straggle along the highway in a barren pine land." For Dean, the northern stretches of Florida where Hurley's headquarters were located "offered little hint" of the stylish living found in Palm Beach and Miami. Dean's Floridian reflection points up another aspect of Hurley's abandonment by Pius XII—the question of Vatican finances and the American church.[5]

Historian John Pollard's excellent study of money and the modern papacy shows that at exactly the time Hurley was moved out of Rome into his financially teetering see, the larger metropolitan dioceses of the Catholic church in the United States were reaching their apogees of financial influence. The dioceses of the East Coast and Midwest were flush with cash, and their bishops wielded great influence in Rome. "United States Catholics," Pollard argues, "were paying a lot of the Vatican's bills" in the 1930s and looked to continue that trend through the 1940s. An American Catholic lay financial elite was emerging along the East Coast and in the industrial belt of the United States. Since it was usually the local bishop who approached wealthy Catholics in support of the pope, appointment to these sees meant instant power back in Rome. With powerful lay Catholics opening their checkbooks, by 1934 America had eclipsed France as the largest contributor to the annual Peter's Pence collection—a voluntary offering by the faithful in support of the pope. Although many Vatican insiders considered Americans uncouth, by 1940 the reality was that American Catholics were contributing as much to the Peter's Pence collection as all other countries combined.[6]

The Peter's Pence collection was a significant tool in the scheme of any bishop's ecclesiastical mobility. During the 1930s, the final act of any bishop visiting Rome was to hand a financial donation to the pope. For American bishops, papal allegiance began to be measured by every shifting decimal point on the check, and by every glad rising of the papal eyebrow. Consequently, by making Hurley the bishop of a missionary see, Pius shrewdly placed another enormous obstacle in the way of his future advancement in the U.S. hierarchy. In fact, Hurley may have weighed this factor. In one of his first acts as bishop, he quickly sent a monetary gift to Pope Pius XII at the Vatican. Along with a note of fealty, Hurley wrote a check to Pius for the sum of 500 dollars—not a paltry gift, but not a lavish one either. In his Vatican notes, Hurley made clear that he understood that 500 dollars was the precise amount expected in donation to a pope when a cleric was made a domestic prelate—a monsignor. Pius never personally acknowledged Hurley's gift. He had Cardinal Maglione reply instead.[7]

Banished to a minor see, Hurley longed to be back in diplomatic circles. He wished for the thrill of being tied up in world events—and he continued to assess the threat of the Nazi drive for world conquest. After working in the Vatican's diplomatic corps, it was difficult for him to come to terms with a homespun southern diocese where sophisticates and multilingual priests were simply not around. "We had no idea who he was," one St. Augustine resident confided. In these early days, if one of his priests failed at a task or lacked urbane sophistication, a shout would go up from the chancery office: "I am surrounded by fools!"[8]

In backwater Florida, Hurley's career began to resemble almost word for word that of the Old Man Marshall character from Richard Harding Davis's famous short story "The Consul." "In the service he had so faithfully followed, rank by rank, he had been dropped, until now he, who twice had been promoted, was an exile, banished to a fever swamp. The great [Vatican] Ship of State had dropped him over the side, had 'marooned' him, and sailed away." With the Holy See having stranded him in an obscure and politically inconsequential see, Hurley knew that his only lifeline back to political viability was anchored in Washington, D.C.[9]

Sensing that the United States was still "right" in its clash with the dictators, he quickly reestablished contact with the State Department and was gently eased back into the craft of diplomacy—this time as a secret worker and spokesperson for U.S. foreign policy interests. If his church had shunted him to the side, his country had not—and there was still much work to do. In the forefront of Hurley's mind was the constant conviction that German Nazism represented the primary threat to all of Christian civilization. For Hurley, explicit antinazism became the categorical imperative of his new episcopacy, regardless of how far away he was from the center of events. Hurley continued to cultivate his Washington contacts and ultimately worked with Roosevelt administration officials stateside to an even greater extent than he had in Rome.

If the objective of Pius XII and Domenico Tardini was to neutralize Hurley's antifascism by appointing him to a backwater bishopric, they severely misunderstood the resourcefulness of the former Cleveland priest. Left to his own devices, from 1940 to 1945 Hurley became the most outspoken critic of American Catholic noninterventionism and arguably the most ardent Catholic supporter of Roosevelt's wartime foreign policy. The final message of his work in Florida, much of it disguised and behind-the-scenes, would stand in contrast to the gracefully nuanced style of Pius XII's Vatican program.

TURNING THE TIDE

Shortly after his arrival in St. Augustine, Hurley received a letter from Governor Spessard Holland inviting him to become officially involved in the state's civil defense efforts. In a gesture of respect, Holland asked Hurley to become a member of the Advisory Committee on Morale of the State Defense Council of Florida. But Hurley had his sights set on a wider ambit than coordinating lights-out and air-raid drills for Florida's Catholics, and declined Holland's offer, citing "present National commitments." "I am under obligation to go frequently to Washington," Hurley explained to the Florida governor, "in connection with certain phrases [sic] of our National War Effort. Your Excellency will understand, I am sure, that the continuance of the work which I already have in hand is perhaps of greater importance than the position which you so kindly offer me." Holland hadn't a clue what Hurley was getting at, and pressed again.[10]

In a reply to Holland's second appeal, Hurley was more blunt. He insisted to the governor that he had more lofty national security goals to meet. "In my own personal capacity, I have been engaged, since my return to America, in arousing the people of this nation to the dangers to us and to Christian civilization which are inherent to totalitarian systems. Upon the advice of higher authority, I must keep myself free for the continuance of this work, placing my long experience in the Orient and in Europe at the service of the President and officials of the State Department with whom I am in close and constant touch." For these reasons he could not possibly sit on "an obscure sub-Committee of the State Defense Council." Holland, still somewhat baffled by the exchange, accepted Hurley's explanation and dropped the issue. What was instrumental about the short exchange was Hurley's admission that he had placed himself "at the service of the President and officials of the State Department" over service to the American bishops, archbishops, and cardinals, who were publicly professing pacifism and political isolationism.[11]

Placing himself at the service of the U.S. government seemed natural, patriotic, and suitable for an Americanized follower of Pope Pius XI who practiced blunt confrontation with Nazism. For Hurley, the war was a worldwide campaign against evil. His thinking coincided nicely with FDR's intent of creating a "theology of war," in the words of George Q. Flynn, that would propel American Catholics into "the Roosevelt diplomatic consensus." According to this "theology of war" argument, Hitler represented a demonic force in the world. Hitler's mission was to conquer all of "Western Christian Civilization." God, in contrast, had specially and providentially guided the United States since its inception. Through diplomacy, the "blessed harmony" thesis of Hurley's youth could be put into action.[12]

U.S. Under Secretary of State Sumner Welles also had an interest in framing foreign policy against the dictators in a "theology of war" context. As the battle against American neutrality heated up, Welles came to see this design as a way to swing Catholics behind FDR's foreign policy. Welles became the State Department's gatekeeper on Catholic matters soon after his March 1940 European tour. As one student of Roosevelt's Catholic policy has put it, "Welles was Roosevelt's State Department link to the National Catholic Welfare Conference (NCWC) and the attitudes of the Catholic-American community—particularly the hierarchy." In Hurley, Welles found a Catholic bishop with strong Vatican ties who was staunchly antifascist. His link to the Secretariat of State could lend prestige and authority to his work in America on behalf of Catholic interventionism. Hurley's correspondence with Welles increased during the prewar period, as did his admiration for the under secretary of state. Only his allegiance to Franklin Roosevelt exceeded his admiration for Welles.[13]

"We have today united in public prayer throughout the diocese," Hurley informed the president by telegram as he started his third term, "beseeching Almighty God that He sustain you in body and soul, that he direct you by His wisdom, and strengthen you with his fortitude to meet and master the perils which beset our beloved land in these days." Remarkably, Hurley's personal message made it through the gauntlet of White House secretaries and the sea of congratulatory messages. FDR's response of "deep appreciation" and "heartfelt gratitude for remembrance in your prayers" must have left Hurley feeling, once again, very gratified. Bolstered by FDR's personal kindness, Hurley began, in the words of Arnold Lunn, "a vigorous radio campaign against isolationists." Both Hurley's radio campaign and other ventures were covertly supported and fueled by the U.S. Department of State.[14]

Before America's entry into World War II, Catholics were the most isolationist and least informed on international issues of the three major religious groups (Protestant, Catholic, and Jewish) in the United States. While social, educational, and economic considerations accounted for Catholic isolationism, important ethnic factors also came into play, "particularly the lesser willingness of Catholics of Irish, German, and especially Italian origins to support Britain against Germany and Italy." Issues such as Lend-Lease support for Britain, the arms embargo of Loyalist Spain, and the congressional decision to aid Russia were political stress points for Catholic support of Roosevelt. Moreover, as Charles C. Tansill has observed, "Catholic leaders did not respond to the summons to enlist the churches in a movement towards intervention."[15]

"Even after most of Europe fell to the Axis," Alfred Hero has argued, "Catholics were least inclined . . . to think that United States vital interests were at stake in a war on the other side of the Atlantic." By late 1940 there emerged a veritable "battle for Catholic public opinion," a battle that pitted a handful of Catholic interventionists, supported by the State Department, against the majority of Catholics—isolationists committed to seeing America stay out of war no matter the cost. The proposed battle would be a colossal one. The influential Jesuit weekly *America,* the Paulist *Catholic World,* and the lay liberal weekly *Commonweal* lined up against President Roosevelt's emerging interventionist foreign policy. Found in the back of nearly every parish alongside the diocesan newspaper, these journals helped shape Catholic opinion at the grass roots and among the lower clergy. Welles's plan was to circumvent these powerful Catholic sources by politicizing Catholic isolationism and moving the debate into the secular press, where the State Department had the upper hand.[16]

In order to do this, Welles initiated a subtle and shrouded system of supplying Hurley with often confidential State Department materials on foreign policy issues. Upon receiving packets of information from Welles, Hurley articulated the government line in a predetermined Catholic setting. The audience was incidental. What mattered to Welles was not the venue, but that Hurley's words were captured in print. Welles's intention was to move the debate from an intraconfessional level to a national one. In this way, the Catholic leadership in the United States would be forced, under public pressure, to take sides conclusively so as to defeat any charges of being unpatriotic. Hurley's Roman collar clothed Welles's scheme in black, forcing the Catholic press to take notice and respond. Through Hurley, Welles was creating a rift in the hierarchy, where formerly there had been none.

Stateside, Hurley was about to embark on the same sort of information-sharing scheme that he had undertaken with William Phillips at the Vatican from 1938 to 1940. This time the risks to his personal safety were much smaller, but the potential consequences from within the U.S. hierarchy were much greater. Hurley activated Welles's scheme by expounding on the crisis of Nazism to highly improbable Catholic groups. One of his first speeches on American foreign policy and Nazism was delivered to a gathering of Benedictine monks, who in that era were usually forbidden to read newspapers or listen to the radio. A local gathering of Catholic women offered a second opportunity to rail against the Nazi foe. For his part, Hurley saw to it that his diocesan paper, the *Florida Catholic*, covered all his foreign policy speeches. This coverage was then sent to Welles at the State Department, who snatched it up and inserted it into various national periodicals.

Welles's idea is notable for a number of reasons. The under secretary understood that the national readership on Catholic topics was ghettoized; in other words, most Catholic writing was undertaken by Catholics for an audience of Catholics. Welles needed to break this pattern if he intended to move Catholics away from their entrenched positions on a national scale. And in the days before television, when the written word was voraciously consumed by nearly all strata of society, it was through national weekly periodicals and national newspapers that news of importance was transmitted. Through this period, Hurley's lowly diocesan paper was transformed into a quotable source for a national audience.

The first use of this system took place in April 1941 at the eleventh annual Florida state convention of the National Council of Catholic Women (NCCW) in Gainesville. The women put aside their deliberations on a resolution forbidding "the wearing of slacks and shorts by women in churches" in order to listen to their new bishop's dinnertime speech, titled "The Nazi—Humanity's Foremost Enemy." Hurley devoted most of his talk to delicately approaching the Catholic moral dilemma regarding the fascist-versus-communist threat.

In a departure from the unofficial American Catholic position, which saw communism as the primary threat to Catholicism, Hurley turned the tables and echoed the conclusion of his 1939 meetings with Pius XI, Chamberlain, and Halifax. "There is a . . . group of men," he told the Gainesville group, "who, wittingly or unwittingly, are engaged in depressing our national spirit. They are those who day in and day out clamor that Communism is America's enemy No. 1. I am convinced that until a few years ago, that was true, and that today Communism is still our enemy. But I am also convinced that, in point of urgency if not in point of teaching, Communism has now ceded its primacy to National Socialism. . . . Today the first enemy of humanity," Hurley proclaimed with a direct condemnation of Hitler, "the killer of our priests, despoiler of our temples, foe of all we love both as Americans and as Catholics—is the Nazi."[17]

Closing his Gainesville address, Hurley once again vowed his loyalty to the Roosevelt administration. Oddly forsaking the leadership in Vatican City, he proclaimed that Catholic unity was wound up in national unity. Not in Rome but "in Washington, at the White House and on Capitol Hill, are the men whom we have chosen to lead us through the dark valley of the world's travail. In the conduct of the nation's affairs, they have the counsel of our Army and Navy. They are patriotic men. They are the embodiment of American unity. Them we will heed, and them we will follow." Hurley's strongly pro-American "little talk" to the Catholic women gathered at Gainesville was transmitted across the central swamplands of Florida to the pages of the nation's newspapers. "Bishop Hurley Scores Nazis" was the headline of the Chicago *New World*. *The Record* of Louisville also gave front-page billing. In the U.S. House of Representatives, Florida Democrat Joseph Hendricks entered the entire NCCW speech into the *Congressional Record*. At the State Department, Welles gave the all-clear for other administration officials to use Hurley as a political wedge in the anti-interventionist Catholic world of early 1941.[18]

Shortly after the Gainesville speech, Secretary of the Navy Frank Knox made what was described as a "fighting speech" at the annual United States Governors' Conference in heavily isolationist, and Irish Catholic, Boston. Waxing theological, Knox asserted that the war in Europe provided the United States "with a God-given chance to determine the outcome of a world-wide struggle." "Now is the time to put into motion the huge machine we have been building," he said while only a few miles from the Quincy Naval Shipyard. For Knox, America was the "City upon a Hill," while Hitler reigned as the "new and modern Genghis Khan." Abruptly, the Presbyterian Knox began to quote "a great leader of the Catholic church in America" as having recently "made an eloquent and appealing declaration" that denied the totalitarian precept that "every man, woman, and child belongs to the State." Knox informed the twenty-eight governors that the unnamed "Catholic prelate" was right on the mark. Appropriating Hurley's "theology of war" diction, Knox proclaimed that America's impending battle was "a war of Satan, a war of the flesh, a war of paganism." In order to thwart Satan, Knox suggested that the U.S. Navy could be employed to clear the North Atlantic of Nazi raiders.[19]

The speech had drastic repercussions for Knox. After the *Boston Herald* carried it on the front page, Massachusetts's Senator David Ignatius Walsh, a prominent Catholic and member of the Senate Naval Affairs Committee, declared that Knox should be formally censured. FDR's foremost foreign policy foe, Montana Democrat Burton K. Wheeler went further, indicating that Knox should "either resign or be thrown out of office." For their part, New England Catholics were mystified about who their unnamed "great leader" could be. Ambitious editors at Portland, Maine's *Church World* informed New England readers that "presumably Knox had in mind Bishop Joseph P. Hurley of St. Augustine, Florida, of whom few northerners have heard." Like American northerners, Europeans were just getting to know about Hurley.[20]

It was across the seas, in a Britain just recovering from the Luftwaffe blitz, that Hurley's speech garnered the most publicity. It drew top billing in the *London Universe*, which reported the Gainesville speech beneath a full front-page headline: "Bishop Exposes Berlin-Moscow Plan of Confusion to Make USA Commit Suicide." *The Tablet,* Britain's foremost Catholic weekly, took the opportunity to criticize American Catholic isolationism and printed the speech in its entirety. Even the isolationist Jesuit weekly *America* reluctantly called it "a timely and practical warning." The State Department could not have been happier with such wide coverage. "Keep up the good work!" Myron Taylor wrote from New York as he read Hurley's "forthright and inspiring" speech.[21]

Buoyed by the success of the Gainesville speech, Welles raised the stakes. In late May 1941 he sent Hurley a package of top-secret State Department documents outlining the Roosevelt administration's policy on the German occupation of Poland. The documents were extraordinarily sensitive. Apparently, they were given secretly to Welles by the foreign minister of Argentina. "You will remember," Welles emphasized to the new bishop, "that he obtained these documents from confidential sources . . . and was particularly anxious that it not be known that he had let me have these copies and, likewise, that no knowledge ever leak out as to the individuals who obtained the information regarding Polish atrocities. . . . I feel entirely warranted," Welles concluded, "in giving you this information for the purposes you and I discussed, since I know that in your hands it will serve a worthy cause."[22]

The exchange was significant because it showed for the first time on record that a highly placed U.S. government official was passing what amounted to be state secrets to an American Catholic clergyman. Welles's allusion to "the purposes you and I discussed" seems to show that an unrecorded earlier meeting had taken place between the two men. This meeting may have cemented Hurley's allegiance to State Department policy over that of the NCWC and the Vatican. As the United States moved toward belligerency, Hurley's strident pro-Americanism contrasted greatly with his pope's strenuous efforts to negotiate a peace.[23]

The sensitivity and confidentiality of the exchange also were extraordinary. Although Hull and Welles had courted Argentine foreign minister José Maria Cantilo for some time, it was only a month before Welles passed his secret documents to Hurley that Cantilo publicly abandoned Argentina's neutrality for a new pro-American policy of "realistic near-belligerency," a concept only tenuously accepted by ordinary Argentines. Consequently, in addition to the potential for a political scandal in Argentina, the still smoldering domestic anticatholicism of the 1940s made Welles's gamble on Hurley's patriotism a remarkable show of trust.[24]

Hurley assured Welles that he could be trusted not to leak the material, and promised to courier the package back to the State Department after his speech. He also informed Welles that he would use the information as the basis for a series of articles in the *Florida Catholic* designed to reveal conditions of life in Poland under Nazi domination. The series was intended to be picked up by the NCWC News Service. While preparing his series, Hurley scheduled a speech on Poland for June 17, 1940, at St. Leo's Abbey in Tampa. He indicated to Welles that the speech would have "for its prime purpose informing Catholics of the terrible conditions existing in Poland."[25]

This time Hurley was straightforward and unsparing in his use of Welles's State Department documentation. In his speech to the diocesan priests and Benedictine monks gathered at the abbey, Hurley suggested that the German occupation of Poland "called back the worst excesses of pagan persecution against the early Christians." This wartime persecution was a religious persecution whereby the German army sought "to exterminate all that is best in the Polish people—their religion, their culture, and national traditions." He went so far as to imply that German soldiers were perpetrating war crimes against the Poles. "Girls of tender age," he graphically informed the priests, "are snatched from the bosom of their families to serve the lusts of the Reich soldier . . . and cases are known of these pitiful children being shot like dogs when exhaustion and disease have rendered them useless for this degraded service."[26]

Since the series originated with a bishop, the National Catholic News Service went ahead and released the speech to all the Catholic diocesan papers. Upon receiving a copy of Hurley's speech, Welles commented to another State Department official that Bishop Hurley was, "in my judgment, one of the two or three outstanding members of the Catholic hierarchy in this country and is wholly and completely cooperative in the field of foreign policy." The rosy esteem of Welles and the European Division at the State Department was not so easily shared in other parts of Washington.[27]

Monsignor Michael J. Ready, head of the NCWC, was shocked to get word of Hurley's Polish persecution speech. This was because Hurley's talk was brought to his attention not by an ecclesiastical source, but by the Polish ambassador to the United States, Jan Ciechanowski. From out of the blue, Ciechanowski wrote to Ready that he was "moved with deep emotion" by Hurley's words. More astonishing to Ready was the fact that two days after Hurley's speech he received his own top-secret packet of material on Poland, but from an entirely different source—Apostolic Delegate Amleto Cicognani.[28]

Hurley now had to explain to Ready how he had written and delivered such a well-informed speech days before the NCWC and the apostolic delegation received the same sort of information. Ready wanted to know where Hurley was getting his material. Not wanting to reveal Welles as his source, Hurley indicated that the speech was "based on information I had received from other sources," aloofly stating that he considered it a "duty to give publication to the facts which came to my attention." He stubbornly refused to name Welles as the source but assured Ready that it was from "a trustworthy agency." "I should not like the people at 3339 Massachusetts Avenue [the address of Cicognani's apostolic delegation] to think that I divulged confidential matters." But Ready's worry was not about Hurley breaching discretion. He was worried that a lone American bishop had done an end-run around both the NCWC and the Vatican—and was working single-handedly with the Department of State. A young bishop flying solo in the charged atmosphere of isolationist prewar America could cause real problems for the American church.[29]

Ready's problems were just beginning. After the St. Leo's Abbey speech, Welles cajoled Hurley to take the administration's message beyond Florida and onto the national stage. "In these times the American people naturally ask whether the cultural and spiritual values inherent in our conception of civilization can be preserved," he appealed to the young bishop, "and they look for guidance to the enlightened leaders in these fields."[30]

Unbeknownst to him, Hurley's friend Father Maurice S. Sheehy, lieutenant commander of the U.S. Chaplain Corps, wrote to William S. Paley at the Columbia Broadcasting System suggesting that Hurley give a nationwide broadcast. Welles seconded the suggestion and wrote to CBS with an assurance that the European Division would reimburse the network for Hurley's travel costs. In late June 1941 Hurley was invited to speak on a national broadcast about the Vatican and American foreign policy. Hurley sought the under secretary's advice in composing his speech. To ensure that he got it right, Welles rushed off the latest State Department press releases and promised to "listen with interest to your forthcoming radio address." Neither the NCWC nor the Vatican's apostolic delegate was informed. It would blindside them completely. Hurley was doing the bidding of Welles solely. To his mind, it was the state that was right, after all.[31]

The idea of a prominent Catholic cleric delivering a speech advocating intervention had been bandied about the State Department since the spring of 1941. With a sense of urgency, Harold Tittman wrote Cordell Hull from the Vatican in late May that the bishops of the United States "were not sufficiently convinced that a Nazi victory meant the destruction of religion." In fact, Tittman averred, "some prominent American ecclesiastics are not as whole-heartedly behind the present policy of their government as they might properly be. The feeling is held that the true situation should be brought forcibly and urgently home to the American ecclesiastics without further delay and in an impressive manner." Welles knew that Hurley now was primed to be a spokesperson on an "impressive" scale. By early June Hurley had also come to the conclusion that war was "inevitable and that we should not wait until Hitler strikes us." His speech "Papal Pronouncements and American Foreign Policy" was slated for thirty minutes over CBS on July 6, 1941.[32]

"MOST REVEREND WAR-MONGER"

Hurley composed his speech only a week before it aired, drafting it while walking in the solitude of Ponte Vedra Beach, a resort area thirty miles north of St. Augustine. As Hurley jotted down his interventionist speech, he could hardly have guessed that within ten months the very same beach would be the site where a landing party of Nazi saboteurs would disembark from a German U-boat, intent on carrying out an improbable attack on America's industrial plants. In July 1941 such dangers were scarcely considered by a neutral U.S. Catholic hierarchy. Although he solicited suggestions from both Mooney and Welles, he did not submit a draft of the speech to either. He arrived in Washington by train one day before his scheduled hookup. Paul Glynn, the station manager at WSJV in Washington, received his copy of the speech only the day before. On July 6 Hurley was seated behind a CBS microphone to offer his own ideas on Catholic church policy, the Vatican, and American foreign relations.

Hurley's broadcast would finally express his own inner conflicts with the new papal policy: he quoted Pope Pius XI as often as he quoted Pius XII. Politically, however, the broadcast was designed to trump Pius XII's nuanced approach with a reclamation of Pius XI's confrontational rhetoric. "We must call things by their right names," Papa Ratti had told his cardinals on Christmas Eve of 1937 in an address on Nazi atrocities. Five years later, in the most publicity-driven speech of his career, Hurley took up Pius XI's call to "name names," this time to the American public.

Pope Pius XII's cryptic condemnations of the Axis were not enough for Hurley, and over the airwaves of CBS he unleashed an explicit attack. "We will call things by their real names," he began in a forthright jab at Pius's policy of shrouded antinazism. This war had been "prepared by the Nazis in cold blood for over six years," he exclaimed. Giving the reigning pontiff his due, he described Pope Pius XII as a man who, "from the first hour of his Pontificate, sought to fling himself across the path of those who wanted war." But now that Pius's outstretched crosier had failed to trip up the Wehrmacht, Hurley signaled his disenchantment with the pontiff's continued reluctance to denounce Germany by name. As in the past, Hurley would not succumb to what he saw as outmoded diplomatic language and methods.

The context of a heightened national security debate provided Hurley the opening for an explicit denunciation of "the murderous hosts of Nazi

Germany." The Nazis, "contrary to solemn treaty, without provocation, and without previous declaration of war, invaded Holland, Belgium, and Luxemburg. . . . This war is Germany's doing, it is a war of stark aggression; a war for European and world domination." Even more, the war was a "revolution of irreligion and paganism set against the Christian ethic and Christian civilization." Hurley's straightforward denunciation of Germany would raise both the eyebrows and the blood pressures of the isolationist U.S. Catholic hierarchy. Symbolizing the disparity between the American bishops and Hurley, when the editors of the *New York Times* were forced to categorize Hurley's speech on their radio page, they listed what was ostensibly a religious speech with the broadcasts designated "National Defense."

In a series of statements that would draw criticism from secular news columnists, Hurley argued that supreme war powers should be entrusted exclusively to the president: "it is manifestly impossible that the day to day decisions which must be taken often in the greatest secrecy should be submitted to the Congress for discussion. Such matters are lawfully the competence of the Executive . . . in his capacity as Chief Executive and Commander in Chief." The conduct of foreign affairs "should be left to the Commander in Chief," he argued, harkening back to his early admiration of the military, "who alone, in constant, loyal communication with the Congress and in consultation with his military advisors, is capable of bringing us safely through the dangers that encompass us." By apparently arrogating to the president the power to place U.S. armed forces in the field without the consent of Congress, Hurley sparked a barrage of controversy.[33]

AFTERMATH: HIERARCHICAL CONFLICT AND PERSONAL INTROSPECTION

"Bishop Hurley has started something," a frantic Wilfred Parsons, S.J., editor of the powerful isolationist Jesuit magazine *America,* wrote to fellow editor Thomas Francis Meehan after Hurley's speech aired. "Publicly he speaks only for himself, but privately he will tell you he speaks the mind of the Pope." The isolationist Father Parsons certainly had reason to worry, and indeed Hurley's speech had "started something." According to historian Gerald P. Fogarty, S.J., the speech created a pronounced division within the hierarchy. Those who were most irate at Hurley's pro-Roosevelt speech were William Cardinal O'Connell of Boston, Archbishop Michael J. Curley of Washington, D.C., and Archbishop Francis J. L. Beckman of Dubuque, Iowa. Their policy had been to call for peace and to reiterate the pope's pleas for nonviolence.[34]

In response to Hurley's speech, Cardinal O'Connell quickly recalled two of his priests working in the missions of Florida. Archbishop Curley protested to Apostolic Delegate Amleto Cicognani that Hurley had failed to request his permission to speak on a Catholic topic within the Archdiocese of Washington. Curley's ire was sparked as the *Washington Post* blared Hurley's speech on the top of its front page on July 7. By thus highlighting Hurley's direct denunciation of Hitler, the editors clearly deemed the speech more important than reports on the European war itself. Reading all these signs from afar, Dubuque's Archbishop Beckman cuttingly dubbed Hurley "the Talleyrand of the Everglades."[35]

Archbishop Beckman became Hurley's most publicly outspoken critic, and wrote a scathing personal reproof of Hurley in his diocesan newspaper, *The Witness.* "Our only appeal is to logic," Beckman wrote in his July 11 editorial criticizing Hurley's broadcast. He called into question Hurley's endorsement of presidential war powers. "If the people of the United States should not be permitted to decide on such a question of vital concern to them as war, do they belong to a democracy or to a dictatorship?"

Later that month Beckman went on a national radio hookup to confute Hurley. During the broadcast he returned to the prevailing Catholic view that the primary threat to America was not Nazism, but communism. Echoing Cardinal Pacelli in his 1936 sparring contest with FDR, Beckman shouted: "Today the mask is off; it is Communism!, Communism!, Communism!, everywhere gaining ground! We are in danger of being slowly poisoned, debilitated, and disarmed by this monstrous malady."[36]

In New York, Archbishop Spellman wrote a personal letter of congratulations to Pope Pius XII on the occasion of his ordination jubilee. Sensing an opening to mediate between the U.S. government and the Holy See, Spellman included various copies of anti-Hurley letters he was receiving from outraged Catholics of the New York archdiocese, as well as newspaper clippings of the Hurley-Beckman dispute. Signing off, Spellman assured Pius XII that Hurley continued to be vocally antifascist. "In short things are in turmoil here. I am striving to do my duty as I see it as a Catholic bishop and to devote myself to the duties of the office without involving the Church in useless and senseless controversies." Spellman never commented to Hurley about his missive to Pius, or why he believed condemning Nazism by name was "useless and senseless."[37]

Other bishops were less reluctant to reply to Hurley. "Your Mein Fuhrer Roosevelt radio address," wrote Bishop John A. Duffy of Buffalo, "will go far to promote disunity among our fellow-Catholics in the United States. It may be invidious to say, but possibly long residence abroad under totalitarian influences has convinced you that the people of a democracy are incapable of deciding matters affecting their nation and their own lives."[38]

Even more acrid letters of protest from all over the country deluged the tiny chancery office at St. Augustine. Postcards addressed to the "Most Reverend War-Monger" and the "Blood Thirsty Devil in Sheep's Clothing" testified to the divided mood of many American Catholics on the foreign policy issues of the day. "How a pole-cat of your stripe ever got into the clergy is a mystery to the citizens of the USA," one Duffy supporter wrote from Buffalo; "Florida would be justified in putting the boots to your southern extremity and dropping you into the depths of some obnoxious sink-hole." "You may be Churchill's Hope, Joy and Pride," a Coughlinite wrote from Detroit, "BUT TO THE MOTHERS OF AMERICA, YOU ARE JUST A PAIN IN THE ---."[39]

A priest who remembered Hurley from Cleveland cut to the core with unbalanced rhetoric highlighting the divisions within the American lower clergy. "The Episcopal ordination did not blot out your excessive pride. It is this pride that now makes you belch—like an ass—half-truths and insane nothings. This pride will bring about your eternal perdition. If you were not blinded by egotism you would realize the impropriety of your gastric effusions on a subject which Cardinals, Archbishops, and senior bishops do not discuss too publicly. But you—a young, homely, sickly prelate—have the audacity to turn Catholics away from the Church with your gnat-brained war mouthings. . . . You ought to be excommunicated. You have about as much faith as a cat's tail."[40]

Although he could shrug off the ad hominem attacks of Coughlinite isolationists, Hurley had to be more concerned about the opinion of the apostolic delegate. He knew from his experience in the Coughlin case that Archbishop Amleto Cicognani held great power in matters of U.S. church policy. As historian George Q. Flynn has observed, Amleto Cicognani was "upset" with the new bishop's public foray into the international affairs. In his personal notes on the broadcast, Hurley noted that Cicognani was "bitterly critical" of the speech. Spurred by Father Coughlin, "acrimonious critics" deluged Cicognani's apostolic delegation in Washington, D.C., with "thousands of letters." Cicognani feared a real "crossing of lines" between Hurley's religious role and his political attitudes. For the pope's representative, it was "inopportune" for American religious leaders to make moral judgments upon political topics.[41]

"I assume that you know that the reaction to Bishop Hurley's talk was most unfriendly at the Apostolic Delegation," Maurice Sheehy wrote to Sumner Welles. "I do not see why the Delegate should be permitted to criticize a bishop for such a fine statement of American principles." Welles indicated to Sheehy that he was deeply disturbed by "the pussy-footing influence of the [Apostolic] Delegation." Both Hurley and Welles were annoyed that Cicognani did not make a public statement in support of the speech. In a pocket notebook that Hurley carried with him on the train trip back to St. Augustine he scribbled: "*Chick* [Hurley's nickname for Cicognani]—*'Don't say any more.'*"[42]

Hurley chafed at Cicognani's new restrictions and became ever more cynical and caustically critical of the apostolic delegate. He began to blame Cicognani for systematically fashioning the very American episcopal neutrality that his speech had aimed to overcome. To Hurley Cicognani was "a political-minded Delegate who chooses Bishops in the only way he knows anything about—by intrigue, by balancing faction against faction, by personal favoritism." Even the American cardinals fell into his ambit. "The result" of Cicognani's control of appointments "is that we get mediocre men. . . . Neutral gray is the color of the U.S. Purple."[43]

Although Cicognani was unaware of Hurley's private thoughts about him, he was deeply distressed by the new Florida bishop's actions. In fact Hurley's outspoken behavior so disturbed Cicognani that he deliberately foiled an impending promotion. At Cicognani's request, and unbeknownst to Hurley, the Florida bishop was taken out of consideration for a Vatican post to head the apostolic delegation in India. Such advancement in the diplomatic corps, Cicognani wrote to Cardinal Maglione at the Secretariat of State, might be construed as lending "explicit Vatican support" to Hurley's remarks.[44]

Cicognani's assessment was partly correct. As apostolic delegate to

India, Hurley would have been raised to the rank of archbishop from monsignor in less than a year—an ascent rivaling only that of Mooney's fifteen years earlier. But while the posting would have moved him up the hierarchical ladder, it also would have jettisoned him halfway around the globe and outside the immediate influence of Sumner Welles and other officials at the U.S. Department of State. The fact that this net result was not considered by Archbishop Cicognani lends weight to the assumption that the apostolic delegation had no idea that Hurley was working so closely with Welles and the State Department. An embittered Father Coughlin sensed otherwise.

Coughlin wasted no time in deriding the "American Talleyrand" in his newspaper *Social Justice*, which devoted its front page on July 14, 1941, to rebutting Hurley's positions. Perhaps recalling Hurley's secret conversation of fraternal correction four years earlier, Coughlin took aim and struck. He denounced Hurley as an "inspired cooperator with Communists and an advocate of American dictatorship." "Since this mitered politician, this non-taxpayer, this scoffer at the 'put up the sword' policy," he argued with wacky prose, "has pole-vaulted into prominence on the crozier of a bishop, be it remembered that the publicity he has gained is merely accidental. Without the crozier, he would still grovel in the solitude of the Everglades. . . . Let's not become afflicted with a Florida sunburn which makes things appear red and causes a fever, sometimes affecting the brain." Finally, Coughlin intuited Welles's influence, encouraging his flock to reject the message of "this clerical Charlie McCarthy."[45]

The fiery rhetoric from Detroit clearly ruffled Mooney. In a rare disagreement with his protégé, Mooney let Hurley know that he was "fearful of the results" of the speech. Hurley recorded that Mooney disagreed with his July 6 assertion that the Constitution gave the president the right to declare war. After a few days, when Mooney cooled back to diplomatic form, he clarified to Hurley that the address was "right, but not clear." Mooney may have been selling him out on the speech. He backed up Cicognani and encouraged Hurley not to respond to anyone, not even to Bishop Beckman. Joseph A. Luther, a Jesuit with connections inside the Detroit chancery and a supporter of Coughlin, secretly wrote with a tone of authority to the editors at *America* about Mooney's true feelings. "Abp. Mooney seems slightly to resent Hurley's attitude, but his only comment was 'we will wait and see what happens.'"

The Detroit headlines certainly caused a headache for the Coughlin-crossed Mooney. Joseph Luther reported that Mooney's prime diocesan consultant on Father Coughlin, Monsignor William F. Murphy, considered the speech "just a cheap political gesture of Hurley's to capture New Deal and Administration favor." Meanwhile Hurley conveyed to Mooney that he would respect his wishes and say nothing.[46]

With very little support coming to him from within the American hierarchy, and now with even his closest ecclesiastical friends turning against him, it is not surprising that Hurley sought consolation and gained confidence from Sumner Welles and some of the nation's highest-ranking government officials. Two days after Hurley's July 6 speech Welles offered Hurley hearty congratulations, characterizing the address as being "of monumental importance" and "of the utmost value at this particular moment in opening the eyes of many millions of the people of the United States to the true facts of the world situation." The under secretary of state closed by saying that he was glad to see that the young bishop was "continuing his diplomatic activity." Whether the "diplomatic activity" was for the United States or the Vatican, Welles never made clear. On July 22 Myron Taylor added his acclamation: the speech was a "very masterly address. . . . It was timely and very well designed to meet an actual situation that existed." Vice President Henry A. Wallace wrote to Maurice Sheehy that Hurley had made "a significant statement."[47]

Other distinguished figures also praised Hurley. At the end of July the popular novelist Taylor Caldwell sent Hurley her warmest congratulations, attaching a carbon copy of a letter she had sent to Archbishop Beckman, in which she called Hurley "a man regarded with deep reverence and love by many." "He has courage and dignity, stature and nobility," she wrote to Beckman of Hurley. "He, like Jesus, will not compromise with evil—you should rise up and like Jesus, call him blessed." The internationally known philosopher Jacques Maritain indicated that it was "a great joy and consolation" to listen to Hurley's speech. Maritain congratulated Hurley for alerting America to the "grave consequences for the future of civilization and Christianity."[48]

The national journalistic response to Hurley's speech was mixed. *Time* magazine devoted its entire religion section of July 14 to the speech. The interventionist editors considered Hurley to be "the first forthright, authoritative Catholic voice . . . against any idea that Hitler's war against

Russia was a holy crusade." Florida Democratic Senator Claude Pepper called Hurley's speech "a very able and outstanding radio address" and entered it into the *Congressional Record*. The influential syndicated journalist Ernest K. Lindley, much to the dismay of the isolationists—and the horror of the hierarchy—underscored Hurley's past connections to the Secretariat of State. "Whether or not Hurley spoke with the express approval of the Vatican," Lindley concluded his syndicated article, "as a personal protégé of the present Pope, it is thought inconceivable that he would say anything which he did not believe to be in thorough harmony with Vatican policy." "Notwithstanding his disclaimer," Lindley wrote in the *Washington Post* after some double-checking, "[Hurley] did in fact present these views with the approval or consent of the Pope."[49]

Thus, the speech spread confusion in the ranks of the American hierarchy and fitted nicely into Welles's plan to create a public alternative to American Catholic isolationism. Welles, Taylor, and Phillips had so "turned" Hurley to the government line that he became a seemingly witting accomplice in this task. Strangely, Hurley seemed unaware of the entrenched isolationism of the American clergy.

"I have had no peace since I made that broadcast," he wrote to Mooney. "Some of the comments by columnists and editorial writers are wide of the mark," he indicated to Welles, "but many others have seized upon the vital parts of the speech,—the necessity for unity and confidence in the Government." "As often occurs in such cases," he understated to Myron Taylor, "the address was the victim of some unfortunate headlines." Indeed, the intensity of the stream of vituperation arriving at his desk in St. Augustine caught him off guard. According to one report, the post office in St. Augustine had to shut down temporarily and bring in extra workers to cope with the bags of mail arriving for the chancery. Hurley's response to his critics was uncharacteristically passive, and certainly informed by Mooney's admonition to keep quiet. He did not even answer the "Mein Fuhrer Roosevelt" letter from Bishop Duffy.[50]

Despite the deluge of negative criticism, Hurley's inner passion and patriotic beliefs were only strengthened. "Nothing has as yet happened to make me regret any of it," he wrote to Mooney only a week after the broadcast. "Even the misleading headlines had the effect of drawing more attention to what I said. I am convinced that someone had to correct the notion that the Church was in some way out of harmony with the policy of the Government; that we were tinged with the color of the dictatorships." For Hurley, the silence of the American bishops as well as the nonconfrontational policy of Pope Pius XII generated broad confusion among noncatholics trying to assess the church's position. It was Roosevelt who was taking the better Christian part by publicly scolding the Nazis. "This nation has cast the die," he wrote in a follow-up editorial justifying his speech. "The men it freely elected as its leaders have decided that the future good of the country lies in the complete defeat of Hitlerism—the Nazi." Aligning himself with U.S. policy in preference to papal foreign policy, he related to Mooney that Washington was ready to pull out all the stops. "I have been resisting some pressure to see the President," he relayed to his uneasy mentor. With Welles smiling, the hierarchy in turmoil, and Catholic war support in the balance, "Papal Pronouncements and American Foreign Policy" promoted Hurley as a candidate for further secret White House missions.[51]

CHAPTER SEVEN

Propagandist in Black

HURLEY AND THE U.S. DEPARTMENT OF STATE

HISTORIANS OF WARTIME PROPAGANDA often make the distinction between "black" and "white" propaganda. On the one hand, white propaganda is largely factual, and its source can usually be identified. The objective is to "spin" or distort the reporting of actual news toward a desired end. Black propaganda, on the other hand, is information that is purported to emanate from a source other than the true one. In at least one sense, black propaganda operates from a position of deceit. For this type of misinformation to be accepted by the target audience, it is imperative that the credibility of the originator be untainted. The chances of its acceptance are increased "if black propaganda comes from an authority within the target audience." In at least one sense, such propaganda is a "black art" used in time of war.[1]

From the spring of 1941 through the spring of 1943, Hurley fitted the bill superbly for Welles, Taylor, and FDR as a Catholic "authority" on international affairs. And it was precisely the international aspect of Hurley's growing fame as a churchman that Welles aimed to harness. After the attack on Pearl Harbor, American Catholics closed ranks behind FDR and the administration's war goals. But Catholic opinion still needed to be shaped in a number of respects, not the least of which were American policy on aid to the Soviet Union, Vatican policy toward Japan, and Catholic sympathy for the Axis in Latin America. Vatican neutrality also continued to vex American policymakers. What Hurley offered the State Department was a direct line to a quotable Catholic source for copy that usually struck against the pose of papal neutrality.

In the months after Hurley's CBS speech, Welles distributed more of the Florida bishop's speeches and statements to the secular press. Among other coups in this secret system was Hurley's formulation of why and how American Catholics could support FDR's Lend-Lease bill proposing military aid to the Soviet Union. This was an extremely thorny issue, since isolationist Catholics felt buttressed in their stand by the prohibition on cooperating with communism contained in the March 1937 papal encyclical *Divini Redemptoris* (On Atheistic Communism). But Hurley claimed that such aid was permissible—and issued the first statement granting Catholic approval for Lend-Lease by an American bishop. Hurley's *Florida Catholic* article appeared nearly two months before a Vatican-sponsored document on the same issue. Further, Hurley's justification for Lend-Lease was framed in terms that no Vatican document dared to use.

Perhaps recalling his disgust when Pius XII refused to name Germany as the aggressor in 1939, Hurley was not going to let isolationist American Catholics similarly off the hook. Hurley named Nazism explicitly as "a rapacious, murderous, power which has loosed a torrent of injustice, violence, and religious persecution upon almost the whole of Europe and which will destroy our Christian civilization the world over unless we oppose it with all our strength." Since Hurley's formulation was printed during the heated congressional debate on Lend-Lease, it was extremely useful to Welles and to FDR, who retained a copy of Hurley's "Russian aid" formula in his official file.[2]

Welles continued to achieve other small triumphs. He single-handedly placed a Hurley letter to the editor in the *New York Times,* assuring the Florida bishop that in this way his views would "get the widest publicity." The missive castigated Father Coughlin as both "unChristian" and "unpatriotic." And although there is no direct evidence suggesting Welles's involvement, the under secretary surely smiled approvingly when Hurley's controversial CBS speech was used verbatim by the *New York Times'* editors to justify FDR's unilateral deployment of American troops to Iceland.[3]

Hurley continued to prove to Welles that he could be trusted to carry out the exact wishes of the State Department. Such independence also showed that he was moving away from the control of the Catholic power structure in the United States. With Hurley on board, Welles now found that he could circumvent the National Catholic Welfare Conference, the apostolic delegate, and any bishops of whom he was unsure. Moreover, as the war continued Welles began to see Hurley as a valuable counterpoise to various Catholics worldwide who remained sympathetic to the Axis. Through various means of black propaganda, Welles would use Hurley as a tool to thwart fascist gains in the worldwide propaganda war.

Buoyed by patriotism, Hurley was a willing participant. In August 1941 a portrait of Welles, with chiseled and steely features, appeared on the cover of *Time* magazine. The under secretary of state's grave countenance appeared on the bas-relief of the Department of State seal—a seal symbolizing the power, international reach, and style of leadership that Hurley admired. Allied to Welles's view that American power should be used abroad, from 1941 through 1943 Hurley deliberately withheld from other American bishops that Welles and other Roosevelt administration officials were the sources of several of his most important public speeches. In other cases, Hurley's name was suppressed in Catholic material used by the Department of State, including one report aimed at influencing the war policy of Pope Pius XII. In at least two cases, Hurley black propaganda operations became presidential decisions.

In late August 1941 Sumner Welles became interested in using the momentum from the CBS speech to promote U.S. policy in Latin America. Welles may have been alerted to the intensity of Catholic profascism there by a series of reports from career diplomat George S. Messersmith. Appointed as ambassador to Cuba in 1940, Messersmith quickly began to report on Nazi infiltration of Latin America and the Roman Catholic church. In one very important confidential eleven-page memorandum, Messersmith outlined to Welles that the lower Catholic clergy in Cuba were being influenced by Spanish Fascists. "Because Germany and Italy aided the Franco Government in the Spanish Civil War," Messersmith pointed out, "a great majority of the clergy are taking the attitude that Germany and Italy are the defenders of the Catholic Church." Messersmith longed for a forthright Catholic statement to set the record straight.

Messersmith recommended to Welles that the State Department ask Pope Pius XII to clarify the situation through a public statement, but he was not hopeful. Having closely monitored Catholic events from Vienna during the 1930s, he was as perplexed as Hurley was by the shift in papal policy under Pius XII. "What is particularly disconcerting," he wrote from Havana, "is that the attitude of the Vatican, which at one time seemed to be so clearly defined, is becoming more and more obscure. If any directives are coming out of Rome to the clergy in the other American Republics, they are coming in a very obscure form. . . . I regret to say, that I have had indications from good sources that directives may actually be coming in the form of instructions not to say anything which might be objectionable to the totalitarian regimes."[4]

Taking his lead from Messersmith, in late June 1941 Welles decided "to talk to the President with regard to the possibility of Bishop Hurley making a trip to the west coast of South America. If the President agrees," Welles confided to Maurice Sheehy, "I shall take pleasure in writing to Bishop Hurley to that effect." Apparently, FDR agreed. On July 10 a Chicago newspaper reported that the State Department was considering asking Hurley "to go south to repeat his views in the Catholic nations of Latin America," commenting that "such a journey would be of tremendous assistance to the United States government in the development of hemispheric solidarity." As yet unaware of Mooney's true feelings about his CBS speech, Hurley wrote to him about Welles's latest plan. "It would be a quiet trip for the purpose of vacation," Hurley explained, "but I would be expected to visit the Bishops in a few of the countries. . . . The request comes from the Under Secretary of State and request from that quarter at this time is not easy to refuse." More tempting for Hurley was Welles's offer to pay for the trip.[5]

When Hurley's friend Father Maurice Sheehy got wind of what Welles was about to do, he rushed off an urgent note to the under secretary behind Hurley's back. Sheehy wanted Welles to provide more for his friend than simply an expense account. "The bishop does not want any official sanction for this trip," Sheehy explained, but "he does expect a little guidance and (may I speak frankly), protection." Perhaps aware that Hurley had already put himself in danger by working for the U.S. embassy in Rome from 1938 to 1940, Sheehy made clear to Welles that "his life would be in danger from the time he left our shores until he returned." Sheehy insinuated that a U.S. naval warship should shadow Hurley's liner.[6]

A few days after Sheehy's request to Welles for "protection," Mooney responded to Hurley's original request for advice on the matter. Mooney was becoming convinced that his diplomatic protégé had been co-opted.

Hurley was now taking orders from the Department of State, or at least he was seriously entertaining offers from outside the Catholic hierarchical orbit. Mooney, seasoned in the ways of the Vatican, now became vocal against Hurley's "crossing of the lines" between church and state. "I advise against it," he warned. "To my mind, it comes to be bad in every way. It would make it impossible to convince anyone that your speech was an independent move on your part. Moreover, it would color everything you might do or say in the future . . . it would advertise you as a government agent."[7]

With Mooney advising that a Latin American trip would be "bad in every way," Welles's proposed trip to South America foundered. Hurley never recorded why he turned down Welles's proposal, or whether Welles informed him about presidential approval for the trip. The decision probably reflected a combination of Mooney's caution and the specter of Archbishop Amleto Cicognani's latest warnings. Hurley continued his diplomatic contacts with Sumner Welles and Myron Taylor, but from that point on he acted independently of other bishops. Mooney's quashing of the Latin American trip had the effect of moving Hurley closer to Welles and terminating any prior solicitation of advice from Catholic quarters. It also set Hurley at odds with developments at the Vatican, even as the United States moved from isolationism toward total war.[8]

Catholic isolationism in the United States ended with the attack on Pearl Harbor on December 7, 1941. On December 23 Edward Mooney, now chairman of the National Catholic Welfare Conference, publicly offered Roosevelt the unanimous support of the American episcopate. Archbishop Beckman, Hurley's constant foe, wanted to dissent from Mooney's statement, but was silenced by Apostolic Delegate Cicognani. Hurley was vindicated in many ways after December 1941. The American hierarchy was placed on a war footing and now echoed much of what Hurley had been advocating since his final days in Rome. But even with the entrance of the United States into the war, problems of Catholic allegiance continued to pop up on the diplomatic radar.[9]

In March 1942 the State Department was abuzz with reports from Japan that confirmed Hurley's opinion that Pope Pius XII was lining up the Holy See on the wrong side of the wartime equation. "We have supreme confidence in victory because we know that we are right," Hurley announced in a speech over NBC exactly one month earlier. Even the

Soviet Union was "on the right side in this war of good against evil." Yet the Vatican was about to establish diplomatic relations with imperial Japan. On March 14 Welles wrote to FDR telling him that "Bishop Hurley was horrified . . . that it was actually true that the Vatican was receiving a diplomatic mission from Japan." Welles fumed, but there was little he could do. On March 27 Ken Harada, then Japan's acting ambassador to Vichy, was appointed special minister to the Vatican. President Roosevelt took the development as a personal insult, coming so closely after Pearl Harbor. The State Department lodged a "strong protest" through Myron Taylor.[10]

Hurley's "horror" at the Vatican anti-Allied move pushed him further into the shadowy world of black propaganda. Fascist press outlets were describing the arrangement as a "Japanese diplomatic victory over the United States," language that made Hurley bristle. To mitigate the Japan fiasco, Hurley made an outright offer to the State Department to prevent any recurrence of anti-American diplomacy at the Vatican. What the State Department really wanted, however, was a bold move of black propaganda to swing Pius XII squarely back into the Allied camp.

THE HAND THAT HOLDS THE PEN: THE "BISHOPS' DRAFT" OF 1942

On September 2, 1942, Hurley enjoyed a luncheon with Myron Taylor at his country estate in Locust Valley, New York. In the middle of a "long and pleasant" conversation, Taylor asked Hurley if he would accompany him on his next official visit to the Vatican. "Since I have been considering this whole matter," Taylor wrote to Edward Mooney about his next meeting with Pius XII, "the thought has often come to me how useful it would be were Bishop Hurley to accompany me." The offer was remarkable, but by running his suggestion by the cautious Edward Mooney, Taylor unknowingly complicated his own plan. Since Mooney still harbored misgivings about Hurley's July 6 CBS speech, he presumably thwarted a Hurley return to Rome.[11]

That summer FDR had ordered Taylor to return to the Vatican in order to present "an explanation . . . as to America's views concerning the war, and beyond" to Pope Pius XII. Hurley would have played an important symbolic role. If Taylor took Hurley back to Rome, he would be presenting more than a written statement to the pope; he would be bringing a physical embodiment of FDR's expectations for American Catholic church policy. A face-to-face encounter between Hurley and Pius XII, arranged by the U.S. government, would speak volumes about FDR's hopes for Catholic policy.[12]

On September 19 Myron Taylor met with the pope for the first time since his departure from Rome in 1940. Taylor flew from Lisbon to Rome in what was rumored to be "a more or less blacked-out" Italian government transport plane and was met in Rome by an equally "more or less blacked-out" Vatican limousine. During his audience Taylor presented Pius XII with a written statement of the U.S. government's position on the war and in particular the position of American Catholics concerning the war in Europe. What was unusual about this five-page statement was that no one in the Roosevelt administration had had any hand in its composition.[13]

The statement that Taylor presented to the pope, ostensibly a U.S. government position paper, was the collaborative product of three American clerics: Joseph P. Hurley, Edward Mooney, and Michael Ready. The statement was drafted without the consultation of any other American bishops. Taylor gave his stamp of approval to the statement in late August. He made neither revisions nor corrections. It was sent to Roosevelt in early September as an official government document. There was no need to have it vetted by the Department of State. It was Hurley's finest act of black propaganda yet.

"It was pleasing to know that Bishop Hurley had taken part," Taylor later wrote to Mooney about the document's composition. Taylor could count on Hurley to give—and perhaps to force—the unadulterated government line as he collaborated with Mooney and Ready. Welles immediately sent a draft copy to FDR. After being cleared by FDR, Secretary of State Hull, and Welles on September 4, the "Bishops' Draft" was presented in its entirety to Pope Pius XII on September 19. Myron Taylor read it to the pope verbatim, just as it had been composed by Hurley, Mooney, and Ready six weeks earlier.[14]

The "Bishops' Draft" was a remarkably forthright statement of American wartime objectives. A declaration of patriotism and determination, and an assertion of ultimate victory, it reveals Hurley's influence throughout. Schematically, the statement strikingly resembled his controversial July 6, 1941, speech. After a preliminary section including brief synopses of *Mit brennender Sorge* and *Summi Pontificatus,* the draft moved toward argumentation grounded in American militarism, antinazism, and a universal call to the American principles of democracy. Shattering Pius's constant calls for immediate peace, the draft echoed defiantly that "the only thing that would make the United States lay down the arms taken up in defense of national security and world decency would be complete and forthright acceptance of the Atlantic Charter and the Manifesto of the United Nations."

The martial rhetoric was assuredly the work of the patriotic Bishop Hurley. "Our shipyards are producing ocean-going ships for combat and commerce at a rate hitherto undreamed of," the document declared, probably signifying Hurley's attempt to neutralize any lingering memories of Vatican awe of the Wehrmacht in 1940. "The entire industry of the world's greatest industrial nation is now directed to one only objective—to manufacture, by mass production methods in which we excel, the implements of war."

The "Bishops' Draft" in effect administered an electric shock treatment designed to move Pius into conceding to American global power. Given the martial prose, Hurley most likely wrote the document's final paragraphs. "We have only begun and yet we have already surpassed the arms output of Germany at her peak," the document boasted. The "Bishops' Draft" concluded with a salvo of militarism: "The world has never seen such an avalanche of war weapons, manned by skilled mechanics and stouthearted freemen, as we shall loose in 1943 and 1944 against the Axis." Hurley's long-held philosophy of unflinching military leadership —the maintenance of virtue in the midst of difficulty—had made its way back into the hands of Pope Pius XII.[15]

An analysis of the "Bishops' Draft" makes clear that Hurley and the other bishops believed that "Christian ideals" were at stake and that the war was being conducted against "the enemies of Christian civilization." If Hitler led the "Panzer divisions of paganism," President Roosevelt was leading "Mr. Chrysler's tanks of Christianity." The "Bishops' Draft" was a manifesto of American Catholic patriotism and allegiance. At the same time, it was an appeal to bring the Vatican to a long-desired appreciation of the moral rectitude of American democracy—and to push the Holy See into abandoning any hint of preordained Nazi domination of Europe.

The "Bishops' Draft" was black propaganda aimed directly at Pope Pius XII. According to archival sources available for confirmation, only

FDR, Welles, and Taylor knew that the document was composed by Mooney, Ready, and Hurley. Given Hurley's cool relationship with Amleto Cicognani, it is probably safe to say that the apostolic delegation would never have recommended that Hurley compose another policy statement. Moreover, since Taylor presented the document to the pope in the name of the U.S. government, the covert composition of the brief seems to show that the top two leaders of the American Catholic hierarchy had come to oppose Pius XII's diplomatic strategy of straddling the Axis and recognizing imperial Japan. In this case, Mooney, Ready, and Hurley had to place deep trust in the secrecy of FDR, Welles, and Taylor. If Pope Pius XII became aware that the highest-ranking prelates in the United States were so out of synch with wartime papal policy, it could have spelled chaos for their ecclesiastical careers. Pius XII probably never knew he was receiving a warning shot from his own bishops.

COUNTERING THE NAZI THREAT IN IRELAND

Hurley's belief that the Allies were engaged in a war to preserve Christian civilization kept him at the beck and call of Welles, who by October 1942 had found yet another assignment for the Florida cleric. This time the State Department needed a declaration to counteract a speech by Joseph Cardinal MacRory of Ireland. The cardinal objected to the presence of American troops recently assigned to staff British submarine bases in Northern Ireland. MacRory carped at the United States from the moment Yankee troops stepped ashore, claiming that their presence marked official U.S. acceptance of the political division of Ireland and of British domination of the northern counties.[16]

"The partition of Ireland," the cardinal stated, "is a flagrant and intolerable injustice against Catholics doomed to live under . . . narrow and unjust domination. When I read day after day, that this war is being fought for the rights and liberties of small nations and then think of my own corner of my country overrun by British and United States soldiers against the will of the nation, I confess I sometimes find it exceedingly hard." The *New York Times* gave play to MacRory's commentary. The fiery cardinal's potential for stirring up anti-British sentiment among Irish Catholics in America unnerved Welles. For Welles, the MacRory statement was a particularly tricky threat. MacRory was the Catholic cardinal-archbishop of Armagh, the historically primatial see located in Northern Ireland. Anti-

British as well as staunchly anticommunist, MacRory was well known to German agents in Ireland for harboring "pro-Axis sympathies."[17]

On the very evening of the cardinal's statement, a Western Union delivery boy rapped on the door of the cathedral rectory in St. Augustine. A telegram from the Office of War Information (OWI) in Washington, D.C., apprising Hurley of Cardinal MacRory's latest pro-Axis statement was handed to the new bishop. OWI, probably informed of Hurley's propaganda value by Welles, was direct: "We would appreciate statement from you for foreign broadcast counteracting bad effect of prelates words among Catholics pointing out mistaken attitude of Cardinal MacRory and explaining necessity for having American soldiers temporarily in Ulster to protect Eire as well as rest of British Isles from German attack and occupation. Please wire collect."[18]

Hurley readily accepted the task, even though for an American bishop from a minor see to tussle publicly with a foreign cardinal would restart on an international scale the disruptions Amleto Cicognani so ardently wished to tamp down in the United States. It was clear that Hurley was no longer taking orders from the apostolic delegate, Mooney, or any other prelate. He was thoroughly aligned with Sumner Welles and taking instructions from the Department of State. Shortly after receiving the telegram, Hurley composed an editorial for the *Florida Catholic* and sent a copy to OWI for broadcast to Ireland. With the Irish editorial and broadcast, Hurley stepped further into the world of black propaganda.

In his telegraphed response Hurley promised his attention but "questioned the prudence" of OWI's having sent an open telegram with no signature. On October 9 the *Florida Catholic* carried Hurley's rebuttal to MacRory's statement. Acknowledging that the partition of Ireland created a problematic situation in light of democratic principles, Hurley directed his editorial toward "the universal issues involved in our struggle against Nazism." After labeling the cardinal's words a "slur" upon Allied war aims, Hurley claimed "that Ireland's civil and religious liberties stand or fall with the fate of the Allies in this titanic struggle." He hoped that the "Christian chivalry" of the Irish people would lead them to "thank God for the presence of their American friends in Northern Ireland." OWI planned a radio broadcast of Hurley's words to Europe.[19]

Welles read the editorial "with utmost interest" and "felt confident that the editorial had accomplished a great deal of good." He believed that Hurley was precisely the antidote to Cardinal MacRory's anti-Americanism, and he came up with a plan for more propaganda. On October 12 Welles sent a personal letter to Roosevelt suggesting a Hurley junket to Ireland. "I wonder if it might not be in fact advantageous if Bishop Hurley were to go to Ireland ostensibly of course on some business not connected with the government. Will you let me know what your judgment may be?" Roosevelt mulled the proposal over, probably impressed that the former Vatican attaché was such an ardent and effective supporter. The president responded to Welles's query by saying, "Yes, but I think that the Administration should have no hand in Bishop Hurley's going to Ireland. . . . I am sure it would do good if he did go, but it should be in a wholly private capacity." Seemingly, FDR gave Welles approval for the State Department to engage in further black propaganda with Hurley. Welles took FDR's permissive view as a go-ahead for a Hurley trip.[20]

On October 29 Welles held a meeting with Monsignor Michael Ready, the general secretary of the National Catholic Welfare Conference. His aim was to have Ready give NCWC approval to the trip, thereby shielding the Roosevelt administration. Putting Ready under intense pressure, Welles told Ready that he had already submitted correspondence on the matter to the president and that FDR had responded favorably. "The situation in Eire is critical for the United States cause due to tremendous propaganda against this country," he argued to an unconvinced Ready. Ready was probably still brooding from being struck from out of the blue by Hurley's editorial and radio broadcast against Cardinal MacRory. With his MacRory statement by OWI, Hurley had again circumvented both the NCWC and the apostolic delegation, and Ready had had enough. He refused NCWC involvement with Welles's scheme.[21]

"I do not think that Hurley is the man," Ready told Welles, "because he has already identified himself as opposed to Cardinal MacRory's views, and the Irish Bishops and leaders would very likely resent an outsider coming to them to define certain issues of the war." Welles was dumbfounded. Even with presidential backing, Ready refused to budge. "It was a long conversation," Ready recorded.[22]

Within the week, Ready advised Mooney about his protégé's latest plot with Welles. Both prelates were genuinely perplexed by Hurley's constant maneuvering around established episcopal protocols. And given what they saw as the July 6, 1941, fiasco, they could not be totally sure what Hurley might say or do. Hurley's former connection to the Holy See, viewed as a prize for Welles, was "an element further confusing the proposed mission,"—or any other mission for that matter.[23]

Mooney was becoming irritated with Hurley's State Department ploys and decided to look after his own interests. He asked Ready to write to Welles stating his own disapproval of the Irish junket. "Archbishop Mooney . . . pointed out that even in our own country Bishop Hurley's trip to Eire would be exploited by some groups to the detriment of the cause"—a veiled reference to the ferociously anti-British Father Coughlin in Royal Oak, and a potential major headache for Mooney if unleashed again on Bishop Hurley. In a conversation with Welles sometime later, Hurley found out that Ready had advised against the trip. Willing and eager to make the trip, Hurley described Ready's intervention with Welles as "a short-circuiting attempt." He remained unaware that Mooney was also a force behind the intervention.[24]

For the American episcopate, the episode spelled out that Amleto Cicognani might have been right—that Hurley was becoming an unrestrained problem. By now Mooney and Ready had to be wondering who was controlling the actions of the bishop of St. Augustine. Did they have a renegade bishop within the ranks? Hurley's private moves, had they been known to Mooney and Ready, would certainly have shocked the prelates. For example, in 1942, during the fall meeting of the American Catholic bishops at the Catholic University of America, Hurley slipped out secretly to rendezvous at the Wardman Park Hotel with Robert Wilberforce, chief religious propagandist for the British Information Services (BIS), and a liaison with British foreign intelligence—MI6. Future uberphilosopher Isaiah Berlin, then Wilberforce's subordinate for American Jewish affairs at BIS, indicated that the British desired to harness the power of the American Catholic political bloc, "because American Catholics were better organized" than any other religious body in the United States. For Hurley, the stakes of his Wardman Park meeting were high. The American bishops, many of whom were of Irish ancestry, would have been outraged had they known that one of their own was meeting with a British agent.[25]

Whatever the bishops might do to try to restrain Hurley, Welles was determined to keep him on his side as the one bishop with whom he could work seamlessly and utilize for State Department black propaganda efforts. As the bishops pushed him aside, Welles knew that Hurley was paying a real price for his alliance with the State Department. By the summer of 1942 Welles, Taylor, and FDR found it appropriate to reward Hurley for his extraordinary allegiance to FDR's global strategy.

SAVING ST. AUGUSTINE

"The City of St. Augustine is faced with a grave economic situation as a result of the war," Hurley wrote on June 3, 1942, to Sumner Welles. "I am informed by members of the local Chamber of Commerce that virtually every independent business in town is headed for collapse unless immediate relief is forthcoming." After the bombing of Pearl Harbor, the citizens of St. Augustine were faced with ominous choices. Tourism was the life source of the town. When the government announced a nationwide program of gasoline and rubber rationing, it might as well have announced the descent of the plague upon northern Florida. During the summer of 1942 the cavernous luxury hotels built by railroad magnate Henry Flagler in the 1800s were sitting vacant, restaurants went dormant, beaches were empty, and small business owners feared the worst.

The only hope was to turn St. Augustine into a Navy town. The Chamber of Commerce sent urgent letters to Senator Claude Pepper and Representative Joe Hendricks. All that came back from Capitol Hill were empty promises and more delay. As economic doldrums began to affect the seaside city, a fierce bidding war emerged between St. Augustine and the city of Daytona over the construction of a proposed naval training school. When the U.S. Navy bypassed St. Augustine in favor of Daytona—citing the availability of airfield space and the proximity of Riddle Aeronautical Academy—the businessmen in St. Augustine felt despair.

When Hurley got word of the situation through cathedral parishioner X. L. Pellicer, a Chamber of Commerce member, he indicated that he would write to his friend Sumner Welles with the hope of getting the U.S. military into St. Augustine. The Chamber of Commerce was unsure just what this new Catholic bishop could do or what he had up his sleeve. Hurley's reputation since arriving in town was that of an aloof, distant "man of the church." His bearing was formal, and his interaction with the local establishment infrequent. Most St. Augustinians knew he had worked for two popes, but how these credentials could translate into a bargain with the U.S. military was anybody's guess. Hurley's friendship with Welles, whom Yale historian Gaddis Smith has ranked "among the half-dozen most influential American career diplomats of the twentieth century," was unknown to the people of St. Augustine. With nowhere else to turn, the city fathers decided to cast their lot with the new bishop.[26]

Hurley's letter to Sumner Welles about the economic plight of St. Augustine was masterly in its power of persuasion. It was a private request for extraordinary federal assistance, a philosophical treatise, an action report, and a business proposal all in one. After spelling out the dire situation and listing the advantages to the government if it were come to St. Augustine, Hurley gently notified Welles that he was even willing to go over the under secretary's head. "It is felt that the President himself, if he knew both of our plight and our possibilities, would be interested in helping us to a solution which would be advantageous to the nation as well as the city."

Welles understood the picture immediately. His action on behalf of Bishop Hurley, in political terms, was instantaneous and overwhelming. He underlined the three pivotal questions that Hurley proposed and aimed to discuss them with him in private. First, Welles needed to explore the feasibility of establishing a school for Army or Navy officers or enlisted men in the hotels of St. Augustine. Second, Hurley asked Welles to survey the possibility of using the port of St. Augustine for Navy or Coast Guard purposes. Third, Hurley suggested the feasibility of expansion and use of the municipal airfield by the U.S. Army Air Corps. Finally, he notified Welles that he would travel to Washington with a small delegation from St. Augustine and meet with him in three days to discuss the military possibilities, which he described as "the salvation of the City's economy as long as the war lasts."[27]

Welles's reception of Hurley was extraordinary—and signifies just how highly he valued Hurley's clandestine work for the State Department. He contacted Orme Wilson, the State Department's liaison to the Army and Navy, and ordered him to set up interviews for Bishop Hurley with all the top logistical brass in Washington. Within two days, Wilson arranged for Hurley to meet with the five top military base decision-makers. John Dillin, a young member of the St. Augustine Chamber of Commerce who was delegated to be Hurley's secretary for the trip, sat captivated by the clout the puzzling new prelate was wielding in the nation's capital. "Bishop Hurley and I had a dandy little meeting here yesterday," he wrote back to St. Augustine in gee-whiz style. "He has made a wonderful set of interviews

—really, the sort of men who can say 'yes' or 'no.' We are going to try to make more calls than I think is humanly possible." An exhausted Dillin wrote to X. L. Pellicer that Bishop Hurley was "a wonderful sport."[28]

Of all the meetings, it was the interview with Rear Admiral Lloyd T. Chalker, the vice commandant of the Coast Guard, that paid off the most. "After considerable discussion," Dillin recorded, "the thought came to Admiral Chalker of the possible establishment of a Coast Guard Training School at St. Augustine. And in this program, I believe that we have hit on the most feasible project of all." Dillin sat spellbound as Hurley, dressed in black, pleaded the case for St. Augustine to the full-dress Coast Guard admiral. The Chalker interview launched the Coast Guard at full steam toward St. Augustine. By August 1942 William R. Kenan, president of the Florida East Coast Hotel Company, leased the palatial Ponce de León Hotel to the Coast Guard for 18,000 dollars. The old hotel would become a premier Coast Guard training academy in Florida. Weeks later the Coast Guard leased the Bennett and Monson Hotels for its Women's Reserve Units, known as SPARS. By September tens of thousands of Coast Guardsmen and women were headed to St. Augustine.

Hurley thanked Welles and Wilson profusely; "if we succeed in our efforts to find a means of municipal livelihood during the war, it will in large part be due to the consideration you have shown us." Upon his return home, the reports of the trip to Washington were sealed in a special "personal and confidential defense projects" file in Hurley's archive. Hurley preferred that his name be kept out of any public discussion, and consequently the story of his role in "saving St. Augustine" has never been told. He made clear that his connections to the government and the defense establishment were to receive no publicity. John Dillin, still wide-eyed, concluded his final report to the Chamber of Commerce with "One more thing . . . If I ever have anyone to work with up here again, I certainly hope it is with Bishop Hurley. He did the finest job that possibly could be done for St. Augustine, in a way that no one else could do it."[29]

Hurley's secret petition for St. Augustine paid enormous dividends for his tiny adopted hometown. Soon, however, the administration would require service from Hurley over the emerging issue of the European Jewish persecutions. At the State Department, this issue was treated just as much as an issue of religion as a matter of state. Hurley's contacts at the State Department now wanted another of his famous "forthright statements"—this time on the particular issue of the Nazi concentration camps.

"ORGIES OF EXTERMINATION"

Since his seminary days, Hurley had exhibited a peculiar and sometimes obsessive opinion about Jews and things Jewish. The Jesuits at St. Ignatius College encouraged young Catholics to admire the accomplishments of individual Jews, while perceiving Jewish social advancement as a threat to Catholic status. Hurley excluded Father Coughlin's antisemitic rantings from his moral compass, while condemning his lack of patriotism and objections to FDR's foreign policy goals. During his time at the Vatican, Hurley worried about the antisemitic paramilitarism of the Christian Front plotters not so much because they aimed to assassinate Jews, but because they cast American Catholics as potential seditionists.

After his posting to St. Augustine in 1940, the young bishop seems to have undergone a shift that took him from cultural antisemitism, to religious sympathy, to a moral and graphic defense of Jews. This shift marks an extraordinary change for someone who had been so close to institutional antisemitism. The breakthrough could have been brought about only by an internal moral reassessment of religious priorities coupled with suggestions from U.S. diplomats that the emerging Jewish persecutions in Europe were becoming another "Catholic problem" for American foreign policy. Hurley's swing to philosemitism involved both religious sensibility and American Catholic patriotism.

Hurley first addressed the European Jewish persecutions in a subdued way in his Gainesville speech of April 1941. His Americanism prompted him to discuss Catholic antisemitism in relation to the Christian Front sedition case. He described Front activities as "that vulgar, hate-inspired, campaign against our Jewish fellow citizens which eventuated in attempts at racial discrimination and mob violence." On June 17, when presenting the situation of German concentration camps in Poland in his speech at St. Leo's Abbey, Hurley referred to the "tens of thousands of other [besides Catholic] political leaders herded off to the living death of Oranienberg, Dachau, and other concentration camps." Interestingly, historian Owen Chadwick has commented that it was not until October 1941, four months after Hurley's speech, that Vatican officials became aware of the horrors that Jews faced in the eastward deportations.[30]

Hurley's next, and his most important, statement on the terror faced by European Jews came in the wake of Pope Pius XII's Christmas Message of 1942. Contemporary analysis of the Christmas Message has been the subject of heated debate among historians and biographers of the pontiff. Its section dealing with the death camps has been described by some papal detractors as "obfuscatory, mentioning neither Jews nor Nazis," and by defenders of Pope Pius XII as carrying with it a "clear denunciation of Nazi ideology." For historian Daniel Jonah Goldhagen, the diplomatic tone of the Christmas Message fell tragically short of a clear condemnation of such systematic moral evil.[31]

The section of Pius XII's Christmas Message dealing with the death camps was relegated to one sentence in the forty-eighth paragraph of the fifty-two-paragraph document. The relevant clause was a statement urging civil social order and international tranquility. "Mankind owes that vow to the hundreds of thousands of persons who, without any fault on their part, sometimes only because of their nationality or race, have been consigned to death or to a slow decline." At the time, both British and U.S. representatives were disappointed by what they considered to be a murky papal one-liner.

British ambassador to the Vatican D'Arcy Osborne commented that the pope had produced a fine encyclical on "special social problems," but otherwise found it useless. More puzzling was the attitude of the French Vichy representative to the Vatican, Léon Bérard, whose function was to justify Vichy antisemitic legislation to the pope. According to historian Owen Chadwick, Bérard, who probably expected an outright condemnation of the Nazi methods, "asked the Pope directly why he had not used the word Nazi in his condemnation." To this question "the Pope replied that if he had mentioned the Nazis by name, he would have had to mention the Communists by name." If the report is true, it shows a surprising level of semantic dexterity on the part of Pius XII. While it is true the pope did not condemn "Communists by name," he did condemn "Marxist Socialism" at length and most vigorously in the Christmas Message. "The Church has condemned the various forms of Marxist Socialism," Pius echoed, "and she condemns them today, because it is her permanent right and duty to safeguard men from currents of thought and influences that jeopardize their eternal salvation."[32]

In late 1942, reactions to the pope's Christmas Message ranged from forceful Axis condemnation to Allied diplomatic frustration. The *New York Times*, presumably after obtaining a primer in papal diplomatic speech from a Vatican source, famously called Pius "a lonely voice in the silence and darkness enveloping Europe this Christmas." "But most listeners seem not to have even noticed the passage in question," Harvard theologian Kevin Madigan has pointed out, "much less to have regarded it as a denunciation of Nazi atrocity."[33]

"The message does not satisfy those circles which have hoped that the Pope would this time call a spade a spade," Hurley's friend Harold Tittman wired Washington, "and discard his usual practice of speaking in generalities." Even though Tittman had been pushing for Pius to name spades since earlier that summer, he added that the message was being described in Vatican circles as "candid and forceful." Later, when Tittman personally told Pius XII that he did not think the statement was clear, Pius registered "surprise."[34]

Historian Michael Phayer, who has skillfully compiled the responses of the Holy See to the inflow of intelligence on the Holocaust, argues that through the end of 1943, the Holy See was reluctant to speak out on the death camps. Cardinal Maglione privately explained that Allied information on the camps could not be verified. Historian José Sánchez has affirmed that Pius "probably knew about the massacres by the end of 1942 . . . and he continued with oblique references in his statements in 1943." The problem was the verification of data.[35]

Papal incredulity and near-cryptic Vatican references to the death-camp issue during 1942 and 1943 lend historical magnitude to an unexamined *Florida Catholic* editorial drafted by Hurley on March 13, 1943, and published on April 9, titled "Let Christians Take the Lead!" Contrary to the tussle within Vatican circles, Hurley's editorial stated that mass extermination of Jews was a concrete fact. In addition, he made it obligatory for Catholics specifically to denounce Jewish extermination as a religious matter of conscience. With graphic description, Hurley called the exterminations—a phenomenon of which few American Catholics were aware— a profound religious issue on which Catholics needed to "take the lead."

The editorial is also significant because it applied what Daniel Goldhagen has called "exterminationist" language specifically to the Jews. Previously, all Catholic statements regarding the plight of Jews used the descriptor "persecutions"—a word that could have been applied to both

Jews and Catholics during the 1920s and 1930s. By employing language such as "slaughter" and "orgies of extermination," Hurley's editorial was forging a new path of description for American Catholics. He had entered Nazi exterminationism of Jews into the Catholic framework. For Hurley, the exterminations were a profound moral evil—and a profoundly Catholic crisis.[36]

Theologically, Hurley fashioned a moral thunderbolt aimed at jolting Catholics from complacency. He argued that "all Christians, Catholic and Protestant alike," were under moral obligation to speak out against the "orgies of extermination" sweeping the occupied lands. With his editorial, Hurley made the camps of extermination—previously a "Jewish issue" —an integral Roman Catholic issue of the greatest moral weight. Using exterminationist language, he described the camps as a "criminal effort to eradicate the Jews."[37]

"For Catholics," the editorial began, "the very basis of our faith is challenged by the orgies of extermination that are going on among the Jews in Europe." In language ripe to fulfill Daniel Goldhagen's call for a moral reckoning, Hurley continued that "Christians would fail in their most fundamental duty if they were to leave this challenge unanswered, if they left it to Jews alone to seek the ways and means to stop the slaughter of their kith and kin." He then moved to the moral question and engaged in a manner of theological thinking that was far-distanced from the wrangling he experienced in St. Peter's Square. "Not the Jews, but the Christians should take the lead in opposing in every way possible the barbarism that rages unchecked in those countries where the hooked cross, symbol of persecution, murder, and torture, still flies."

The editorial was framed in the context of leadership. The implication was that if Catholic silence continued on the issue of the exterminations, Protestants were likely to achieve a moral high ground over Catholics. For Hurley, this was another indirect poke at what he perceived as Pius XII's abdication of leadership. "All Christians, and especially those who have the fullness of the Christian Faith," should "deem it an honor to take up the defense of the Jews."

Over a year later Hurley would write an equally striking editorial, titled "Anti-Semitism: Our Problem." In it he reiterated the moral argument and made a further appeal for leadership among Catholics. Commenting on the continued and rapid growth of antisemitism, he argued: "what is more disturbing is the growth of indifference, almost approaching acquiescence, on the part of those who should be in the front lines combating it." The Roman Catholic church needed to assume the lead over the Protestant churches, beat back indifference, and head to the "front lines" of the battle against Jewish extermination and antisemitism. But who should lead the forces in battle?[38]

"The Papacy," according to the March 1943 draft editorial, had assisted Jews "in the past," and that tradition required the papacy to do so again. This may have been Hurley's way of juxtaposing what he considered to be Pius XI's vocal support of Jews before the war with Pius XII's near silence on the same issue. Hurley's 1943 editorial acknowledged that Protestants had so far been at the forefront of condemning the persecutions—but now it was time for Catholics to "take the lead." Hurley "expected" the papacy to take on this mission, an indication that he did not think enough was yet being done. Since "the papacy and the body of the Faithful have interposed themselves in the past against the Jews and their persecutors," it was "therefore in accordance with the tradition of the Church . . . in the present sad juncture [to] expect them to take measures for the protection of Jews." Hurley's rejection of antisemitism was a remarkable philosophical shift. Faced with the effects of arguably the greatest moral evil of the twentieth century, he shed his 1930s perspective and was compelled to change his thinking on the Jews. In early 1943 his words offered an isolated, conscience-driven, authentically Christian and public response to what would come to be known as the Holocaust.[39]

More importantly, since in 1943 the systematic murder of European Jewry had not yet been morally categorized by Catholic theologians, Hurley's words ring prophetic. As historian Peter Novick has pointed out, "the murderous actions of the Nazi regime, which killed between five and six million Jews, were too real, but 'the Holocaust' as we speak of it today was largely a retrospective construction, something that would not have been recognizable to people at the time." But Hurley's language makes clear that he understood the evil nature of arguably the vilest aspect of the Final Solution—the death camp. As he embarked on an effort to swing the Roman Catholic church to a defense of the Jews, he was doing something completely new. American newspapers published very little about the Holocaust during the war, mainly because reports were either hard to verify or hard for ordinary Americans to believe. In light of these complications, the "orgies of extermination" language and the appearance of Hurley's moral imperative raise further questions about the sources and timing of the editorial.[40]

Michael Phayer has noticed that precisely during the spring of 1943, the Holy See was receiving multiple reports of genocide at the camps, but points out Pius's "failure to exercise leadership regarding genocide." Pius "never spoke out himself in any significant manner on behalf of the Jews nor circulated the courageous statements of bishops who did speak out among the church hierarchy"—including Hurley's. What, then, triggered Hurley's graphic and early "moral beckoning"? How could Hurley speak with such moral certainty about Jewish exterminations in Florida when even the Vatican was struggling to figure out the situation in Europe?[41]

It is difficult to trace the origin of Hurley's editorial, but there are two possible sources. First, material for the editorial may have come from a frustrated Harold Tittman in Rome, through confidential State Department channels. After getting nowhere with Pius XII regarding the clarity of his Christmas Message, he may have been looking for other ways to get State Department information on the camps out. Hurley was the obvious candidate. As in previous cases, Taylor or Tittman could have simply handed top-secret information to Hurley for his use, with the understanding that Hurley would return the documents after fashioning his statements. As before, they trusted that Hurley would not leak their information. Second, the editorial could have been commissioned by Hurley's consecrator, Cardinal Maglione, who was under increasing pressure from the U.S., French, and British governments for a Vatican statement of deeper moral clarity on the Jewish concentration camps.[42]

Although there is no documentary proof that either the Holy See or the United States was involved, the possibility that a nudge came from the Holy See's secretary of state seems remote. On March 16, 1943, three days *after* Hurley composed his editorial for publication in the *Florida Catholic*, Cardinal Maglione wrote to the bishop of Fribourg to obtain information on deported Jews, "concerning whom there are no positive data." Furthermore, if the Holy See had been behind the Hurley editorial, it could have adequately publicized the clarion call through the offices of the apostolic delegate in conjunction with the NCWC News Service.[43]

The second scenario, of U.S. government prompting and intelligence-sharing, seems much more likely. At the time, Hurley maintained close contact with Myron Taylor and frequently traveled to Taylor's winter home on Ocean Drive in Palm Beach, Florida. Taylor was in touch with Harold Tittman at the Vatican via secure State Department cable. Historian Susan Zuccotti has shown that both Tittman and Taylor, using various firsthand reports, were working feverishly in the late fall of 1942 to have Pius move forward on a statement condemning the Jewish executions. Quoting German sources, an Associated Press report from September 1942 indicated that in his final audience with Pius after handing him the "Bishops' Draft," Taylor asked the pope to publicly support a U.S. condemnation of the persecution of Jews in Vichy France.[44]

If, as before, Hurley was used as a tool by American diplomats, what, then, about publicity? How to explain the fact that Hurley's moral protest stayed put in the Sunshine State and was not carried in the national press, unlike so many of his previous statements? One factor could be that Myron Taylor was much less adept at working media and press contacts than Sumner Welles, who seems not to have been consulted on the death-camp editorial. At the time, Welles was embroiled in a homosexual scandal and experiencing a rift with Secretary of State Hull. That scandal would result in Welles's release from government service in the summer of 1943. In the end, the editorial may have been a last resort by Taylor and Harold Tittman to get their information on the exterminations to a Catholic source who mattered. Unfortunately for Tittman and Taylor, the publicity nexus of earlier days was breaking down. Sadly, what ranks as the first and perhaps only moral reckoning of the Nazi death camps by an American Catholic bishop was relegated to the pages of a small Catholic newspaper outside any orbit of real influence.

HURLEY *USQUE JUSTIFICATUS:* AMERICAN CATHOLICISM AT WAR'S END

The events of 1945 seemed to offer further justification for Hurley's forceful denunciation of Nazi barbarism. The opening of the concentration camps throughout Europe revealed the full systematic horror of the Nazi death machine. During the war, Hurley refused to let his posting to St. Augustine stand in the way of his continued diplomatic activity, even though his years in St. Augustine blurred the lines of diplomatic loyalty. Had Mooney and Ready not got wind of Hurley's moves, there is every reason to believe that he could have gone ahead with trips to both Latin

America and Ireland with the specific approval of either the pope or the American bishops. Even faced with these setbacks, Hurley continued actions of black propaganda throughout the war years. As Pope Pius XII shifted Vatican policy away from the policy of Pope Pius XI, Hurley became more strongly convinced that "the Church was wrong and the state was right." At the center of so much controversy from 1938 to 1941, by 1945 Hurley could stand above strife and take his place as a soothsayer of right thinking.

As Hurley stood vindicated, the Vatican reassessed its wartime philosophy. If it had been somewhat suspicious of American democracy and religious liberty before World War II, the experience of the war had taught the bitter lesson that the democracies at least allowed the Catholic church to survive and even prosper. In the aftermath of war, two powers were left standing—the United States and Soviet Russia. Pius XII and others at the Vatican had no difficulty determining where their interests lay. Putting aside their ideological ambivalence about the United States, an important shift in Vatican attitudes took place; the argument that Hurley had crafted in the "Bishops' Draft" had been validated. Now the Vatican looked to the United States as the sole protector of Christian civilization.

The only problem for the Vatican was that America's wartime ally, the Soviet Union, also reigned supreme. The Soviet victory foreshadowed communist domination of a predominantly Catholic eastern Europe. To Pope Pius XII, the specter of atheistic communism spreading throughout Europe now appeared more real than ever. The Vatican adapted its international policy to this new world situation.

Harold Tittman concluded that the pope suddenly became pro-American and looked to America as a defense against the communist behemoth. Filippo Bernardini, Vatican nuncio to Switzerland, observed that the "Pope was emphatic that the Holy See must 'look to the United States' and that many more non-Italian prelates should be brought to the Holy See in important positions." To combat communism, Pius XII scoured the diplomatic rolls for American clerics who could work hand in hand with U.S. officials.[45]

CHAPTER EIGHT

A Parallel Endeavor against Communism

THE UNITED STATES AND THE VATICAN IN
TITO'S YUGOSLAVIA

"IN 1945," former Office of Strategic Services officer Martin S. Quigley has written, "Yugoslavia was a country of particular concern for the Pope, [Under Secretary of State for Ordinary Affairs Giovanni Battista] Montini, and [Under Secretary of State for Extraordinary Ecclesiastical Affairs Domenico] Tardini. Officials at the Vatican were sure that true peace would not come to areas of Europe taken over by the communists, if there were efforts to enforce Russia's domestic policy against religion." On the ground in Yugoslavia, Catholics also operated under a cloud of fear, and some expected reprisals for Nazi collaboration if a communist system were imposed. Franklin Lindsay, a member of the Office of Strategic Services (OSS) who headed the U.S. Military Mission to Yugoslavia, reported during the summer of 1945 that "Slovene clerics were beginning to organize an underground in Croatia and Slovenia." This was the beginning of the controversial Krizari paramilitary movement among Catholic clergy, an aggressive response to Marshal Tito's "desire to minimize if not abolish the jurisdiction of the Vatican over the Catholic Church in Croatia and Slovenia."[1]

In Rome, Pope Pius XII knew that he needed to move world opinion against communist gains in eastern Europe. According to one Vatican diplomatic source, "the United States was in the driver's seat" after World War II, and the pontiff began to scour his ranks for American clerics to bring into the diplomatic corps of the Holy See. In a move that would have been inconceivable as few as four years earlier, the same church diplomats who had agreed to submarine Hurley's diplomatic career after his 1941 CBS speech cast their eyes to unsung St. Augustine and pulled Bishop Joseph Patrick Hurley back into the formal ranks of Vatican diplomacy.

In January 1945, four months before Hitler's demise, Hurley was summoned to the Vatican by Pope Pius XII and informed of his impending appointment as regent *ad interim,* or acting chief, of the apostolic nunciature in Belgrade, Yugoslavia. He was surprised by the nomination. He had been away from diplomacy for five years, had little "official" Vatican training in diplomacy, and none at all in Balkan affairs. The area's culture, politics, history, and religious diversity was terra incognita to the bishop of St. Augustine, Florida. The Vatican, however, was not looking for cultural sensitivity. In appointing Hurley to Yugoslavia, the Holy See sought someone who could work smoothly with the Americans in the overall struggle against communism.

To this end, the Vatican vested Hurley with the full diplomatic authority of a nuncio. Thus, Hurley became the first non-Italian to be raised to the rank of nuncio in the history of papal diplomacy. Yet, Pius XII shrewdly utilized the office of regent. While official Vatican sources are silent on the precise executive powers possessed by a regent, there is some evidence to suggest that Pius may have been viewing regency in the same terms as its formal secular diplomatic counterpart. In such a case, regency would be granted by the pope under his official title as sovereign of the State of Vatican City. Since the Holy See and the Vatican City are separate entities, Hurley would be directly connected to the pope as supreme spiritual head of the Catholic Church, yet also technically detached from the administrative apparatus of the Holy See.

In secular diplomacy, a regent acts in the name of—and may invoke identical power as—the sovereign or head of state. The rank of regent is little known and infrequently used in papal diplomacy. However, as a consummate diplomat, Pius XII could have been arming Hurley with such powers for emergency use. If this was what Pius was doing, Hurley would have the power to negotiate treaties with the Yugoslav state, make appointments, and even settle jurisdictional disputes. These were powers Pius XII prudently believed might be needed if communications were cut off or dangerous conditions prevailed. And Hurley did employ many of these tactics during the time of his regency.[2]

Hurley's appointment as regent was also useful for Yugoslavia's new communist dictator, Marshal Josip Broz Tito. Since Hurley was not a papal nuncio, his diplomatic position would not conflict with Tito's drive for an atheistic state system. Finally, and perhaps most ironically for Pope Pius XII, historian Peter Kent has shown that it was precisely Hurley's public wartime antinazism that made him an acceptable choice for Marshal Tito.[3]

Hurley's appointment was publicly announced on October 22, 1945, just one month after the American embassy in Belgrade began operation. The Vatican newspaper, *Osservatore Romano*, explained that Hurley's mission would be chiefly concerned with gathering information on the Yugoslavian episcopate. "This appointment makes it possible for the Holy See . . . to reestablish normal contacts with the Episcopate of that country after a period of almost complete interruption caused by war conditions." Almost in passing, the announcement mentioned Hurley's mission to Marshal Tito's newly formed Federative People's Republic of Yugoslavia. No mention was made that it was Tito himself who had taken the initiative and requested Vatican representation in Belgrade—a fairly strong signal of the new dictator's willingness to search for common ground.[4]

Suspicion, rather than cooperation, drove U.S. interests. Not surprisingly, as soon as Hurley's assignment became public, U.S. government agencies expressed an "official interest" in his new assignment. In the fall of 1945 Hurley was encouraged to attend a set of meetings in Washington with War Department officials to "bring him up to date on the political, social and economic conditions of Yugoslavia." There is no record that Hurley informed the Vatican or any American bishops about these meetings. U.S. intelligence officials considered themselves fortunate in having an American asset ready-made to head behind the Iron Curtain. Major Daniel J. Ryan of the Army Intelligence Corps and Brigadier General Louis Fortier, a former military attaché in Belgrade, met with Hurley for a series of intelligence briefings in early November 1945. These contacts are remarkable since there is currently no published account or record of a Vatican diplomat ever meeting with U.S. government intelligence officers prior to posting. Ryan and Fortier also were certainly developing Hurley to act as an intelligence agent for the United States. Hurley readily accepted this role. To his mind, it was a continuation of the noble work he had done with William Phillips and Sumner Welles during World War II.[5]

Harold Tittman, Myron Taylor's assistant in Rome, also contemplated Hurley's departure for Belgrade. While the mission was "naturally considered a difficult one," Tittman wrote of his friend, he was rather skeptical about the appointment, noticing Hurley's deficiencies in preparation. The job "would seem to require much tact and a realistic understanding, not only of the political regime of Yugoslavia," he wrote to the State Department, "but also of the problems confronting both the United States and Western European nations in that country." Among the problems confronting Western policy in Yugoslavia 1945 were long-standing religious and national struggles. These were vast issues that Hurley was only just beginning to comprehend.[6]

When Hurley began his trip to Belgrade in late December 1945, he entered a region of the world that had been the scene of religious conflict and violent fragmentation for over a millennium, dating back to the Roman empire. Jozo Tomasevich, the preeminent historian of wartime Yugoslavia, employs the language of complexity and entanglement to describe the wartime situation. In his magisterial work, *War and Revolution in Yugoslavia, 1941–1945,* Tomasevich describes the area assigned to Hurley as multiconfessional, multinational, and rife with "competing religious traditions." "The bloody confrontations among the various nations, national minorities, and religious groups in Yugoslavia during the war," Tomasevich points out, "often had their roots in antagonisms that reached deep into the past." Unaware of the complexities that he would face, Hurley believed that his posting would involve dealing only with the immediate political legacy of World War II.[7]

On April 6, 1941, German bombs had rained down on Belgrade. The Axis powers took control of the region on April 17, 1941, and created the Independent State of Croatia (Nezavisna Drazava Hrvatska, the NDH) under the puppet governance of Ante Pavelić, the leader of the fascist Ustasha terrorist group. Pavelić has been described as a passionate Croat who was also "passionately anti-Serb, anti-Semitic, and anti-Communist." Many Croatians wanted an independent state, Tomasevich avers, "but the state they obtained was a [Nazi] puppet state, independent in name only."[8]

Given their subservience to the Serbs between the two world wars, many Croatian nationalists were delighted by this development. Croats who yearned for an autonomous Croatian state finally had their hopes fulfilled in the NDH. The Catholic hierarchy, firmly grounded in Croatian nationalism, praised the new leader and his government. The young arch-bishop of Zagreb, Aloysius Stepinac, commented that it was "easy to see the hand of God at work" in the creation of the NDH.[9]

For Ante Pavelić, the hand of God could be pressed into the service of his new state. Niccolò Machievelli's dictum that the true prince must always at least "appear pious" underpinned many decisions of the leader Ante Pavelić. The Ustasha chief always had priest-ministers in his retinue, maintained a chapel in his residence, and acquired personal priest-tutors for his children. To all appearances, he was a devout Catholic. Disturbing for Vatican interests was that Pavelić's NDH was composed of Croatian fascists who carried out some of the most deplorable atrocities of World War II. Within two years of its founding, however, the NDH would have to contend with new strategic realities.

During 1943 an improbable military turn raised grave concerns for Pavelić, Catholics in Croatia, and the Vatican. The communists, under their redoubtable wartime leader Josip Broz Tito, began to score con-siderable victories in the ground war. By 1943 Tito's brigades, under the command of the Partisan Committee of Liberation, commonly known as the Partisans, had garnered the support of the Allies. By early 1945 the communist Tito had ousted the Nazi puppet Pavelić and aimed to reign supreme in Yugoslavia. The Allies offered his new government speedy recognition.

THE METAMORPHOSIS OF AN ANTINAZI

Tito's ascendance as the new communist overlord in Croatia changed Roman perceptions drastically, and the Vatican busily reformulated its policy in the Balkans. Pius XII was certain that the communists would exact harsh reprisals upon the Croatians—all Catholics—who had collabo-rated with the wartime puppet Ustasha regime. "Some Catholic priests," Stella Alexander has pointed out, "identified themselves with the Usta-sha government, collaborating fully with it, while others gave it qualified support." Consequently, when dealing with the democracies, the Vatican began to accentuate the Catholic and Croatian cultural characteristics of former Ustasha members rather than draw attention to their wartime Na-zism. Domenico Tardini spelled out this new emphasis in a conversation with Myron Taylor in May 1945. He argued, naïvely, that the "clergy and prominent Catholics" fleeing the communists were "constantly persecuted only because they refuse to share the communist point of view." In light of the communist threat, the Vatican either forgot or rationalized away any former associations of Croatian Catholics with the Ustasha. For the Vatican, and later for Hurley, the external communist threat subsumed any sober reflection on prior Nazi collaboration. For the Holy See, the shift was to view former members of the former NDH as Croats and more especially as Catholics.[10]

For Hurley, the new circumstances in Yugoslavia produced a bizarre reversal of his vociferous morally based antinazism. The switch was quick and remarkable. Now that Hitler had been defeated, the Nazi was no longer "enemy No. 1 of America and the world." By 1945, communism ascended to the despotic throne abdicated by Nazism and tightly gripped the "dagger held at the throat" of Western Christian civilization. As Hurley settled into his mission in Belgrade, a peculiar swing toward Croatian nationalism became evident.[11]

Much of his new ideology was based in an assessment of Croatian nationalism as a manifestation of ordinary patriotism. Yet Hurley had no idea that Croatian nationalism defined itself against many unique cultural and religious variables. In Hurley's mind, the Croatians were a "historic people," who were "once again . . . gloriously justifying their age-old title as *antemurale Christianitatis*." This metaphor fitted neatly into Hurley's conceptual framework. The notion of the *antemurale Christianitatis* was used to accentuate the civilizational divide between East and West. Described by one scholar as "a myth of historical courage and power," the device portrayed Croatia as the "forward wall of Christendom," as "the easternmost rampart of Christian Europe, and . . . the sole defender of the West against the East." For Hurley, Croatia became the new defensive battleground, previously against Serbs and Islam, now against encroaching communism.[12]

For Hurley, Cardinal Mercier's integration of patriotism into religious expression now assumed priority. Hurley never admitted to Catholic Croatian complicity in the Ustasha reign of terror. His new appropriation of Croatian nationalism made it impossible for him to acknowledge that Croatian Catholics could have perpetrated the wartime atrocities attributed to them. In Hurley's Americanized Catholic worldview, it was inconceivable that Catholics could become the agents of evil. In private, he referred to the Ustasha "bestiality" (the quotation marks are Hurley's) as though atrocities had never been committed.[13]

The most explicit example of Hurley's abrupt philosophical transformation from an avid antinazi to a tolerant Ustasha apologist is found in a personal letter to Howard J. Carroll, Michael Ready's successor as the general secretary of the National Catholic Welfare Conference. "It will be remembered that the discontented elements in that country turned against the Government with disastrous results in 1941," Hurley pointed out to Carroll. This was a reference to Croatian resistance to Serbian hegemony within the interwar Kingdom of Serbs, Croats, and Slovenes. With an exculpation of the Croatian Ustasha, he continued, "it is of no avail to say that they sided with Nazi Germany—they thought that they were turning against an oppressive government, and they knew then, as we know now, that they were also fighting Communism. Communism was as great a threat to them then as it is to us now. In the period between 1941 and 1945, the Croatian people were defending their country, their existence and their freedom in the face of the assault of the Red Beasts, the barbarians of the twentieth century."[14]

For Hurley, Croatian anticommunism became the hallmark of Croatian Catholicism. Catholic theological anticommunism melded with the current siege concepts of Croatian nationalism to create an inflexible, authoritarian, and unswerving religious hybrid. The inflexibility of this new theological equation made perfect sense to Hurley. It was intellectually simple, putting aside cultural, ethnic, historic, and ecumenical factors. Since his diplomacy had been anchored in diplomatic firmness since the Mylapore Agreement, he was ready to commit to the hard-line Croatian Catholic view. Over time, Hurley would absolve the wartime Croatian Catholic hierarchy and enter into common cause with the Croatian bishops against Marshal Tito, a dictator he would soon meet face to face.[15]

On January 21, 1946, Hurley arrived at the nunciature in Belgrade and prepared to present his diplomatic credentials to Marshal Josip Broz Tito. As he had expected, the interview was far from cordial. Tito delayed him for a full hour. He sat nervously in the lobby of government headquarters. "Tiger —Tito's fierce police dog, was my companion," he later recalled. "I sat and said the Rosary—the joyful mysteries. And smiled. And calmed down." From the start, the two men both disturbed and distrusted each other.[16]

To Hurley, Tito was the evil commander of the Yugoslav Red Horde. According to his religious philosophy, Tito, a Croatian whose mother once wished him to become a priest, could never, as a baptized Roman Catholic, perpetrate such a vicious persecution upon his coreligionists. In Hurley's mind, Tito was the personification of evil and had no claim to Catholicity. According to reports, his Partisans had already executed innumerable priests by firing squad. Privately, Hurley aligned Tito with all the worst of his early prejudices: "Who is Tito?" he asked himself, "A Ukrainian Jew?"[17]

PRO PATRIA, PRO DEO: THE U.S.-VATICAN NEXUS IN YUGOSLAVIA, 1946

Shortly before he was sent to Yugoslavia, Hurley was advised by Montini at the Vatican to "cooperate to the utmost of his ability with the Allied diplomatic representatives at Belgrade." "Cooperation to the utmost" was aimed at gaining some scores in the area of diplomacy. Amid the restrictions of a regime inimical to both the United States and the Vatican, such cooperation did not rule out low-level anticommunist espionage. Myron Taylor accurately described the sort of cooperation that Washington could expect from Hurley. While Hurley was in Yugoslavia "ostensibly only [for] religious matters," he could also "be counted on to carefully observe Tito-Stalin political relations." Taylor was certain that Hurley would, as he had done for Welles, work secretly to promote the U.S. position.[18]

Hurley's mission to Belgrade was only a part of the complex Vatican strategy to enlist the United States in a common alliance against communism. "Outside official circles," diplomatic historian John Lewis Gaddis has written, "the hierarchy of the Catholic Church constituted the most vocal center of skepticism regarding Soviet ideological intentions." In the postwar world, the Vatican believed it was entering into another "parallel endeavor" with America, this time to thwart the spread of communism. "In fact," one State Department official remarked after a conversation with Archbishop Cicognani, "he all but stated that we [the United States] were the Church's greatest ally and greatest hope against communism."[19]

In Belgrade the strategizing between Hurley and U.S. officials was intended to be covert. While attending official diplomatic functions, parties, and receptions, Hurley's policy was not even to speak to those U.S. embassy officials present lest Tito suspect him of "working for the

Americans." But he met with those officials secretly, supplying them with reports, maps, data, and information on both Catholic and Yugoslav activities. His information was gleaned from conversations conducted with Catholic bishops and priests who reported on local political events and Catholic trends. Hurley was a ready-made fit for such endeavors, since he needed no special language training. In the early days of his posting he conducted conversations with Croatian and Slovene clerics in Latin, the Roman Catholic clerical lingua franca, and quickly prepared reports for the Americans. Such espionage activities were all part of the high-stakes game against communism.[20]

Hurley was convinced that Tito's secret police were spying on the nunciature from the day he moved in. "Every light bulb that needs changing receives the attention of the Yugoslav Foreign Office," he once joked to a colleague. In view of the fact that two U.S. embassy workers were jailed on espionage charges in early 1946, his continued resolve to work with the American embassy was daring if not heroic. Moreover, signaling that any espionage activity was now a game of life and death, three Yugoslav nationals found guilty of passing military secrets to the United States were condemned and executed by firing squad in early 1947.[21]

But was the intelligence Hurley was funneling to the Americans useful? British historian Ann Lane has concluded that because of the obstacles involved, *any* information culled from "discussions with individuals opposed to the existing regime" was precious. Hurley, who was passing along information gathered from Croatian and Slovene bishops opposed to Tito, was clearly a prime source of intelligence for the American embassy—and for the president of the United States. "Bishop Hurley of Florida . . . with whom I have collaborated in effective ways," Myron Taylor reported to President Truman, "is reporting that the conditions in Yugoslavia are, to use the Pope's own word, 'terrible.'" Taylor promised Truman "a full report" on the Yugoslav situation, adding that he was being aided "to the fullest extent" by Hurley. "This of course," he assured the president, "is done in a most secret and confidential way."[22]

While Hurley and the Vatican were supplying Washington with genuine intelligence, the Americans were supplying Hurley's nunciature with crucial assistance. For example, early in the relationship an arrangement was made whereby the Vatican's official correspondence would be sent to Rome via the American diplomatic pouch. This agreement was particularly beneficial to the Vatican, since it was thought that the chances of the Yugoslav authorities violating the American pouch were virtually non-existent. The arrangement was also remarkable in that the United States was allowing a foreign state to transmit its secrets through American diplomatic channels. This cozy relationship only reinforced Pius's perception that the two states were partners in the battle against world communism. In operation, the relationship was fostered by President Truman's new ambassador to Yugoslavia, Richard C. Patterson.[23]

Patterson was a Roosevelt appointee, Ivy League educated, and the wartime chairman of RKO Pictures. Hurley admired his World War I service record, for he had served under Hurley's childhood military hero, General John J. Pershing. On the personal side, the ambassador and the Vatican regent were exactly the same height and size (5 feet 7½ inches) and shared a passion for golf. Both could be blunt, and both were convinced that Tito was an unscrupulous dictator who had to be dealt with firmly. Indeed, as early as November 1945 Patterson was convinced that a hard line was necessary in combating the "hostile attitude of this regime toward America."[24]

In the early days of his posting, Patterson even may have allowed Hurley to engage in a little psychological warfare. When the Office of War Information decided to act on a Yugoslav Foreign Office invitation to sponsor free public showings of "some first-class American films in Belgrade," the embassy surprised communist officials by first screening the 1943 film *The Song of Bernadette*. Although the movie had won five Academy Awards, the story of a peasant girl's spiritual relationship with an apparition of the Virgin Mary was deemed by the OSS "not to be precisely the best choice for a city in the throes of political struggle in which the religious issue plays a prominent part."[25]

The cooperative personal relationship emerging between Hurley and Patterson was described in one of the embassy's first reports. "He is believed to have a high standing among high churchmen in the Vatican," Patterson relayed to Secretary of State James F. Byrnes about Hurley, "to be a personal friend of Cardinal Spellman of New York, and is a close personal advisor of His Holiness, the Pope. He is a very friendly man, easy to get along with, speaks fluent French and Italian, as well as some German, and has a quick Irish temper." Though overestimating Hurley's advisory role to Pius XII and his link to Cardinal Spellman, the embassy staff correctly perceived that Hurley was an estimable Vatican insider. This assessment was fortunate, for soon Hurley would need to use his prestige at the U.S. embassy to affect Yugoslav policy toward the Holy See.[26]

Within a month of the presentation of his credentials to Marshal Tito, the Vatican was forced to deal with its first crisis. On February 13, 1946, Hurley's office received word that four nuns, members of the Sisters of Charity, had been condemned to death by a state tribunal in Gospić, Croatia. Hurley knew that the accusations were grave and foreboding. The sisters were charged with complicity in the murder of wounded Partisan soldiers who were being cared for at their hospital in Otačac in September 1942. According to reports, a raiding party of Nazi-backed Ustasha soldiers had broken into the hospital at night and killed about twenty Partisans. At their trial, one of the Partisan soldiers offered to testify that the sisters had had nothing to do with the raid, but he later recanted under pressure. In the end, the tribunal ordered the death sentences to be carried out within ten days.

Bishop Hurley immediately made "personal representations" to the Yugoslav Foreign Office, but was rebuffed and delayed. Hurley believed that only the mighty arm of the United States could save the sisters from imminent death. "Because of the universal reputation in which the Sisters, and especially hospital Sisters are held," Hurley frantically wrote to Ambassador Patterson, "this case will have the widest repercussions throughout the civilized world if the sentence is carried out." Vatican diplomacy was racing to come to terms with Tito's new form of state persecution. "Every instinct of religion, humanity, and chivalry cries out against the act contemplated," Hurley wrote in an exquisite melding of theological and international principles. Forcing the United States to face church-state relations in Yugoslavia head-on, he warned Ambassador Patterson that the crisis "may well constitute a test case to whether the Yugoslav government is determined to exterminate the Catholic religion in this country."[27]

In response, the embassy put the case on the high priority list. Patterson requested "instructions as to further steps" from Secretary of State Byrnes within hours of receiving Hurley's report. In the meantime the lawyers handling the case for the sisters filed an appeal of the death sentence at the Superior Court in Zagreb.[28]

In early April the Zagreb court commuted the sentences of three of the sisters to twenty years' imprisonment. For reasons that are unclear, the fourth Sister of Charity, Sister Zarka Ivasic, had her death sentence upheld and was executed by firing squad on April 7, 1946. For publicity reasons, the Yugoslavs kept the sentences secret for over a month. On May 21 the nunciature asked Ambassador Patterson to intercede in the case, saying that the Vatican would "welcome representations for clemency and commutation of the sentences of the other three." Patterson, shocked at the outcome of the trial and the execution of Sister Ivasic, noted to Washington that "it would be well to make them." In an unparalleled show of support for the Vatican, Secretary Byrnes's response was quick and decisive. "On humanitarian grounds," he wrote within hours of receiving Patterson's report, "the Department is disposed to authorize you to approach Yugoslav government with a view to obtaining clemency for the Sisters. . . . You may, when a suitable opportunity arises, express the interest of the United States Government in the case and state that the exercise of executive clemency should not fail to be well regarded in the United States."[29]

Although the outcome for Sister Zarka Ivasic was tragic, diplomatically the Vatican could not have wished for more. On September 6 Ambassador Patterson personally made the Vatican's pitch for executive clemency. In an *aide-mémoire* he specifically laid out to Tito that any further action against the sisters would meet with severe disapproval by the United States. Unexpectedly, Tito offered a compromise on the three surviving sisters: their twenty-year sentences to hard labor would be revoked if they refused to wear their habit, became laicized, and worked only as nurses in state hospitals. In diplomatic terms, Tito's proposal ranked as a watershed event in the history of U.S.-Vatican relations. At no time since the establishment of the Myron Taylor mission in 1939 had the United States used its political clout and good offices with another head of state to effectuate a concrete negotiated outcome on behalf of the Holy See.[30]

"Humanitarian grounds" notwithstanding, this was surely a major diplomatic win for the Vatican. Through late 1946, the relations between the U.S. embassy and Hurley's nunciature remained cooperative. President Truman, not yet committed to the State Department's emerging communist "containment" policy, instructed Patterson to use "a two-fisted, tough policy with Tito." The president's boxing metaphor was agreeable to Hurley. Under Truman's mandate, Patterson continued to criticize Tito for his lack of respect for basic freedoms and for human-rights violations. This phase would become the high-water mark of U.S.-Vatican cooperation.[31]

While Hurley saw eye-to-eye with Patterson regarding Tito and the "two-fisted approach," he had his own hands full. "So far we have not really gotten to grips with the government. They complain that the Bishops and clergy are *politicanti* [amateur politicians] and out of sympathy with the regime. We counter by saying that it is hard to have much sympathy with a regime which has killed and imprisoned hundreds of priests, and which has despoiled the church of all its possessions. . . . Of course, the charge used against us is always collaboration with the occupier and treason against the actual government." Hurley was not about to consider the possibility of Catholic collaboration with the Nazis. The Vatican, in contrast, seemed to be weighing other options.[32]

"IF YOU STRIKE THE SHEPHERD"

Archbishop Aloysius Stepinac of Zagreb was arguably one of the most controversial Catholic clerics of the entire Cold War. Since the end of World War II, scholars, journalists, and popes have decried and defended the complex history of the archbishop of Zagreb. Stepinac had been the highest-ranking Catholic leader in Croatia during the war and was already a controversial figure by the time he met Hurley in early 1946. His actions during World War II relating to the forced conversion of Orthodox Serbs to Roman Catholicism, alleged antisemitism, and alleged collaboration with the Ustasha left him beleaguered by a tortured legacy.[33]

Stepinac's biographer Stella Alexander has observed that a "triple myth" emerged around the Cold War bishop. Alexander points to various religious, ethnic, and political myths that sprang up around later interpretations of Stepinac's life. Remarkably, Hurley's place has either been deemphasized or simply left out of the historical debate, even though he was a principal shaper of various points of the triple myth. His interactions with Tito, his reports to the Vatican, and his conversations with Pius XII were extremely important in fashioning Stepinac's regional cult and broadcasting his image to the world.[34]

By late 1945, Stepinac posed the most serious threat to Tito's plan for the state consolidation of religion. While he had not always publicly sided with the NDH during World War II, he had maintained close ties to the regime. His enthusiasm for the new puppet state conditioned his public response to the government. In his capacity as chaplain to the armed forces of the NDH—the equivalent of Archbishop Spellman's position in the United States—he appeared publicly with many high-ranking Ustasha officers, creating a disturbing photographic record for later propaganda efforts. By 1943, however, Stepinac seemed to be falling out with Ante Pavelić and felt compelled to protest the latter's barbarous treatment of Serbs and Jews.[35]

Personifying Hurley's 1943 call for a moral defense of Jews in the face of extermination, Stepinac preached a sermon in March of that year denouncing the persecution of Jews because "their family shrine was not in accordance with the theories of Nazism." Though preached two years after the anti-Jewish legislation was introduced, Stepinac's March 1943 sermon did blast "the registration of Jews, the confiscation of their property," and "the wearing of marks of distinction" under force of law. In fact, the Stepinac sermon was so condemnatory of Nazi-inspired antisemitic laws that when it was rebroadcast over Vatican Radio the U.S. Office of War Information recycled excerpts for its own use.[36]

Many scholars, however, believe that Stepinac could have done more to criticize the Pavelić regime, and that most of his criticism of the Ustasha regime was always done "quietly and tactfully." Stepinac failed to be as tactful in his denunciations of the Tito regime. In fact, by the spring of 1945 he was vociferously preaching against atheistic communism.[37]

Stepinac emerged as a true political problem for Tito during the fall of 1945, when it became clear that as the principal leader of Croatia's Catholics he would not enter into a *modus vivendi* with the government. "The government desires to minimize if not abolish the jurisdiction of the Vatican over the Catholic Church in Croatia and Slovenia," OSS agent Franklin Lindsay reported privately to former president Herbert Hoover. As expected, Archbishop Stepinac steadfastly refused to go along with Tito's plan to create a national church. There would be no dialogue, no search for common ground, no cooperation at any level.[38]

Eyeing Tito as a new and godless enemy, Stepinac rejected any outward appearance of diplomacy. In September 1945 he began a yearlong process of gradually infuriating Tito when he convened a bishops' conference and released a scathing pastoral letter—to be read from the pulpits—enumerating multiple instances of government oppression. The letter was, as historians describe it, "a massive frontal attack, in all-out defiance of the government." In response, Tito ordered that Stepinac's spiritual assault be countered in a less metaphysical way—with bullets.[39]

"As the Archbishop was proceeding by automobile to attend a religious ceremony," Myron Taylor's office reported, "the prelate's car was stoned and then sprayed with machine gun fire." Taylor's office informed Washington that "the hostility shown by the communists" was "causing Archbishop Stepinac to fear for his safety and his life." By the time Hurley arrived in Belgrade the machine-gunning had stopped, but Tito knew that Stepinac was not going to play the silky game of diplomacy. In fact, during Hurley's second meeting with the dictator, Tito launched into a tirade against the Zagreb archbishop.[40]

"If Marshal Tito expected Bishop Hurley to be over-awed by his unexpected and outspoken attack on Stepinac, he must have been disappointed," Ambassador Patterson recorded in his unpublished memoir. According to Patterson, Hurley met with Tito in early February 1946 and told him "plainly of the ill treatment the Catholic Church was receiving from his regime, citing imprisonment and execution of priests and sisters, often without trial and seldom if ever with a fair trial; successive steps by the regime to abolish religious teaching in schools; police surveillance of almost every bishop in the country and the forced discontinuance of those liberties which the church was accustomed to enjoy 'in every democratic country.'" True to his fighting mentality, Hurley did not flinch during his interview and remained steadfast as "the Marshal listened with an air of studied distraction." The indomitable Tito must have been flabbergasted when the diminutive American bishop concluded their conversation by saying "that it would be well if the Marshal would reflect upon . . . a change of attitude."[41]

If Tito was hoping that the Vatican might send him a deft diplomat who aimed at a workable solution, he was disabused of this notion after meeting Hurley. Hurley's enumeration of regime abuses was nothing more than a rehash of Stepinac's September pastoral letter. Both Stepinac and Hurley used their own "two-fisted" approach with Tito. Hurley's confrontational style of diplomacy convinced Tito that he should appeal over Hurley's head. In late February 1946 Tito used his Foreign Office to send a message to Pope Pius XII to get Stepinac out of Yugoslavia. Hurley was dead set against the removal of Stepinac. If he were to leave, it would mean more than a Vatican diplomatic shuffle—it would mean the symbolic capitulation of the Holy See to Tito's communist state. More importantly, it would be a blow to Croatian Catholic nationalism—a chink in the vaunted *antemurale Christianitatis*.[42]

In midsummer 1946 Hurley received word through unofficial Vatican channels that Pope Pius XII was seriously considering removing Archbishop Stepinac from Zagreb. The quiet extraction of Stepinac would remove a number of complications for Pope Pius XII as he rolled out his new postwar strategy of aligning with the West. Stepinac himself reflected on the precarious nature of his position to U.S. diplomats early on. While he regretted the photographic record of his interactions with Ustasha officials (now widely posted on various Internet websites), he noted to American vice-consul Theodore Hohenthal that it was "unavoidable that the head of the Church would have contact with the head of the State." Stepinac recalled attending the first meeting of Tito's Croatian provisional assembly, "and that on his arrival, pictures were taken of him" and flashed to newspapers all over the country "for the obvious purpose of convincing the people that he supported the regime." Such admissions confirm Stepinac's entangled public position and his potential for becoming a problem if Pius wished to secure a *modus vivendi* with Tito. Moreover, press accounts seem to confirm that Stepinac's diplomatic value was being reconsidered by the Vatican in 1946. A front-page *Washington Post* story announced the "unofficial viewpoint" at the Vatican that because of the obligations of his ecclesiastical position, Stepinac "undoubtedly would have come into contact with [Nazi] occupation forces." At the same time, the Vatican disputed charges of outright collaboration. Given these emerging complications, would Pius ease Stepinac up and out of Zagreb?[43]

When Hurley got word that such deliberations were being contemplated, he was incensed. For Hurley, the mere mention of contact and collaboration with the Nazis was just another proof that Pope Pius XII was beginning to back down. Stepinac was under fire, literally, and now was no time to surrender or show weakness. "Communism," he wrote in his diary years later, "It is tough. We must be tough to defeat it: *Delenda*. We must stand firm."[44]

Stepinac was a fighter against atheistic communism—a footsoldier in Hurley's anticommunist cosmos. "Stubborn—tough—immovable" is how he summed up his strategy for dealing with Tito. Anything less would mean a "compromise in the Kingdom of God." As Pacelli had done in

1940 when the two men butted heads on Nazism, so now the pope was willing to symbolically "cave in" to the communists. Hurley responded to the rumor by ordering his secretary to arrange a meeting with Pope Pius XII. The next day he flew to Rome for an emergency summit.[45]

Hurley met with Pius in the library of the papal apartments, a corner room with windows overlooking St. Peter's Square. Hurley was quick, direct, and forceful. The two men talked over the Stepinac situation for forty-five minutes. Hurley pleaded the case that Stepinac had to stay put in Yugoslavia as the standard-bearer for Catholic theological anticommunism. He was adamant. As the meeting ended, Hurley sternly "reminded" Pius that "Aloysius Stepinac was the hero of the church in the Balkans—if you strike the shepherd, the sheep will be scattered."[46]

Simplifying matters greatly, Hurley placed the future unity of all Balkan Catholicism in Pius's hands. Pius, perhaps recalling how he had spurned Hurley's vocal antifascism in 1939 and 1940, now listened to him intently. The pope thanked Hurley for coming, and Archbishop Stepinac stayed in Zagreb. After many years, Hurley had finally won a battle with Eugenio Pacelli.

Hurley's flint-faced opposition to Pius's removal of Stepinac in 1946 seems difficult to reconcile in light of Hurley's past success with clerical exiles. In 1940 he had been secretly instrumental in moving Benito Mussolini's original political nemesis, the Italian antifascist priest Dom Luigi Sturzo, out of his European exile to the unlikely haven of Jacksonville, Florida. Hurley provided Sturzo with accommodation along the scenic St. John's River, hospital care, and other resources. From Florida, Sturzo carried on a vibrant prodemocracy campaign, wrote books, and gained further esteem worldwide.[47]

But his strong position on Stepinac was probably due to Stepinac's status as an archbishop—a position Hurley had long equated with spiritual generalship. Added to this was probably his lingering personal estimation that Pope Pius XII was weak. "Christianity is not a religion of *soft sentiment*," he later remarked in writing about Stepinac; it was "a religion of strong men—of valiant men—of heroes."[48]

Another factor that must be weighed was Stepinac's public role as a Croatian patriot. Catholics, and especially priests, who sympathized with Tito were not necessarily seen by their priestly brethren as procommunist, but rather as "anti-Croat." If Stepinac stayed and fought Tito, he would be showing a Croatian patriotism commensurate with his Catholic stamina. For Hurley, true patriotism relied not only on fealty to one's nation but also on steadfastness. In Hurley's thinking, Cardinal Mercier's famous 1914 treatise *Patriotism and Endurance* melded theological patriotism with staunch resistance to the foes of Catholicism. Regardless of papal reevaluation, Stepinac would have to stay and fight.[49]

After Hurley's intervention with Pius, patriotism and endurance seemed to be winning the day. In the fall of 1946, contrary to his original inclination, Pius XII kept Archbishop Stepinac in Zagreb to play the role of the Christian hero. When Marshal Tito finally realized that Stepinac would not be moving, he became enraged at the Vatican. Moreover, he was genuinely perplexed by the Vatican's position. Banking on Hurley's reputation as an antinazi, he had expected more from the American bishop. He was unaware of Hurley's new blindness to Catholic clerical collaboration during the war. In a show of force, Tito decided to move against Stepinac directly.

"The going here in Y. is not easy," Hurley wrote to Edward Mooney on September 17, 1946. "The arrests and 'trials' of priests continue, accompanied by a reign of terror. No one knows when his door will be knocked on in the dead of night." Just hours after Hurley penned those words, Archbishop Stepinac was roused from his sleep at the archepiscopal palace in Zagreb and placed under arrest by Tito's secret police.[50]

On the evening of his arrest, Stepinac called in the U.S. consul in Zagreb, Theodore Hohenthal, for consultation. Stepinac expected that the Americans would have to take his final message of persecution to the world. In what would be his final hour of freedom, Stepinac told Hohenthal his thoughts about Joseph Patrick Hurley and military stamina. "When I told him I had seen . . . Bishop [Hurley] in Gorizia . . . he grew reminiscent (unusual for him) and talked about his experience in World War I at Gorizia, where his regiment was in continuous action for ten months and sustained very severe losses." According to Hohenthal, Stepinac was sure that "the signal had been given" by Tito for a new war to begin, a campaign to "murder . . . his priests and bishops . . . on a much larger scale than heretofore." Though "utterly unconcerned about his own safety," he made "this coming reign of terror . . . the main point of his message to me," Hohenthal reported.[51]

Stepinac was less perceptive about Tito's intentions. At the beginning of their conversation Stepinac remarked to Hohenthal that "he was certain the OZNA [the Yugoslav secret police] would come for him, but he did not believe it would happen immediately." On this point he was tragically wrong. Hohenthal reported that Stepinac's arrest might have occurred "immediately following my visit."[52]

Hurley must have been in a frenzied state when the press broke the news of Stepinac's arrest on September 18 with front-page stories worldwide. Not to his diplomatic credit, at the time of the arrest Hurley was out of the country and miles away. Apparently falling back on his custom as a young Roman diplomat, he had taken the month of September off for a holiday in Switzerland, most likely at his favorite villa overlooking the restful waters of Lake Lugano. Stepinac, too, was puzzled by the bishop's absence; after all, Stepinac's secretary had been arrested weeks earlier and put on trial—a trial that was part of Tito's plan for amassing evidence against him.

Indeed, Hurley's long and conspicuous absence from the Belgrade nunciature may have prompted Tito to undertake the arrest precisely when the Vatican's regent was out of country. The timing played to Tito's advantage, since Hurley's absence precluded direct Vatican representations to the Yugoslav Foreign Office and any potential assistance from the U.S. embassy. Caught unawares and away from his post when Stepinac was incarcerated, Hurley was rushed back via Rome, and under the piercing gaze of Pope Pius XII. A savvy Vatican Press Office spun the Belgrade regent's presence in the Eternal City by declaring the situation so grave that Pope Pius XII personally "sent Bishop Joseph P. Hurley to investigate."[53]

Archbishop Stepinac's arrest moved the Vatican's battle with the Yugoslav state to a new level. A "savage battle of wills" was about to begin, and the first clashes spilled out into the press. On September 18 the Zagreb newspaper *Vijestnik* claimed that Stepinac was "the supreme head of all the dark and bloody crimes" committed by profascist bands since the end of the war. *Osservatore Romano* countered on September 20 "in what was one of the newspaper's swiftest reactions to a political event." For the first time Stepinac was referred to as a martyr. "We think of Archbishop Stepinac arrested and being sent to trial; we think of his pastoral virtue, his patriotism," *Osservatore Romano* expressed in prose strikingly similar to Hurley's melding of patriotism and religion; "We think of this unconquerable defender of truth, of the Catholic faith, of national aspirations, and of the Christian civilization of his people." From September 30 until October 11, 1946, Stepinac was tried in a school gymnasium in Zagreb in the presence of Hurley and his staff.[54]

Historians will not be able to fully reconstruct Hurley's role in the Stepinac trial until the official Vatican archival documents on the event are released. But it is likely that Hurley fashioned Stepinac as a symbolic figure of Croatian patriotism valiantly symbolizing Catholic opposition to communist tyranny. Hurley saw Stepinac as a modern-day national martyr for the faith—another Thomas à Becket or St. John Fisher. His first pretrial visit to the incarcerated Stepinac at Lepoglava prison reflected this outlook.

"As Bishop Hurley prepared to leave Archbishop Stepinac's cell, Archbishop Stepinac leaned forward in an effort to kiss Bishop Hurley's episcopal ring." This breach of protocol caught Hurley off guard (Hurley, a bishop, would normally have been obliged to kiss the ring of Stepinac, an archbishop). Hurley immediately withdrew his hand and asked Stepinac why he wished to kiss the ring. "You are the representative of the Holy Father, who is above all bishops," Stepinac replied. Upon hearing this, Hurley bent down on one knee and kissed Stepinac's own episcopal ring, saying, "Then I must do this because you are a martyr for your Catholic people." The Croat hero-martyr role was cast.[55]

In his conversations with both Pius and Tito, Hurley held up Stepinac as a *dramatis persona* of postwar Catholic anticommunism. As Stepinac's trial got underway in September 1946, Bishop Hurley and his nunciature staff were busy taking notes on the trial and producing the proper symbolism. In front of over 600 onlookers, every day during the trial, Hurley rose from his seat toward the front of the courtroom and bowed deeply as Stepinac and his guards walked past. This public show of obeisance from a Vatican official rankled the regime and gained attention worldwide.

On October 11 the verdict of Tito's kangaroo court was handed down. Stepinac was found guilty on all counts and sentenced to sixteen years' hard labor at the infamous Lepoglava prison north of Zagreb. International Catholic reaction to the sentence was widespread and swift. Catholic sources quickly condemned the verdict through such secular press outlets as *Le Figaro, Le Monde,* and the *New York Times. Osservatore Romano* likened Stepinac to the crucified Christ. Hurley, convinced now that Stepinac had been martyred as much for his patriotism as for his Catholicism, gave a short interview as he left the courtroom. "This man, whom I venerate, is the [Cardinal] Mercier of our time!" The trial, according to Hurley, was "one of the most important events of the century."[56]

As he prepared his reports for Rome, the Florida bishop must have been saddened that America, the country that had feted Cardinal Mercier, the patriotic Belgian resister of the Boche, had barely registered a weak protest on behalf of Stepinac. Lacking recourse to either economic retribution or military intervention, and now doubtful of American support, Hurley used the only weapon at his command—the spiritual barb. He would nettle the Tito regime through symbolic gestures of defiance.

The day after the Stepinac verdict was announced, Hurley successfully petitioned the Vatican to excommunicate any Catholic who had been involved in the trial. The issuing body, the Vatican's Sacred Congregation of the Council, was called into special session for the first time in seventy-five years. Aimed directly at Marshal Tito, a baptized Catholic, its decree of excommunication was the first "blanket excommunication" since the Napoleonic era. The excommunication was so sweeping and swift that some historians have wondered why a similar excommunication was not applied to Hitler during World War II. Shortly after the excommunication was delivered, Hurley took another symbolic swipe at the regime by conferring a highly publicized "apostolic benediction and blessing" on Archbishop Stepinac's seventy-five-year-old mother.[57]

In response to Hurley's irritating religious maneuvers, Tito hit back hard with violent harassment. "Bishop Hurley participated in the consecration of auxiliary Bishop Vovk at Ljubljana," T. J. Hohenthal reported to the State Department; the ceremony "was performed on schedule, despite the fact that a tear gas bomb was set off in the church during the consecration which caused the participants and the congregation great physical irritation." In the wake of the tear-gas incident, the Yugoslav government unleashed press attacks, physical intimidation, and restrictions on Hurley and the nunciature.[58]

By early 1948 Bishop Hurley had emerged as the primary thorn in the regime's side. A recently declassified 1948 secret report from "an Allied intelligence agency operating in Trieste," most likely the British Special Operations Executive, offers a firsthand account of Hurley's role in effecting the serious rift in church-state relations. In his capacity as regent, Hurley began appointing Croatian clerics to bishoprics "without an advance notification being sent either to the state authorities or members of the religious board." These ecclesiastical counterstrokes, made within his discretionary powers as regent, aggravated Tito to the hilt. In the 1948 report, designated "Secret Control—For U.S. Officials Only," the source, "Informant No. 1," indicated that Tito was "highly indignant over this action." The episcopal appointments "clearly show that there is a chasm dividing the state and church with a still deeper chasm between Tito and the papal nuncio Hurley."[59]

"The representatives of the Croatian provincial government," the informant reported, "repeatedly stated . . . that the main obstacle to a settlement between the state and Church is the papal nuncio Hurley who is an American and consequently unfamiliar with Balkan conditions and what is more he does not want a settlement at all." Through 1948 the "chasm" between Hurley and Tito deepened further. But larger political events were at work. The Allied intelligence report presented a more troubling situation for Hurley. It demonstrated that either the British or the Americans had placed a spy in the nunciature. The description of nunciature activities was so accurate that any move Hurley made would now be telegraphed to the Allies. In the relationship with his country Hurley had always been the practitioner of low-level espionage for the Allies, never the target of Allied professional espionage. The thought that the Allies could spy on one of their own probably never occurred to him. In 1948, as Tito began to disrupt the geopolitical framework of postwar Europe, U.S. interests would begin to diverge further from those of the Vatican.[60]

CHAPTER NINE

Betrayal in the Balkans

THE STEPINAC CASE

"I AM NOW SEEING the motion picture of totalitarianism for the fourth time," a despondent Hurley wrote to Edward Mooney shortly after the Stepinac verdict. "Japan, Italy, Germany, Yugoslavia—the colors have changed, but it is the same theme. In this last showing, however, the technique is far more perfect." "The story is one of unquestionable persecution," he confided, "and of a gradual liquidation planned in a knowing and efficient way: the terror is tangible." With Tito's reign of terror working at full steam, Hurley wondered about the silence of the United States on Archbishop Stepinac.[1]

In late 1946 State Department officials still were reluctant to take a stand on the guilt or innocence of the Zagreb archbishop. Hurley's friend, the sympathetic Ambassador Patterson, would state publicly only that "everything possible was being done." The State Department's first and only official response to the Stepinac trial came an embarrassing nine days after the verdict was announced. In a statement issued by Acting Secretary of State Dean Acheson on "U.S. Interest in Civil Liberties in Yugoslavia," the State Department condemned the lack of due process at Stepinac's trial as well as his loss of basic civil liberties. In what must have been a blow to Hurley, the U.S. statement made no mention of Stepinac's guilt or innocence. Acheson's vague civil-liberties statement was the only public utterance the State Department would ever make concerning Archbishop Stepinac.[2]

Unofficially, Acheson commented to the *New York Times* on October 23 that although the fairness of the Stepinac trial "left a great deal to be desired," the United States would make no official protest. For nearly sixty years thereafter, as the case became a perennial flash point in U.S.-Yugoslav relations, all government officials were directed back to Acheson's nebulous civil-liberties statement of 1946.[3]

Patterson and Acheson's virtual silence on Stepinac may have been due to their reception of information from other sources, which seemed to contradict the public absolution that the Holy See, under pressure from Hurley, was granting to Stepinac. Through its own channels, the State Department was in possession of documents that seemed to cast doubt on the archbishop's complete innocence during World War II. These were the reports of the American vice-consul at Zagreb, Peter Constan.

In an agreement worked out between Charles Thayer of the Office of Strategic Services and Tito in December 1944, Constan and Karl Norden became the first State Department officials to enter Yugoslavia. By the time of the Stepinac trial, Constan had served longer in the country than any other U.S. political official. Since Stepinac's trial was taking place in Zagreb, Constan was tabbed to file the official reports. Constan's remarks have never been reviewed in connection with the Stepinac trial or subsequent historical debate. They are important because they contributed to the formulation of the United States' long-standing policy on Stepinac. In his reports, Constan indicated that, at best, the United States should be skeptical of Stepinac's claims of innocence. This was a particularly surprising observation given that Constan was well known as a hard-line anticommunist.[4]

On October 3, 1946, during the final hours of the trial, Archbishop Stepinac was granted thirty minutes to give his "last word." Since Stepinac had chosen to remain mute throughout the trial, it was reasonable to assume that this "final say" would be a forceful statement of his innocence. "His speech was not directly a defense speech," Constan noted with an air of puzzlement; "he offered no proof that he had not committed the acts of which he is accused, no explanations or excuses." Constan seemed baffled by Stepinac's lack of rejoinder. He noticed, for example, that instead of defending himself, Stepinac "broke into a stinging counter-indictment against the regime." Constan believed that Stepinac's diatribe against the Tito regime certainly "should establish that Archbishop Stepinac is an ardent Croat patriot fighting for freedom and he is not a traitor to his people"—a conclusion that was never in doubt. On the whole, Constan "came away with the definite impression that Archbishop Stepinac had in certain ways erred," that he had "shown too much tolerance, perhaps sympathy, toward the Independent State of Croatia, and in that way may have given a certain amount of comfort to the enemy."[5]

Giving comfort to the enemy during wartime was a serious offense, and at the time of the Stepinac trial it was an even more explosive issue. As it happened, while Archbishop Stepinac was on trial in Zagreb, the United States was in the process of expanding its standards on exactly what constituted "comfort to the enemy." From 1943 until 1947, the Supreme Court was considering whether an intellectual commitment to the goals of an enemy country rose to the level of "aid and comfort." In the celebrated *Haupt* case of 1947, Justice Robert H. Jackson made clear that although a subject "may intellectually or emotionally favor the enemy and harbor sympathies or convictions disloyal to this country's policy or interest," treason could be assigned only in cases of overt action. Outside the scope of its ruling, the Court added a clear condemnation of "disloyalty" to the American interests, a buzzword that would resonate throughout the 1950s.[6]

Wartime collaboration by Stepinac was hard for the Americans to assess. Initially, Hurley argued from silence on the Stepinac case. Hurley "considers it significant, that Tito made no charges against [the] Archbishop's conduct during occupation," the Belgrade embassy reported after Hurley's first meeting with Tito. When Hurley discussed Stepinac two weeks later, embassy counselor Harold Shantz noted that "Bishop Hurley stoutly defended the actions of Stepinac during the war and believed him innocent of any real collaboration charges." Shantz did not prod Hurley to distinguish between "collaboration" and "any real collaboration," but given the fact that the same distinctions were being argued at the Supreme Court, only steps away from the Department of State, it is no wonder that the United States chose to stay mum. Constan's simple reference to even "a certain amount of comfort" coupled with Shantz's qualified collaboration raised red flags in Washington.[7]

On top of this, and more important still, the Americans were in possession of a secret source attributed to Stepinac that raised serious doubt about the archbishop's public utterances. On September 9 Stepinac composed a secret seven-page memorandum and without Hurley's knowledge transmitted it to the American consul at Zagreb, Theodore H. Hohenthal. On September 26 Hohenthal notified the State Department that he had received a "secret memorandum prepared by Archbishop Stepinac." He transmitted the memo as Enclosure No. 2 of his consular report and labeled it "Archbishop's Memorandum." This memorandum has never been reviewed in all of the voluminous literature of the Stepinac case.[8]

Presumably, since all the press outlets were covering the trial of Stepinac's secretary, Father Ivan Salic, the archbishop knew when he wrote the memorandum the precise testimony and charges that would be leveled against him. Since Stepinac refused to speak at his trial, with the exception of his "last word," which was largely unconnected to the charges, the memorandum would become the archbishop's last-ditch effort to present his case and to save him from any future harm. It is not known if Stepinac alerted Hurley to the existence of the "Archbishop's Memorandum" or if he kept a copy of the memo for himself.

In light of the rigged proceedings and subsequent execution of the Chetnik leader Draza Mihailovic four months earlier, Stepinac surely considered the "Archbishop's Memorandum" his last freely composed message and a matter of life and death. In fact, toward the end of Stepinac's own trial, British ambassador Charles Peake visited with Marshal Tito and impressed upon him that the West would certainly register its indignation were Stepinac to receive the same punishment as Mihailovic. Reportedly, Tito responded to Peake that the Yugoslavs "would not be such fools as to kill an Archbishop."[9]

But the Vatican believed that Tito had other ideas. "Shoot the Archbishop," was the advice Foreign Minister Vladimir Velebit gave Tito shortly after Stepinac's arrest, and before his trial. Hurley's nunciature was informed that while Velebit had it in mind to execute the Croatian Stepinac as a countermeasure for the execution of the Serb Mihailovic, he "could not shoot him because of world public opinion." The memorandum that Stepinac handed to Hohenthal was, then, a desperate cry for American assistance.[10]

The first section of the "Archbishop's Memorandum" was an ideological exposition in which Stepinac identified himself as a martyr to communism. According to Stepinac, his impending trial represented more than a personal saga—it was "a clash between Catholicism and Communism,

which are today two of the most opposed concepts of life in the world."
With a nod to Croatian nationalism, he argued that his removal as archbishop of Zagreb "would pierce the heart of the Croatian soul." A trial
conviction "would leave clear the road which leads to the inner organization of the Church," he argued, "in order to subdue the Church to the will
of the regime, which today is internationally known as the most faithful
disciple of the Soviet regime." "The regime does not like to lead an open
fight," Stepinac offered in an ironic observation before his very public
show-trial; "because of world opinion it is afraid to do so."[11]

What was frustrating for the Americans who were analyzing the archbishop's secret statement was the fact that even in this secret memorandum Stepinac was unwilling or unable to offer any new evidence of his
innocence. On hot-button topics, he invariably referred back to statements
already published in his diocesan newspaper. There were many points
later brought up at his trial that he dismissed out of hand, logically garbled,
or simply left unclear. While the Americans agreed that Stepinac had been
unjustly tried and imprisoned, the secret memorandum in their possession offered no new argumentation, evidence, or verification.

A more perplexing and potentially grave situation for the Americans
who reviewed Stepinac's memorandum was his explanation of why he
agreed, at the behest of NDH leaders shortly before the fall of the Independent State of Croatia, to hide several trunks of Ustasha archival material in
the basement of his episcopal palace. Although he ultimately handed over
the archives to the Croatian Communist Party leader Vladimir Bakarić, it
was alleged at his trial that the Ustasha archives were placed with Stepinac
in anticipation that the fleeing Ustasha forces would one day regroup and
return to establish an anticommunist state once the war was over. Since
a plan did exist for an Ustasha return (known as Operation Krizari), the
safety of the Ustasha archives would have been crucial to the successful
installation of a nationalist government.[12]

The "Archbishop's Memorandum" gives the first indication of Stepinac's thinking on this matter. In his memo, Stepinac stated plainly that he
placed the archives of the NDH Ministry of Foreign Affairs in the cellar of
his palace "in order to save them from Allied aerial bombardment." This
was a baffling admission for the Americans, since the United States had
been an Allied power during the war. Such political fuzziness seems to
indicate that Archbishop Stepinac did not understand the wartime impli-

cations of such a move. Even more, he may have misunderstood that the Americans' emerging anticommunism did not necessarily translate into a break with Allied wartime political aims. Perhaps the decisive complication for Stepinac was that when hammering out the Italian armistice in 1943, U.S. diplomats fought hard to make the secreting of enemy archives a war crime. "The concealment of archives, records, plans, or any other documents or information" became a prosecutable offense under United Nations rules.[13]

Stepinac was acting out of sympathy and intense national feeling. Regardless of political naiveté, it was clear to the State Department officials who were reading the "Archbishop's Memorandum" that his discussion of events only reconfirmed Peter Constan's observations from the trial that, though unjustly tried, Stepinac may have given "a certain amount of comfort to the enemy" during wartime. Since the State Department, unlike Hurley, was not concerned about making Stepinac a martyr, it kept its judgments secret and moved on to formulate the next major foreign policy shift in Yugoslavia, a shift that would have major ramifications for Vatican relations and Hurley's diplomatic status.[14]

"SO MUCH DUST IN THE EYES"

"I am engaged on the first trenches of the battle where the forces of Christ are locked in deadly combat with those of Satan," Hurley wrote back to a friend in St. Augustine during the fall of 1947. At about the time that Hurley was "locked in deadly combat with . . . Satan" in Yugoslavia, the State Department was preparing a new team of diplomats to send to Belgrade. On April 9, 1947, the Senate confirmed the appointment of Cavendish Welles Cannon to replace Richard C. Patterson as ambassador to Yugoslavia. Second-in-command and counselor of the embassy was Robert Borden Reams. In June 1948, Reams, acting as counselor of embassy, noticed a subtle shift on the part of the Yugoslavs toward the Soviets. Gauging various Soviet-Yugoslav actions, Reams became convinced that there were rumblings underneath the surface of communist harmony. Much to the State Department's surprise, Reams was vindicated on June 28, 1948, when Stalin publicly expelled Tito from the Communist Information Bureau, or Cominform, international communism's propaganda organization, which until then had been headquartered in Belgrade.[15]

Writing to Washington, Reams described the Tito-Stalin split as "the

most significant event here since United States recognition." He concluded that the schism might "afford us the opportunity to penetrate
and disunite [the] Soviet bloc." Reams urged that America be prepared to
offer economic assistance to Tito. In the Belgrade nunciature, the ever-
suspicious Hurley rejected Reams's opinion as preposterous.[16]

"The ideological indictment of the Kominform [sic] against Tito,"
Hurley wrote to Edward Mooney, "is merely dust in the eyes, he is guilty
of schism, not heresy." To Hurley, Tito remained communist even after
the split. What he was guilty of was political separation from Stalin, not
ideological revolt. Tito's expulsion from the Cominform was inconsequential in terms of Vatican policy. The move did not reduce communist
oppression against the Catholic church. Somehow Hurley had to get this
message to the Americans. Since the embassy was silent on the Stepinac
issue, he decided to play a different card. Now deeply suspicious of the
American team in Belgrade, he circumvented State Department officials
altogether and turned to his old friend Myron Taylor. In a last-ditch effort
to persuade America not to be duped by Tito's schism, Hurley petitioned
Taylor to bring the Catholic view to President Truman.[17]

On July 25, 1948, Taylor submitted to President Truman a sixteen-page
confidential report composed by Hurley titled "The Controversy between
the Komonform [sic] and the Communist Party of Yugoslavia." "From
the style of this report I am confident that I know very well the author
with whom for years past I have worked in close cooperation both at the
Vatican in Rome and in America," Taylor confided to Truman. "I am certain of his ability, good judgment, and trustworthiness." Much as with
the "Bishops' Draft" six years earlier, Taylor was kind enough to submit
a Hurley report to a state leader as the work of his own office. This way,
Hurley's report on the Tito-Stalin split reached the president, the exact
person he needed to influence. Taylor was sure that Truman would "find
the document of interest."

"In its present phase," Hurley opened his summary, "the controversy
is clearly a family quarrel among avowed Communists." Drawing on the
language of Catholic theology to make his point, he alerted Truman that
internal communist oppression remained unchanged. Indeed he warned
that "close examination of the accusations and detailed reply would lead
one to believe that there is no serious 'doctrinal' divergence in the attitude
and actions of the Yugoslavs." Tito the communist had not changed his

ways merely because of an internal power struggle. "The attempt to make the controversy appear as one of 'doctrine' is, then," Hurley reiterated to Truman, "so much dust in the eyes. . . . One may reasonably conclude, that the controversy is basically one of discipline and not of 'doctrinal' principle."

Candidly and prophetically, Hurley feared that a divorce from the Soviets might "throw Yugoslavia into the arms of the Western Powers who could easily supply her wants." Further, Russian sanctions might "also greatly increase the magnetism of the Marshall Plan which has already exerted considerable influence on Yugoslav economists." Despite the fact that Truman had already begun to agree with Reams's policy evaluation, Hurley hoped that Truman would not be deceived by what was essentially an "issue of Communist discipline." He hoped in vain. Truman, in the midst of recovering his political fortunes after the disastrous 1946 elections, was looking for a way to poke Stalin in the eye. Yugoslavia was too tempting an opportunity for him to pass up.[18]

Perhaps with some foreboding, all Hurley could do now was to sit and await Truman's response to the Tito-Stalin split. "I do not look for an early relaxation of the persecution," Hurley informed Mooney not long after writing his report; "on the contrary, for tactical reasons, the pressure seems to be applied more strongly against the Church during the past few months." Hurley's observations proved correct. As historian Lorraine Lees has pointed out, in the months immediately after the Tito-Stalin split the government revived its antireligious campaign.[19]

Adding to this ever-deepening sense of isolation at the nunciature, the American embassy determined to reassess its operational relation to Hurley's own mission in Belgrade. The new American decision reflected a small part of what one historian has termed a "diametric reversal in diplomatic relations between Yugoslavia and the United States." The tight relationship between the nunciature and the American embassy was about to end. For Hurley, the first sign of a reversal came in the exchange of intelligence.[20]

As was the custom during the ambassadorship of Richard Patterson, the U.S. embassy and the Belgrade nunciature frequently shared intelligence and opinion in their common crusade against communism. In 1948 Reams began to take a closer look at the material coming from the nunciature. Unknown to Hurley and the Vatican, Reams started to question the validity of Hurley's accounts.

"It is extremely difficult for the Embassy to establish the validity of reports of this nature," Reams informed the European division at the State Department. "It is felt that the lack of substance in these reports greatly limits their usefulness as documentation of anti-church activity in Yugo-slavia." In the most candid appraisal of Vatican intelligence reports since the inception of Hurley's mission, Reams concluded: "They appear to contain the usual type of material which is commonly identified as having originated with propaganda organizations." Hurley apparently remained unaware of this critical reappraisal and downgrading of his information; he continued to supply the Americans with numerous reports.[21]

On June 30, 1948, the State Department reviewed the economic repercussions of the Tito-Stalin split and formulated a new policy. The United States would no longer scrutinize Yugoslavia's domestic policies. "Its internal regime is basically its own business," the official statement read. "The character of the regime would not . . . stand in the way of a normal development of economic relations." Tito now had a green light to maintain his regime of fear and repression against Catholics while simul-taneously looking to the West for economic aid. The days of U.S. political pressure in conjunction with Hurley and Vatican interests were over. In February 1949, shortly after taking the helm as secretary of state, Dean Acheson described the new economic ties with Yugoslavia as "a reward for its stepping outside the Soviet bloc." Hurley believed all of this to be nonsense. His country, formerly—and in all other cases—unabashedly anticommunist, was abandoning him, and he did not know why.[22]

In May 1949 the Yugoslavs tested the new American policy by request-ing twenty-five million dollars from the U.S. Export-Import Bank. To Hurley, Tito was galloping down Wall Street on a Trojan horse while the United States willingly disregarded the principles of religious freedom as set forth in the Atlantic and United Nations Charters. Cast aside were all of Welles's former promises, FDR's assurances, and Hurley's harmonic vision of American foreign policy. After 1948, Hurley became infuriated at what he saw as a sellout of American principles. His Americanized view of symmetry between U.S. democratic principles and Roman Catholic theological aims was being rent asunder.

"If we want to have strength in Yugoslavia, we must restore civil and religious rights," Hurley wrote as the Export-Import Bank loan was being negotiated. For Hurley, the question was a clear case of exacting a quid pro quo for religious and civil liberties. Now, in Yugoslavia, the wartime rhetoric of liberty and democratic justice did not seem to apply. "We are now on the verge of choosing to disregard ethical principles and the clear commitments of the United Nations Charter." "If we follow the plan suggested we MAY strengthen Jugoslavia by helping Jugoslavs to help themselves," he confided to his notes. "If we give the money as the bill proposes, without any strings, we weaken both ourselves and Yugoslavia. The facts of universal violations of human rights are well known. We have had lamentable experience in helping Communist regimes without insisting on decency."[23]

Hurley's shock at and dissatisfaction with the policy shifts of 1948 and 1949 seem to confirm Harold Tittman's 1945 assessment of the Vatican regent's insufficient diplomatic preparation for his Balkan assignment. His naiveté about the limits of national-interest diplomacy, Balkan religious history, and the American policy readjustments testify to his inability to adapt to changing diplomatic circumstances. Writing in 1994 Kenneth Sinclair-Loutit, who was a United Nations Relief and Rehabilitation official in postwar Belgrade, commented that Hurley "seemed to be completely lost once he stepped outside of the small American community in Belgrade . . . and was not at all familiar with European politics."[24]

Moreover, Hurley was deeply impressed by a Croatian nationalism that so easily grafted Roman Catholicism to it as an external identifier. In Belgrade he accentuated Stepinac's national patriotism to override crucial questions about Catholic clerical collaboration during the war. "As citizen and Patriot," Hurley later lionized Stepinac, "sprung from that glorious Christian people who for long centuries have been the Southern bulwark of the True Faith—the Croats—the Antemurale Christianitatis—Stepinac gives the world hope."[25]

Arriving in the Balkans in 1945, Hurley had seen no conflict between Croatian hyperpatriotism and Roman Catholic theological principles. By touting Archbishop Stepinac as "the Cardinal Mercier of our times," he was in fact equating Stepinac's embrace of Croatian national aspiration—signified by his early political acceptance of the NDH—with Mercier's honorable bonding of "patriotism and endurance."

As Hurley grappled with these concepts, Tito began to accelerate his campaign against the Catholic church. In this new phase of intimidation, he made a concerted effort to subordinate the church to the state. Priest assassinations, arrests, and executions moved to a new level. By 1949 Tito's regime could no longer legitimately claim wartime collaboration as a pretense for murder and imprisonment.[26]

In June 1949 the situation became so serious and the nunciature so isolated that Hurley decided to solicit the help of Myron Taylor once more. One last time, Hurley prepared a report for Taylor to convey to President Truman. This was Hurley's final attempt to influence U.S. foreign policy in Yugoslavia. His confidential "Memorandum on the Religious Situation in Yugoslavia since January, 1947" was a final effort to sway the chief executive toward a humanitarian, and essentially procatholic, understanding of the Yugoslav situation. "The religious situation in Yugoslavia continues to be grave," the twenty-page memo opened. Hurley then listed the various executions, arrests, imprisonments, and other crimes perpetrated against Yugoslav Catholics. The memo was placed on Truman's desk on June 14, accompanying a letter from Taylor assuring the president that the memo would "prove of interest" to him.[27]

President Truman's reply to Taylor on June 17 was confusing. On the one hand, he specifically lauded the thorough investigations and substance of the "Religious Situation in Yugoslavia" memo. "These reports are authoritative," Truman confessed, "and therefore extremely valuable." Yet, despite conceding the "authoritative" nature of the reports, Truman suggested nothing to help alleviate the grim situation for Catholics. The second half of Truman's response to Taylor consisted of personal pleasantries, family gossip, and sentimental chatter, with nary a word about policy nor even a sympathetic remark about the Yugoslav civil-rights record toward Catholics. Later that summer, after Tito dissolved his joint Soviet air and transport companies, the United States granted Yugoslavia its coveted twenty-million-dollar Export-Import Bank loan. Hurley never wrote to Truman again.[28]

BREAKING POINT

In 1983 Milovan Djilas recalled that directly after the Partisans came to power in Belgrade, many top communists "were taken by the idea of developing and strengthening a 'national Catholic church'—a church that would break away from the Vatican. There was even mention of . . . certain priests leaning in that direction." Following the Stepinac trial, the state attempted to organize the lower clergy into "professional organizations of priests, a sort of clerical trade union" in sympathy with the goals of the government. Tito tried endlessly to negotiate state concerns with both individual bishops and Hurley's nunciature. Convinced that the higher clergy were devoted to the Vatican, the state looked to the priests' unions as a way to infiltrate the church, make it more "national," and bring the Catholic people under its aegis.[29]

On this score, Hurley fought Tito tooth and nail. The fight over the "priests' associations" was probably his most significant achievement in the realm of ecclesiastical diplomacy. And, ironically, it was his one Balkan diplomatic success which, over the long haul, was most underappreciated by both the United States and Pope Pius XII. Using the diplomacy of determination, Hurley sustained the Yugoslav Catholic bishops' morale, headed off a splintering of the clergy, and kept Yugoslav Catholicism from succumbing to a state-sponsored hybrid church. The establishment of a national church would have confused the faithful, fractured unity, and set up an ersatz Catholic church, undercutting the Vatican's religious authority for generations.

When Dr. Bozo Milanovic founded the first Catholic Priests' Association in 1948, Hurley's influence among the bishops ensured that the membership remained small. Traveling widely throughout the country, Hurley reminded the Croatian and Slovene bishops that their first and final allegiance was to the pope of Rome. A growing concern for Hurley in 1948 was the budding Slovene Priests' Association, which had been founded in Maribor by the maverick priest Rev. Joseph Lampret. This group established an Organizing Committee and founded its own weekly journal, *Bilten,* with Lampret as editor.

In May 1949 the Organizing Committee of the Slovene Priests' Association presented Hurley with a list of demands, which included the official dismissal of Bishop Gregorij Rozman of Ljubljana, who was known to have "collaborated fully with the Germans and the Slovene anti-Partisan forces" (Rozman fled to Austria in 1945 and later settled in Cleveland, Ohio), and the cessation of "lying broadcasts" over Vatican Radio. In a brilliant move aimed to disintegrate the group's collective power, Hurley received the members of the committee individually at the nunciature. Since he already had a reputation as a feisty and imperious fighter, none of the renegade priests looked forward to meeting Hurley face to face. In private, he questioned them on their politics, asked if they belonged to the Communist Party, and accused them of acting under pressure from the secret police. He had what was described as a "sharp exchange" with Father Lampret. Hurley's special tactics deflated the Priests' Association's claims to unity, and the group began to fizzle.

Hurley's exchange with Lampret reflected his own deep suspicions. He believed that Lampret had been thoroughly co-opted by the state, was the ringleader of the Priests' Association, and was most likely a communist. In condemning Lampret to the Vatican, Hurley continued to equate religion and Croatian nationalism. "Lampret is no good and should have been excommunicated two years ago," he wrote to Domenico Tardini; "he is a traitor to his faith and to his nation." During July and August the Priests' Association held meetings all over Slovenia to protest Hurley's behavior and to air its demands.[30]

Hurley viewed such pressure as just so much more persecution. "It takes the form of endless interrogations, for hours and hours at a time, to almost all our priests," he wrote to Mooney in early 1949. "The purpose is to break them down in order to force them to collaborate. This in itself is merely a stage in the road to a national church." Unflinching priests were "tortured and imprisoned, in some cases killed, either judicially, or extra-judicially. The pressure is so terrible," he informed Mooney, "that the strongest spirits are close to the breaking point, and nervous collapse is frequent."[31]

But in the wake of the Stepinac case and the Tito-Stalin split, Hurley's work on this matter seems to have been underappreciated by the Vatican. Largely as a result of the diplomacy of determination, within the year the government's campaign to prop up the Priests' Association began to wane. "It was clear," historian Stella Alexander has pointed out, "that if the church and the government were to move towards a *modus vivendi* different methods must be used." Hurley made clear to Tito that he was not about to buckle, and soon the government in Belgrade came to understand that it needed to negotiate with bishops and not with the priests.[32]

Hurley's strategy of uncompromising diplomacy kept the Catholic church of the Balkans together. His efforts were all behind the scenes, and there is no clear evidence in any Vatican documents, public or personal, that officials in Rome even understood their significance. Elsewhere the creation of communist national churches became a tremendous problem (and remains so today) for the Holy See, particularly in China and later in Cold

War Cuba. Ultimately, Hurley's unheralded efforts in 1949 safeguarded one of the ancient ecclesial marks of Roman Catholicism—unity.

As Hurley grappled with Tito over a national church, another battle was heating up on a formerly unthinkable front. In 1949 the U.S. embassy in Belgrade initiated a series of talks aimed to take away the one diplomatic chip that Hurley had fought so hard to secure—the symbolic figure of the martyr Stepinac. More than three years after his trial, American diplomats still could not rid themselves of the thorny Stepinac problem.

Hurley's constant reports to Rome, his courtship of increasingly influential American bishops, and the impressive press campaign waged by the National Catholic Welfare Conference all kept Stepinac at the forefront of American Catholic anticommunist efforts. New York's publicity-conscious Archbishop Spellman did not help State Department officials when naming his newest educational endeavor Archbishop Stepinac High School. "There is a new crime in the world—the crime of believing in God," Monsignor Fulton Sheen thundered at the dedication of the White Plains school. "This school is dedicated to such a 'criminal,' who like Christ, suffered under Pontius Pilate." With such flourish, the name of Stepinac was, by 1949, folding itself into the pious lives of ordinary American Catholics.[33]

On May 1, 1949, the Knights of Columbus sponsored an Archbishop Stepinac "loyalty parade" of 100,000 Catholics in New York City. On the same day another 100,000 protesters wended their way down O'Connell Street in Dublin, Ireland. In response to these demonstrations, the Senate Foreign Relations Committee passed a resolution calling on the United States to seek relief for Stepinac through the United Nations. Both the House of Representatives and the Senate passed resolutions in the summer of 1949 calling on the United States to take action to free Stepinac— and directly link economic aid to the imprisoned archbishop. Stepinac was becoming a cult figure of communist martyrdom. Hurley's hopes were being fulfilled. The U.S. publicity battle seemed to be the only public battle that Hurley was winning in his war against Tito.[34]

The Hurley publicity wins on Stepinac were frustrating to a Belgrade embassy that dearly wanted to relate to the Tito regime without having to worry about the human-rights problem of Stepinac. The worldwide public-relations blitz during the spring and summer of 1949 compelled the newest U.S. ambassador in Belgrade, George V. Allen, to come to terms with the thorny Stepinac issue. For Catholics, domestic consumption of Truman's "wedge" policy in Yugoslavia was faltering over Stepinac. Ambassador Allen wanted Stepinac released from jail, and Hurley worked intensely to cut him off.

"Beware of conditional release of Stepinac," Hurley scribbled in his diplomatic notes. "No 'political' concession." Any compromise with Tito on Stepinac was "a propaganda move which will settle nothing and only further deceive us [Catholics?]. . . . Allen pushes for it," he remarked in exasperation, "most unwisely. You cannot cure cancer with a salve." To Hurley, a Stepinac release would "settle nothing." Hurley was probably still unsure whether Pope Pius XII would order such a release. Complicating matters was that the languishing Stepinac vowed that he would leave captivity only under a direct order from the pope. When the aggressively anticommunist *New York World Telegram* broke a story on October 3, 1949, that Tito was about to "free Archbishop Stepinac," and that "Vatican sources" believed the general veracity of the report, Hurley again felt as if his legs were being cut out from under him by the pope he had warned of just such dangers.[35]

On the ground in Belgrade, the losses multiplied. The erosion of the church continued. The best Hurley could do was mount pinprick attacks against a communist behemoth, now flush with American dollars. After four years the situation seemed as obstructed and mired as ever. Hurley consistently castigated the Tito regime; at the same time he criticized the American betrayal—and held deep suspicions about Ambassador Allen. Perhaps out of frustration or perhaps out of fear, he began to cast his suspicions westward. As the *annus horribilis* of 1949 wound to a close, Hurley reassessed the policies of those whom he had been sent to represent. The old method of having the Vatican publicize the oppression was wearing thin. The Holy See was beginning to sit on Hurley's reports. As the situation worsened, Hurley looked for a scapegoat. He believed that Eugenio Pacelli was not willing to prosecute a two-front war against the State Department and Tito's communist regime. As the silence from Rome worsened, he again aimed his criticisms, as he had in 1940, obliquely at Pope Pius XII.

By late 1949 more published news reports indicated that the Vatican was considering going ahead with a conditional release for Stepinac. A dejected Hurley began to question Vatican policy, including the policymakers

at the top of the Vatican hierarchy. "It is saddening—and maddening—
to be forced to admit that the major fault lies with ourselves," he wrote
to Mooney in December. "The center is completely and precisely well-
informed. But they either are incapable of doing anything, or they do not
want to." With words that harked back to his 1940 assessment of Pius XII,
he went on: "We still have a chance, if only we had some vision and courage." His obscure yet critical references to the "center" and to "Rome"
were most likely allusions to Pius XII. Moreover, his final opinion was that
"the old, deplorable principle that we can win battles without fighting—a
national [Italian?] weakness—is again being invoked."[36]

Hurley's criticisms became less circumspect as he watched his efforts
to thwart communism meet with resistance in the Vatican. "I am dismayed at the thinking—more at the lack of decisive, timely, action at
Rome," he again unburdened to Mooney. "I have sought to rally them
from their hand-wringing passivity; have accused them in official reports
of wasting their time on futile post mortems instead of using intelligent
and vigorous remedies while the patient is still alive; have urged them
to call in some priests or prelates or laymen who are capable of directing
a useful news agency; have taunted them with the sepulchral ineptitude
and incompetence of the Vatican Radio."[37]

As he did in his editorial on the death camps, Hurley couched the
discussion of leadership comparatively with other organized religions,
suggesting that Roman Catholicism's principal leader now ran the risk
of failing in leadership. In Yugoslavia, it was the Orthodox church, which
was in some way "looking to us for the lead." "The bishops and priests"
were "holding fast," Hurley informed Mooney with the flourish of military
metaphor. "In our very danger, there is a great opportunity—if we only
had greatness." In wishing for "greatness" and true leadership at "the
center" of the Vatican, Hurley was again wishing out loud that Pius XII
might claim a more "intelligent and vigorous" place on the religious
battlefield.[38]

Hurley's pointed criticisms of Vatican policymakers surely damaged
his status in Rome. "How easy it is," diplomatic historian Harold Nicolson observed, "for a diplomat to find himself in disagreement with the
policy of his government. Yet even if he 'assents with civil leer,' he should
know full well that this attitude is in fact an act of silent disloyalty." In his
multivolume history of diplomacy, Nicolson called loyalty one of the most

important attributes of the diplomat. But from Belgrade, it was appearing that Hurley's "leer" was far from civil and his "disloyalty" far from silent. Dunning letters to the Vatican complaining of "sepulchral ineptitude," incompetence, and "hand-wringing passivity" could hardly tip the scales of perceived loyalty in his favor.[39]

As his standing at the Vatican became imperiled, Hurley also worried that those at the "center" were leaving him to twist in the wind. He saw silence and compromise as a lack of dedication in the battle to defeat evil. Little did he realize that his own diplomacy of confrontation was now out of step with the policy of Pope Pius XII, who was acting as his own secretary of state. As early as 1948 the secret Allied intelligence report on church-state relations indicated astutely that from "Informant Number One's" point of view, "the Vatican is more conciliatory and it is Hurley's attitude toward Yugoslavia that is stiff." Likewise, the lack of attention to Hurley's suggestions in Rome signaled that his tenure as a diplomat was about to end.[40]

In May 1949 the Vatican began making plans for Hurley's departure from Belgrade. In a move that sounded an ominous note, Monsignor Pietro Sigismondi was named counselor of the nunciature on May 30. On June 3 the Italian newspaper *Il Quotidiano* denied "rumors and speculation in the press that possible changes in the diplomatic situation between Yugoslavia and the Holy See are about to take place." The Italian daily reported that "the assignment of Monsignor Sigismondi to the Belgrade post is one of the normal rotations among diplomatic personnel of the Vatican." Such defensive posturing did not bode well for the beleaguered Florida bishop. Later that month, Hurley officially agreed to relinquish his position as regent.

To replace him, the Secretariat of State sent one of its rising stars—the Italian Monsignor Silvio Oddi. Wise and affable, Oddi was a midlevel diplomat in the Secretariat of State. But there were complications. At the time of his appointment, Oddi was only thirty-nine years old. In addition, it seems that the Secretariat of State never informed Hurley that Oddi was its choice to be his replacement.[41]

In his memoirs, Silvio Cardinal Oddi explains that he was "entrusted with the Belgrade nunciature in June of 1949." But Hurley's correspondence bears out that he stayed at the nunciature as regent through August 1950. "He had asked to be replaced," Oddi wrote innocently of Hurley, "but when he saw me arriving, he protested." Perhaps recalling the importance of the impressive arrival of Archbishop Paolo Marella in Tokyo, Hurley looked quizzically at Oddi as he landed on the nunciature doorstep. "A bishop cannot be replaced by a simple monsignor!" Hurley objected to a baffled Oddi. In a brazen move, Hurley apparently kept Oddi out of the nunciature for over a year.[42]

On August 28, 1949, Joseph McGeough, who had Hurley's old job at the American desk at the Secretariat of State, wrote to Hurley and informed him that he had "inquired in a general way about the situation in Belgrade and present plans and learned (confidentially) that the status quo actually existing will probably be continued, at least for the present. At any rate I understand that DT [Domenico Tardini] will be writing you about this." Now under secretary of state for extraordinary ecclesiastical affairs, Tardini was adamant that Hurley leave Belgrade. Vatican policy had changed. For reasons of strategy, Oddi needed to become the point man in Yugoslavia. The usefulness of having an American in Belgrade had run its course. As a result of Hurley's stubbornness, the Holy See was being thrown off its new policy course, and Vatican officials were becoming distressed. "The Secretariat of State had to intervene," Oddi wrote in a likely reference to Pope Pius XII, who acted as his own secretary of state from 1944 to 1958, "to convince him to leave his residence in Belgrade." Over a year after he was assigned, Oddi took the helm at the nunciature. "In summary," Oddi explained with diplomatic understatement in his memoir, Hurley's welcome "was not a very warm one."[43]

On September 10, 1950, McGeough informed Hurley in Switzerland that "an official letter is going out to you . . . indicating the possibility or advisability of your coming over [to Rome] *per congedarsi* [on account of getting the sack]." On the advice of McGeough, Hurley traveled to Rome but had to cool his heels for a whole month before Pius agreed to see him in private audience. As in 1940, Pius had to find a way to "elevate" him without promoting him. To smooth out the affair, McGeough notified Hurley "that the Holy Father has in mind the presentation of a special gift as a fitting remembrance of your valued service." In late September the feisty Irish-American and the perceptibly pallid pontiff met in a personal audience and exchanged cordialities after a diplomatic dénouement.[44]

The meeting was tense. Pius understood that Hurley had placed his life in danger early in the mission. Before 1948 he had performed well

in persuading the United States to intervene on the side of the Holy
See. Later in his posting to Yugoslavia, Hurley had represented Vatican
policy seamlessly in dealing with Tito's consolidation of priests' unions.
He had traveled widely, reassured the beleaguered Croatian and Slovenian
bishops, faced a gas attack, and stood up to a dictator. Yet Pius also had
his concerns. Hurley's initial understanding of the Stepinac case was
deeply flawed, and his absence from Belgrade during Stepinac's arrest
a monumental gaffe. What marred Hurley's image the most as he met
with Pius were his recent antipapal ramblings and his bizarre behavior
toward Silvio Oddi, who, though a young monsignor, was a representative
of Pius XII himself.

As a token of esteem and appreciation, the pope bestowed on Hurley
a ruby ring, a gold, emerald-encrusted chalice, and the title of archbishop
ad personam, meaning that he was granted the title of archbishop but could
not claim an archbishopric. In commemoration of his service behind the
Iron Curtain, Pius awarded Hurley the Papal Medal of the Order of Pope
St. Sylvester. But while these distinctions were outwardly prestigious,
ecclesiastically they rang hollow. In the Pontifical Orders of Knighthood,
the Order of St. Sylvester ranks lowest, is sometimes bestowed upon laymen, and can even be awarded to noncatholics. The title archbishop *ad
personam* was an ecclesiastical nicety, since his see was not raised to an
archbishopric. It was perhaps a final jab by Pius to show disapproval
of Hurley's own whining about ecclesiastical rank. Typically, given the
sensitive nature of his assignment and the good work he had done in it,
Hurley would have been kept on in the diplomatic corps, moved to a larger
American see, or even raised to the rank of cardinal. Instead he was sent
back to tiny St. Augustine.[45]

For his part, Hurley looked forward to returning to St. Augustine.
His experiences fighting communism in Yugoslavia had drained him
physically and emotionally. To his mind, Stepinac and the other Croatian
priests who had perished at the hands of the communists were martyrs
for the faith. They had fought the battle and won it through unheralded
moral superiority. In parallel fashion, Hurley vowed to fight the same
"savage battle" against communism outside the Iron Curtain and in his
own backyard. In the fall of 1940 Hurley had dedicated himself to fighting
Nazism and Vatican "passivity" in conjunction with the Department of
State. Ten years later, as he made his way back to the United States, the

Florida bishop vowed to take on domestic communism as fiercely as he had countered Nazism. This time, however, there would be no "parallel endeavor" with the State Department. Hurley had been betrayed in the Balkans. As far as he was concerned, it was precisely the Department of State that was the problem.

CHAPTER TEN

Standing Alone between Church and State

ARRIVING BACK IN St. Augustine in the fall of 1950, Hurley was, as one contemporary described him, "a changed man." He had become more conservative, and much more critical of his country's foreign policy. The American abandonment in Yugoslavia spelled a drastic political reorientation for the archbishop. He felt spurned by his country, its Democratic president, and the party of his earliest political allegiance—the party of Roosevelt. He was politically dislocated, cut asunder from the tenets of Americanism, patriotism, and religious parallelism that he had so eagerly imbibed since his youth. There was no longer a harmonic convergence between Catholic ideals and U.S. political realities.

After returning from his Belgrade posting, Hurley began to share the emerging minority conservative Republican critique of communist expansion, which supported the concept of an aggressive "rollback" of communism rather than its mere "containment." This new orientation set him at odds with the Department of State. Ironically, the government agency he had so willingly sacrificed so much for during World War II and the beginning of the Cold War was now the agency he would engage in battle. The economic "buyout" in Yugoslavia—and the attendant sacrifice of American religious principles—"was the worst buy since Teheran and Yalta, when we lost the Balkans, E. Germany, and the Baltics."[1]

After 1945, Hurley believed that the communists had ascended the throne of tyranny and were now Christianity's "enemy No. 1." In this perception Hurley was no different from many other Catholics. Patrick Allitt has noticed that this change occurred on a broad scale among many American Catholics after World War II. "In the interests of the wartime alliance with Stalin against Hitler, American war propagandists [including Hurley] portrayed the Russians as heroic allies and as determined, sincere patriots. As diplomatic relations between the victors worsened in the years after 1945, American images of Stalin changed rapidly; by 1950, most Americans regarded Stalin and communism with almost the same horror they had reserved for Hitler and Nazism five years before."[2]

After 1948 Yugoslavia became the exception to this rule. Everywhere Hurley looked in the Cold War West, he saw Catholic theological anticommunism squaring agreeably with the rising tide of American political anticommunism. Historian Donald Crosby showed that early strains of Catholic antiradicalism led, by the late 1940s, to a growing convergence "between the views of Catholic leaders and those of American Cold War leaders generally." Patriotism played a crucial role. "When Soviet communism emerged as America's chief foreign rival in the late 1940's," John Haynes has argued, "Catholic anticommunism echoed American Cold War patriotism. . . . American Catholics, in expressing anticommunism, simultaneously affirmed both their Catholicism and Americanism."[3]

Since Hurley's experience was the lone Cold War exception to this rule, the opposite equation held true. The more he attempted to derail America's pro-Tito policy in Yugoslavia, the more he was branded "unpatriotic" by State Department officials. Such a situation had been heretofore unthinkable for the bishop. Yugoslavia's Cold War exceptionalism spelled a chaotic patriotic dissonance for the man who had risked so much for the U.S. government. Through the 1950s, with unflagging determination, Hurley used aggressive public and private means to try to turn American policy. Patriotic passive aggression was his new rule.

His behind-the-scenes anticommunist actions during the 1950s were numerous, creative, and daring. Three examples of his personal battles with the Department of State included a forceful struggle with Ambassador George V. Allen, the commissioning of a historic humanitarian mission to Archbishop Stepinac, and an aggressive theologically anticommunist intervention in 1959 that reverberated from south Florida all the way to the halls of the Kremlin.

THE STRANGE CASE OF AMBASSADOR ALLEN

Through 1951, the United States continued to funnel economic aid to Tito, and the tenor of U.S. government relations with Yugoslavia took on a rather congenial outward appearance. On December 6 Ernie Hill, a reporter for the *Chicago Daily News,* published some controversial remarks by the new U.S. ambassador, George V. Allen, whom Hurley had known in Belgrade. As a former assistant secretary of state, Allen possessed a status that underscored the importance of the new U.S. relationship with Tito. Hill's interview of Ambassador Allen occurred in the midst of a new round of rumors that Archbishop Stepinac was about to be released from prison.

"Slav People Cool to Stepinac Release: Many Still Believe Archbishop Gave Aid to Nazis during War," blared the headlines from Chicago. Hill's column argued for Stepinac's release, also a primary aim of Allen's. "This does not mean that we approve of his activities during the war," Allen explained to Hill; "the Archbishop accepted the title of Vicar Marshall of the Croatian Army, which collaborated with the Nazis. Some five to seven hundred thousand Yugoslavs were killed by Nazi collaborators. Stepinac's part in all this is unquestioned. While we disapprove of jailing clergymen, the Yugoslavs had adequate reason from their viewpoint for trying and condemning him."[4]

Without realizing it, Allen had stirred up a hornets' nest of Catholic controversy. His remarks seemed to officially sanction the injustice of Stepinac's trial. The National Catholic Welfare Conference was outraged, and immediately turned to Hurley for guidance. "As far as I know," one NCWC insider wrote to Hurley, "you are, for all practical purposes, the Church in Yugoslavia." On December 7, 1951, Under Secretary of State James E. Webb sent a priority telegram to Allen in Belgrade advising him to clam up on the Stepinac issue. "Apparently, this story is causing quite a stir among Catholic circles in the United States." The hero Stepinac— martyr, patriot, and "Croatian Mercier"—had been slandered in public, and this time by an American diplomat.[5]

On December 10 the State Department composed a "Restricted Security Memorandum" to define its position on the Ernie Hill story, "which was causing quite a flurry among the Catholic Hierarchy of the country." When Ambassador Allen was contacted to provide his side of the story, he revealed confidentially "that Hill was a careful reporter and that he had no quarrel with [the] interpretation of his remarks." In a separate long telegram to then Secretary of State Dean Acheson, Allen pointed out again that "Hill is a careful newspaperman and I do not think any attempt at correction or denial would be useful or appropriate." In a comment divulging his true opinion of Stepinac, Allen let loose that "the general purport of his [Hill's] article is not far out of line." In other words, Allen believed that Archbishop Stepinac had collaborated with the Nazis during World War II.[6]

Keeping his identity secret, Hurley bombarded the ambassador with personal attacks. His letters and statements appeared above the name of Father John J. Fitzpatrick, the executive editor of the *Florida Catholic*. Fitzpatrick, a conscientious pastor and editor, was hardly an expert on the complexities of Yugoslav internal or foreign policy, and so it is more than likely that Hurley colluded with Fitzpatrick to have the letters sent to State Department. For the next year, letters bearing the signature of "Father Fitzpatrick" of St. Augustine bombarded State Department officials— everyone from Ambassador Allen to the secretary of state.

On December 14, 1951, the *Florida Catholic* printed an editorial bearing the title "The Strange Case of Ambassador Allen." The editorial was carried nationally by the NCWC News Service and appeared in a host of diocesan newspapers. Carrying Fitzpatrick's name, the editorial alleged that Allen had "become the Voice of Titoist Yugoslavia. . . . Mr. Allen has been passing out to his visitors what he is told by the Agitprop of the Communist Party in Yugoslavia." The editorial charged that Allen had relinquished his professionalism as an American diplomat. "Seemingly he looks upon himself as the chief propagandist for the 'forced conversion' to Titoism of the American people."[7]

Through December 1951, the George V. Allen controversy simmered as the NCWC brushed off the explanations of both Under Secretary of State Webb and Secretary of State Acheson as "courteous but most unsatisfactory." Hurley steeled the NCWC for a long fight, describing Archbishop Stepinac as a victim of a vicious American "communist" propaganda campaign. "No man in modern times has been so maligned by Communist propaganda and the garbling of the news by Western and American press correspondents, not a few of whom are at least fellow travelers." Hurley urged the NCWC to take up these observations with Acheson one last time. "Keep the question open," he urged. If the State Department rebuffed them one more time, "I think the entire correspondence should be brought to the attention of the President."[8]

In the end, the NCWC decided against bringing the president into the fray. Hurley, however, refused to give up his aggressive pursuit of Ambassador Allen. Over the next two years he played a shrouded cat-and-mouse game with Allen, attempting to embarrass and trap him in his own words. In early 1952, when Allen addressed the prestigious National Press Club in Washington, D.C., Hurley composed a series of stinging questions about Stepinac and U.S. foreign policy. "Give him no quarter," Hurley scribbled at the bottom of a letter to his Catholic "plant" in the Press Club's audience; "he is a selfish, ambitious, utterly unprincipled person." When one of Hurley's questions about Allen's Ernie Hill column made it through the Press Club censors, it clearly threw the ambassador, leaving him to stumble through the complexities of the Stepinac issue in front of the gathered international press correspondents. Hurley took satisfaction in having won his latest joust.[9]

Within weeks of embarrassing Allen at the National Press Club, Hurley struck again. Getting wind that Allen was to appear on the Jesuit Edmund Aloysius Walsh's weekly television show *Georgetown University Forum*, he wrote to Walsh with more tough questions. Father Walsh agreed to pester Allen for Hurley. This time Hurley unleashed a barrage of questions about the case of Slovene bishop Anton Vovk. One month earlier, while conducting a pastoral visit to Novo Mesta, Slovenia, Vovk had been doused with gasoline and set on fire. For political reasons, doctors at the local hospital had refused to treat him even though the burns threatened his life. Unfortunately for Allen, he knew little about the case.

When Walsh informed Allen that Bishop Vovk "was attacked by a local group of rowdies . . . [who] threw gasoline oil on him and nearly incinerated him on the spot!" the ambassador was again caught off guard. He first deflected the question by asserting that religious matters were internal issues of state, then produced an answer exonerating the Tito regime by arguing that the central government could not be responsible for what a group of "local rowdies" did to a visiting bishop. Hurley's subversive badgering on Stepinac and now Vovk unnerved Allen and the State Department.[10]

On March 17, 1952, "at the suggestion of the Secretary of State's Office," Ambassador Allen privately met with NCWC general secretary Howard J. Carroll to resolve the festering problems of Stepinac and Vovk. Contradicting the secret information contained in his two telegrams to the State Department in December 1951, Allen lied to Carroll and told him "that he had formed no opinion concerning Archbishop Stepinac's alleged activities during the war. . . . Mr. Hill purported to quote me on matters on which I had not formed any opinion whatever." The ambassador indicated that he was "profoundly disturbed and quite understood the perturbation of Catholic circles in the country." Afterward, a won-over Howard Carroll urged Hurley to let Allen off the hook. With some reluctance, Hurley finally acquiesced. But he would not wait very long to counterattack on a new front.[11]

ATOMIC THEOLOGY: THE 1953 STEPINAC MEDICAL MISSION

"Cardinal Stepinac is dying: Tito wants him to die" blasted the first line of an urgent telegram from St. Augustine sent out to all the American bishops. In June 1953 four Yugoslav doctors examined Stepinac, who by then had been elevated by Pius XII to the rank of cardinal. They found him suffering from a rare and incurable blood disease known as polycythemia rubra vera (PRV). The Yugoslav doctors advised moving Stepinac out from his house arrest in Krasic, Croatia, to a large medical facility in Fiume. Stepinac refused to leave Krasic, since to do so he would have to ask permission of the Yugoslav government. "This I will not do," Stepinac made clear, "because I do not consider myself guilty before the Communists." His physicians were distressed by his obstinacy.[12]

In 1953 the usual treatment for PRV entailed a combination of blood-letting along with doses of arsenic. The fact that arsenic was used to treat PRV has presented a delicate sidelight on the current martyrdom cult surrounding Stepinac. When tests were run on Stepinac's remains in 1998 in conjunction with his possible elevation to sainthood, minor traces of arsenic were detected. The presence of the substance generated a flurry of semiofficial statements and numerous press reports contending that Stepinac had been slowly poisoned while in jail. For some, his death in 1960 was "almost certainly as a result of poisoning by his Communist captors."[13]

By the early 1950s, arsenic was giving way to atoms. In 1951 a promising experimental treatment was being perfected in California at the Livermore Laboratories. The head scientist at the Department of Radiological

Medicine was Dr. John H. Lawrence, brother of the Nobel Prize–winning physicist Ernest Lawrence, and a formidable scientist in his own right. Lawrence's new method for treating PRV was to administer small doses of the radioactive isotope phosphorus 32 (P-32). The latest experiments were promising. But the possibility of getting a P-32 isotope treatment to Stepinac seemed nil. It would involve transporting radioactive material thousands of miles, introducing it behind the Iron Curtain, and administering the doses to a controversial but technically condemned war criminal.

If Stepinac were to travel to the United States for such treatment, Tito would never allow him back into Yugoslavia. Tito hoped that the decline of Stepinac's health would do what he was unable to do by threats and pressure —force the cardinal out of the country. Stepinac adamantly refused, and since Pope Pius XII was reluctant to order him out, Tito encountered the prospect of instantly creating a dying martyr.[14]

On July 18 *Osservatore Romano* reported that the archbishop's health "could now be considered critical." The next day Hurley unveiled a plan "to use the good offices of the United States government to obtain permission from the Yugoslav government for an American medical specialist to visit and treat His Eminence." Archbishop Karl J. Alter, the new chairman of the Administrative Board of the NCWC, alerted Apostolic Delegate Amleto Cicognani. Cicognani most likely passed the plan up to Pope Pius XII or a subordinate in the Secretariat of State for final approval. In late July Cicognani informed Alter that there was "no objection on the part of the Holy See" to Hurley's strategy. An emergency NCWC appropriation of 8,000 dollars was wired to Hurley in St. Augustine. In great haste, telegrams from St. Augustine were sent out to all members of the American hierarchy "earnestly begging [them] to intervene . . . with President Eisenhower . . . to make it possible to send a specialist to the bedside of Cardinal Stepinac."[15]

Hurley implored Eisenhower to lend the power of his office to the scheme. "In order to save the life of this illustrious and heroic confessor of the faith," he wired the president, "I beg you to use your good offices to obtain from the Yugoslav government *Laissez-Passer* for a physician. I am confident, Sir, that your powerful help will be appreciated by millions of the persecuted and will bring a special blessing upon you as it will reflect honor upon our country." With the telegrams sent off and the search for a competent medical authority under way, Hurley finally advised Cardinal Stepinac that "everything in our power will be done to bring to you the specialized aid which your malady requires, and I pray that we may be successful."[16]

Again operating behind the scenes, Hurley generated enormous publicity for his plan. First, he targeted a set of U.S. senators who he believed would be friendly to the cause. Since the name Stepinac was by now ingrained in the Catholic consciousness of the nation, senators scrambled to add their names to Hurley's list—and win Catholic votes in the process. Hurley's telegram was read on the floor of the U.S. Senate and published in the *Congressional Record*. Democrat Hubert Humphrey wired "Father Fitzpatrick" that he was "completely in sympathy and was urging President Eisenhower and Secretary Dulles to obtain safe conduct and facilities for specialists to aid Cardinal Stepinac." An unlikely quartet of senators responded to the call. Republican Senators Joseph R. McCarthy and Barry Goldwater wired that they were "looking into the matter," and Democratic Senators Mike Mansfield and Hale Boggs advised that they were "immediately contacting President Eisenhower and Secretary Dulles." Powerful noncatholics such as Senator Leverett Saltonstall of Massachusetts urged the president "to get the proper doctors to the bed-side of the Cardinal."[17]

At the White House, Colonel Paul T. Carroll, the liaison officer who also served as Eisenhower's staff secretary, was put in charge of managing the mechanics of Hurley's uncommon request. Around July 18 the devoutly Catholic Carroll informed Archbishop Hurley that the president had given him the go-ahead to seek a visa for an American physician to visit Stepinac. Carroll then handed matters off to General Walter Bedell Smith, the under secretary of state. Bedell Smith carried out negotiations with the Yugoslav ambassador, Vladimir Popovic, to secure the necessary visa. As Bedell Smith was making his presentation to the Yugoslavs, Hurley notified the State Department that a doctor had been chosen to carry out the sensitive medical mission.[18]

Earlier in the week, Hurley had traveled to Cleveland to consult with some of the finest physicians of his home city, including his niece's husband, Dr. Frank Dzurik, of the Cleveland Clinic. Dzurik explained to Hurley what Dr. John Lawrence was doing in California. Since Hurley hoped to humiliate Tito and save Stepinac at the same time, Dr. Lawrence was the perfect Cold War fit. As director of the Donner Laboratory of Medical Physics at the University of California, Lawrence carried immense international prestige. In addition, as a member of the U.S. Atomic Energy Commission, he symbolized American scientific supremacy. To round out the plan, a sprinkle of holy water was needed. It was decided that Lawrence, a Lutheran, should be accompanied on his mission by Dr. John F. Ruzic, a Croatian-American Catholic who was chief surgeon at Holy Cross Hospital in Chicago. The next step was to contact the Yugoslavs.

Yugoslav ambassador Popovic seemed accommodating if not impressed by the high-level American reaction to Stepinac's health. He assured Walter Bedell Smith that a visa was on the way. In exchange for the visa, the White House agreed to state publicly that "Dr. Lawrence requested the visa privately"—a move that would take the Yugoslav Foreign Office off the hook. Within hours, Drs. Lawrence and Ruzic, along with their six millicuries of P-32, were allowed free passage to the ailing Stepinac. Hurley immediately informed Howard Carroll at the NCWC and Patrick A. O'Boyle, the archbishop of Washington, D.C. "AB O'Boyle and Msgr. Carroll of NCWC," Paul Carroll penned in his White House notes, "are as happy as a couple of bed bugs."[19]

With the departure to Yugoslavia of Drs. Lawrence and Ruzic, Hurley had single-handedly forced presidential action and alleviated the earlier sense that he had been abandoned by the nation's commander-in-chief. He also convinced Pius XII that the value of saving Cardinal Stepinac was worth disrupting diplomatic protocols. By sheer force of will, Hurley had awakened the U.S. Congress to the cardinal's plight and forced the hand of a formerly reluctant Department of State. On July 26, 1953, Dr. Lawrence administered a small injection of P-32 to Cardinal Stepinac. According to reports, the treatment immediately ameliorated his condition.[20]

Although Hurley believed he had moved a mountain of government obstruction, the State Department also had a stake in seeing the cardinal cured. In 1951, developments in nuclear science and medicine were pivotal in projecting the image of the United States as a world power. Cold War media hype boomed that Dr. Lawrence's P-32 treatments would someday cure everything from cancer to polycythemia. Mass-circulation magazines repeated the claims. As the State Department knew, taking on Cardinal Stepinac as a patient would bolster such assertions and ramp up American prestige worldwide. Dr. Lawrence's group at the Donner Laboratory also shared in benefits from the Stepinac visit. Always on the lookout to publicize his experiments, Lawrence had a knack for making atomic medicine newsworthy. By such devices as the Stepinac trip, he was able to cultivate much-needed funding for his research.[21]

After Dr. Lawrence administered his doses of P-32, Hurley breathed a sigh of relief in Cleveland. But before he had time to celebrate, his massive public-relations coup was upset. As he reached across the breakfast table for his copy of the *New York Times* at the Hotel Cleveland, he spied the above-the-fold front-page news: "Two U.S. Doctors Prescribe for Stepinac; Describe Condition as Relatively Good." The report from Zagreb, complete with a large photo of a smiling Dr. Lawrence, then added more disconcerting news. During a press conference in Zagreb, Lawrence had told the international press corps that the cardinal's condition was "not serious" and that he expected him to "get along." Unwittingly derailing Hurley's calculated plan to publicly cast Stepinac in the role of dying martyr, the politically blameless Lawrence added that the Yugoslav communist doctors treating the cardinal were doing a good job and were largely responsible for Stepinac's "relatively good condition."[22]

"Respectfully and urgently request," read the rather panicked telegram from Hurley to Lawrence, "that American newspaper correspondents be told quote no comment now. . . . Best interests of all concerned will be served by withholding comment until after consultations in New York." Unfamiliar with the international ideological concern over Stepinac, Lawrence had no clue that his straight medical assessment and praise for fellow professionals would cause a political backlash.[23]

Meanwhile Lawrence and Ruzic finished their treatment of Cardinal Stepinac. "The moment I saw him I realized I was in the presence of a thoroughly good man," Lawrence wrote in his diary as he wrapped up his visit. "A man of great courage . . . a man who gave the appearance that he would gladly become a martyr." Lawrence administered the P-32 to Stepinac for three days. As he was leaving the cardinal's home he told Stepinac that his prognosis was good, but that "if he could take a calmer view of communism and avoid getting upset, he might get along better." Lawrence flew to Rome and delivered a medical report to Pope Pius XII. "The Pope considers Cardinal Stepinac one of the most inspiring leaders in the spiritual struggle against communistic enslavement."[24]

Hurley flew to New York, met with the returning doctors at Idlewild

Airport, and consulted with them to compose a statement for public release. The new statement contradicted the earlier rosy *New York Times* report. This time the prognosis was grave and threatening. "We are of the opinion that due to the mental stress and strain being constantly experienced by the Cardinal," the doctors emphasized, "medical therapy will be less effective in his present environment."[25]

In the end, Hurley pulled off another public-relations victory. Even the Vatican acknowledged the importance of the medical visit. "The sentiment here, and this authoritatively," reported Monsignor Joseph McGeough from the American desk at the Vatican, "was that the initiative of the intervention of the American surgeons was excellent both from the evident charitable and religious motive and also from the political one." The Catholic cause had been preserved, the communists stymied, Tito foiled, and the cardinal temporarily restored to health. Lawrence was able to publicize the use of his radioisotopes to a worldwide press corps. Yet after the media blitz of the doctors' visit to Stepinac subsided, Hurley's thinking underwent a sudden change.

Instead of expressing gratitude to the State Department, Hurley inexplicably began to castigate it for what he perceived as its unwillingness to help Stepinac. The State Department "did not want to make an effort to save the life of the great hero," he claimed. Posing again as "Father Fitzpatrick," he wrote a letter to Walworth Barbour, director of the State Department's Office of Eastern European Affairs, alleging "coolness . . . reluctance . . . [and] . . . hostility" toward "our endeavor to alleviate the condition of that authentically great man who is Cardinal Stepinac." Barbour was astounded by the ungrateful critique from St. Augustine.[26]

He forwarded Hurley's "Father Fitzpatrick" letter to Walter Bedell Smith. The under secretary of state took up the issue with Howard Carroll of the NCWC, arguing that the barb from St. Augustine was "both unreasonable and uncharitable," especially since the "Department of State . . . was bending every effort toward accomplishing, what . . . partook [in] the nature of a minor miracle." Bedell Smith closed his letter to Carroll "as a Catholic," explaining that he could not see any "specific grounds for complaint."[27]

On November 9, 1953, Bedell Smith received a five-page fusillade from Hurley writing again as Father Fitzpatrick. The letter chilled Catholic relations even further. Incensed that Bedell Smith would write "as a Catholic,"

Hurley launched into a bitter tirade against American policy toward Yugoslavia and the United States' failure to castigate Tito over the Stepinac case. Bedell Smith was the recipient of all Hurley's disgust accumulated since the "sellout" of 1948.

"The maintenance of contact with the enemy and the exertion of constant pressure upon him is a concept which you, as one of our most distinguished and successful generals, understand very well," the "fighting" Florida bishop presumptuously warned the former four-star. "Many of our most capable diplomats are in full agreement with our contention that we failed to apply this primary principle in our dealings with Marshal Tito at a time when we were in a very favorable position. Let us not, therefore, lose our sense of proportion about the amplitude of our victory in the affaire Stepinac."[28]

Bedell Smith was outraged by the "Father Fitzpatrick" missives. The case was moved up to Deputy Under Secretary of State Robert D. Murphy, a Catholic trained by the Jesuits at Marquette University. Murphy was an astute observer of Yugoslav politics, and what was probably unknown to Hurley was that in August 1944 Murphy had conducted extensive face-to-face meetings with Tito on the island of Vis. As a member of Eisenhower's London staff, Murphy had helped to lay the foundation for U.S.-Yugoslav policy. In a particularly candid series of long letters, Murphy took it upon himself to explain the finer points of Yugoslav diplomacy. "Our present policies," Murphy assured the Florida cleric, "do not mean that the traditional attitude . . . in favor of . . . human rights and liberties as we understand them, including complete freedom of religion, has been in the slightest degree diminished." Murphy was sure that his official summary of policy would put an end to the Yugoslav religious controversy.[29]

He was proved wrong. Hurley and Father Fitzpatrick unleashed another barrage of criticism. "This is a Communist government, by definition . . . it is against everything we Christians stand for, and is determined to exterminate us." This was Hurley's simple profession of faith: communism was evil, expansionist, and a common foe. In the past, American government officials had always stood shoulder to shoulder with American Catholics in combatting foreign "isms" bent on the destruction of the West. In Yugoslavia this simple equation was failing to function. The end result for Hurley was cynicism and distrust of government.[30]

"Have you become so naïve," Father Fitzpatrick wrote, echoing Hurley, "as to believe [that Tito does not aim to crush the Catholic church] merely because some Communist diplomat says so, and because such a statement is echoed by a pink American diplomat and pink American correspondents? It would be interesting to know," he sniped, "whether the incomplete information your letter contains was procured by the personal investigation of a trusted American diplomat, or whether it is a hand-out from the Yugoslav Press Office."[31]

"The injection of the words 'pink' and 'naïve,'" Murphy shot back, "into our correspondence is not appreciated. . . . Our national policy toward a given country is established not by one or two individuals, pink or otherwise, but by a highly organized effort . . . presided over by the President. . . . We intend to cooperate [in religious matters] to the extent that the framework of our national policy permits." In other words, Catholic concerns were subordinate to larger U.S. policy issues.[32]

The case was closed. Murphy's forthright response made it clear that any further overtures from Florida to the State Department would go unheeded. With this in mind, Hurley quietly bowed out of the policy realm and restricted his anticommunist efforts to campaigns within his own jurisdiction, where his words had some influence on opinion and events. Using his regional Catholic connections, the *Florida Catholic,* and the power of his episcopal authority, Hurley would look for other ways to make waves up in Washington.

FOR WHOM THE BELLS TOLL

In May 1957 Archbishop Hurley was invited to Washington, D.C., to "occupy a place in the sanctuary" at St. Matthew's Cathedral during the Requiem Mass for Wisconsin Senator Joseph R. McCarthy. Washington's Archbishop Patrick A. O'Boyle gave the eulogy for the controversial anticommunist. With the exception of O'Boyle, Hurley was the highest-ranking Catholic prelate in attendance. He was conspicuously silent on this publicity-steeped occasion, standing quietly in mourning. After the Mass he offered no public comments. Yet his willingness to make the long trip from Florida to Washington was significant, suggesting a personal relationship with the Wisconsin senator, although there is no written record of one in Hurley's personal archive.[33]

McCarthy and Hurley did agree on at least one thing: the State Department was full of "pink" and communist-inspired diplomats. Hurley's attendance at McCarthy's funeral signals his identification as a McCarthy-ite anticommunist. One element that set Hurley apart from Senator McCarthy, however, was that his suspicions of communist infiltration of the State Department were based in a violent personal collision over the Tito-Stalin split. Hurley's misgivings about communists in the State Department were firsthand, visceral, and sealed as early as 1948—nearly two years before McCarthy's first wild public assertions about communist infiltration of the State Department.

Hurley's attendance at McCarthy's funeral was not the first time he paid him tribute, however. In 1954, when McCarthy assailed the U.S. Army with allegations that it was harboring subversives, Hurley was there to back him up at what proved to be the turning point in the senator's public support. Typically, Hurley drew upon martial metaphors. His front-page editorial "General Patton and Senator McCarthy" compared McCarthy's notorious interrogation of Army officers with Patton's infamous 1943 slap of a hospitalized, shell-shocked soldier.

"General Patton was tough. He tolerated no foolishness in the . . . business of war. . . . He sought out the enemy and destroyed him." Likewise, McCarthy was "a tough, hard-driving American when it comes to facing America's enemies. . . . Almost single-handedly he has awakened the nation to the serious threat of communism—the enemy within." In McCarthy, Hurley saw a true patriot who was being denounced by "professors from the halls of Red universities . . . commentators of pink radio and TV networks, by dubious personalities in even in the Army and State Department." McCarthy was the new Patton—"a valiant fighter." Like Patton, McCarthy was "quick with the indignant word and the resounding, well-merited slap."[34]

Though silent at his funeral, Hurley dedicated the front page of the *Florida Catholic* on May 10, 1957, to McCarthy, "the illustrious soldier, Senator, and Christian patriot." Hurley's McCarthyism and distrust of the State Department stayed with him well after he returned from Washington. Just over a year after praying for McCarthy's soul, Hurley took it upon himself to flex his anticommunist muscles and spark the notice of the State Department one last time.

In January 1959 Hurley followed with great interest the travels of the first deputy of the Soviet Union, Anastas I. Mikoyan. In a celebrated junket to the West, the communist leader made his way around the United States on a highly publicized two-week "holiday tour." Soviet premier Nikita Khrushchev had sent Mikoyan not only to meet with President Eisenhower and Secretary of State John Foster Dulles, but also to forge contacts with high-ranking American business leaders.

The chief exponent of increasing the Soviet Union's trade with foreign countries, Mikoyan planned to visit Florida on January 20. His objective was to inspect a state-of-the-art orange juice processing plant and a frozen fruit packaging plant near Tampa. Instead of hospitality, Mikoyan received a delicately veiled threat of violence and an unwelcome warning from the Florida Catholic community headed by Archbishop Hurley.

Hurley was determined to do everything within his ecclesiastical power to dissuade Mikoyan from visiting Florida. In early 1959 he issued a circular letter to priests of the diocese concerning the Mikoyan visit. This was a "Special Order," and under the signature of his Chancellor, Rev. John P. Burns, the archbishop spelled out his battle plan. All of Florida's priests were called to the "front lines."

"We understand that Mikoyan, the Russian Communist, will be in Tampa on 20 January. The Most Reverend Archbishop desires that our priests and people join together on that occasion in a solemn act of religious intercession for the repose of the souls of the tens of millions ruthlessly done to death by Mr. Mikoyan and his associates. It is recommended that this intercession be made through the Holy Sacrifice of the Mass. It is further recommended that the church bells be tolled on this occasion. It would cause tragic discouragement in the hearts of our suffering brethren behind the Iron Curtain, if we were not to manifest our profound sentiments of Catholic solidarity with them on this mournful occasion when Mikoyan defiles the soil of Florida."[35]

The archbishop's protest left nothing to chance. Hurley himself would synchronize and direct the "tolling of the bells." Every Roman Catholic church in the state of Florida—from the lowliest mission station to the historic old cathedral in St. Augustine—was to toll its bells as soon as the Russian stepped aground at Tampa airport. Additionally, Hurley hoped to produce a loud and lengthy clanging of church bells throughout downtown Tampa at the very time the Mikoyan delegation was touring the city. Hurley knew well the symbolic value of tolling bells and of their meaning to people associated with the Balkans. The theological symbolism was powerful, going back to the siege of Constantinople in 1453. This was another clerical call to arms. When Hurley's plan was leaked to the Associated Press, the news service called the impending event "a massive religious intercession."[36]

Hurley also utilized the *Florida Catholic* both to publicize his own opposition to Mikoyan and to persuade the State Department to call off the proposed visit. In the January 16 issue he ran an editorial titled "Unwelcome 'Guest.'" The most remarkable feature of the editorial was its unremitting use of the rhetorical device known variously as preterition or paralepsis. The device, used to most famous effect by Cicero, involves announcing that the speaker (or, in this case, the writer) will "pass over" the mention of dire acts or events, actual or possible—and, by that very mention, bringing them to the audience's attention. Hurley employed this device to offer a subtly veiled threat of violence to the Russian deputy premier.

As if fresh from a reading of Aristotle's *Rhetoric,* Hurley began: "We sincerely hope that there will be no violence touched off by his appearance in our state." He then let loose with a melding of Cold War imagery and classic Catholic McCarthyism. "When the blood-drenched hand of Mikoyan grips the hands of benighted Americans, can it be in friendship? When the Red Russian trader talks commerce, can it be for any other reason than to build a more devastating Kremlin monster-machine with which to grind into dust . . . modern America? Yes, it is not a time for violence." In follow-up commentary, Hurley prodded that "Catholics of Florida do not wish to see violence done to Mikoyan while he is in the state, but neither do they approve of him leaving the United States with the impression that he is welcome here." Hurley's veiled but "blood-drenched" threats deeply affected diplomats in Washington.

"Mikoyan Has Talk with Eisenhower; FLORIDA TRIP CANCELED," read the front-page headline of the *New York Times* on January 18, 1959. The stated reason for canceling Mikoyan's Florida trip was the organized protest of Archbishop Joseph Patrick Hurley. The State Department knew all about Hurley's damage potential, and informed the Russians about the bumptious Florida bishop's anticommunism. From the moment Mikoyan set foot in the United States, there were reports about "worried State Department officials" who feared the possibility of physical violence directed at the deputy premier. Ten days before Mikoyan was due to touch down at Tampa, President Eisenhower appealed for "the courtesy Americans usually show visitors," as administration officials "were fearful that dem-onstrations . . . would get more and more violent . . . as Mikoyan toured the country." Hurley's threatening imagery was the final straw. The State Department knew enough of the man behind the talk to realize that the Soviet–State Department delegation would be taking a real chance if it set foot in Florida.[37]

Deeply impressed with the success of Hurley's anti-Mikoyan venture, in September 1959 William F. Buckley Jr.'s fledgling *National Review* trans-lated Hurley's captivating imagery onto its cover page. As the September 1959 Camp David summit loomed, a cartooned and smiling President Eisenhower shook the "blood-drenched hand" of Nikita Khrushchev. Ear-lier, Hurley had made known to *National Review* editors that he wished to sponsor another "tolling of the bells" as the Soviet premier met with the president. Apparently, he was gagged by higher authorities, presumably at the NCWC, who were falling out with his robust anticommunist ma-neuvers. In the September 12 issue of the *National Review* editor L. Brent Bozell featured a full-column statement by Hurley in which the arch-bishop warned Catholic anticommunists not to be muzzled, presumably as he had been, "while the Red enemy penetrates our lines and carries on an insidious devastating war." Bozell called it a "splendid statement" and promised to push for another "national campaign" of bell-tolling as future Soviet visits unfolded.[38]

Throughout the 1960s Hurley continued to assess world politics as a Cold Warrior bishop. He never stopped commenting privately on world affairs. After 1960, however, his commitment to affecting high-level di-plomacy waned. He no longer had access to high-level policymakers in government. A new set of diplomats had assumed control in the State De-partment. Lacking concern for the international political power of Catholi-cism, that regime passed Hurley by. Hurley steadily turned his attentions to the unique spiritual and social concerns of his burgeoning diocese.

CHAPTER ELEVEN

Last Years, Final Struggles

THE 1960s should have seen Hurley move into his final years at a relaxed pace. He had served the church well as an administrator, bishop, and diplomat. Pope Pius XII had died in 1958 at Castel Gandolfo outside Rome, and Hurley perhaps believed that he could finally put away his misgivings about Pius's earlier political choices. Pius's successor, Angelo Roncalli, took the name Pope John XII and breathed fresh air into the church with his jovial and warm personality. Now bereft of a personal relationship with the pope, by the early 1960s Hurley seemed content to be back in Florida. His energies were devoted to the creation of a Catholic historical museum in St. Augustine, a massive expansion of his diocesan school system, and a renewed commitment to his flock in the Sunshine State. He was content in Florida, and no longer harbored any ambitions to move either up the East Coast or back to Cleveland. He was beginning to consider himself a true Floridian. But if a number of serene golden years were what he was after, religious and political circumstances would prevent him a quiet exit. Much of his inner turmoil was tied to a new financial dislocation in his diocese.

As early as 1940 Hurley had looked at Florida's future and determined that real estate would be the number-one commodity after the war. When Florida real estate prices were cheap during the war, he began to buy small parcels of land for future development as parishes. Slowly at first and with limited resources, he eventually became a major player in the high-stakes Florida real estate game.

Through the 1950s Hurley schooled his pastors in the art of buying real estate. Getting wind of the federal government's intention to build the Eisenhower Interstate System, he instructed his pastors to buy at least seven acres of land within three miles of each proposed interchange. "Tell Father Nolan that I congratulate him on his new property purchase," Hurley wrote to a lieutenant. "If he were to make three or four more similar purchases . . . my congratulations would know no bounds." One hundred fifty-five acres were purchased in St. Petersburg alone in 1950—and such transactions continued each year through the 1950s. Tracts as large as 65 and 72 acres were set aside for diocesan use. In one case Hurley bought a 200-acre parcel and considered turning it into a golf course. Throughout the 1950s Hurley concluded purchases of at least 300,000 dollars' worth of property each year.[1]

Hurley displayed an insatiable drive to raise funds and plow the people's pennies into Florida real estate. By 1954 he had transformed the Catholic church in Florida into a financial giant dwarfing the combined capital assets of both the Florida National Bank of Jacksonville (three million dollars) and the Barnett National Securities Corporation (just over one million dollars). And the buying continued through the late 1950s. Humbly posing as simple country pastors, Hurley's real-estate-savvy monsignori unobtrusively went about the peninsula buying prime 100-acre parcels in the blink of an eye, many of them in south Florida. Neither the other bishops of the United States nor the apostolic delegate in Washington had any real idea what Hurley was doing in his "missionary see." They presumed him irrelevant after his diplomatic career stumbled in 1950.[2]

Perhaps other bishops failed to notice what he was doing because real estate investment was drastically contrary to traditional American Catholic investment practices. Since the late nineteenth century the only "investing" any other American bishop had ever done was in either stocks or bonds. The trend in American diocesan financing was always to diversify strategies in blue-chip investments and keep focused on the long term. Hurley's decision to place his entire diocesan investment capital in a single commodity was truly novel and ultimately providential, but this strategy would soon cause him tremendous stress and personal anxiety as Roman officials, viewing Florida's booming demographic growth, sought to impose a new administrative order on the territory. This would create a legal and fiscal nightmare for Hurley.[3]

"THE RAPE OF ST. AUGUSTINE"

In early 1958 the Holy See concluded that population trends in Florida demanded that the Diocese of St. Augustine be divided in two, creating another diocese in south Florida. Peculiarly, given that the lines of communication in Florida perennially ran vertically from north to south, the Holy See decided to create the Diocese of Miami by ecclesiastically splitting the state horizontally, near Orlando, Florida. Hurley was neither advised nor consulted about this move. Apparently Vatican planners, including Pope Pius XII, who made the final decision to divide the diocese, had written off Hurley as inconsequential.

When the creation of the Diocese of Miami was announced in early 1958, its new bishop, Coleman F. Carroll, naturally expected the assets from the Diocese of St. Augustine to be comprised of "stocks, bonds, mortgages, and other forms of intangibles." According to church practice and canon law, these assets were to be divided right down the middle. Little did Bishop Carroll know that Hurley's investments lay in very tangible and desirable tracts of Florida real estate. When Bishop Carroll's attorney informed Hurley that the deeds to *all* the church property in the sixteen southernmost counties "should be executed to transfer title," groans went up in the chancery in St. Augustine. In 1958 Hurley had exactly 159 gigantic undeveloped "spec," or speculation, properties in south Florida.[4]

Bishop Carroll, his lawyer Clyde Atkins, and the apostolic delegate were shocked to learn that Hurley's diocese had absolutely no stocks and bonds to transfer to Miami. At first Carroll was horrified to think that he would have to start building his new diocese from scratch and was deeply upset with Hurley for investing all of his massive fundraising in Florida's "good ground." But initial shock soon turned to incipient covetousness as lawyers and accountants began to check the record of holdings. They nearly fell off their chairs when tallying the returns on Hurley's unearned increment. Since 1940, the return on his purchases had skyrocketed astronomically beyond any conceivable blue-chip investment.

Consistent with his fighting spirit, Hurley was obsessed with claiming his fair share for his new northern Diocese of St. Augustine. If he could not recoup something from the south Florida purchases, he believed, his north Florida diocese would "be stripped of everything save its history." To keep Bishop Carroll at bay, in 1959 Hurley created the Catholic Burse Endowment Fund, Inc., a "paper" holding corporation of the Diocese of St. Augustine. He began signing over the south Florida deeds to the Catholic Burse Endowment Fund—effectively signing the disputed southern lands over to himself. The public transfer of deeds aroused a storm of protest from Miami diocesan officials. Accusations of "obstructionist tactics" were fired back and forth between Miami and St. Augustine. Eventually the signing over of deeds was stopped, the apostolic delegate was called in, and both sides hunkered down for what was to become a long and hotly contested duel of episcopal authority and ecclesiastical legal procedure.[5]

At every turn, Hurley refused to back down. In August 1959 the Vatican stepped in. The Sacred Consistorial Congregation set up a three-man commission to adjudicate the dispute. In May 1960 the commission ruled that Hurley was to sign over all landed property to Bishop Carroll, with monetary remuneration assessed at the "book value" of the original purchase price. Tens of millions of dollars of appreciation were swept away with the stroke of a pen. Moreover, the decision went contrary to all prior adjudications dealing with stocks or bonds, in which the appreciative value was halved. "Archbishop, you don't need a lawyer," Hurley's attorney Daniel A. Naughton quipped after reading the memo from the commission; "you need a sheriff—these people are robbers!" Hurley was given thirty days to start deeding over the lands.[6]

Hurley refused, and a second Vatican commission was constituted, this time with a number of American cardinals and archbishops reviewing the case. Their decision was to be final and would be backed by the Sacred Consistorial Congregation in Rome. Through tactics of delay and counterappeal, Hurley kept this second commission at work for the next four years. According to one diocesan source, Archbishop Egidio Vagnozzi, then apostolic delegate to the United States, warned Hurley from the outset that "from this there shall be no appeal." Finally, on July 2, 1964, the commission's recommendation was delivered: the lands of the Diocese of St. Augustine were to be handed over to the Diocese of Miami at "book value." Hurley "assembled his attorneys on the following Monday to prepare an appeal."[7]

As if defying the apostolic delegate had not been enough, in a wildly

symbolic move aimed at winning Pope Paul VI's heart, Hurley jetted all
his diocesan consultors to Ostia, Italy—the place of St. Augustine's legen-
dary fourth-century rapturous mystical vision of God. There the pope
was reportedly greatly taken aback when he saw Hurley and his whole
entourage smiling and waving from a distance as he toured the town. On
August 28, the Feast of St. Augustine, the entire coterie sent unsolicited
written greetings to the pope and hand-delivered them to the Vatican. At
the same time, Hurley began to feel that Archbishop Cicognani—whose
frosty response to his 1941 speech no doubt still festered—was behind
"the decision." In 1961 the authoritative Amleto Giovanni Cicognani
was appointed secretary of state of the Holy See. "V. [Vagnozzi] said that
Cicognani was losing his grip at the end of his Washington tour," Hurley
penned, "and then they made him Secretary of State! What is the 'book
value' of Cicognani?" he wondered.[8]

In 1962 Hurley met Cicognani at a public function in Chicago. When
he offered his congratulations on being named secretary of state, "he
threw my hand aside," Hurley recorded. "He was petulant when I grinned
[back] at him." Ultimately, Hurley's would prove to be a lone voice crying
in the Everglades. A third and irrevocable decision would be promulgated
in Rome. "If this case is settled on the basis of the book value," Hurley
wrote hyperbolically, "it will go down in history as the most outstanding
case of injustice in the whole history of the Catholic Church in the United
States. . . . This is the rape of St. Augustine."[9]

On November 18, 1965, Hurley received word from Rome that any
further appeal would be thrown out. The news came from his old friend
G. B. Montini, now reigning as Pope Paul VI. "It goes without saying that
we accept the decision of the Holy See," Hurley wrote "with customary
discipline and obedience." Weary and worn, the embattled bishop finally
capitulated. "I was threatened to be amenable," he later wrote in his diary,
"or 'suffer the consequences'"—a possible reference to his removal as
bishop or other grave measure.[10]

The subdivision of the diocese consumed Hurley's energies for seven
years. Moreover, his support structure of years past was crumbling. His
beloved mentor, Edward Cardinal Mooney, died on October 25, 1958, just
two months after the deliberations with Miami got underway. Hurley was
now seventy years old and needed rest. Surely, he believed that his golden
years would be quiet and tranquil. The church, however, was anything

but tranquil during the 1960s, and the tumult of church transformation gave Hurley little time to rest.

A CHURCH TRANSFORMED: VATICAN II

On January 25, 1959, Pope John XXIII announced his decision to convene a general ecumenical council at the Vatican in what one commentator termed "a gesture of serene boldness." The move by Pope John was truly courageous. Inside the church, new theological currents were wending their way stealthily below a surface of monolithic theological stability. When the "spirit and dialectic"—a spirit of questioning previously held theological principles—eventually surfaced at Vatican II from 1962 to 1965, the church found itself in the midst of what historian Philip Gleason has described as "a spiritual earthquake."[11]

For a Cold Warrior bishop such as Joseph Patrick Hurley, the council augured changes for the worse for world Catholicism. In responding to the call of the council, Hurley acted quickly in 1962 to assemble an entourage and attend each session. Theologian Raymond E. Brown, S.S., a Sulpician priest of the Diocese of St. Augustine and a future member of the Pontifical Biblical Commission, recalled that Hurley would discuss the theological concerns with him after each evening's dinner. "Hurley was very interested in all that was going on, but his own tendencies were conservative." Moreover, "his friends on the Roman scene—particularly Alfredo Ottaviani—were conservative and he hoped that they would succeed."[12]

Hurley's contribution to the council reflected his conservative views. His first active involvement came on September 22, 1965, during the fourth and final session. He was dismayed by what he saw as an attempt to overlook the conspicuous threat of communism in conjunction with inordinate attention to the Holocaust and Jewish relations. At the forefront of his mind was the case of Cardinal Stepinac. In his only oral declaration at the council, Hurley reproached his fellow bishops for speaking out vigorously in defense of the Jews while leaving their persecuted Catholic brethren behind the Iron Curtain to languish in communist jails. "It has been put forth that we must speak of the persecution of the Jews," he declared to the bishops. "Are we not, then, allowing ourselves to be silent concerning the persecution of our own Catholic brothers?" Hurley implored the council to undertake a "solemn declaration of honor to the modern day Martyrs and Confessors" of the faith behind the Iron Curtain—the "silent church" still under the yoke of communist persecution. Misreading the times, Hurley was unaware that theological anticommunism was being de-emphasized at the council. Moreover, any de-emphasis of the Holocaust was not where the council was heading.[13]

Earlier, in November 1963, as the document that would become the landmark Jewish-Christian statement *Nostra Aetate* (In Our Times; October 28, 1965) was being debated, Hurley had written briefly on "Anti-Semitism" in his notebook. "The anti-defamation people sometimes do more harm than good in their over-persuasiveness." In a very strange recommendation, he suggested that "they should bow out and hand the job over to [the comedian] Buddy Hackett. He is wholesome, delightfully Jewish. You cannot be anti-Jew with him around." That such thoughts were penned as the "potentially epochal" document on Christian-Jewish relations was being reviewed shows a stunning undercomprehension of the document's importance. "No God, No morals, Sensuality," he scratched despondently above his comments on Jews and antisemitism.[14]

Social disruptions were taking place all across the theological landscape. By the end of Vatican II Hurley would see his old protector, Alfredo Cardinal Ottaviani, publicly challenged by another cardinal. A spontaneous round of applause for Ottaviani's rival—as progressives defiantly broke the conciliar protocols—was described as the most dramatic moment of the council, "an electric moment," as one St. Augustine priest observed. And through it all, the "silent church" of communist persecution was moved entirely out of the debate.[15]

Peter Hebblethwaite has argued that the theological conservatives at the council objected to what was being put forth by the progressive bishops because they determined much of the new theology not to be authentically "Christian." The conservatives were shocked to see that traditional theology based in divine-command ethics was being eroded by a theology more in sympathy with human nature. Hurley shared this view. "There is a natural theology," he commented privately, "but *America* Catholics—*Commonweal* [liberal] Catholics have substituted nature for grace; psychology for morality."[16]

New theologians gradually came to the fore at Vatican II. Thinkers such as Karl Rahner, S.J., Rev. Hans Küng, and John Courtney Murray, S.J., took the mantle as the latest generation of Catholic theological lights. Hurley, sulking and distraught at the boldness of the new theologians, could only comment gloomily. "The clerical 'teen-agers' are jubilant about their victory. Like the Sisters, they behave like bobby-soxers. Scream at every call for freedom—every clamor for youth. They are the followers of Küng, Rahner, et al., as American girls were of Sinatra. . . . Hans Küng is to theology," he added, "what Elvis Presley is to music." Theologian and council expert John Courtney Murray, S.J., was "incapable of a simple, declarative sentence" and "a master of double-talk."[17]

"It occurred to me," Hurley's young priest-secretary recalled about his time at Vatican II, "that during the Council Hurley had few friends." The Yugoslav bishops were the only church delegation that seemed to respond to him warmly. Surrounded by priests from his diocese who knew little of his secret diplomacy at Rome or in Yugoslavia, he became more detached from the council proceedings. Other American bishops could not begin to comprehend the battles he had fought against Marshal Tito, and most especially on behalf of Cardinal Stepinac. "Hurley was brilliant in many ways," his former Vatican II secretary recalled, "but a loner who had to be in charge at all times." As the 1960s wore on, Hurley found that he could not control the social, religious, and cultural forces that clashed with his pronounced conservatism.[18]

The socioreligious commotion of the council did not forsake Hurley when he returned to Florida in 1965. Even as he was digesting Vatican II, he was thrust into the eye of a storm in St. Augustine involving perennial questions of race, theology, social justice, and southern culture. Now Hurley was faced with a rare opportunity for spiritual and public leadership.

IN THE EYE OF THE STORM

"St. Augustine became a landmark in the Civil Rights era when the Reverend Martin Luther King, Jr., and the Southern Christian Leadership Conference (SCLC) selected it as a target city in 1964," historian David R. Colburn has written. King's activity in St. Augustine foisted both Hurley and the tiny resort city directly into the path of the oncoming civil-rights hurricane. During the summer of 1964 King intended to make St. Augustine "a major area of civil rights activity and media attention."[19]

King and his advisors understood St. Augustine's history when they selected it as a "target city." Part of their calculation included a role they hoped Catholicism would play. Unlike many southern cities, St. Augustine had a very large Catholic population, accounting for at least one-third of the city's churchgoers. "More than any other church," Colburn has written, "the Catholic church had the greatest opportunity to influence the racial response of the community." Andrew Young, executive director of the SCLC, noticed the potential influence for good that the Catholic church might bring to bear in St. Augustine. "In as Catholic an area as St. Augustine," Young noted privately, "the Church could be a big influence."[20]

There are indications in the historical record that as the violence escalated and national media attention focused on St. Augustine in the summer of 1964, King had it in mind to ask Hurley to act as a co-arbitrator for the civil-rights marchers. This meant that King would temporarily share a role with Hurley as a civil-rights negotiator. Since King's staff considered Hurley "the most important religious figure in the community," he would be called upon to create an alliance for civil rights.[21]

On June 11, 1964, King arrived in St. Augustine and began his efforts in earnest. He was arrested as he tried to integrate Monson's Motor Lodge, a popular hotel in the heart of the town. Violence grew through June as thirty consecutive days of sit-ins, evening marches, and swim-ins made national television news. On June 25 Klansmen mounted a bloody attack on a group of SCLC workers as they prepared for a sit-in. "This reign of terror cannot be stopped short of intervention by the Federal Government," King cabled the Justice Department, beseeching it to "do something about the brutality and violence" in St. Augustine.[22]

Finally, with the open violence demanding a response, King made a direct appeal to Hurley. "Dear Sir," the long June 11 telegram read, "recent events in St. Augustine belie the concept of democracy and ridicule the American dream of freedom and dignity for all mankind." King presumed to ask Hurley to use his leadership and high standing in the community to work for change. Since King had written the telegram from his cell in the St. John's County jail, he hoped that as a Christian leader of high standing Hurley would step forward alongside the now leaderless marchers. "Hatred and violence reigned in America's oldest city," King wrote in part. "Will you use your good will and influence . . . to unite the forces of reason and humanity within the city to bring about a just solution to the racial crisis here[?]" Put off by what he saw as the audacity of Dr. King, Hurley made no immediate reply.[23]

The SCLC, however, kept the pressure on Hurley. On June 18 Andrew Young contacted the St. Augustine chancery in order to arrange for a face-to-face meeting between Dr. King and Archbishop Hurley. Hurley was now posed with a dilemma, since he had not yet responded to King's June 11 telegram. Anxious to avoid the embarrassment of not responding to a public figure then being considered for the Nobel Peace Prize, Hurley nevertheless continued to balk at a personal meeting and instead whisked off a telegram in response to King's. His aim was to contrast Catholic prestige with what he understood as King's lawless behavior. "The Catholic Church in St. Augustine has used its influence consistently to achieve equal justice under law and Christian Fraternity among people of different races. All our churches are open to all people. We have taught the lesson of justice and fraternity not only in words but also by example. . . . The best interests of St. Augustine will be served in the difficult period of transition by refraining from any act which might occasion or perpetuate ill will or hatred among our people. Joseph P. Hurley." This was the only contact that Archbishop Hurley would ever have with King.[24]

As argued elsewhere, King's unsuccessful courtship of Hurley shaped how the SCLC would relate to Catholic bishops as the movement went forward. New tactics were devised and episcopal leadership circumvented in creative ways as Catholics took a more prominent role in the marches, particularly at Selma, Alabama, in March 1965. After St. Augustine and his jail-cell rebuff, King would not take Christian sympathy—and particularly the Christian sympathy of American Catholic bishops—for granted. King seemed genuinely puzzled by Hurley's lack of response. For his part, Hurley was revolted by King's use of "massive non-violence which invariably led to violence."[25]

The violence and turmoil of 1964 left Hurley discouraged and drained. He became bewildered and shocked by what he saw occurring in his beloved church, his adopted hometown, and the world. Distress at the council had been followed by civil disobedience at home. As Florida Catholic historian Michael McNally has pointed out, "the burdens of office were beginning to wear on him visibly." What Archbishop Hurley really needed in 1965 was rest and mental relaxation, things that neither his church nor his country was willing to offer during the final months of his life.[26]

In October 1967 Hurley traveled to Rome to attend the international Synod of Bishops called by Pope Paul VI. Although Hurley approached the trip as a working vacation, the specter of communist persecution hung over the inaugural worldwide gathering of bishops. Stefan Cardinal

Wyszynski of Poland famously was refused permission by the Polish communists to travel to Rome and attend the all-important synod. In Kraków, a little-known archbishop, Karol Wojtyla, announced his own personal boycott of the synod and protested the communist action against his mentor Wyszynski. Blessing this move, Pope Paul VI commanded that Wojtyla's name be inscribed on the attendance lists of the synod, even though he was not present. Hurley was impressed by this strong show of anti-communist Catholic solidarity. "The power is in Catholic Poland," he penned thoughtfully. In a startlingly accurate premonition of Wojtyla's ascent to the papacy as Pope John Paul II in 1978, and his role in fracturing international communism twenty-five years later, Hurley dashed off his final thoughts of late October 1967: "Poland—Catholic Poland—will break the teeth of Communism—will win over Russia."[27]

At the same time, recollections of his work under Pope Pius XII flooded back. To Hurley, Pius was hardly the fighter that Wyszynski, Wojtyla, and Paul VI were proving to be. He recalled his final showdown with Pius, almost fifteen years earlier, over the Lawrence and Ruzic medical mission to the ailing Cardinal Stepinac in 1953. "Pius XII did not want to receive Drs. Lawrence and Ruzic," he confided to his diary. "I was asked to keep them out of Rome." Pius, according to Hurley, wanted "to avoid the impression that they were sent by the Holy See." Characteristically, Hurley had stared down Pius and ordered the doctors' entourage to head for Rome. "But they went to Rome and were kindly received," he divulged as if airing one final triumph over a dithering Pius. "Thus," he recorded, "the Holy See did not want to make an effort to save the life of a great hero."[28]

As the bishops' synod wore on, Hurley would have his own health issues to confront. In late October he became ill and sought the counsel of some Italian doctors. At the Gemelli Hospital in Rome, Hurley's doctors informed him that he was suffering from anemia and advised that if he felt well enough, he should travel back to the United States and consult his personal physicians. Hurley jetted back to Florida on October 27, but during the journey he became more seriously ill. Arriving in Orlando, he had to be removed from the plane on a stretcher and rushed to hospital. There doctors concluded that the original diagnosis was completely wrong: Hurley was suffering from acute leukemia, and it would be his terminal disease.

On October 30, 1967, Archbishop-Bishop Joseph Patrick Hurley died at Mercy Hospital in Orlando. His closest associates repaired to the hospital and prayed in its chapel. This was a fitting gathering place, since some years earlier Hurley had dedicated the altar to his mother, Anna Durkin Hurley. The *New York Times* chronicled Hurley's life in two columns, accentuating his time in Belgrade. Hurley, however, would have been more appreciative of William F. Buckley Jr.'s tribute on the pages of the *National Review.* The father of modern conservatism called Hurley "among the most adamant and outspoken critics of Communism in the United States," primarily "since he knew first hand its potential for evil." New tributes would take form within the St. Augustine cathedral sanctuary.[29]

A Requiem Mass was celebrated for Hurley at the historic cathedral in St. Augustine on November 6. Paul J. Hallinan, archbishop of Atlanta and a native Clevelander, was the principal celebrant. In Rome, Pope Paul VI was reportedly deeply saddened to hear of Hurley's death, calling him "a collaborator in days past." Hurley's former auxiliary, Bishop Thomas J. McDonough, preached the eulogy. "In any walk of life," McDonough concluded, "his talents would have been recognized and utilized." McDonough's observation was correct. In fact, during his lifetime Hurley strode two distinct paths. For the historian, Hurley's life is consequential precisely because of his service to both church and country. At various times his life melded the two. At other points, service to country seemed to gain the upper hand. His patriotism, the product of an "Americanized" immigrant church, informed his perceptions of Vatican clumsiness in dealing with the dictators. Throughout his career, questions about the reconciliation between church and state, allegiance to a Roman perspective or to an American imperative, loomed large. His military instincts—perhaps a tribute to his initial vocation—left him to fight in the breach between papal tiara and American flag.[30]

In the era before World War II, Hurley was the most vocally antifascist, pro-American, and prodemocratic prelate stationed in the Vatican. In retrospect, since we now understand the full evil of Nazism, Fascism, and the death camps, his antifascist attitude may strike modern readers as only fitting, obvious, and proper. But in the context of the time, which was marked by American incomprehension about the death camps and the delicacy of Pope Pius XII's diplomacy, he stands out as a broadcaster of realities, a forecaster of truth, and a man of moral courage. His conscious and daring decision to work secretly with William Phillips inside the Vatican indicates a greater allegiance to his own country's antifascist foreign policy than to the policies of a church which he considered ambivalent.

Hurley's resolute antifascism did not, however, prevent him from maintaining a tragic myopia concerning Catholic-Jewish relations. His strange idiosyncratic personal attitude concerning the Jewish people in the 1930s led to disastrous results when dealing with the antisemitic radio priest, Father Charles E. Coughlin. In the end, Hurley's patriotism won out over his religious sensibilities. His memorandum to G. B. Montini and the Congregation for Extraordinary Ecclesiastical Affairs, urging that Coughlin be silenced for his "unpatriotism," was deeply flawed in view of the Nazi regime's European use of Coughlin as a propaganda tool. Yet, writing from Rome, his observations and advice on the Coughlin question offer to historians of twentieth-century America for the first time the notion that Father Coughlin cannot be viewed strictly as a domestic American Catholic problem.

At the same time, Hurley's writings reveal that U.S. diplomatic officials were also forced to deal with the international ramifications of the Coughlin phenomenon. Government officials believed that the pope and his curia could exercise power over the ornery midwestern priest, and they were frustrated with the Vatican's hesitancy. They also failed to recognize that the Holy See might be concerned about a Fascist backlash. In contrast, by early 1943 Hurley's prejudices, absorbed in the immigrant neighborhoods of Cleveland, had so lessened that he could see, where Pope Pius XII publicly could not, that the death camps of Europe were a strict issue of Catholic Christian social consciousness.

Hurley's secret work stateside from 1940 to 1945 tied him to the U.S. Department of State more than any other bishop in the country. The lines of allegiance became so blurred that by 1941 even his mentor Archbishop Mooney questioned whether his allegiances were lining up squarely with the Holy See. After 1941 Hurley began to distance himself from the cautious Mooney and to meet privately with U.S. officials. Unbeknownst to even the most powerful American bishops, he engaged in black propaganda efforts at the behest of the State Department, the Office of War Information, and the president. Under Secretary of State Sumner Welles was instrumental in "turning" Hurley toward a predominantly pro-Roosevelt position—spurning Vatican wartime neutrality—and becoming an effective Catholic propagandist for the administration.

Of all Hurley's contact with the U.S. government, his collaboration with the U.S. embassy in Belgrade probably represents his most daring, comprehensive, and, for a time, effective diplomacy. From 1945 to 1948 Hurley and his staff worked with a sense of naïve cheerfulness in conjunction with American Cold War diplomatic planners. It was Hurley who, at what seems to be the first time on record, influenced the U.S. government to make direct representations to a host country's head of state on behalf of the Vatican. All this changed in 1948. As U.S. policy moved from confrontation to political "containment," Hurley became disillusioned with the government he had presumed for so long was in parallel accompaniment with Vatican Cold War interests. As the United States nestled up to communist dictator Marshal Josip Broz Tito, he was horrified to learn that the United States would no longer be supportive of the Christian goals he believed were inherent in good government. The "blessed harmony" of earlier days had fragmented disastrously, with America apparently no longer guided by Christian principles.

Hurley was also dissatisfied with the course of Vatican policy in the Balkans. Early in his mission, he had believed that Pope Pius XII was willing to compromise with Marshal Tito over Archbishop Stepinac, thereby exhibiting a weakness that Hurley had identified as far back as the 1930s. He also may have felt that Pius underappreciated the ecclesiastical battle he had waged in the Balkans. The gem-studded chalice that the pope presented to Hurley in 1950 was unceremoniously deposited at the Catholic Student Center in Gainesville, Florida—far from the high-profile and historic cathedral in St. Augustine. During the 1960s, while on a visit to Gainesville, Hurley asked to view the chalice. But "from the way he spoke and viewed it, it was obvious that he did not give it any personal value," a diocesan curate recalled puzzledly.[31]

The break between Tito and Stalin deepened Hurley's cynicism. He began to adopt McCarthyite language in his correspondence with U.S. State Department officials. His later years were consumed with fighting the politically generated hybrid of "Titoism" at home and alerting America to the internal dangers of communism. After his 1953 medical mission to the languishing Cardinal Stepinac, he stopped dwelling on the bad blood that existed between himself and Pope Pius XII. Dismissing the pontiff as a weak fighter against communism, Hurley turned his considerable clandestine talents to the domestic scene. In 1959, through a masterstroke of black propaganda of the type he had perfected during World War II, the feisty bishop of St. Augustine, Florida, single-handedly prevented a member of the Soviet Politburo from setting foot in Florida.

In terms of church-state relations, Hurley embodies the "assimilation problematic" central to the cultural investigations of historian Philip Gleason. Formed in an era when Roman Catholic philosophy, practice, patriotism, and even prayer melded harmoniously with American ideals, Hurley's allegiance to the American system and the "blessed harmony" between the two was shaken to the core as American Catholics entered the 1960s. The tensions that emerged throughout Hurley's career were grounded in the reconciliation of his Catholic identity with American pluralism, both political and—especially in his dealings with Dr. Martin Luther King Jr.—cultural. His clashes with Pope Pius XII reflect his difficulties in reconciling American patriotism and American Catholic socialization with papal authority.

In March 1964 Pope Paul VI appointed the Vatican's first permanent observer to the United Nations, thereby endorsing that body's support for human rights. In January 1984 President Ronald Reagan appointed a Catholic layman, William A. Wilson of California, as the first U.S. ambassador to the Holy See. Ostensibly these new diplomatic contacts marked the end of the secrecy that characterized the Hurley years. Yet at both the United Nations and the State Department, Vatican policy sometimes collides with U.S. foreign policy on issues such as population control and just-war doctrine. For all their intensity and goodwill, formal diplomatic relations with the Holy See have not yet swept away the tensions of American Catholic identity in the life of the nation. Many of these abiding tensions are reflected in the life, the work, the struggles, and the diplomacy of Archbishop-Bishop Joseph Patrick Hurley.

NOTES

The following abbreviations are used in the notes.

AAD   Archives of the Archdiocese of Detroit

ADSA   Archives of the Diocese of St. Augustine

ADSS   *Actes et documents du Saint Siège relatifs à la seconde guerre mondiale,*
          ed. Pierre Blet, Angelo Martini, Robert A. Graham, and Burkhart
          Schneider, 11 vols. (Rome: Libreria Editrice Vaticana, 1965–1981)

FRUS   *Papers Relating to the Foreign Relations of the United States* (Washington,
          D.C.: U.S. Government Printing Office, various years)

HAMC   Hurley Administration Microfilm Collection, ADSA

MAUC   Mooney Administration Uncataloged Collection

NCCJ   National Conference of Christians and Jews

NCCIJ   National Catholic Conference for Interracial Justice

NCWC   National Catholic Welfare Conference

PSF   President's Secretary's File

RG   Record Group

USNA   U.S. National Archives, Archives II, College Park, Maryland

INTRODUCTION

1. Rev. Michael J. McNally has chronicled Hurley's important pastoral role in twentieth-century Florida Catholicism. See his *Catholicism in South Florida* (Gainesville: University of Florida Press, 1982) and *Catholic Parish Life on Florida's West Coast, 1860–1968* (St. Petersburg, Fla.: Catholic Media Ministries, 1996).

2. W. Thomas Larkin, "25 Who Mattered," *St. Petersburg Times Turn Magazine,* November 28, 1999, http:www.sptimes.com/News/112899/Floridian/25 _who_mattered.shtml (accessed February 26, 2007).

3. Frank J. Coppa, introduction to "Pope Pius XII and the Cold War: The Post-War Confrontation between Catholicism and Communism," paper presented at the conference "Religion and the Cold War," Royal Institute of St. Catherine's, London, March 3, 2000.

4. Guenter Lewy, review of Saul Friedländer, *Pius XII and the Third Reich: A Documentation, Political Science Quarterly* 81 (1966): 681.

5. Philip Gleason, "The Catholic Church in American Public Life in the Twentieth Century," *Logos* 3 (2000): 87.

6. Ibid.; William A. Halsey, *The Survival of American Innocence: Catholicism in an Era of Disillusionment, 1920–1940* (Notre Dame, Ind.: University of Notre Dame Press, 1980), 2.

7. Michael Williams, *American Catholics in the War* (New York: Macmillan, 1921), quoted in Gleason, "Catholic Church in American Public Life," 88.

8. T. Michael Ruddy, *The Cautious Diplomat: Charles E. Bohlen and the Soviet Union, 1929–1969* (Kent, Ohio: Kent State University Press, 1986), 1.

9. Joseph P. Hurley, "Let Christians Take the Lead!" editorial, *Florida Catholic*, April 9, 1943.

10. *The Times* (London), July 5, 1940.

CHAPTER 1. A PRIEST IN THE FAMILY

1. William L. Shirer, *Berlin Diary: The Journal of a Foreign Correspondent* (New York: Alfred A. Knopf, 1941), 514; *Ciano's Diary, 1939–1943*, ed. Malcolm Muggeridge (London: W. Heinemann, 1947), 277.

2. Caroline Phillips's notes on a conversation with Italian foreign minister Galeazzo Ciano, diary "Rome, February 25, 1940 to July 11, 1940," n.d., Caroline Drayton Phillips Papers (hereafter Caroline Phillips Papers), box 5, Schlesinger Library, Radcliffe Institute, Harvard University; Caroline D. Phillips journal, September 13, 1939–February 24, 1940, [2], ibid. Phillips was somewhat hopeful when Cardinal Pacelli was elected Pope Pius XII, trusting that he would stand up to the dictators when she wrote in her diary on March 4, 1939, that "Cardinal Pacelli was elected Pope . . . to the joy of everyone except perhaps Hitler and the Duce. . . . He has a heavy burden to bear and he has the qualities of leadership with holiness and austerity, I think." I am grateful to Mrs. Caroline Drayton Phillips's daughter, Mrs. Anne Bryant, for allowing me to view the 1940 journal.

3. Diary "Rome, February 25, 1940 to July 11, 1940," n.d., Caroline Phillips Papers, box 5. The best study of the meeting is John S. Conway's "The Meeting between Pope Pius XII and Ribbentrop," *Canadian Catholic Historical Review* 25 (1968): 103–116. Conway accurately calls the meeting a mutually "unsuccessful diplomatic encounter."

4. Caroline Phillips's notes on a conversation between Pius and Ribbentrop, as told to her by William Phillips, in diary "Rome, February 25, 1940 to July 11, 1940," March 29, 1940, box 5; unnamed correspondent inscription on news-

clipping titled "Vaticano," n.d., General Correspondence Folder, February–July 1940, ibid., box 3.

5. Robert E. Sherwood, *Roosevelt and Hopkins: An Intimate History* (New York: Harper, 1948), 398.

6. Joseph P. Kennedy to Sumner Welles, July 17, 1939, Joseph P. Kennedy Papers Collection, series 8.2.7, box 110, Sumner Welles folder, John F. Kennedy Presidential Library, Boston; John S. Conway, "Myron C. Taylor's Mission to the Vatican, 1940–1950," *Church History* 44 (1975): 85.

7. George J. Gill, "The Myron C. Taylor Mission, the Holy See, and 'Parallel Endeavor for Peace,' 1939–1945," *Records of the American Catholic Historical Society of Philadelphia* 98 (1987): 30.

8. On the interview see personal notes, 1940, Papers of Archbishop Joseph P. Hurley (hereafter Hurley Papers), ADSA; on the paucity of information about the meeting see Gerald P. Fogarty, S.J., *The Vatican and the American Hierarchy from 1870 to 1965* (Wilmington, Del.: Michael Glazier, 1982), 266. The official Vatican diplomatic documents mention nothing of Taylor's final interview; see *ADSS*, vol. 4.

9. "Diplomats on the Move," *Time*, September 2, 1940, 38.

10. Andrew M. Greeley, *The Irish Americans: The Rise to Money and Power* (New York: Harper & Row, 1981), 75; Lawrence J. McCaffrey, *The Irish Diaspora in America* (Bloomington: Indiana University Press, 1976), 61; U.S. Census Office, "Statistics for Selected Industries in Cuyahoga County, 1880," in *Report of the Manufacturers of the United States at the Tenth Census* (Washington, D.C.: Government Printing Office, 1882), table III, 9–14.

11. George W. Potter, *To the Golden Door: The Story of the Irish in Ireland and America* (Boston: Little, Brown, 1960), 138; Mrs. Mercedes Hurley Hughes, interview with author, February 15, 1997.

12. Loretta Hurley to Mercedes Hurley Hughes (copy), April 29, 1977, author's collection; *Cleveland City Directory* (Cleveland: Cleveland Directory Company, 1889), 9.

13. *New York Times*, January 9, 1932, 20; *Plat-Book of the City of Cleveland, Ohio, and Suburbs* (Philadelphia: G. M. Hopkins, 1912), plate 29; Samuel P. Orth, *A History of Cleveland, Ohio*, vol. 1 (Chicago: S. J. Clarke Publishing, 1910), 49; Soundex, 1910 Ohio Census, Cuyahoga County (enumeration district 0269, family 0155), microform reel 640-h, Western Reserve Historical Society, Cleveland.

14. *Plat-Book of Cleveland*, map 29; William G. Rose, *Cleveland: The Making of a City* (Cleveland: World Publishing, 1950), 389.

15. *Cleveland City Directory*, 1909; 1910 Ohio Census, Cuyahoga County.

16. James Gibbons, "Patriotism and Politics," *North American Review* 204 (1892): 392; Andrew Greeley, *The Catholic Experience: An Interpretation of the History of American Catholicism* (Garden City, N.Y.: Doubleday, 1967), 33; Winfred Garrison, *Catholicism and the American Mind* (Chicago: Willett, Clark, & Colby, 1928), 8.

17. Jay P. Dolan, *In Search of American Catholicism: A History of Religion and Culture in Tension* (New York: Oxford University Press, 2003), 86, 96; *One Hundred Years of Holy Name* ([Cleveland]: [Holy Name parish], 1954), Holy Name parish folder, Archives, Diocese of Cleveland, [4]; Ohio Historical Records Survey Project, Work Projects Administration, *Parishes of the Catholic Diocese of Cleveland* (Cleveland: Cadillac Press, 1942), 48.

18. G. C. Kniffin, *Assault and Capture of Lookout Mountain,* souvenir pamphlet (Lookout Mountain, Tenn.: W. E. Hardison, n.d.), [1]; 1966 notebook, HAMC, reel 28.

19. Patricia McNeal, *Harder than War: Catholic Peacemaking in the Twentieth Century* (New Brunswick, N.J.: Rutgers University Press, 1992), 2; *Catholic Peacemakers: A Documentary History,* II, ed. Ronald G. Musto (New York: Garland Publishing, 1996), 281–284.

20. David Van Tassel and John J. Grabowski, eds., *The Encyclopedia of Cleveland History* (Bloomington: Indiana University Press, 1987), 136; Loretta Hurley to Mercedes Hurley Hughes, April 29, 1977; "Nominations," n.d., Robert Johns Bulkley Papers, MS 3310, container 3, folder 4, Western Reserve Historical Society, Cleveland.

21. Bulkley to Hurley, November 20, 1912, Hurley Papers, ADSA.

22. Bulkley to Hurley, December 2, 1912, ibid.

23. Bulkley to Hurley, December 20, 1912, ibid.

24. Hurley India diary, 1930, n.d., Hurley Papers, ADSA.

25. *Brassey's Encyclopedia of Military History and Biography* (Washington, D.C.: Brassey's, 1994), 129; *The Sheaf* (Rochester, N.Y.: St. Bernard's Seminary, 1967), 46, Archives of the Diocese of Rochester, N.Y.

26. *The Self-Made Man, The Best Course,* and *Why Catholics Do Not Lead,* pamphlets, Hurley Papers, St. Ignatius College folder, ADSA; Donald P. Gavin, *John Carroll University: A Century of Service* (Cleveland: Kent State University Press, 1985), 38–75.

27. *Piles of Money,* pamphlet (Cleveland: St. Ignatius College, n.d.), [1], Hurley Papers, St. Ignatius College folder, ADSA; James W. Reites, S.J., "St. Ignatius Loyola and the Jews," *Studies in the Spirituality of Jesuits* 13 (1981): 29; Arendt quoted in James Bernauer, "The Holocaust and the Search for Forgiveness: An Invitation to the Society of Jesus," ibid., 36 (2004): 27–37; Vincent A. Lapomarda, S.J., *The Jesuits and the Third Reich* (Lewiston, Maine: Edwin Mellen Press, 1989), 77.

28. *Piles of Money,* [2]. One influence on this score seems to be a Jesuit dependence on Abelardian medievalism that held up the Jewish work ethic to Catholics for emulation. See George E. Ganss, *St. Ignatius' Idea of a Jesuit University: A Study in the History of Education* (Milwaukee: Marquette University Press, 1956), 128–129.

29. *St. Ignatius College Catalogue, 1914–1915* (Cleveland: St. Ignatius College, 1915), ADSA; notebook marked "Oratory" [St. Ignatius College, 1915], Hurley

Papers, ADSA; Dr. Vincent T. Lawler to Hurley, June 22, 1915, Hurley scrapbook I, ibid.

30. Gavin, *John Carroll*, 52; Edward R. Kantowicz, *Corporation Sole: Cardinal Mundelein and Chicago Catholicism* (Notre Dame, Ind.: Notre Dame University Press, 1983), 183; Neal Garnham, "Both Praying and Playing: 'Muscular Christianity' and the YMCA in Northeast County Durham," *Journal of Social History* 35 (2001): 401; Clifford Putney, *Muscular Christianity: Manhood and Sports in Protestant America, 1880–1920* (Cambridge, Mass.: Harvard University Press, 2001), 9; *Why Catholics Do Not Lead* (Cleveland: St. Ignatius College, n.d.), [1], Hurley Papers, ADSA.

31. *Catholic Universe Bulletin*, November 15, 1940.

32. News clippings, Scrapbook I, Hurley Papers, ADSA; Photographic Archive, ibid.; 1965 notebook, HAMC, reel 28.

33. Thomas Gaffney to Hurley, November 14, 1915, Hurley Papers, ADSA; Robert John Bulkley to Hurley, May 11, 1915, and January 7, 1916, ibid.

34. *Catholic Universe Bulletin*, November 19, 1940.

35. "Chronicle of the Scholastic Year 1915–1916," in *Liber Status Alumnorum, Seminarii S. Bernardi, Roffae, New York*, vol. 2: *1913–1934*, St. Bernard's Seminary folder, Archives of the Diocese of Rochester, N.Y.; Tom Hogan to Hurley, February 9, 1917, Hurley Papers, ADSA.

36. J. J. Hartley to Bishop John P. Farrelly, April 27, 1916, John P. Farrelly Papers, Educational Institutions Collection, St. Bernard's Seminary folder, Archives, Diocese of Cleveland.

37. Gary Edward Polster, *Inside Looking Out: The Cleveland Jewish Orphan Asylum, 1868–1924* (Kent, Ohio: Kent State University Press, 1990), 52–56; Van Tassel and Grabowski, *Encyclopedia of Cleveland History*, 573; Jack Wertheimer, *Unwelcome Strangers: East European Jews in Imperial Germany* (Oxford: Oxford University Press, 1987), 92.

38. Frederick J. Zwierlein, *Talks to Men and Women on the World of Today* (Rochester, N.Y.: Art Print Shop, 1946), 32–33; Rev. Charles E. Coughlin, "Why Leave Our Own," *Brooklyn Tablet*, January 28, 1939.

39. St. Bernard's Seminary notebook, 1916, Hurley Papers, ADSA.

40. Catholic source contemporary with events, interview with author, May 16, 1996; *Alerte!* folder, Hurley Papers, ADSA; Hurley to "Bud" Walsh, October 1929, bound notebook, ibid.

41. David A. Gerber, ed., *Anti-Semitism in American History* (Urbana: Illinois University Press, 1986), 3; Leonard Dinnerstein, *Anti-Semitism in America* (New York: Oxford University Press, 1994), 35.

42. Liberty Bond placard, Hurley Papers, ADSA; Raymond Hurley to Joseph Hurley, May 9, 1918, ibid.

43. Civil Service records file, 1917–1918, ibid.

44. *Catholic Universe Bulletin*, November 15, 1940; *Cleveland Plain Dealer*, January 8, 1932.

45. *Catholic Universe Bulletin*, May 30, 1919; Ronald J. Rychlak, "Goldhagen v.

Pius XII," *First Things: A Monthly Journal of Religion and Public Life* 42 (2002): 38.

46. Francis Cardinal Bourne, *The Voice of Belgium: Being the War Utterances of Cardinal Mercier* (London: Burns & Oates, 1917), 4; *New York Times,* October 17, 1919.

47. John A. Gade, *The Life of Cardinal Mercier* (New York: Scribner's, 1934), 131–145; Robrecht Boudens, *Two Cardinals: John Henry Newman and Désiré Joseph Mercier* (Louvain: Louvain University Press, 1995), 271.

48. Henry B. Leonard, "Ethnic Tensions, Episcopal Leadership, and the Emergence of the Twentieth Century American Catholic Church: The Cleveland Experience," *Catholic Historical Review* 71 (1985): 394–395.

49. *Catholic Universe Bulletin,* March 10, 1922.

50. Translation from the Latin of a postcard from Mooney to unknown recipient, transcribed in cover letter from R. I. Kinnane to Hurley, October 14, 1959, Hurley Papers, ADSA. Mooney's most ardent supporter at the North American College was the rector, Charles A. O'Hern.

51. Edward Mooney, farewell address to St. Patrick's parish, Youngstown, 1923, Mooney Administration, series 4, box 41, folder 3, AAD; R. I. Kinnane to Hurley, October 14, 1959, Hurley Papers, ADSA.

52. Vital Statistics Record for Joseph P. Hurley, Archives, Diocese of Cleveland; Mooney to Hurley, March 14, 1927, Hurley Papers, ADSA; Leo J. Miltner, M.D., December 3, 1932, medical report, Peiping Union Medical College, Peiping, China, ibid.

53. Registration card, Faculté des Lettres de Toulouse, 1926–1927, Hurley Papers, ADSA; notebook, "19th Century Problems Diplomatique," ibid.

54. *Catholic Universe Bulletin,* January 15, 1926.

55. Mooney to Hurley, January 6, 1927, Hurley Papers, ADSA.

56. On Powers and Mooney see John Stark Bellamy, *Angels on the Heights: A History of St. Ann's Parish, Cleveland Heights, Ohio, 1915–1990* (Cleveland: Privately printed, 1990), 36–37.

57. John M. Powers, "Log of the Belgenland Cruise," entries for December 9, March 15, and April 17, 1928, collection of Mrs. Mercedes Hurley Hughes. I am grateful to Mrs. Mercedes Hurley Hughes for allowing me to view a copy of this travel diary.

58. Mercedes Hurley Hughes to author, February 5, 2000.

59. "Five Year Diary," August 2, 1930, Hurley Papers, ADSA.

CHAPTER 2. DIPLOMATIC OBSERVER

1. Hugald Grafe, *History of Christianity in India: Tamilnadu in the Nineteenth and Twentieth Centuries* (Bangalore: Church History Association of India, 1990), 35. The Sacred Congregation of the Propaganda Fide was founded on January 5, 1622, by Pope Gregory XV. It was assigned the mission of spreading the Catholic faith to all areas of the world where the Christian gospels had not been preached or where a hierarchy had not yet been established.

2. *Annuario Pontificio* (Vatican City: Tipografia Poliglotta Vaticana, 1913), 278; Robert A. Graham, S.J., *Vatican Diplomacy: A Study of Church and State on the International Plane* (Princeton: Princeton University Press, 1959), 126; David J. Alvarez, "The Professionalization of the Papal Diplomatic Service, 1909 to 1967," *Catholic Historical Review* 75 (1989): 243.

3. Hugald Grafe, *History of Christianity in India* (Bangalore: Church History Association of India, 1982), 72; Randall quoted in Thomas E. Hachey, ed., *Anglo-Vatican Relations, 1914–1939: Confidential Annual Reports of the British Ministers to the Holy See* (Boston: G. K. Hall, 1972), 146.

4. [F.] Givergis, *The New Diocese of Tiruvella* (Ernakulam, India: I. S. Press, 1931), 9; Eugene Cardinal Tisserant, *Eastern Christianity in India: A History of the Syro-Malabar Church from Earliest Time to the Present* (Calcutta: Orient Longmans, 1957), 159; Mar Ivanios to Hurley, February 27, 1931, Hurley Papers, ADSA.

5. Hurley to Bud Walsh (copy), October 1929, black bound diary, Hurley Papers, ADSA. Hurley's habit was to transcribe in this diary copies of all the letters he sent to Walsh.

6. Hurley diary, October 12, 1929, Hurley Papers, ADSA. For Hurley's description of the altar servers see Hurley to Walsh, October 1929.

7. India diary, n.d., HAMC, reel 29.

8. Robert F. McNamara, *History of the Diocese of Rochester, 1868–1968* (Rochester, N.Y.: Diocese of Rochester, 1968), 387.

9. Mooney to Bishops of India, circular letter, February 14, 1931, Mooney Administration, series 4, AAD; Bishop Lawrence Casey to Rev. Robert F. McNamara (copy), January 10, 1967, author's collection. I am grateful to Father McNamara for sharing a copy of this letter from his residential files.

10. Edward Mooney to "Caro Mio [probably Father John J. Casey, secretary to Cardinal Hayes]," November 26, 1931, HAMC, reel 29; McNamara, *Diocese of Rochester*, 583 n. 18.

11. James M. O'Toole, *Militant and Triumphant: William Henry O'Connell and the Catholic Church in Boston* (Notre Dame, Ind.: University of Notre Dame Press, 1992), 70; Anthony Rhodes, *The Vatican in the Age of the Dictators, 1922–1945* (London: Hodder and Stoughton, 1973), 307.

12. Hurley to Mooney, April 10, 1933, AAD. Constantin Yurenev was sent to Berlin in 1937, recalled to Moscow in 1938, and shot on Stalin's orders in 1938. On Yurenev's service in Rome see Alexander Barmine, *One Who Survived: The Life Story of a Russian under the Soviets* (New York: Putnam, 1945), 152.

13. Audience with Emperor of Japan, 1931 (typewritten transcript in French), Mooney Administration, series 4, box 41, folder 4, AAD; Hurley to Mooney, December 12, 1933, MAUC, box 3, AAD.

14. Akira Iriye, "Japan's Policies toward the United States," in *Japan's Foreign Policy, 1868–1941*, ed. James William Morley (New York: Columbia University Press, 1974), 445; Justus D. Doenecke, ed., *The Diplomacy of Frustration: The Manchurian Crisis of 1931–1933 as Revealed in the Papers of Stanley K.*

Hornbeck (Stanford, Calif.: Hoover Institution Press, 1981), 18; *Saionji Harada Memoirs,* quoted in Yale C. Maxon, *Control of Japanese Foreign Policy: A Study of Civil-Military Rivalry, 1930–1945* (1957; reprint, Westport, Conn.: Greenwood Press, 1973), 238.

15. Shunsuke Tsurimi, *An Intellectual History of Wartime Japan, 1931–1945* (London: KPI, 1986), 12; Sung-Gun Kim, "The Shinto Shrine Issue in Korean Christianity under Japanese Colonialism," *Journal of Church and State* 39 (1997): 503.

16. George H. Minamiki, S.J., "The Yasukuni Shrine Incident and the Chinese Rites Controversy," *Catholic Historical Review* 66 (1980): 205. The controversy surrounding the cultural adaptation of Christianity in China and Japan is known familiarly as the "Chinese Rites Controversy." "On its most general level," D. E. Mungello observes, "the Rites Controversy posed the question of whether it is necessary to change a culture in order to adopt a foreign religion." Specifically, it asked whether the Chinese (and Japanese) who adopted Christianity also had to adopt Western culture; "Introduction," in *The Chinese Rites Controversy: Its History and Meaning,* ed. D. E. Mungello (Netteta, Germany: Steyler Verlag, 1994), 3.

17. George Minimiki, *The Chinese Rites Controversy from Its Beginnings to Modern Times* (Chicago: Loyola University Press, 1985), 141.

18. Diary entry, October 17, 1932, Papers of Joseph C. Grew, MS Am 1687 (57), by permission of the Houghton Library, Harvard University.

19. Richard H. Drummond, *A History of Christianity in Japan* (Grand Rapids: W. B. Eerdmans, 1971), 323; diary entry, October 31, 1932, Papers of Joseph C. Grew, MS Am 1687 (58), by permission of the Houghton Library, Harvard University.

20. Mooney to Archbishop Paolo Marella, December 2, 1933, AAD; Henry L. Stimson to Joseph Grew (telegram), January 18, 1933, in *FRUS,* 1931–1941, 1: 109; Errol MacGregor Clauss, "The Roosevelt Administration and Manchukuo, 1933–1941," *Historian* 32 (1970): 596.

21. Mooney's last-minute appointment to the Rochester see may have been precipitated by an administrative change at the apostolic delegation in Washington. In March 1933 Pietro Fumasoni-Biondi, the former apostolic delegate to Japan, was called to Rome. He was replaced by Archbishop Amleto Giovanni Cicognani, who did not arrive in Washington until May 22, 1933. Bishop John Francis O'Hern of Rochester died on the day of Cicognani's arrival. The search for a successor to O'Hern was begun amid the exigencies of the administrative change at the delegation. The apostolic delegate plays a crucial role in the selection of bishops, a secret and lengthy process that must gain final approval both from the Congregazione per i vescovi (Congregation for Bishops) in Rome and from the pope.

22. Mario Oliveri, *The Representatives: The Real Nature and Function of Papal Legates* (Gerrards Cross, U.K.: Van Duren, 1981), 76. In 1969, in the declaration *Sollicitudo Omnium Ecclesiarum* (The Care of All the Churches), the

Holy See finally created an official category for the position Hurley was holding, naming it "substitute." "Those who, although they exercise their mission both to the Local Churches and the State, are nevertheless 'substitutes,' provisional Representatives, in the temporary vacancy or in the absence of a Head of Mission," the declaration read.

23. George Bull, *Inside the Vatican* (New York: St. Martin's Press, 1982), 131–132. The normal progression through the ranks of papal diplomacy called for a young priest to study for two years at the Pontificia Academia Nobili Ecclesiastica and start as an attaché at a papal nunciature. Chiefs of mission were normally chosen from the ranks of counselors of mission and named papal chamberlains, or monsignors. Chiefs of mission or counselors were hardly ever chosen from the ranks of the secretaries or auditors. See Peter C. Van Lierde, *The Holy See at Work: How the Catholic Church Is Governed* (New York: Hawthorne Books, 1962), 234.

24. Harold Nicolson, *Diplomacy* (London: Oxford University Press, 1950), 232.

25. Hurley to Mooney, October 23, 1933, MAUC, box 3, AAD.

26. Thomas B. Morgan, *The Listening Post: Eighteen Years on Vatican Hill* (New York: G. P. Putnam's Sons, 1944), 181.

27. Hurley to Mooney, February 20, 1933, MAUC, box 3, AAD.

28. Ibid.

29. Minimiki, *Chinese Rites Controversy*, 121; Hurley to Mooney, October 4, 1933, MAUC, box 3, AAD. The islands in Kagoshima Bay were of great military and tactical value to the Japanese. The Allies also recognized this fact. In 1945 the American Sixth Army proposed that the first stage of the planned invasion of Japan, "Operation Olympic," be staged from the islands in Kagoshima Bay. See Gerhard L. Weinberg, *A World at Arms: A Global History of World War II* (Cambridge: Cambridge University Press, 1994), 871.

30. John D. Meehan, *The Dominion and the Rising Sun: Canada Encounters Japan, 1929–1941* (Vancouver: University of British Columbia Press, 2004), 15–25, 110.

31. Hurley to Mooney, October 4, 1933, MAUC, box 3, AAD.

32. Ibid. Ironically, after his death in 1940 Marler would be criticized for a perceived "pro-Japanese bias" and an unwillingness to stand up to the military government. On this see James Eayrs, *The Art of the Possible: Government and Foreign Policy in Canada* (Toronto: University of Toronto Press, 1961), 135–136.

33. Hurley first used the term "persecution of Catholics" in his October 4, 1933, letter to Mooney. The concept of the "silver spoon" diplomat, born to wealth and a member of the "Eastern establishment," is treated in David K. Johnson, *The Lavender Scare: The Cold War Persecution of Gays and Lesbians in the Federal Government* (Chicago: University of Chicago Press, 2006), 67. Johnson mentions U.S. Under Secretary of State Sumner Welles as the prototype silver-spoon diplomat. Hurley would later work closely with Welles.

34. W. Cameron Forbes quoted in Gary Ross, "W. Cameron Forbes: The

Diplomacy of a Darwinist," in *Diplomats in Crisis: United States–Chinese–Japanese Relations, 1919–1941*, ed. Richard Dean Burns and Edward M. Bennett (Santa Barbara, Calif.: ABC-Clio, 1974), 51; Hurley to Mooney, February 2, 1933, MAUC, box 3, AAD; *Nippon Catholic Shinbun*, November 26, 1933, Hurley Papers, ADSA.

35. Hurley to Mooney, November 12 and December 12, 1933, MAUC, box 3, AAD.

36. Hurley to Mooney, November 12, 1933.

37. Ibid.; Paolo Marella to Mooney, March 21, 1934, ibid.

38. Marella to Mooney, March 21, 1934; Photographic Archive, Hurley Papers, ADSA.

39. Marella to Mooney, October 12, 1933, MAUC, box 3, AAD.

40. Schrembs to Mooney, November 25, 1933, ibid.; Hurley to Mooney (telegram from M.S. *Asama Maru*), March 19, 1934, ibid.

41. Mooney to Schrembs, November 28, 1933, ibid.

42. Robert F. McNamara, *The American College in Rome, 1855–1955* (Rochester, N.Y.: Christopher Press, 1956), 596.

43. Thomas J. Reese, S.J., *Inside the Vatican: The Politics and Organization of the Catholic Church* (Cambridge, Mass.: Harvard University Press, 1996), 175.

44. Hurley to Doc [Mooney], October 11, 1934, MAUC, box 9, AAD.

45. Ibid.; John F. Pollard, *Money and the Rise of the Modern Papacy: Financing the Vatican, 1850–1950* (Cambridge: Cambridge University Press, 2005), 136–157.

46. Hurley to Doc [Mooney], November 15, 1934, MAUC, box 3, AAD.

47. Hurley to Doc [Mooney], November 15, 1934, and November 12, 1933, ibid. Schrembs prided himself on his singing, musical talent, and hymn-writing. In 1928 he published the *Diocesan Hymnal* (New York: J. Fischer), which was well received in Catholic circles nationwide; *Cleveland Plain Dealer*, February 3, 1935.

48. Alvarez, "Professionalization of Papal Diplomatic Service," 240; Hurley to Mooney, November 15, 1934, MAUC, box 3, AAD.

49. Alvarez, "Professionalization of Papal Diplomatic Service," 246; Robert I. Gannon, *The Cardinal Spellman Story* (Garden City, N.Y.: Doubleday, 1962), 47.

50. Peter C. Van Lierde, *The Holy See at Work: How the Catholic Church Is Governed* (New York: Hawthorne Books, 1962), 155; Graham, *Vatican Diplomacy*, 142; "Named to Vatican Post," *New York Times*, November 17, 1934.

51. *Annuario Pontificio* (Vatican City: Typis Polyglottis Vaticana, 1936), 725; Heinrich Scharp, *How the Catholic Church Is Governed* (New York: Herder & Herder, 1960), 62.

CHAPTER 3. SILENCING CHARLIE

1. "Father Coughlin's Residence Bombed," *New York Times*, March 31, 1933, 3. The *New York Times* did Coughlin no favors by publishing his exact street address in the article.

2. David M. Kennedy, *Freedom from Fear: The American People in Depression and War* (New York: Oxford University Press, 1999), 230; Marshall W. Fishwick, "Father Coughlin Time: The Radio and Redemption," *Journal of Popular Culture* 22 (1988): 33.

3. The best summaries of the Catholic church's handling of Coughlin are found in Donald Warren, *Radio Priest: Charles Coughlin, the Father of Hate Radio* (New York: Free Press, 1996); and Leslie Woodcock Tentler, *Seasons of Grace: A History of the Catholic Archdiocese of Detroit* (Detroit: Wayne State University Press, 1990). Also see Sheldon Marcus, *Father Coughlin: The Tumultuous Life of the Priest of the Little Flower* (Boston: Little, Brown, 1973); and Charles J. Tull, *Father Coughlin and the New Deal* (Syracuse, N.Y.: Syracuse University Press, 1965).

4. Marcus, *Father Coughlin*, 45.

5. Hurley handwritten personal notes, ca. 1940, Hurley Papers, ADSA.

6. Earl Boyea, "The Reverend Charles Coughlin and the Church: The Gallagher Years, 1930–1937," *Catholic Historical Review* 81 (1995): 213; "Bishop Michael Gallagher's Written Statement on Father Charles E. Coughlin Issue of October 25, 1937," typescript (copy), Hurley Papers, box 53, folder MC1, ADSA.

7. Albert Fried, *FDR and His Enemies* (New York: St. Martin's Press, 1999), 62.

8. Boyea, "The Reverend Charles Coughlin," 213. Hurley never gave a specific date or location of his conference with Coughlin. When Mooney asked for detailed information on the meeting he responded: "As to the memorandum of my conversation with Coughlin, I have not been able to locate it." This was probably a dodge by Hurley so that he did not have to put any quotations from an internal Vatican report into an outgoing personal letter. See Hurley to Mooney, October 12, 1937, MAUC, box 9, AAD.

9. Joe [Hurley] to Doc [Mooney], July 13, 1937, MAUC, box 9, AAD.

10. Tull, *Father Coughlin and the New Deal*, 64–137.

11. Woodcock Tentler, *Seasons of Grace*, 327.

12. Hurley to Mooney, November 21, 1937, MAUC, box 9, AAD.

13. Hurley to Mooney, October 12, 1937, ibid.; *New York Times*, July 27 and September 3, 1936.

14. Joe [Hurley] to Doc [Mooney], November 25, 1937, MAUC, box 9, AAD. *Osservatore Romano* is the official newspaper of the Vatican. The pope appoints its editor, who reports to the Holy Father or his secretary of state. It is the most important source in understanding the Vatican's public position concerning issues of the Holy See's foreign policy.

15. *Osservatore Romano*, September 3, 1936.

16. "Vatican Voices," *Time*, August 17, 1936, online digital archive, http://www.time.com/time/magazine/article/0,9171,756480,00.html (accessed April 14, 2007).

17. Tull, *Father Coughlin and the New Deal*, 145.

18. Ibid., 173.

19. Mary Christine Athans, *The Coughlin-Fahey Connection: Father Charles E. Coughlin, Father Denis Fahey, C.S.Sp., and Religious Anti-Semitism in the United States, 1938–1954* (New York: Peter Lang, 1991), 164–165.

20. Warren, *Radio Priest*, 251.

21. Tull, *Father Coughlin and the New Deal*, 197; Ronald Modras, "Father Coughlin and Anti-Semitism: Fifty Years Later," *Journal of Church and State* 31 (1989): 233; Rev. Charles E. Coughlin, "Persecution-Jewish and Christian," in *Am I an Anti-Semite? Nine Addresses on Various "isms"* (Detroit: Condon Printing, 1939).

22. Tull, *Father Coughlin and the New Deal*, 198.

23. *Time*, December 19, 1938. The Catholic panel denouncing Kristallnacht included Archbishop John J. Mitty of San Francisco; Bishop John Mark Gannon of Erie, Pennsylvania; Bishop Peter Ireton of Richmond, Virginia; and the Catholic governor of New York, Alfred E. Smith. The panel was arranged by Rev. Maurice S. Sheehy of the Catholic University of America. A transcript of the broadcast was published in the *New York Times* on November 17, 1938, and was introduced by a multicolumn front-page article. The biographies of Coughlin overlook this important Catholic hierarchical response to Kristallnacht.

24. Tull, *Father Coughlin and the New Deal*, 199; Warren, *Radio Priest*, 260; Woodcock Tentler, *Seasons of Grace*, 336.

25. Doc [Mooney] to My Dear Joe [Hurley], December 22, 1938, Mooney Administration Uncataloged Collection, box 9, AAD. The suspense and interest of the December 11, 1938, rebroadcast were heightened by Coughlin's personal introduction, a drawn-out defense against a Jewish critic who had accused the priest of being "a sadist." Coughlin interpreted the comment as a rap on his priestly celibacy and argued at the top of his voice that he was "not a sexual pervert." Explaining sexual sadism to his audience in graphic detail, Coughlin insisted that he never "gained sexual gratification in witnessing the sufferings of others." Such frank sex talk over the national airwaves by a priest was extraordinary, and Mooney's moral sensibilities surely bristled. Rev. Charles E. Coughlin, "Let Us Consider the Record," radio broadcast of December 11, 1938 (Broomall, Pa.: Catholic Counterpoint, 2000), audiocassette.

26. Mooney to My Dear Joe [Hurley], December 22, 1938, MAUC, box 9, AAD.

27. Ibid. It is possible that Mooney's order, published in the *Michigan Catholic*, calling for "prayers for the persecuted" on the Sunday after Kristallnacht, was a direct response to Coughlin's speech.

28. Mooney to Joe [Hurley], December 26, 1938, MAUC, box 9, AAD.

29. Hurley to Doc [Mooney], December 26, 1938, ibid.

30. Joe [Hurley] to Doc [Mooney], January 16, 1939, ibid.

31. Ibid. On Gemelli and antisemitism see Wiley Feinstein, *The Civilization of the Holocaust in Italy: Poets, Artists, Saints, and Anti-Semites* (Madison, N.J.: Fairleigh Dickinson University Press, 2003), 217–218.

32. Harry Fornari, *Mussolini's Gadfly: Roberto Farinacci* (Nashville: Vanderbilt University Press, 1971), xi; The *Manifesto of German Racism* was promulgated by Mussolini in July 1938. Essentially, the decree announced that Italians were Aryan in origin and biologically different from Jews and Africans, who were considered to be racially "extra-European"; quoted in Meir Michaelis, *Mussolini and the Jews: German-Italian Relations and the Jewish Question in Italy, 1922–1945* (Oxford: Clarendon Press of Oxford University Press, 1978), 240.

33. Farinacci quoted in Fornari, *Mussolini's Gadfly*, 187; Richard A. Webster, *The Cross and the Fasces: Christian Democracy and Fascism in Europe* (Stanford: Stanford University Press, 1960), 110. Papal historian Frank Coppa has called the battle over the schools a "Fascist struggle with the Catholic church for the minds of the young"; see Frank J. Coppa, "From Liberalism to Fascism: The Church-State Conflict over Italy's Schools," *History Teacher* 28 (1995): 137.

34. D. A. Binchy, *Church and State in Fascist Italy* (1941; reprint, Oxford: Oxford University Press, 1970), 625.

35. Roger Griffin, "The 'Holy Storm': Clerical Fascism through the Lens of Modernism," *Totalitarian Movements and Political Religions* 8 (2007): 214. On Farinacci and the Catholic press see Michaelis, *Mussolini and the Jews*, 141.

36. *New York Times*, January 17, 1939; William A. Mueller, "Coughlin and the Nazi Bund," *Look*, September 26, 1939, 10–15.

37. *New York Times*, March 7 and November 20, 1939. Three years earlier Hurley had dismissed Clinchy when he came to the Vatican hoping to create a coalition with the Catholic church against antisemitism. Describing Clinchy as "an agent of a nonsectarian organization," he warned Mooney to be skeptical of the National Council of Christians and Jews (NCCJ). Hurley described the NCCJ as "a Jewish move to head off a persecution of Jews in the United States," an ironic comment given that arguably the most malicious treatment of Jews in the prewar United States was perpetrated by the professedly Catholic and Coughlin-inspired Christian Front. Hurley to "Doc" [Mooney], September 11, 1935, Mooney Administration Uncatalogued Collection, box 9, AAD.

38. Louis D. Gross to Pope Pius XI, telegram (copy), *Jewish Examiner*, June 20, 1939; Hurley Vatican notebook, n.d., HAMC, reel 28.

39. *New York Times*, January 26, 1939.

40. Anthony Joseph Drexel Biddle to FDR, memorandum, January 12, 1939, in Donald B. Schewe, ed., *Franklin D. Roosevelt and Foreign Affairs: Second Series, January 1937–February 1939*, vol. 13 (New York: Clearwater Publishing, 1979), 118; Jay Allen to George S. Messersmith, January 26, 1939, George S. Messersmith Papers, item 1139, Special Collections, University of Delaware Library, Newark; Lewis Browne quoted in "Coughlin Says Nazis Will Yield to Papacy," *New York Times*, March 6, 1939; FDR quoted in Joseph P. Kennedy

diary, February 9, 1939, Joseph P. Kennedy Papers Collection, box 91, folder: Diary, Feb.–March 1939, John F. Kennedy Presidential Library, Boston.

41. Julius Streicher quoted in William C. Kernan, *The Ghost of Royal Oak* (New York: Free Speech Forum, 1940), 23; Richard Steigman-Gall, *The Holy Reich: Nazi Conceptions of Christianity, 1919–1945* (Cambridge: Cambridge University Press, 2003), 125; Carol D. Schulz and Eve Nussbaum Soumerai, *Daily Life during the Holocaust* (Westport, Conn.: Greenwood Press, 1998), 281.

42. Boyea, "The Reverend Charles Coughlin," 224–225.

43. R. Lieber, "Tardini, Domenico," in *New Catholic Encyclopedia*, vol. 13, 2nd ed. (Detroit: Gale, 2003), 759. By this time Tardini would have been one of the "bosses" that Hurley referred to in his January 16, 1939, letter to Mooney as dismissive of the outcry about the speech. This attitude allowed Hurley to shield Pope Pius XI from the severity of the crisis.

44. Hurley Vatican notes, n.d., HAMC, reel 28.

45. Peter R. D'Agostino, *Rome in America: Transnational Catholic Ideology from the Risorgimento to Fascism* (Chapel Hill: University of North Carolina Press, 2004), 83–85.

46. Hurley to Mooney, January 16, 1939, MAUC, box 9, AAD; *New York Times*, September 12, 1940.

47. "Notes of Mgr. Hurley of the Secretariat of State," in *The Holy See and the War in Europe: March 1939–August 1940*, ed. Pierre Blet, Angelo Martini, and Burkhart Schneider (Washington, D.C.: Corpus, 1965), 352.

48. "Arsenal Siezed by G-Men," *Binghamton Press*, January 14, 1940, author's collection. I am grateful to my father, Dr. Gordon V. Gallagher, for sending me my grandfather's scrapbook of Father Coughlin–related clippings wherein this item was found.

49. Theodore Irwin, *Inside the "Christian Front"* (Washington, D.C.: American Council on Public Affairs, n.d.), 1, John C. Metcalfe Collection, box 2, folder: Christian Front, Hoover Institution Archives, Stanford, Calif.; J. Edgar Hoover [Washington] to E. J. Connelley [New York Field Office], January 31, 1940, "Christian Front" subject file, U.S. Federal Bureau of Investigation, Washington, D.C.; Athan G. Theoharis, *The FBI: A Comprehensive Reference Guide* (Phoenix: Oryx Press, 1999), 23. I am grateful to Dr. John J. Fox Jr., the Federal Bureau of Investigation's official historian, for providing a copy of FBI director J. Edgar Hoover's report on the Christian Front case.

50. Notes of Monsignor Hurley of the Secretariat of State, in Blet, Martini, and Schneider, *The Holy See*, 352. This volume is one of eleven in the *Actes et documents du Saint Siège relatifs à la seconde guerre mondiale (ADSS)*, ed. Pierre Blet, Robert A. Graham, Angelo Martini, and Burkhart Schneider, and was released by the Holy See in response to accusations made in Rolf Hochhuth's 1963 play, *Der Stellvertrete*, concerning Pope Pius XII's silence in the midst of the Holocaust. Another work, Saul Friedländer's *Pius XII and the Third Reich: A Documentation*, rev. ed. (New York: Knopf, 1966), also spurred the Holy See to authorize the selective release of these documents

from its Archivo Segreto. See *Italian Foreign Policy, 1918–1945: A Guide to Research and Research Materials,* ed. Alan Cassels (Wilmington, Del.: Scholarly Resources, 1982), 140–141.

51. Hurley Vatican notes, n.d., HAMC, reel 28.

52. Blet, Martini, and Schneider, *The Holy See,* 352; Franklin D. Roosevelt to Myron Taylor, memorandum, February 13, 1940, Official File, folder 76b: Church Matters, Subfile: X-Refs, 1940–41, Franklin D. Roosevelt Library, Hyde Park, N.Y. Interestingly, FDR's thinking mirrored that of C. Everett Clinchy and the fledgling National Conference of Christians and Jews. In early 1940 the National Catholic Conference for Interracial Justice (NCCIJ) published a report titled "Anti-Semitism Leads On to Anti-Christianism." The thesis of this report was that a spike in antisemitic behavior by Catholics would result in a sharp rise in anticatholicism across the country.

53. "Opinion for His Excellency Mons. *Sostituto,*" HAMC, reel 30.

54. Hurley Vatican notes, n.d., HAMC, reel 28.

CHAPTER 4. AN AMERICAN MONSIGNOR IN MUSSOLINI'S ITALY

1. Caroline Drayton Phillips, 1938 diary, May 3, 1938, Caroline Phillips Papers, box 5, Schlesinger Library, Radcliffe Institute, Harvard University.

2. David F. Schmitz, *The United States and Fascist Italy, 1922–1940* (Chapel Hill: University of North Carolina Press, 1988), 191.

3. Joe [Kennedy] to Sumner Welles, April 5, 1939, Papers of Sumner Welles, Office Correspondence 1920–1943, folder 11, Joseph P. Kennedy File, Franklin D. Roosevelt Library, Hyde Park, N.Y.

4. Jay Pierrepont Moffat to Cordell Hull, October 27, 1938, Papers of Jay Pierrepont Moffat, MS Am 1407 (vol. 13), by permission of the Houghton Library, Harvard University.

5. David J. Alvarez, "The United States, the Vatican, and World War II," *Research Studies* 40 (1972): 239–250.

6. William Phillips, *Ventures in Diplomacy* (Boston: Beacon Press, 1952), 251.

7. James Hennessey, S.J., "American Jesuit in Wartime Rome: The Diary of Vincent A. McCormick, S.J., 1942–1945," *Mid America* 56 (1974): 47; Amanda Smith, ed., *Hostage to Fortune: The Letters of Joseph P. Kennedy* (New York: Viking, 2001), 479.

8. William Phillips diary, William Phillips Papers, MS Am 2232, 55M-69 (vol. 17), 2704–2786, by permission of the Houghton Library, Harvard University.

9. Ibid.; Joseph P. Kennedy to Sumner [Welles], July 17, 1939, Papers of Sumner Welles, Office Correspondence 1920–1943, folder 11, Joseph P. Kennedy File, Franklin D. Roosevelt Library.

10. 11 January–6 May 1938 diary, May 5, 1938, Caroline Phillips Papers, box 5, Schlesinger Library, Radcliffe Institute, Harvard University; Arnaldo Cortesi, "Rome Thinks Visit Will Oil the Axis," *New York Times,* May 2, 1938; Ruth Ben-Ghiat, "Italian Fascists and National Socialists: The Dynamics of

an Uneasy Relationship," in *Art, Culture, and Media under the Third Reich,* ed. Richard A. Etlin (Chicago: University of Chicago Press, 2002), 266.

11. 11 January–6 May 1938 diary, May 5, 1938, Caroline Phillips Papers, box 5. Hurley later used the "Crooked Cross" imagery in his editorial "Let Christians Take the Lead!" *Florida Catholic,* April 9, 1943.

12. *The Times* (London), January 14, 1939; "Rome Visit," January 13, 1939, [4], Archives of the First Earl of Halifax, Edward Frederick Lindley Wood, Earl of Halifax, microfilm S830, Foreign Office Papers, Private Collections, vol. 319, Lamont Library, Harvard University.

13. Ministry of External Affairs, *Documents diplomatiques français, 1932–1939* (Paris: Imprimerie Nationale, 1979), series II, vol. 13, 655; Alan Campbell Johnson, *Viscount Halifax: A Biography* (New York: Ives Washburn, 1941), 502. Papal historian Frank J. Coppa has indicated that Pius XI may have been leaning in this direction as early as June 1937: "Indeed, Nazism seems to have displaced Communism as Pius XI's major concern." See Frank J. Coppa, "Two Popes and the Holocaust," in *Remembering for the Future: The Holocaust in an Age of Genocides,* ed. John K. Roth and Elisabeth Maxwell-Meynard (New York: Palgrave, 2001), 400.

14. Hurley quoted in interview with Monsignor John P. McNulty, July 17, 1995, St. Petersburg, Fla. Monsignor McNulty served as Bishop Hurley's personal secretary in the Belgrade nunciature from 1945 to 1950.

15. Joe [Hurley] to Doc [Mooney], December 26, 1938, MAUC, box 9, AAD; Joe [Hurley] to Mike [Michael J. Ready], October 2, 1939, NCWC Papers, Records of the General Secretary, series 10, box 21, folder 4, American Catholic History Research and University Archives, Catholic University of America.

16. Jay Pierrepont Moffat diary, vol. 41: July 28–December 1938, Papers of Jay Pierrepont Moffat, MS Am 1407 (vol. 42), by permission of the Houghton Library, Harvard University; Gerald P. Fogarty, S.J., "Roosevelt and the American Catholic Hierarchy," in *FDR, the Vatican, and the Roman Catholic Church in America, 1933–1945,* ed. David B. Woolner and Richard G. Kurial (New York: Palgrave Macmillan, 2003), 26.

17. *Osservatore Romano* was established in 1861 in an attempt to present the Catholic opinion amid the rise of nationalism and secular liberalism; Thomas B. Morgan, *A Reporter at the Papal Court: A Narrative of the Reign of Pope Pius XI* (New York: Longmans, Green, 1937), 238.

18. William Phillips diary, September 2, 1938, William Phillips Papers, MS Am 2232, 55M-69 (vol. 17), 2704–2714, by permission of the Houghton Library, Harvard University.

19. Ibid.; Hurley Vatican notebook, September 12, 1938, HAMC, reel 28.

20. Anthony Rhodes, *The Vatican in the Age of the Dictators, 1922–1945* (London: Hodder and Stoughton, 1973), 238; Philip V. Cannistraro, ed., *Historical Dictionary of Fascist Italy* (Westport, Conn.: Greenwood Press, 1982), 381.

21. William Phillips diary, William Phillips Papers, MS Am 2232, 55M-69 (vol. 17), 2705, by permission of the Houghton Library, Harvard University.

22. Radio Bulletin NR 22, Washington, January 27, 1939, to U.S. Embassy in Rome, January 28, 1939, Hurley Papers, ADSA. The Hurley notation is in the upper left corner. On Italian intelligence actions see David Alvarez, *Spies in the Vatican: Espionage and Intrigue from Napolean to the Holocaust* (Lawrence: University Press of Kansas, 2002), 212–215.

23. Journal of Caroline Drayton Phillips, September 13, 1939–February 24, 1940, journal in possession of Mrs. Anne Bryant; Eleanor Packard Reynolds, *Balcony Empire: Fascist Italy at War* (New York: Oxford University Press, 1942), 228; Hurley [Rome] to "Dear Doc," n.d., Archives of the Archdiocese of Detroit.

24. MacGregor Knox, *Mussolini Unleashed, 1939–1941: Politics and Strategy in Fascist Italy's Last War* (Cambridge: Cambridge University Press, 1982), 123; D. A. Binchy, *Church and State in Fascist Italy* (1941; reprint, Oxford: Oxford University Press, 1970), 662.

25. *New York Times*, January 28, 1939.

26. William Phillips to Sumner Welles, January 28, 1939, Papers of Sumner Welles, Office Correspondence, folder 7, Franklin D. Roosevelt Library; Radio Bulletin NR 22, "Address by Mr. Welles—Some Aspects of Our Foreign Policy," January 28, 1939 [U.S. Embassy], Rome, Hurley Papers, ADSA.

27. *The Ciano Diaries, 1939–1943: The Complete, Unabridged Diaries of Count Galeazzo Ciano Italian Minister for Foreign Affairs, 1936–1943,* ed. Hugh Gibson (New York: Howard Fertig, 1973), 111.

28. Warren F. Kimball, *The Most Unsordid Act: Lend-Lease, 1939–1941* (Baltimore: Johns Hopkins Press, 1969), 17.

29. *Osservatore Romano*, September 23, 1939, 1.

30. Richard A. Webster, *The Cross and the Fasces: Christian Democracy and Fascism in Europe* (Stanford: Stanford University Press, 1960), 142; "Italians Arrest Writer for Vatican City Paper," *New York Times*, September 8, 1939, 1; Herbert L. Matthews, *The Fruits of Fascism* (New York: Harcourt, Brace, 1943), 264.

31. Cordell Hull, *Memoirs* (New York: Macmillan, 1948), 713; Gerald P. Fogarty, S.J., *The Vatican and the American Hierarchy from 1870 to 1965* (Wilmington, Del.: Michael Glazier, 1985), 260.

32. Hull, *Memoirs*, 714.

33. William Phillips diary, William Phillips Papers, MS Am 2232, 55M-69 (vol. 21), 3475, by permission of the Houghton Library, Harvard University. Unfortunately, the Hurley archives do not contain this letter from President Roosevelt.

34. Camille M. Cianfarra, *The Vatican and the War* (New York: E. P. Dutton, 1944), 34, 146.

35. Sherman S. Hayden, "The Foreign Policy of the Vatican," *Foreign Policy Reports* 19 (1944): 284. Interestingly, Hayden provided a review copy of his article to Hurley before its publication.

36. Parts of the sketches of Pope Pius XI and Eugenio Pacelli rely on papal

historian John Pollard's excellent portraits in *Money and the Rise of the Modern Papacy: Financing the Vatican, 1850–1950* (Cambridge: Cambridge University Press, 2005), 127–130.

37. Martin S. Quigley to author, March 5, 1999.

38. An excellent survey of the historiographical controversy about Pacelli's greater fear of communism than of Nazism is found in José M. Sánchez, *Pius XII and the Holocaust: Understanding the Controversy* (Washington, D.C.: Catholic University of America Press, 2002), 103–107.

39. *Catholic Universe Bulletin*, News Clippings folder, n.d., Hurley Papers, ADSA; *New York Times*, October 1, 1936, 1.

40. Fogarty, *The Vatican and the American Hierarchy*, 246. Fogarty's assessment differs drastically from that of Rabbi David G. Dalin, who argues without citation that the specific aim of the meeting was to silence Coughlin. See Rabbi David G. Dalin, *The Myth of Hitler's Pope: How Pope Pius XII Rescued Jews from the Nazis* (Washington, D.C.: Regnery, 2005), 57. Although he was not silenced until 1942, Coughlin did observe a hiatus on his public speeches while Pacelli was in the country; John Cornwell, *Hitler's Pope: The Secret History of Pius XII* (New York: Viking, 1999), 176–177.

41. Harlan Phillips, oral history interview with Florence Kerr, October 18, 1963, Washington, D.C., Smithsonian Archives of American Art, http://www.aaa .si.edu/collections/oralhistories/transcripts/kerr63.htm#top (accessed January 26, 2006). The Kerr interview was restricted by the Smithsonian Institution until 1999. Historians and biographers of Pope Pius XII may have overlooked this important account, most likely because of a Federal News Service stenographer's phonetic transcription of Pacelli's name from the audio tape as "Pachelli." Ms. Karen B. Weiss, Information Resources Manager, Smithsonian Institution, telephone conversation with author, June 30, 2006.

42. Pacelli quoted in Alfred W. Klieforth to Jay Pierrepont Moffat, March 3, 1939, Papers of Jay Pierrepont Moffat, MS Am 1407 (vol. 16), by permission of the Houghton Library, Harvard University.

43. Ibid. When Hitler entered the German Workers' Party he was an informer assigned to the Political Department of the German army's VII (Munich) District Command, Bavarian Regiment Four. An excellent synopsis of Hitler's early ideological shifts and his initial left-wing dalliance is found in Ian Kershaw's epic *Hitler: 1889–1936 Hubris* (New York: W. W. Norton, 1999), 118–125. For a full discussion of Hitler and the German Workers' Party, see the first chapter of Geoffrey Stokes's *Hitler and the Quest for World Dominion* (New York: St. Martin's Press, 1986), 4–29.

44. Alfred W. Klieforth to Jay Pierrepont Moffat, March 3, 1939, Papers of Jay Pierrepont Moffat, MS Am 1407 (vol. 16), by permission of the Houghton Library, Harvard University.

45. Frank J. Coppa, *The Papacy, the Jews, and the Holocaust* (Washington, D.C.: Catholic University of America Press, 2006), 142–186.

46. Owen Chadwick, *Britain and the Vatican in the Second World War* (Cambridge: Cambridge University Press, 1986), 57; Peter C. Kent, *The Lonely Cold War of Pope Pius XII: The Roman Catholic Church and the Division of Europe, 1943–1950* (Montreal: McGill–Queens University Press, 2002), 15–17.

47. Domenico Tardini, *Memories of Pius XII* (Westminster, Md.: Newman Press, 1961), 73–75. The distinction between the political policies of the two popes is expertly presented in Peter C. Kent, "A Tale of Two Popes: Pius XI, Pius XII, and the Rome-Berlin Axis," *Journal of Contemporary History* 23 (1988): 589–608.

48. Hurley Vatican II notebook marked "1965," HAMC, reel 28.

49. Eugenio Cardinal Pacelli quoted in Dorothy Thompson, *Let the Record Speak* (Boston: Houghton Mifflin, 1939), 296.

50. On the relationship between Hurley and Cardinal Pacelli: Rev. Frank Mouch, telephone conversation with author, March 29, 2007. Father Mouch was named assistant chancellor of the Diocese of St. Augustine in 1963.

51. Hurley to Walter Foery, Bishop of Syracuse, N.Y., May 5, 1943, HAMC, reel 30. One of the only named references to Pacelli in Hurley's diaries is a recollection that "Cardinal Pacelli was devoted to Wagner's music—the sturdy, triumphal, surging kind"; Hurley notebook, HAMC, reel 28; Paul L. Rose, *German Question/Jewish Question: Revolutionary Anti-Semitism from Kant to Wagner* (Princeton: Princeton University Press, 1990), 378.

CHAPTER 5. "SPIES EVERYWHERE"

1. William Phillips diary, February 2, 1940, William Phillips Papers, MS Am 2232, 55M-69 (vol. 25), 3686, by permission of the Houghton Library, Harvard University.

2. NCWC news release (copy), June 1966, Hurley Papers, ADSA.

3. Harold H. Tittman to Hurley, June 7, 1962, HAMC, reel 28; *New York Times,* February 27, 1940.

4. Elisa A. Carrillo, "Italy, the Holy See and the United States, 1939–1945," in *Papal Diplomacy in the Modern Age,* ed. Peter C. Kent and John F. Pollard (Westport, Conn.: Praeger, 1994), 138; Myron C. Taylor to Giovanni B. Montini, March 26, 1940, Papers of Myron C. Taylor, box 10, Franklin D. Roosevelt Library, Hyde Park, N.Y.

5. John F. Morley, *Vatican Diplomacy and the Jews during the Holocaust, 1939–1943* (New York: Ktav, 1980), 130–131; *New York Times,* September 23, 1939.

6. William M. Harrigan, "Pius XII's Efforts to Effect a *Détente* in German-Vatican Relations, 1939–1940," *Catholic Historical Review* 49 (1963): 189. On Italy and U.S. dollars for the purchase of construction materials abroad see Joseph P. Kennedy diplomatic diary, March 10, 1940, Joseph P. Kennedy Papers Collection, box 92, Folder: March 1940, John F. Kennedy Presidential Library, Boston.

7. Cordell Hull to FDR, June 18, 1940, PSF, Diplomatic Correspondence: Vatican, box 51, Franklin D. Roosevelt Library. A *note verbale* is a communication

that is less formal than a signed note and more formal than a memorandum. It is unsigned, but it is customary to conclude it with a conventional
expression of courtesy; Secretariat of State to FDR (copy), note verbale
[no. 7515, April 26, 1940], Hurley Papers, ADSA.

8. Cordell Hull to FDR, June 18, 1940, PSF, Diplomatic Correspondence:
Vatican, box 51, Franklin D. Roosevelt Library; on Hull's anticatholicism see
diary entry, March, 2, 1939, Jay Pierrepont Moffat, Moffat diaries, vol. 42,
by permission of the Houghton Library, Harvard University; Myron Taylor
to Luigi Cardinal Maglione, note verbale, June 18, 1940, PSF, Diplomatic
Correspondence: Vatican, box 51, Franklin D. Roosevelt Library.

9. Michael R. Marrus, *The Unwanted: European Refugees in the Twentieth
Century* (New York: Oxford University Press, 1985), 267.

10. Harrigan, "Pius XII's Efforts," 186; on Hurley's hurried translation of
the English version see Camille M. Cianfarra, *The Vatican and the War*
(New York: E. P. Dutton, 1944), 197.

11. Hurley handwritten personal notes, 1940, Hurley Papers, ADSA.

12. Maurice Sheehy to Sumner Welles, June 11, 1941, Papers of Sumner Welles,
box 73, folder 5, Franklin D. Roosevelt Library.

13. Hurley personal notes, 1940, Hurley Papers, ADSA; Hurley diaries, n.d.,
HAMC, reel 28.

14. Arnold Lunn, *Come What May: An Autobiography* (Boston: Little, Brown,
1941), 337; Lunn, *Memory to Memory* (London: Hollis and Carter, 1956), 165;
"The Vatican on Conscientious Objectors," *The Tablet* 176 (1940): 31. New
research indicates that Vatican Radio was given the freedom to broadcast
some pro-Allied programming from 1940 through 1942; Jacques Adler,
"The 'Sin of Omission'? Radio Vatican and the anti-Nazi Struggle, 1940–
1942," *Australian Journal of Politics and History* 50 (2004): 396–406.

15. Raymond Jonas, *France and the Cult of the Sacred Heart: An Epic Tale for
Modern Times* (Berkeley: University of California Press, 2000), 171–180;
241–242.

16. For the Latin text with sectional demarcations see *Acta Apostolica Sedis* 31
(1940): 426. Father Ronald Knox's edition was published as *Encyclical Letter
Summi Pontificatus of Our Most Holy Lord Pius by Divine Providence Pope XII
of That Name* (London: Catholic Truth Society, 1939).

17. Flynn, *Roosevelt and Romanism*, 119.

18. Leslie Woodcock Tentler, *Seasons of Grace: A History of the Catholic Archdiocese of Detroit* (Detroit: Wayne State University Press, 1990), 353; Hurley
loose handwritten notes, 1940, Hurley Papers, ADSA.

19. Hurley to Doc [Mooney], July 25, 1940, HAMC, reel 30; personal notes
related to July 25 letter, Hurley Papers, ADSA.

20. Personal notes, 1940 (draft of the July 25 letter to Mooney), Hurley Papers,
ADSA; personal notes related to July 25 letter, ibid.

21. Tittman quoted in Rhodes, *Vatican in the Age of the Dictators*, 264; Pierre
Blet, *Pius XII and the Second World War* (New York: Paulist Press, 1999), 134.

In rendering Pius's voice, Blet relies heavily on the notes and recollections of Domenico Tardini. The personal perspective of Pius is disclosed largely through parsed public statements and previously published official sources.

22. Hurley handwritten personal notes, 1940, Hurley Papers, ADSA, copies in author's possession. Here Hurley uses the term "auditor" in the Italian sense of the word, that is, as one who receives and responds to reports.

23. Hurley draft of letter to Mooney, July 25, 1940, HAMC, reel 30; personal notes, 1940, Hurley Papers, ADSA.

24. 1940 notes, HAMC, reel 30. In 1940 Montini, arguably the prime antifascist in the curia, believed a German victory to be inevitable. His statement seems to be a political assessment of military realities rather than a philosophical compromise. See Richard J. Wolff, "Giovanni Battista Montini and Italian Politics, 1897–1933: The Early Life of Pope Paul VI," *Catholic Historical Review* 71 (1985): 227–247.

25. Unbound notes, HAMC, reel 30; personal notes, 1940, Hurley Papers, ADSA.

26. Hurley personal notes, "Last days in Rome," n.d., HAMC, reel 30.

27. Thomas J. Reese, S.J., *Archbishop: Inside the Power Structure of the American Catholic Church* (San Francisco: Harper & Row, 1989), chap. 1. For the Hurley timeline see *St. Augustine Record,* November 26, 1940; Carlo Cardinal Rossi to Hurley (photocopy), August 16, 1940, Archival Administrative Folders, ADSA.

28. Philip Matthew Hannan, *Rome: Living under the Axis: A Look Back at a Turbulent Time in History through the Letters of a Young Seminarian and Future Archbishop, 1936–1940* (McKees Rocks, Pa.: St. Andrew's Productions, 2003), 212; personal notes, 1940, Hurley Papers, ADSA.

29. "Diplomats on the Move," *Time,* September 2, 1940, 38; Rev. Joseph A. Luther to Rev. Francis X. Talbot, S.J., [2], July 10, 1941, *America* Archives, Special Collections, Georgetown University Library.

30. "Hurley Elevation in Vatican Likely: Clergymen Here Look for Consecration by Pope," *Cleveland Plain Dealer,* August 24, 1940; Hurley personal notes, HAMC, reel 30.

31. "Pope Appeals for Modesty: Assails 'Tyranny of Style,'" *Washington Post,* October 7, 1940, 1.

32. Alvarez, "The United States, the Vatican and World War II," 240; "Memorial Masses for Archbishop Hurley," NCWC News Service, October 30, 1968, NCWC Papers, Obituary Files, American Catholic History Research and University Archives, Catholic University of America.

33. *Biographical and Heraldic Dictionary of the Catholic Bishops in America,* ed. Gerard Brassard, vol. 2 (Worcester, Mass.: Stobbs Press, 1960), 153; *Oxford Latin Dictionary,* ed. P. G. W. Glare (London: Oxford University Press, 1983), 2073, 166.

34. "Hurley Becomes Bishop," *New York Times,* October 7, 1940; invitation list for consecration, October 6, 1940, Hurley Papers, box 145, ADSA.

35. "Pope Receives Mgr. Hurley," *New York Times*, October 8, 1940; Tittman to "My dear Bishop [Hurley]," n.d., Hurley Papers, box 145, ADSA.

36. Amanda Smith, ed., *Hostage to Fortune: The Letters of Joseph P. Kennedy* (London: Viking, 2001), 310–320; Susan Zuccotti, *Under His Very Windows: The Vatican and the Holocaust in Italy* (New Haven: Yale University Press, 2000), 268–269. Ignace Jan Paderewski, former premier of Poland and world-class pianist, was also a passenger on the ship.

CHAPTER 6. AN AMERICAN BISHOP IN PRESIDENT ROOSEVELT'S COURT

1. *Catholic Review* (Baltimore), August 23, 1940; "Tribute Paid to New Prelate by State Head," *St. Augustine Record*, November 26, 1940.

2. Michael V. Gannon, *The Cross in the Sand*, 2nd ed. (Gainesville: University of Florida Press, 1983), 26.

3. *Official Catholic Directory* (New York: P. J. Kenedy, 1940).

4. "Bishop Hurley Is Formally Installed," *Florida Catholic*, November 29, 1940, 1; "Tribute Paid to New Prelate by State Head," *St. Augustine Record*, November 26, 1940.

5. Edward King, "The Great South," *Scribner's* 9 (1874): 11; Annie Roberston MacFarlane, "A St. Augustine Episode," *Harper's* 65 (1882): 438; Nina Oliver Dean, "It's More than Miami," *New York Times*, January 21, 1940.

6. John F. Pollard, *Money and the Rise of the Modern Papacy: Financing the Vatican, 1850–1950* (Cambridge: Cambridge University Press, 2005), 137.

7. Ibid., 136–138. In his Vatican notes Hurley explained: "In computing fees for a Domestic Prelacy, the Italians have hit on a system which speaks volumes of their opinion of Americans: If the fee is £500 for an Italian, it is $500 for an American. They will explain that it is calculated in the currency of the country. But it is not £500 for the Englishman"; Hurley handwritten notes, Hurley Papers, ADSA.

8. J. D. Usina, interview with Julie Crum of the *St. Augustine Catholic*, 1995, audiocassette, side 2 of 2, ADSA; Rev. Frank M. Mouch, e-mail message to author, October 17, 2003.

9. Richard H. Davis, *The Consul* (New York: Charles Scribner's Sons, 1911), 11.

10. Hurley to Spessard Holland, January 17, 1942, Hurley Papers, box 48, folder I1, ADSA.

11. Hurley to Holland, February 7, 1942, ibid.

12. George Q. Flynn, *Roosevelt and Romanism: Catholics and American Diplomacy, 1937–1945* (Westport, Conn.: Greenwood Press, 1976), 186.

13. Leo V. Kanawada Jr., *Franklin D. Roosevelt's Diplomacy and American Catholics Italians and Jews* (Ann Arbor: UMI Research Press, 1982), 64.

14. Hurley to Roosevelt (telegram), January 20, 1941, President's Personal File 7303, Bishop Joseph P. Hurley Folder, Franklin D. Roosevelt Library, Hyde Park, N.Y.; Roosevelt to Hurley, January 22, 1941, ibid.; Arnold Lunn, *Memory to Memory* (London: Hollis and Carter, 1956), 165.

15. Alfred O. Hero Jr., *American Religious Groups View Foreign Policy: Trends in*

Rank and File Opinion, 1937–1969 (Durham, N.C.: Duke University Press, 1973), 12; Charles C. Tansill, *Back Door to War: The Roosevelt Foreign Policy 1933–1941* (1952; reprint, Westport, Conn.: Greenwood Press, 1975), 600.

16. Hero, *American Religious Groups,* 23; Mark Lincoln Chadwin, *The Hawks of World War II* (Chapel Hill: University of North Carolina Press, 1968), 248; Justus D. Doenecke, *Storm on the Horizon: The Challenge to American Interventionism* (Lanham, Md.: Rowman & Littlefield, 2000), 7.

17. Hurley, speech at NCCW Florida state convention, April 30, 1941, Hurley Papers, ADSA.

18. U.S. Congress, House, "Extension of Remarks of the Honorable Joe Hendricks," 77th Cong., 1st sess., *Congressional Record* 87, pt. 11 (May 8, 1941): A2176–77.

19. Alan Frazer, "Time to Act, Knox Asserts," *Boston Herald,* July 1, 1941; "Knox Talk Cheers Italy," *New York Times,* July 2, 1941.

20. James Reston, "Senators Call on President to Rebuke Knox," *Boston Herald,* July 2, 1941; *Church World,* July 18, 1941.

21. *London Universe,* June 20, 1941; *The Tablet,* June 21, 1941; *America,* May 17, 1941; Taylor to Hurley, July 2, 1941, Hurley Papers, box 31, folder T, ADSA.

22. Sumner Welles to Joseph P. Hurley, June 5, 1941, Papers of Sumner Welles, box 69, folder 10, Franklin D. Roosevelt Library.

23. Memorandum of conversation, Sumner Welles and Michael J. Ready, June 21, 1941, NCWC Papers, Records of the General Secretary, series 10, box 22, folder 23, American Catholic History Research and University Archives, Catholic University of America. Before World War II, the highest point of church-state contact for Catholics sympathetic to the Roosevelt administration was the 1939 State Department–sponsored Latin American junket of Bishop James H. Ryan of Omaha, Nebraska, and Monsignor Maurice Sheehy of the Catholic University of America in Washington, D.C. The two prelates met with FDR in Miami before departing for Latin America in order to counteract Nazi propaganda that portrayed the United States as a Protestant country unfriendly to Catholics.

24. David Scheinin, "The Closet Ally: Argentina," in *Latin America during World War II,* ed. Thomas M. Leonard and John F. Bratzel (Lanham, Md.: Rowman & Littlefield, 2006), 184. *Time* magazine used the term "realistic near-belligerency" to describe Argentine neutrality before Pearl Harbor; "Army of Amateurs," *Time,* June 9, 1941, online digital archive, http://www.time.com/time/magazine/article/0,9171,795331-1,00.html (accessed April 22, 2007).

25. Hurley to Welles, June 26, 1941, General Records of the Department of State, RG 59, file 860C.00/885, USNA.

26. Hurley, untitled speech delivered to the priests of the Diocese of St. Augustine at their annual retreat at St. Leo's Abbey, Tampa, Fla., June 17, 1941, Hurley Papers, ADSA.

27. Welles, confidential memorandum, June 30, 1941, General Records of the Department of State, RG 59, file 860C.00/885, USNA.

28. Jan Ciechanowski to Michael J. Ready (copy), June 21, 1941, Hurley Papers, box 59, folder A1, ADSA.

29. Hurley to Michael J. Ready, June 23, 1941, ibid.

30. Welles to Hurley, July 5, 1941, General Records of the Department of State, RG 59, file 860C.00/885, USNA.

31. Sumner Welles to Rev. Maurice Sheehy, June 30, 1941, Papers of Sumner Welles, Maurice Sheehy Files, box 73, folder 5, Franklin D. Roosevelt Library; Welles to Hurley, July 5, 1941, Hurley Papers, box 145, folder D16, ADSA.

32. Harold Tittman to Cordell Hull (telegram), May 28, 1941, Papers of Myron C. Taylor, box 10, Franklin D. Roosevelt Library; Rev. Maurice S. Sheehy to Sumner Welles, June 11, 1941, Papers of Sumner Welles, Maurice Sheehy Files, box 73, folder 5, Franklin D. Roosevelt Library.

33. Joseph P. Hurley, "Papal Pronouncements and American Foreign Policy" (speech delivered over the Columbia Broadcasting System Network at Washington, D.C., July 6, 1941), Hurley Papers, box 31, ADSA. For Hurley's verbatim lifting of antinazi rhetoric from Pope Pius XI see A. J. Hoover, *God, Britain and Hitler in World War II: The View of the British Clergy, 1939–1945* (Westport, Conn.: Praeger, 1999), 71.

34. Excerpt of letter from Wilfrid Parsons to Thomas Francis Meehan, July 16, 1941, General Correspondence Files, Joseph P. Hurley, box 15, folder 3, *America* Archives, Special Collections, Georgetown University Library; Gerald P. Fogarty, S.J., *The Vatican and the American Hierarchy from 1870 to 1965* (Wilmington, Del.: Michael Glazier, 1982), 272.

35. Hurley to Mooney, July 13, 1941, Hurley Papers, box 145, ADSA; *Washington Post*, July 7, 1941.

36. *The Witness*, July 11, 1941; "Archbishop Pleads against U.S. Entry into Foreign Wars," *Florida Catholic*, August 3, 1941.

37. Archbishop Francis J. Spellman to Pope Pius XII, September 4, 1941, in *ADSS*, 1: 182.

38. Bishop John A. Duffy to Hurley, July 8, 1941, Hurley Papers, box 31, ADSA.

39. Charles F. Mysert to Hurley, n.d., Hurley Papers, box 33, folder M, ADSA; James E. Murphy to Hurley, July 9, 1941, ibid.

40. Rev. Francis C. Boyle to Hurley, July 7, 1941, Hurley Papers, ADSA.

41. "July 6, 1941 Speech," personal notes, n.d., reel 30 HAMC; Flynn, *Roosevelt and Romanism*, 87.

42. Rev. Maurice Sheehy to Sumner Welles, September 11, 1941, Papers of Sumner Welles, Maurice Sheehy Files, box 73, folder 5, Franklin D. Roosevelt Library; "July 6, 1941 Speech," personal notes, n.d., HAMC, reel 30; Hurley pocket notebook (1941), Hurley Papers, ADSA.

43. Hurley unbound notebook, cabinet 6, drawer 1, ADSA. Purple was the color associated with the office of cardinal and came into ceremonial fashion under Pope Benedict VIII in the early eleventh century. The cardinal was vested with a red hat and a purple gown. Purple represented the color of

blood running through the veins. The metaphor was that cardinals would be of a mind to have their own blood spilled in order to maintain the articles of the Christian faith. In the old language, one was "raised to the purple" on being appointed a cardinal.

44. Cicognani to Maglione, August 11, 1941, *ADSS*, 5: 140–141.

45. *Social Justice,* July 14 and 28, 1941.

46. "July 6, 1941 Speech," personal notes, n.d., HAMC, reel 30; Rev. Joseph A. Luther, S.J., to Rev. Francis X. Talbot, S.J., July 11, 1941, Joseph P. Hurley folder, Wilfrid Parsons, S.J., Papers, Special Collections, Georgetown University Library; Hurley to Mooney, July 13, 1941, Hurley Papers, box 145, ADSA.

47. Welles to Hurley, July 8, 1941, Hurley Papers, box 31, ADSA; Taylor to Hurley, July 22, 1941, ibid.; Henry A. Wallace to Maurice Sheehy, July 8, 1941, ibid., box 145, folder E1.

48. Taylor Caldwell to Hurley, July 31, 1941, Hurley Papers, box 31, folder C, ADSA; Jacques Maritain to Hurley, July 9, 1941, ibid., folder M.

49. *Time,* July 14, 1941; U.S. Congress, Senate, "Extension of the Remarks of the Honorable Claude Pepper of Florida," 77th Cong., 1st sess., *Congressional Record* 87, pt. 14 (December 4, 1941): A5446–47; Ernest K. Lindley, "Bishop Hurley in Flaying Nazis May Have Set Forth the Settled Policy of the Papacy," *Brooklyn Eagle,* July 11, 1941, Clippings File, Joseph P. Hurley, box 15, folder 2, *America* Magazine Archives, Special Collections, Georgetown University Library; *Washington Post,* July 11, 1941, 9.

50. Hurley to Mooney, July 13, 1941, Hurley Papers, box 145, ADSA; Hurley to Sumner Welles, July 14, 1941, Papers of Sumner Welles, box 69, folder 10, Franklin D. Roosevelt Library; Hurley to Myron C. Taylor, July 19, 1941, Hurley Papers, box 31, folder T, ADSA; J. D. Usina, interview with Julie Crum of the *St. Augustine Catholic,* 1995, audiocassette, side 2 of 2, ADSA.

51. Hurley to Mooney, July 13, 1941, Hurley Papers, box 145, ADSA; Hurley editorial, *Florida Catholic,* July 13, 1941.

CHAPTER 7. PROPAGANDIST IN BLACK

1. Susan A. Brewer, *To Win the Peace: British Propaganda in the United States during World War II* (Ithaca: Cornell University Press, 1997), 5; Norman Polmar and Thomas B. Allen, *Spy Book: The Encyclopedia of Espionage,* 2nd ed. (New York: Random House, 2004), s.v. "Black Propaganda"; Stanley Newcourt-Nowordworski, *Black Propaganda in the Second World War* (Stroud, U.K.: Sutton, 2005), 1–5.

2. *Florida Catholic,* September 26, 1941. Hurley's editorial of September 26 mirrored, to a large extent, the reasoning of Rev. Edgar R. Smothers, S.J., who introduced the three moral antecedents for lending aid to Russia as early as 1939. See Edgar R. Smothers, S.J., "The Moral Aspects of Certain Relationships with Russia," *Ecclesiastical Review* 101 (1939): 50–54; and George Q. Flynn's summary of Smothers in *Roosevelt and Romanism:*

Catholics and American Diplomacy 1937–1945 (Westport, Conn.: Greenwood Press, 1976), 171–172. For the Hurley formula and FDR see Papers of Sumner Welles, William L. Langer and S. Everett Gleason Files, Franklin D. Roosevelt Library, Hyde Park, N.Y. See also Langer and Gleason, *The Undeclared War: 1940–1941* (1953; reprint, Gloucester, Mass.: Peter Smith, 1968), 797.

3. *New York Times*, March 28, 1942, and July 8, 1941; Hurley to Sumner Welles, Papers of Sumner Welles, box 79, folder 9, Franklin D. Roosevelt Library.

4. George S. Messersmith [Havana] to Sumner Welles, confidential memorandum, May 16, 1941, George S. Messersmith Papers, item 1459, Special Collections, University of Delaware Library, Newark.

5. Sumner Welles to Maurice S. Sheehy, June 30, 1941, Papers of Sumner Welles, Maurice Sheehy Files, box 73, folder 5, Franklin D. Roosevelt Library; "U.S. May Send Florida Bishop on Latin Tour," *Chicago Daily Times*, July 10, 1941; Hurley to Mooney, July 13, 1941, Hurley Papers, box 145, ADSA; memorandum of conversation, Michael J. Ready and Sumner Welles, July 17, 1941, NCWC Papers, Records of the General Secretary, series 10, box 22, folder 23, American Catholic History Research and University Archives, Catholic University of America.

6. Maurice S. Sheehy to Sumner Welles, July 10, 1941, Papers of Sumner Welles, Maurice Sheehy Files, box 73, folder 5, Franklin D. Roosevelt Library.

7. Mooney to Hurley, July 16, 1941, HAMC, reel 30.

8. *New York Enquirer*, 18 August, 1941. The *New York Enquirer* received its initial funding from William Randolph Hearst in 1926. Editor William Griffin, a former advertising man, was arrested for sedition in July 1942 in the same raids that detained the fringe religious leaders William Dudley Pelley and Gerald B. Winrod. These detentions briefly overshadowed the trial of the Nazi saboteurs discovered on Ponte Vedra Beach, Florida.

9. Gerald P. Fogarty, S.J., *The Vatican and the American Hierarchy from 1870 to 1965* (Wilmington, Del.: Michael Glazier, 1982), 276.

10. The move caused deep Allied mistrust for many years. In 1950 the issue came up in a conversation between British diplomats and Domenico Tardini. "The pope had to accept a Personal Representative from the Emperor of Japan," Tardini argued, "because of the precedent of Myron Taylor." Still uncomfortable about the 1942 messiness, Tardini was forced to skew the facts. Harada was not a "Personal Representative to His Holiness" but a special "Minister to the Holy See," a recognized rank in Vatican diplomacy and one of much greater import than Taylor's. See Sumner Welles to Franklin D. Roosevelt, memorandum, March 14, 1942, PSF, Departmental File: State Department, box 77, Franklin D. Roosevelt Library; John Somers Cocks to Western Department, "United States Representation to the Holy See," in *British Documents on Foreign Affairs: Reports and Papers from the Foreign Office Confidential Print*, vol. 26, ed. Denis Smyth (Bethesda, Md.: University Publications of America, 1983), 314. For Hurley quotes see untitled radio

broadcast of Joseph P. Hurley, National Broadcasting Corporation Network, Catholic Committee of the South, Richmond, Va., April 25, 1942, Hurley Papers, box "sermons, notes, talks," ADSA.

11. Taylor to Mooney, September 2, 1942, AAD.

12. Myron C. Taylor, ed., *Wartime Correspondence between President Roosevelt and Pope Pius XII* (New York: Macmillan, 1947), 68. Hurley's copy of this work is inscribed from Taylor "With enduring recollection and highest esteem"; library of the diocesan archives, ADSA.

13. Harold H. Tittman Jr., "Vatican Mission," *Social Order* 10 (1960): 116.

14. Taylor to Mooney, September 2, 1942, AAD. In a September 4 memo to FDR, Welles wrote: "Myron Taylor has handed me the attached draft which is the work of Archbishop Mooney, Bishop Hurley of Florida, and Monsignor Ready. He proposes to use it as a basis of his conversation with the Pope upon his arrival at the Vatican"; Sumner Welles to Franklin D. Roosevelt, memorandum, September 4, 1942, PSF, Diplomatic Correspondence: Vatican, box 51, Franklin D. Roosevelt Library.

15. A copy of the "Bishops' Draft" that Welles submitted for FDR's approval can be found in PSF, Diplomatic Correspondence: Vatican, box 51, Myron Taylor folder, Franklin D. Roosevelt Library.

16. Brian Barton, *Northern Ireland in the Second World War* (Belfast: Ulster Historical Foundation, 1995), 124–125.

17. *New York Times*, September 28, 1942; John P. Duggan, *Neutral Ireland and the Third Reich* (Totowa, N.J.: Barnes and Noble, 1985), 125; Dermot Keogh, *The Vatican, the Bishops and Irish Politics 1919–1939* (Cambridge: Cambridge University Press, 1986), 178–181.

18. Edith Iglauer, Office of War Information Security, to Hurley (telegram), n.d., Hurley Papers, box 36, folder B1, ADSA.

19. Thomas J. McDonough (Bishop Hurley's secretary) to Edith Iglauer, Office of War Information (telegram), September 29, 1949, ibid.; *Florida Catholic*, October 9, 1942.

20. Sumner Welles to Joseph P. Hurley, October 12, 1942, Papers of Sumner Welles, box 79, folder 9, Franklin D. Roosevelt Library; Sumner Welles, memorandum, October 12, 1942, President's Personal File 7303, Bishop Joseph P. Hurley Folder, Franklin D. Roosevelt Library; Sumner Welles to Franklin D. Roosevelt, General Records of the Department of State, RG 59, file 811.34541E/8A, USNA; Franklin D. Roosevelt, personal memorandum, October 12, 1942, President's Personal File, 4996, ibid.

21. "Memorandum for the Files," October 29, 1942, memorandum of conversation between Welles and Ready, NCWC Papers, Files of the General Secretary, series 10, box 22, folder 24, American Catholic History Research and University Archives.

22. Ibid.

23. Ready to Welles (copy), November 7, 1942, ibid.

24. Ibid.; Hurley handwritten notes, HAMC, reel 30.

25. Nicholas John Cull, *Selling War: The British Propaganda Campaign against American "Neutrality" in World War II* (New York: Oxford University Press, 1995), 10–11; Wilberforce to Hurley, October 24, 1942, Hurley Papers, box 55, folder C19, ADSA; Martin T. Gilligan (Hurley secretary) to Wilberforce, October 28, 1942, ibid., folder C20; Michael Igniateff, *Isaiah Berlin: A Life* (London: Chatto & Windus, 1998), 104.

26. Gaddis Smith, review of Benjamin Welles, *Sumner Welles: FDR's Global Strategist* (New York: St. Martin's Press, 1997), *New York Times Book Review,* January 25, 1998.

27. Hurley to Welles, June 3, 1942, Papers of Sumner Welles, box 79, folder 9, Franklin D. Roosevelt Library.

28. From June 8 through June 10 Hurley conducted meetings with Lieutenant Commander F. E. Weld of the Bureau of Aeronautics; Colonel D. R. Stinson, Army Assistant for Base Services; Lieutenant Colonel H. B. West of U.S. Army Munitions; Rear Admiral Chalker of the U.S. Coast Guard; and Captain F. U. Lake of the U.S. Navy.

29. For John T. Dillin's reports see HAMC, reel 16, folder 53 M-1, Correspondence: St. Augustine Defense Projects Special File, ADSA.

30. Hurley, untitled speech delivered to the priests of the Diocese of St. Augustine at their annual retreat at St. Leo's Abbey, Tampa, Fla., on June 17, 1941, Hurley Papers, ADSA; Owen Chadwick, "The Pope and the Jews in 1942," in *Persecution and Toleration,* Studies in Church History, vol. 21, ed. William J. Shields (Oxford: Blackwell, 1984), 469.

31. Murray Teitel in Joseph Bottum, Martin Rhonheimer, and Murry Teitel, "Another Skirmish in the Pius Wars," *First Things: A Monthly Journal of Religion and Public Life* 45 (2004): 7; Ronald J. Rychlak, "Goldhagen v. Pius XII," ibid., 42 (2002): 38; Daniel Jonah Goldhagen, *A Moral Reckoning: The Role of the Catholic Church in the Holocaust and Its Unfulfilled Duty to Repair* (New York: Knopf, 2002), 41–42.

32. Osborne and Bérard quoted in Chadwick, "The Pope and the Jews in 1942," 470–471; Pope Pius XII, "The Internal Order of States and People," Christmas Message, 1942, Eternal Word Television Network, http:www.ewtn.com/library/PAPALDOC/P12CH42.HTM (accessed June 12, 2006). In a chillingly ironic section, given the contemporary debate generated by the document, Pius argued that Catholics could not remain morally silent regarding the call for social justice that was at the heart of Marxism even though it was expressed in atheistic terms: "In spite of the fact that the ways they [Marxist workers] followed were and are false and to be condemned, what man, and especially what priest or Christian, could remain deaf to the cries that rise from the depths and call for justice and a spirit of brotherly collaboration in a world ruled by a just God? Such silence would be culpable and unjustifiable before God, and contrary to the inspired teaching of the Apostle."

33. Kevin Madigan, "What the Vatican Knew about the Holocaust, and When,"

Commentary 112 (2003): 50. Most scholarly discussions of the 1942 Christmas Message in the postwar period were silent on its application to the destruction of European Jews. Up to the late 1960s, the contents of the message were deemed valuable for Pius's thoughts on Christian marriage and the nascent development of a Catholic social doctrine on human rights. See Clement S. Mihmunovich and Alvin Werth, *Papal Pronouncements on Marriage and the Family* (Milwaukee: Bruce, 1955), 2; David A. Boileau, *Principles of Catholic Social Teaching* (Milwaukee: Marquette University Press, 1998), 44.

34. Tittman quoted in Chadwick, "The Pope and the Jews," 471.

35. Michael Phayer, *The Catholic Church and the Holocaust, 1930–1965* (Bloomington: Indiana University Press, 2000), 47–50; José M. Sánchez, *Pius XII and the Holocaust: Understanding the Controversy* (Washington, D.C.: Catholic University of America Press, 2002), 46.

36. In November 1942 the American bishops, as the National Catholic Welfare Conference, made a stirring statement against the Jewish persecutions. Although the statement was buried in a larger document, it was nevertheless important. "Since the murderous assault on Poland . . . there has been a premeditated and systematic extermination of the people of this nation," the bishops stated. "The same satanic technique is being applied to many other peoples," they asserted, "[including] the Jews in conquered countries and upon defenceless people not of our faith." The bishops' document, titled "Victory and Peace," was a lengthy treatise on Catholic war aims. The point on Jewish persecutions was made toward the middle of the statement, and buried among other weighty Catholic considerations. It did not stand out or receive much publicity at the time, and consequently has been ignored as a practical American Catholic castigation of Nazi methods. The statement is published in full in "American Catholic Responses to the Holocaust: An Exchange between David S. Wyman and Eugene J. Fisher," *Journal of Ecumenical Studies* 40 (2003): 386–389.

37. Hurley draft of editorial sent to G. R. Brunst, March 13, 1943, Hurley Papers, box 50, folder 1, ADSA. The draft was published verbatim as "Let Christians Take the Lead!" in the *Florida Catholic* on April 9, 1943. Exterminationist descriptions were exceedingly rare for Christians. On July 9, 1942, the Anglican cardinal-archbishop of Westminster, Arthur Hinsley, asserted in a radio broadcast that "in Poland alone, the Nazis have massacred 700,000 Jews since the outbreak of war." Hinsley protested the Jewish persecutions publicly until his death in March 1943, calling for "speedy deeds" by Catholic officials. Hinsley did not make protest against the camps a fundamental religious and moral obligation, as Hurley's editorial spells out. Hinsley's speech was welcomed with gratitude by England's Jewish community, while only a single Catholic paper grudgingly admitted the sufferings of Jews. See Thomas Moloney, *Westminster, Whitehall and the Vatican: The Role of Cardinal Hinsley, 1935–1943* (Wells, U.K.: Burns & Oates, 1985), 220.

38. Hurley, editorial, "Anti-Semitism: Our Problem," *Florida Catholic,* June 23, 1944.

39. Hurley to G. R. Brunst, March 13, 1943, Hurley Papers, box 50, folder 1, ADSA; Hurley, "Let Christians Take the Lead!"

40. Peter Novick, *The Holocaust and Collective Memory: The American Experience* (London: Bloomsbury, 2000), 20.

41. Phayer, *Catholic Church and the Holocaust,* 109.

42. A third but less substantial possibility is that the information on the death camps was handed to Hurley by the British Information Service's Robert Wilberforce during their secret Wardman Park Hotel meeting in late October 1942. Hurley's archive contains only correspondence indicating that a meeting with Wilberforce took place, not the substance of the conversation. During 1942 British codebreakers compiled four "thick" dossiers chronicling Nazi killings of Jews for use by the Foreign Office. The dossiers along with "working aids" were sent to the Foreign Office, via MI6, "sometime in 1943." See Michael Smith, "Bletchley Park and the Holocaust," *Intelligence and National Security* 19 (2004): 271.

43. Pierre Blet, S.J., *Pius XII and the Second World War According to the Archives of the Vatican* (Mahwah, N.J.: Paulist Press, 1999), 162. Blet asserts that by June 1943, Pius XII continued to issue measured statements on the topic of the death camps "in the very interest of those who suffer so as not to make their position even more difficult and intolerable than previously." This quasi-utilitarian position is at odds with Hurley's thesis, which was based on a fundamental moral response demanded by each Christian's vocation. Moreover, what Hurley described as a zero-sum game resulting in mass death could hardly have made it "even more difficult and intolerable" for Jews in the camps; Madigan, "What the Pope Knew," 49.

44. Susan Zuccotti, *Under His Very Windows: The Vatican and the Holocaust in Italy* (New Haven: Yale University Press, 2000), 103–107; Hurley to G. R. Brunst, March 13, 1943, Hurley Papers, box 50, folder A1, ADSA; "After War Plans Made with Pope," September 23, 1942, Associated Press clipping, Hurley scrapbook, ibid.

45. Fogarty, *Vatican and the American Hierarchy,* 310.

CHAPTER 8. A PARALLEL ENDEAVOR AGAINST COMMUNISM

1. Martin S. Quigley, *Peace without Hiroshima: Secret Action at the Vatican in the Spring of 1945* (New York: Madison Press, 1991), 59–60; Franklin Lindsay to Herbert Hoover, report, "Developments in Yugoslavia, March–August, 1945," Franklin Lindsay Papers, box 9, folder 23, Hoover Institution Archives, Stanford, Calif. Lindsay was chief of the U.S. Military Mission in Yugoslavia in 1944 and 1945.

2. Ernest Satow, *A Guide to Diplomatic Practice* (London: Longmans, 1957), 117; Hyginus Eugene Cardinale, *The Holy See and the International Order* (Gerrards Cross, U.K.: Colin Smythe, 1976), 146. In June 1950 Pius's shrewd

game with regents began to backfire when the Rumanian communist government expelled Hurley's fellow American regent ad interim, Archbishop Gerald P. O'Hara. Citing regency as the pretext, the Rumanian Ministry of Foreign Affiars ousted O'Hara because "being but the diplomatic representative of the Vatican City . . . [he could] not speak on behalf of the Christian world." See Romulus Boila and Alexandre Cretzianu, *Captive Rumania: A Decade of Soviet Rule* (New York: Praeger, 1956), 197.

3. Peter C. Kent, *The Lonely Cold War of Pope Pius XII: The Roman Catholic Church and the Division of Europe, 1943–1950* (Montreal: McGill–Queen's University Press, 2002), 159. Within Pius's system, the appointment also had advantages. For one, it allowed Pius to appoint Hurley to a high diplomatic post without officially raising him to the rank of archbishop, the usual ecclesiastical rank for a nuncio. Of course, Pius had been ready to do this back in 1941, but Hurley's interventionist July 6, 1941, speech dissuaded him from moving Hurley up the ecclesiastical ladder.

4. *Osservatore Romano*, October 22, 1945. The Vatican newspaper's rendering of diplomatic events during the war was technically correct but somewhat at variance with actual circumstances. Ramiro Marcone, while officially an apostolic visitor without full diplomatic credentials, was nonetheless recorded on the diplomatic list of the Independent State of Croatia during World War II, was afforded the diplomatic courtesies usually accorded representatives of the Holy See, and made the rounds of official receptions and occasions sponsored by the Nazi puppet state. On Tito's request to the Vatican see Harold Shantz [Belgrade] to Secretary of State (telegram), February 23, 1946, General Records of the Department of State, RG 84, Belgrade Legation and Embassy Files, box 71, Secret File: Stepinac Case, 1946, USNA.

5. Colonel John E. Duffy to Hurley, November 5, 1945, Hurley Papers, box 147, folder D3, ADSA.

6. Tittman to Secretary of State, October 26, 1945, General Records of the Department of State, RG 59, file 860.H.404/10–2645, USNA.

7. Jozo Tomasevich, *War and Revolution in Yugoslavia, 1941–1945: Occupation and Collaboration* (Stanford: Stanford University Press, 2001), x. Tomasevich's book will be the standard text on World War II Yugoslavia for many years. Tomasevich writes extensively on the role of the churches and, because of his long historical view, offers a balanced account of the religious, ethnic, and ideological struggles. For the role and history of Roman Catholicism in wartime Yugoslavia see especially 87–101, 532–534, and 551–575.

8. Stella Alexander, "Yugoslavia and the Vatican, 1919–1970," in *Papal Diplomacy in the Modern Age*, ed. Peter C. Kent and John F. Pollard (Westport, Conn.: Praeger, 1994), 155; Tomasevich, *War and Revolution in Yugoslavia*, 55.

9. Stella Alexander, *Church and State in Yugoslavia since 1945* (New York: Columbia University Press, 1979), 20.

10. Stella Alexander, "Croatia: The Catholic Church and Clergy, 1919–1945," in *Catholics, the State, and the European Radical Right*, ed. Richard J. Wolff and

Jörg K. Hoensch (New York: Columbia University Press, 1987), 35; Tardini quoted in Myron Taylor to Secretary of State (telegram), May 19, 1945, General Records of the Department of State, RG 59, Myron C. Taylor Papers, box 29, USNA.

11. Hurley, speech at NCCW Florida state convention, April 30, 1941, Hurley Papers, ADSA; Hurley quoted in Avro Manhattan, *Catholic Imperialism and World Freedom* (London: Watts, 1952), 227.

12. For Hurley on *antemurale Christianitatis* see Hurley to Ivan Meštrović, October 10, 1953, Ivan Meštrović Microfilm, box 8, folder 9, University of Notre Dame Archives, Notre Dame, Ind. On the concept of *antemurale Christianitatis* see David Bruce MacDonald, *Balkan Holocausts? Serbian and Croatian Victim-Centered Propaganda and the War in Yugoslavia* (Manchester: Manchester University Press, 2002), 114–118.

13. Hurley handwritten speech, n.d., NCWC Papers, Records of the General Secretary, series 10, box 26, folder 20, American Catholic History Research and University Archives, Catholic University of America.

14. Hurley to Howard J. Carroll, February 5, 1952, ibid., box 27, folder 6; [Hurley] speech, "Bleiburg-Maribor: Croatian Super Katyn," n.d., Yugoslavia Folder, ADSA. The typescript matches the font on Hurley's typewriter and presumably was either written or reviewed by Hurley.

15. John R. Lampe, *Yugoslavia as History* (Cambridge: Cambridge University Press, 1999), 110; Hurley confidential letter to Ivan Meštrović, October 10, 1953, Ivan Meštrović Microfilm, box 8, folder 9, University of Notre Dame Archives, Notre Dame, Ind.

16. Hurley diaries, notebook Z5, Hurley Papers, ADSA.

17. Richard West, *Tito and the Rise and Fall of Yugoslavia* (New York: Carroll & Graf, 1994), 28; Hurley handwritten marginalia in galley proofs of Richard Pattee's *The Case of Cardinal Aloysius Stepinac*, [13], Hurley Papers, box 150, ADSA.

18. Franklin C. Gowen to Secretary of State, January 8, 1946, General Records of the Department of State, RG 59, Myron C. Taylor Papers, box 28, Confidential Correspondence File, USNA; Patterson to Gowen, January 25, 1946, General Records of the Department of State, RG 84, Belgrade Legation and Embassy Files, box 71, 840.4, Secret File: Catholic Church, USNA; Taylor characterized in Franklin C. Gowen to Secretary of State (telegram), January 15, 1945, General Records of the Department of State, RG 59, Myron C. Taylor Papers, box 28, Confidential Correspondence File, USNA.

19. John Lewis Gaddis, *The United States and the Origins of the Cold War, 1941–1947* (New York: Columbia University Press, 1972), 52; Memorandum of a Conversation (Confidential) Regarding United States Relations with the Vatican, April 3, 1947, J. Graham Parsons Papers, box 1, folder 8, Special Collections, Georgetown University Library.

20. Rev. John P. McNulty, interview with author, April 18, 1995. Many of these reports may be found in General Records of the Department of State, RG

84, Belgrade Legation and Embassy Files, as well as the Yugoslavia Files, files 840.H to 860.H400, 1945–1950.

21. Thomas A. Hickok to Secretary of State James F. Byrnes, January 7, 1947, in *FRUS*, 1947, 4:744–746.

22. Ann Lane, *Britain, the Cold War and Yugoslav Unity* (Sussex: Academic Press, 1996), 64; Myron C. Taylor to Harry S. Truman, June 25, 1946, White House Central Files: Confidential File, State Department, Myron C. Taylor Papers, box 44, Harry S. Truman Presidential Library, Independence, Mo.

23. Secretary of State to Myron Taylor, March 7, 1946, General Records of the Department of State, RG 59, Myron C. Taylor Papers, box 28, Confidential Correspondence File, 1944–1947, USNA.

24. *FRUS*, 1945, 5: 1291.

25. Charles W. Thayer, *Hands across the Caviar* (Philadelphia: Lippincott, 1952), 153.

26. Harold Shantz [Belgrade] to Secretary of State, April 3, 1946, General Records of the Department of State, RG 59, file 860H.404/4-346, USNA.

27. [Hurley] report, "For the Attention of the American Ambassador," n.d., General Records of the Department of State, RG 84, Belgrade Legation and Embassy Secret File: Catholic Church, box 71, file 840.4, USNA.

28. Patterson [Belgrade] to American Representative at Vatican City (telegram), February 14, 1946, ibid.

29. Harold Shantz [Rome] to Secretary of State (telegram), June 5, 1946, ibid.; telegram received, May 21, 1946, ibid.; Secretary of State to American Embassy, Belgrade, telegram received, June 12, 1946, ibid.

30. Telegram received, Acheson to Patterson, May 16, 1946 (see Patterson's notations in pencil), ibid. Hurley's intervention on behalf of the sisters ranks as perhaps the swiftest U.S. response to a Vatican request on record. In May 1943 Pope Pius XII had written a personal letter to President Roosevelt beseeching him to desist from an Allied aerial bombardment of Rome. This maneuver, which met with failure, was a public one and quickly drew a great deal of press reporting. See Pierre Blet, S.J., *Pius XII and the Second World War: According to the Archives of the Vatican*, trans. Lawrence J. Johnson (New York: Paulist Press, 1999), 203–209.

31. Truman to Patterson quoted in Lorraine M. Lees, *Keeping Tito Afloat: The United States, Yugoslavia, and the Cold War* (Pittsburgh: University of Pennsylvania Press, 1993), 6; *FRUS*, 1946, 6: 923.

32. Hurley to Mooney, May 28, 1946, AAD.

33. Jozo Tomasevich rightly describes the historiography on Cardinal Stepinac as "voluminous." Currently, the historiography on Stepinac has devolved into near polemics, with defenders and detractors lining up with equal vigor at every historical turn. The Cold War produced a flood of defensive books about the imprisoned cleric. In the early 1990s, as Yugoslavia descended into ethnic warfare and political breakup, Stepinac emerged again as a symbol of either heroism or criminality. In 1998, when raised to near-sainthood

by Pope John Paul II, new protests erupted. For a scholarly treatment of
the Stepinac case see Stella Alexander's well-balanced biography, *The Triple
Myth: A Life of Archbishop Alojzije Stepinac* (New York: Columbia University
Press, 1987); and Alexander, "Yugoslavia and the Vatican, 1919–1970." Schol-
arly critics of Stepinac include Carlo Falconi, *The Silence of Pope Pius XII*
(Boston: Little, Brown, 1970); Menachem Shelah, "The Catholic Church in
Croatia: The Vatican and the Murder of the Croatian Jews," *Holocaust and
Genocide Studies* 4 (1989): 323–327; and Michael Phayer, *The Catholic Church
and the Holocaust, 1930–1965* (Bloomington: University of Indiana Press,
2000), 31–47. Prominent polemists include Viktor Novak, *Magnum Crimen:
Pola Vijeka Klerikalizma u Hrvatskoj* (1948; reprint, Belgrade: Nova Knjig,
1986); and Vladimir Dedijer, *The Yugoslav Auschwitz and the Vatican: The
Croatian Massacre of the Serbs during World War II* (Buffalo: Prometheus
Books, 1992). Richard Pattee wrote the Vatican-sponsored defense of Stepinac, *The Case of Cardinal Aloysius Stepinac* (Milwaukee: Bruce Publishing,
1953). A postbeatification defense, written at the suggestion of Pope John
Paul II, is Giampaolo Mattei's *Cardinal Alojzije Stepinac: A Heroic Life in
Testimony of Those Who, Together with Him, Were Victims of the Persecution
of Communist Yugoslavia* (Zagreb: Glas Koncila, 2005).

34. Alexander, *The Triple Myth.*
35. Jill A. Irvine, *The Croat Question: Partisan Politics in the Formation of the
Yugoslav Socialist State* (Boulder: Westview Press, 1993), 100.
36. "Bishop in Croatia Flays Censorship and War on Jews," NCWC radio news
service report, *Florida Catholic,* July 16, 1943. On the Vatican's lack of condemnation see Milan Ristović, "Yugoslav Jews Fleeing the Holocaust, 1941–
1945," in *Remembering for the Future: The Holocaust in an Age of Genocide,*
ed. John K. Roth and Elisabeth Maxwell (New York: Palgrave, 2001), 519.
37. Menachem Shelah, "The Catholic Church in Croatia: The Vatican and the
Murder of the Croatian Jews," in *Remembering for the Future: Working Papers
and Addenda,* ed. Yehuda Bauer, vol. 1 (Oxford: Pergamon Press, 1989), 274.
38. Franklin Lindsay to Herbert Hoover, report, "Developments in Yugoslavia,
March–August, 1945," 6, Franklin Lindsay Papers, box 9, folder 23, Hoover
Institution Archives.
39. Stella Alexander quoted in Kent, *Lonely Cold War,* 106.
40. Franklin C. Gowen to Secretary of State (airgram), January 10, 1946, Myron
C. Taylor Papers, General Records of the Department of State, RG 59, box
30, file: Telegrams and Airgrams Sent, 1946–49, USNA.
41. "The Trial of Archbishop Stepinac," undated typescript, 136, Richard C.
Patterson Papers, box 4, Miscellaneous Folder, Truman Library.
42. George Seldes, *Witness to a Century* (New York: Ballantine, 1987), 432.
43. Conversation of Zagreb vice-consul Theodore J. Hohenthal with Archbishop
Stepinac quoted in Harold Shantz to Secretary of State, September 21, 1946,
General Records of the Department of State, RG 59, Myron C. Taylor

Papers, box 34, file: Stepinac Case, 1946, USNA; *Washington Post,* September 20, 1946, 1.

44. Hurley diaries, notebook "1963 Varia I," entry for "Communism," Hurley Papers, ADSA.

45. Ibid.

46. Author interview with unnamed source, May 6, 1999. I am grateful to this source for sharing the gist of the Pius XII–Hurley conversation.

47. U.S. Office of Strategic Services, Foreign Nationalities Branch Files, microfiche INT 171T-810 (Bethesda, Md.: University Publications of America, 1988); Luigi Sturzo, *Corrispondenza Americana, 1940–1944,* ed. Leo S. Olschki (Florence: Istituto Luigi Sturzo, 1998), 49.

48. Hurley diaries, notebook marked "1961–2–3," Hurley Papers, ADSA.

49. Josef Korbel, *Tito's Communism* (Denver: University of Denver Press, 1951), 157; Jill A. Irvine, *The Croat Question: Partisan Politics in the Formation of the Yugoslav Socialist State* (Boulder: Westview Press, 1993), 236–238.

50. Joe [Hurley at Rome] to *Eminentissimi* Doc [Mooney], September 17, 1946, AAD.

51. Theodore J. Hohenthal report transcribed in Harold Shantz [Belgrade] to Secretary of State, September 21, 1946, General Records of the Department of State, RG 59, Myron C. Taylor Papers, box 34, file: Stepinac Case, 1946, USNA. Copies of this report were sent to the War Department and to U.S. Naval Intelligence.

52. Ibid.

53. Joe [Hurley] to *Eminentissimi* Doc [Mooney], September 17, 1946, AAD. Hurley began this letter: "I'm returning to Belgrade tomorrow after a month in Switzerland and a few days in Rome." Theodore Hohenthal to Secretary of State, September 18, 1946, RG 84, Belgrade Legation and Embassy Files, box 71, General Files, Secret File: Stepinac Case, 1946, USNA. On Hurley's absence from the country see also "Pope Dispatches U.S. Bishop to Aid of Yugoslav Prelate," *Washington Post,* September 20, 1946, 1; Franklin C. Gowen to Secretary of State (telegram), September 18, 1946, General Records of the United States Department of State, RG 59, Myron C. Taylor Papers, box 30, USNA; "Archbishop Seized," *Facts on File World News Digest,* July 27, 1946, Facts on File World News Digest (FACTS.com), http://www.2facts.com/ (accessed July 22, 2005).

54. *Osservatore Romano* statement quoted in *New York Times,* September 21, 1946.

55. Msgr. John P. McNulty, interview with author, April 18, 1995, St. Petersburg, Fla. I am grateful to the late Monsignor McNulty for graciously sharing his recollections, and to the Diocese of St. Petersburg.

56. *Osservatore Romano,* September 20, 1946; *Washington Post,* October 12, 1946.

57. "Imprisonment of the Archbishop of Zagreb: Why Those in Any Way Responsible Have Been Excommunicated," *The Tablet* 188 (1946): 196–198.

The Holy See excommunicated on three separate counts, but it was the fact that a lay court had passed judgment on an ecclesiastical person and so "directly impeded the exercise of his ecclesiastical jurisdiction" that was the real charge.

Historian Margherita Marchione has argued that during World War II Adolf Hitler "incurred automatic excommunication" under the identical canons. But apparently neither the Holy See nor the Sacred Congregation of the Council bothered to issue a formal decree for Hitler, an omission that has prompted a small but lively modern historical debate. See "Sacred Congregation of the Council," *Acta Apostolica Sedis* 38 (1946): 401; *The Times* (London), October 15, 1946; Margherita Marchione, *Pope Pius XII: Architect for Peace* (Mahwah, N.J.: Paulist Press, 2000), 24, 44–45; Peter Godman, *Hitler and the Vatican: Inside the Secret Archives That Reveal the New Story of the Nazis and the Church* (New York: Free Press, 2004), 155–161. James Carroll reviews the history of excommunications and discusses the topic of an excommunication of Hitler by Pope Pius XII as an important point in *Constantine's Sword: The Church and the Jews—A History* (Boston: Houghton Mifflin, 2001). On Hurley's blessing of Stepinac's mother see *New York Times,* October 14, 1946.

58. T. J. Hohenthal to Secretary of State, December 31, 1946, General Records of the Department of State, RG 59, Myron C. Taylor Papers, box 28, Confidential Correspondence File, USNA.

59. Robert P. Joyce, Political Advisor, British–United States Zone, to Cavendish W. Cannon, March 17, 1948, General Records of the Department of State, RG 84, Belgrade Legation and Embassy Files, 1948, box 117, Secret File 840.4: Anti-Catholic Incidents, USNA.

60. Ibid.

CHAPTER 9. BETRAYAL IN THE BALKANS

1. Hurley to Mooney, November 23, 1946, AAD.

2. Patterson quoted in *New York Times,* October 24, 1946; "U.S. Interest in Civil Liberties in Yugoslavia," *Department of State Bulletin* 15 (1946): 725.

3. From the 1950s to the 1990s the Stepinac case continued to pop up on the U.S. diplomatic radar. During the early 1960s Senator Lyndon Baines Johnson became deeply interested in the case and received hundreds of letters from a national constituency. As late as 2005, Cardinal Stepinac's legacy entered the U.S. State Department's International Religious Freedom Report. In April 2004 the head of the Croatian Bishops' Conference Justice and Peace Commission called for an apology by Cable News Network (CNN) for indicating during coverage of the funeral of Pope John Paul II that "many perceived Stepinac as close to the country's World War II Nazi puppet regime." CNN refused to comply with the request, stating that "they merely reported about his life"; U.S. Department of State, Bureau of Democracy, Human Rights and Labor, International Religious Freedom Report, Report

on Croatia, November 8, 2005, http://www.state.gov/g/drl/rls/irf/2005/
51546.htm (accessed February 26, 2007).

4. On Peter Constan's anticommunism see Constan to Patterson, memorandum, "Observations of the 1945 Election," Peter Constan Papers, box 1,
Election in Yugoslavia file, Manuscript Division, Library of Congress, Washington, D.C.; see also Constan's memoranda on the Mihailovic trial in the
same collection.

5. Peter Constan, "The Zagreb Trials: Trial of the Archbishop of Zagreb,
Dr. Aloysius Stepinac," General Records of the Department of State, RG 59,
Myron C. Taylor Papers, box 34, Miscellaneous Subject Folder: Stepinac
Case, 1946, USNA; Hohenthal to Secretary of State (telegram), October 3,
1946, General Records of the Department of State, RG 84, Belgrade Lega-
tion and Embassy Files, box 71, Secret File: Stepinac Case, 1946, file 840.4,
USNA.

6. David P. Currie, "The Constitution in the Supreme Court: The Second
World War, 1941–1946," *Catholic University Law Review* 37 (1987): 23. *Haupt
v. United States* overturned a 1945 decision in *Cramer v. United States* that
two witnesses were needed to testify to the same overt act. Thus, *Haupt* lowered the requirements for treason prosecutions against American nationals.

7. Harold Shantz [Belgrade] to Secretary of State (telegram), February 23, 1946,
General Records of the Department of State, RG 84, Belgrade Legation
and Embassy Files, box 71, Secret File: Stepinac Case, 1946, USNA; Shantz
[Belgrade] to Secretary of State, April 3, 1946, General Records of the Department of State, RG 59, 860H.404/4-346, USNA.

8. Hohenthal [Zagreb] to Secretary of State, General Records of the Department of State, RG 59, Myron Taylor Papers, box 34, file: Stepinac Case,
1946, USNA. The "Archbishop's Memorandum" is enclosure no. 2 of dispatch no. 1, dated September 26, 1946.

9. Tito quoted by Peake in Dianne Kirby, *Church, State and Propaganda: The
Archbishop of York and International Relations, a Political Study of Cyril Forster
Garbett* (Hull: University of Hull Press, 1999), 163.

10. "Communism: Yugoslavia," informal notes, NCWC Papers, Office of the
General Secretary, series 10, box 26, folder 20, American Catholic History
Research and University Archives, Catholic University of America. The
notes are written in Bishop Hurley's hand. On Ivo Politeo see Hurley hand-
written marginalia in galley proofs for Richard Pattee, *The Case of Cardinal
Aloysius Stepinac*, [26], Hurley Papers, box 150, ADSA.

11. Hohenthal to Secretary of State, September 26, 1946, USNA. Some of the
points outlined in the "Archbishop's Memorandum" bear close resemblance
to a long press release issued by Zagreb's vicar general, Monsignor Franjo
Salis Seewis, shortly after Stepinac's conviction. See Giampaolo Mattei,
*Cardinal Alojzije Stepinac: Heroic Life in Testimony of Those Who, Together
with Him, Were Victims of the Persecution of Communist Yugoslavia* (Zagreb:
Glas Koncila, 2005), 59.

Missed by all biographers of Stepinac is that his major and repeated defense claim, that his "conscience was clear," rested on the then theologically correct tenet that all interactions with the NDH would have been morally acceptable because the NDH was a civilly constituted state. Both the *Catechism of the Council of Trent* and St. Thomas Aquinas's *Summa Theologie* understood Catholic church-state relations from a deferential position to the state, especially if state constitutions were civilly accepted and the state was not overtly atheistic. As the *Catechism of the Council of Trent* put it, "To some it belongs to govern . . . to others, to be subject and obey." Stepinac's point on conscience was derived from this prevailing theology. In his "last word" at trial, Stepinac argued from the normative civil-religious perspective when he said: "We could not ignore the authority here, even if it were Ustasha." Tellingly, Stepinac asserted to the prosecution: "You have a right to call me to account for action since May 8, 1945," VE Day and the day Tito's Partisan movement officially adhered to the general armistice and declared peace— thereby claiming civil legitimacy. An activist theology confronting unjust regimes and unjust laws did not yet exist in 1946.

12. Michael Phayer, *The Catholic Church and the Holocaust, 1930–1965* (Bloomington: Indiana University Press, 2000), 170; Vjekoslav Perica, *Balkan Idols: Religion and Nationalism in Yugoslav States* (Oxford: Oxford University Press, 2002), 27.

13. United Nations, Italian Military Armistice, September 3, 1943, *American Journal of International Law* 40 (1946): suppl. 1, United Nations Documents, 9.

14. Walworth Barbour, "Trial of Archbishop Stepinac," position paper, November 1, 1946, General Records of the Department of State, RG 59, Records Relating to Yugoslavia, box 1, file 660, USNA. Released through the United States Freedom of Information Act, hereafter USFOIA.

15. Hurley memorandum to Thomas J. McDonough, October 21, 1947, Diocesan Development Fund folder, Hurley Papers, ADSA; Charles G. Stefan, "The Emergence of the Soviet-Yugoslav Break: A Personal View from the Belgrade Embassy," *Diplomatic History* 6 (1982): 387.

16. *FRUS*, 1948, 4: 1073.

17. Hurley to Mooney, September 17, 1948, AAD.

18. Myron C. Taylor to Harry S. Truman, July 25, 1948, White House Central Files: Confidential File, State Department, Myron C. Taylor Papers, box 1, file: Reports—1948, Harry S. Truman Library, Independence, Mo.

19. Hurley to Mooney, September 17, 1948, AAD; Lorraine M. Lees, "American Foreign Policy toward Yugoslavia, 1941–1949" (Ph.D. diss.: Pennsylvania State University, 1976), 143.

20. John R. Lampe, Russell O. Prickett, and Ljubisa S. Adamovic, eds., *Yugoslav-American Economic Relations since World War II* (Durham, N.C.: Duke University Press, 1990), 13.

21. Transmittal letter of Reams to J. Graham Parsons, quoted in Parsons to Secretary of State, February 14, 1948, General Records of the Department of

State, RG 59, file 860H.404/2-1448, USNA. Reams's exchange also reveals that the United States had infiltrated the nunciature and was now cognizant of Hurley's moves; Franklin C. Gowen to Secretary of State, July 25, 1949, ibid., file 860H.404/7-2549.

22. Lorraine M. Lees, "The American Decision to Assist Tito," *Diplomatic History* 2 (1978): 410.

23. Hurley, "Comments on Proposal to Extend Aid to Yugoslavia," handwritten speech, NCWC Papers, Files of the General Secretary, series 10, box 26, folder 20, American Catholic History Research and University Archives.

24. K. W. C. Sinclair-Loutit, "Understanding the Balkan Conflict," *Contemporary Review* 264 (1994): 230.

25. Archbishop Joseph P. Hurley quoted in *The Man of God and His People: First Anniversary Commemoration of the Death of Cardinal Stepinac* (Cleveland: United American Croatians, 1961), [11].

26. Dean Acheson to Harry S. Truman, memorandum, October 6, 1952, PSF, Secret File: Foreign Affairs—Yugoslavia, Truman Papers, Truman Library.

27. "Memorandum on the Religious Situation in Yugoslavia since January, 1947," dated June 1949, White House Central Files: Confidential File, State Department, Myron C. Taylor Papers, box 2, file: Reports—1949, Truman Library; Myron C. Taylor to Harry S. Truman, June 14, 1949, ibid., box 49, folder 1.

28. Harry S. Truman to Myron C. Taylor, June 17, 1949, ibid., box 49, folder 1.

29. Milovan Djilas, *Rise and Fall* (New York: Harcourt Brace Jovanovich, 1985), 39.

30. Hurley to Domenico Tardini (copy), May 15, 1947, NCWC Papers, Records of the General Secretary, series 10, box 26, folder 18, American Catholic History Research and University Archives.

31. Hurley to Mooney, March 4 and December 12, 1949, AAD.

32. Stella Alexander, *Church and State in Yugoslavia since 1945* (New York: Columbia University Press, 1979), 124, 128.

33. Sheen quoted in *New York Times*, September 13, 1948.

34. H. W. Brands, *The Specter of Neutralism: The United States and the Emergence of the Third World, 1947–60* (New York: Columbia University Press, 1989), 156–157; Philip Jenkins, *The Cold War at Home: The Red Scare in Pennsylvania, 1945–1960* (Chapel Hill: University of North Carolina Press, 1999), 172–175.

35. Hurley notes, "Yugoslavia," n.d., Hurley Papers, ADSA. On Stepinac's release only under order from Pope Pius XII, see Silvio Oddi, *Il tenero mastino di Dio: Memorie del Cardinale Silvio Oddi* (Rome: Progetti museali editore, 1995), 55.

36. Hurley to Mooney, December 12, 1949, AAD.

37. Ibid.

38. Hurley to Mooney, March 4 and December 12, 1949, AAD.

39. Harold Nicolson, *Diplomacy* (London: Oxford University Press, 1939), 124.

40. Robert P. Joyce, Political Advisor, British-U.S. Zone (Trieste), to Cavendish W. Cannon, March 17, 1948, General Records of the Department of State, RG 84, Belgrade Legation and Embassy Files, 1948, box 117, Secret File 840.4: Anti-Catholic Incidents, USNA.

41. *Il Quotidiano* quoted in *Florida Catholic,* June 3, 1949, 1.

42. In May 1949 the *New York Times* reported that Hurley would soon be leaving Belgrade after "he performed an outstanding diplomatic job, according to Vatican sources." The same sources indicated that Hurley "might wish to return to his diocese in St. Augustine after nearly four years of intense work." In December 1952, when commenting on the severing of diplomatic relations between the Holy See and Yugoslavia, the *Cleveland Plain Dealer* indicated that Hurley had vacated his post "in June 1950 on sick leave." These reports are in line with Silvio Oddi's rendering of events in his published memoir. See "Papal Nuncio Likely to Leave Yugoslavia," *New York Times,* May 31, 1949; "Yugoslav Dictator Ousts Papal Envoy," *Cleveland Plain Dealer,* December 17, 1952; Silvio Oddi, *Il tenero mastino di Dio: Memorie del Cardinale Silvio Oddi* (Rome: Progetti museali editore, 1995), 53–57.

43. Joseph McGeough to Hurley, August 28, 1950, Hurley Papers, box 149 B, folder 19, ADSA; Oddi, *Il tenero mastino di Dio,* 53–57. I am grateful to Brian J. Gallagher for his assistance in translating Oddi's memoirs.

44. McGeough to Hurley, September 10, 1950, Hurley Papers, box 149 B, folder 26, ADSA.

45. Hyginus Eugene Cardinale, *Orders of Knighthood, Awards and the Holy See,* ed. Peter Bander van Duren (Gerrards Cross, U.K.: Van Duren, 1985), 57; Peter Bander van Duren, *Orders of Knighthood and Merit: The Pontifical, Religious and Secularized Catholic-founded Orders and their Relationship to the Apostolic See* (Gerrards Cross, U.K.: Colin Smythe, 1995), 105. Hurley's two fellow Americans behind the Iron Curtain followed upward paths. Gerald P. O'Hara was appointed nuncio to Ireland in 1951 and apostolic delegate to Great Britain in 1954. Aloisius Muench became a cardinal after his diplomatic tenure expired in 1959.

CHAPTER 10. STANDING ALONE BETWEEN CHURCH AND STATE

1. Monsignor John P. McNulty, interview with author, April 18, 1995; Hurley handwritten speech, n.d., NCWC Papers, Records of the General Secretary, series 10, box 26, folder 20, American Catholic History Research and University Archives, Catholic University of America.

2. Hurley to Mooney, September 17, 1946, AAD; Patrick Allitt, *Catholic Intellectuals and Conservative Politics in America, 1950–1985* (Ithaca: Cornell University Press, 1993), 24.

3. Richard Gid Powers, *Not without Honor: The History of American Anticommunism* (New York: Free Press, 1995), 51; Donald F. Crosby, S.J., "The Politics of Religion: American Catholics and the Anti-Communist Impulse," in *The Specter: Original Essays on the Cold War and the Origins of McCarthyism,* ed.

Robert Griffith and Athan Theoharis (New York: New Viewpoints, 1974), 20; John E. Haynes, *Red Scare or Red Menace? American Communism and Anticommunism in the Cold War Era* (Chicago: Ivan R. Dee, 1996), 95.

4. *Chicago Daily News,* December 6, 1951.

5. Monsignor Paul F. Tanner to Hurley, May 10, 1958, NCWC Papers, Records of the General Secretary, series 10, box 57, folder 4, American Catholic History Research and University Archives; Webb to American Embassy, Belgrade, December 7, 1951, General Records of the Department of State, RG 59, Records Relating to Yugoslavia, file 660 (Stepinac), USNA (released through USFOIA).

6. "Conversation with Ambassador Allen re *Chicago Daily News* Despatch from Belgrade," December 10, 1951, General Records of the Department of State, RG 59, Records Relating to Yugoslavia, file 660 (Stepinac), USNA; Belgrade to Secretary of State (telegram), December 10, 1951, ibid.; "Restricted Security Memorandum," December 10, 1951, ibid.

7. "The Strange Case of Ambassador Allen," *Florida Catholic,* December 14, 1951. The editorial was carried by the NCWC News Service on December 17, 1951. The words "forced conversion" were placed in quotes because Hurley knew that the forced conversion of Orthodox Serbs to Roman Catholicism was a major charge leveled against Archbishop Stepinac during his trial in 1946.

8. Hurley to Howard J. Carroll, February 5, 1952, NCWC Papers, Records of the General Secretary, series 10, box 27, folder 6, American Catholic History Research and University Archives.

9. Hurley to Paul F. Tanner, March 4, 1952, ibid.

10. "Our Problems in Yugoslavia," transcript, *Georgetown University Forum,* March 9, 1952, Edmund A. Walsh, S.J., Papers, box 5, folder 339, Special Collections, Georgetown University Library.

11. Memorandum of a Conversation, Howard J. Carroll and George V. Allen, March 17, 1952, General Records of the Department of State, RG 59, file 660 (Stepinac), USNA (released through USFOIA).

12. Rev. John J. Fitzpatrick, telegram to all cardinals, archbishops, and bishops, July 16, 1953, ADSA; *New York Times,* July 11, 1953. Stepinac had been elevated to cardinal by Pius XII on November 29, 1952. The Yugoslav government, regarding the elevation as a political snub, broke off formal diplomatic ties with the Vatican on December 16.

13. Nathaniel I. Berlin and Louis R. Wasserman, "Polycythemia Vera: A Retrospective and Reprise," *Journal of Laboratory and Clinical Medicine* 130 (1997): 366; "Stepinac: Hero or Collaborator?" *BBC News Europe,* October 3, 1998, http://news.bbc.co.uk/1/hi/world/europe/185761.stm (accessed June 19, 2005); *Our Sunday Visitor's Encyclopedia of Saints* (Huntington, Ind.: Our Sunday Visitor Press), s.v. "Aloysius Stepinac," 71. In 1952 the *Yale Journal of Biology and Medicine* published a groundbreaking article identifying the trigger for PRV as psychological stress. The study concluded that if a person

was placed in environmental conditions that increased mental stress, PRV could result. Since the Holy See refused to order Stepinac to leave Yugoslavia, the stressors of his condition in detention naturally worsened. See Berlin and Wasserman, "Polycythemia Vera," 366, 372.

14. Silvio Oddi's memoir reveals that Stepinac refused to leave Yugoslavia voluntarily, and would do so only if personally directed by the Pope. Hurley, of course, would not have supported such a move.

15. *New York Times,* July 19, 1953; NCWC Office of the General Secretary, memorandum, July 21, 1953, NCWC Papers, series 10, box 27, folder 3, American Catholic History Research and University Archives; John J. Fitzpatrick, telegram to all cardinals, archbishops, and bishops, July 16, 1953, Hurley Papers, ADSA.

16. Hurley to Eisenhower (undated telegram) and Hurley to Stepinac (undated telegram), Hurley Papers, ADSA.

17. U.S. Congress, Senate, Senator James E. Murray reading telegram concerning medical assistance for Cardinal Stepinac, 83d Cong., 1st sess., *Congressional Record* 99, pt. 7 (July 17, 1953): 9039; Hubert H. Humphrey to John J. Fitzpatrick, July 16, 1953 (copy), "Telegrams Received" Folder, Hurley Papers, ADSA; Wilton B. Persons to Leverett Saltonstall, July 23, 1953, White House Central Files: Confidential File, 228A, box 894: Stepinac, Truman Papers, Harry S. Truman Presidential Library, Independence, Mo.

18. Personal notes of John P. McNulty, n.d., Hurley Papers, ADSA.

19. Paul Carroll notes, July 20, 1953, White House Central Files: Official File, 228 and 228A, box 894: Stepinac, Truman Papers, Truman Library.

20. *New York Times,* July 26, 1953. Statistically, patients who contract polycethemia rubra vera survive an average of six to eight years after diagnosis. Stepinac lived another seven years. Lawrence never claimed that the P-32 treatment was more than a palliative. During the 1960s Lawrence's P-32 treatment came under scrutiny by some specialists who claimed that P-32 patients showed a higher susceptibility to contracting leukemia.

21. Gregg Herken, *Brotherhood of the Bomb: The Tangled Lives and Loyalties of Robert Oppenheimer, Ernest Lawrence, and Edward Teller* (New York: Henry Holt, 2002), 19; Department of Energy Oral Histories, "Human Radiation Studies: Remembering the Early Years," oral history of Donner Lab Administrator Baird D. Whaley, August 15, 1994, http://www.eh.doe.gov/ohre/roadmap/histories/0479/toc.html (accessed May 4, 2006).

22. *New York Times,* July 28, 1953.

23. Hurley to John H. Lawrence (undated telegram), Hurley Papers, ADSA; *New York Times,* July 26, 1953.

24. John H. Lawrence, "My Visit to Aloysius Cardinal Stepinac," report, John H. Lawrence Papers, BANC MSS 87/86, Bancroft Library, University of California, Berkeley.

25. "Restraint under Which Cardinal Forced to Live Given as Cause of Condition," NCWC News Service, August 3, 1953.

26. John J. Fitzpatrick [presumably Hurley] to Walworth Barbour, September 1, 1953, NCWC Papers, Records of the General Secretary, series 10, box 27, folder 3, American Catholic History Research and University Archives; Hurley personal notes, HAMC, reel 30.

27. Walter Bedell Smith to Howard Carroll, September 8, 1953, NCWC Papers, Records of the General Secretary, series 10, box 27, folder 3, American Catholic History Research and University Archives; Carroll to Bedell Smith, October 19, 1953, ibid.

28. John J. Fitzpatrick [presumably Hurley] to Bedell Smith, October 19, 1953, ibid.

29. Robert Murphy to John J. Fitzpatrick, June 4, 1954, ibid.

30. John J. Fitzpatrick [presumably Hurley] to Robert Murphy, June 28, 1954, ibid.

31. Ibid.

32. Robert D. Murphy to John J. Fitzpatrick, July 12, 1954, ibid.

33. The issue of contact between Hurley and McCarthy is a tantalizing one given Hurley's "betrayal" by the State Department in Belgrade in 1948. While there is no written evidence of personal contact between Hurley and McCarthy in any documents in Hurley's archive, complete verification is not possible, since McCarthy's Senate subject files and personal subject files for the period are still sealed as of this writing. There is, however, a copy of a May 1957 tribute by Hurley in McCarthy's official funeral clippings file. See Joseph R. McCarthy Papers, series 12, box 65, Department of Special Collections and University Archives, Marquette University.

Historian Patrick McNamara has expertly chronicled and analyzed the alleged Catholic connections to McCarthy's first ideas about using the issue of communist infiltration of government agencies for political purposes. McNamara de-emphasizes the 1950 assertions of journalist Drew Pearson that the Jesuit priest Edmund A. Walsh was the source of McCarthy's idea for a "crusade" against communists in the State Department. One of the stronger arguments downplaying Walsh's involvement with McCarthy was that the Jesuit never was known either to coach or to meet secretly with government officials or politicians—in contrast to Hurley. See Patrick McNamara, *A Catholic Cold War: Edmund A. Walsh, S.J., and the Politics of American Anticommunism* (New York: Fordham University Press, 2005), 157–160.

34. *Florida Catholic,* May 7, 1954.

35. John P. Burns as Chancellor, circular letter to diocesan priests, January 14, 1959, Hurley Papers, ADSA.

36. André Gerolymatos, *The Balkan Wars: Conquest, Revolution, and Retribution from the Ottoman Era to the Twentieth Century and Beyond* (New York: Basic Books, 2002), 48; "Mikoyan Visit Hit by Catholic Group," *Florida Times Union,* January 17, 1959.

37. *New York Times,* January 18, 1959; "Ike Asks Mikoyan Be Given Courtesy," *Florida Times Union,* January 9, 1959.

38. Hurley statement in *National Review,* September 12, 1959, 319; *National Review,* September 26, 1959 (cover); L. Brent Bozell to Archbishop Joseph P. Hurley (telegram), September 2, 1959, Hurley Papers, ADSA.

CHAPTER 11. LAST YEARS, FINAL STRUGGLES

1. Hurley [Belgrade] to McDonough, July 7, 1946, ADSA; Hurley notebook, "Miami Controversy, 1964," HAMC, reel 29; "Real Estate Purchased and in the Process of Being Purchased" [1950], box 151, ADSA.

2. *Moody's Bank and Finance Manual,* ed. John Sherman Porter (New York: D. B. McCruden, 1956), 345, 420.

3. Edward R. Kantowicz, *Corporation Sole: Cardinal Mundelein and Chicago Catholicism* (Notre Dame, Ind.: Notre Dame University Press, 1983), 38.

4. Hurley was particularly worried about the "undeveloped lands" located in the new Diocese of Miami. These lands included 200 acres of property at Golden Glades, 150 acres in northern Dade County, and the entire campus of what is now St. Thomas University in Miami. Hurley had also accumulated nearly 400 acres of undeveloped cemetery property in south Florida.

5. Daniel A. Naughton to John P. Burns, February 5, 1959, Hurley Papers, ADSA; "Meeting of the Delegates of the Diocese of St. Augustine and the Diocese of Miami, Held at St. Mary's Cathedral Rectory, Miami, February 17, 1959," HAMC, reel 31.

6. Quote attributed to Naughton (undated), Hurley's personal notebook, HAMC, reel 28.

7. Rev. Frank M. Mouch, e-mail message to author, March 30, 2007.

8. "1964 Notebook," HAMC, reel 29; personal notebook "For Keeping," ibid.

9. Hurley to Carlo Cardinal Confalonieri, March 4, 1965, HAMC, reel 31; "1964 Notebook," HAMC, reel 29; Hurley-Cicognani exchange in HAMC, reel 28.

10. Hurley to Carlo Cardinal Confalonieri, Secretary of the Sacred Consitorial Congregation, November 24, 1965, HAMC, reel 31; Hurley personal notebook "For Keeping," reel 29.

11. Giuseppe Alberigo, ed., *History of Vatican II* (Maryknoll, N.Y.: Orbis, 1995), 1; Philip Gleason, "Catholicism and Cultural Change in the 1960's," *Review of Politics* 34 (1972): 91–107.

12. Rev. Raymond E. Brown to author, August 7, 1996, audiocassette, in author's possession.

13. *Acta Synodalia Sacrosancti Concilii Oecumenici Vaticani II,* vol. 4, pt. 2 (Vatican City: Typis Polyglottis Vaticanis, 1977), 190.

14. "Anti-Semitism" personal notes, HAMC, reel 28.

15. Catholic source contemporary with events, interview with author, May 16, 1996.

16. Peter Hebblethwaite, *Pope John XXIII: Shepherd of the Modern World* (New York: Doubleday, 1985), 487; Hurley personal notebook, HAMC, reel 28.

17. Notebook II, 1964, HAMC, reel 29; Hurley personal notebook, HAMC, reel 28.

18. Rev. Frank M. Mouch, e-mail message to author, March 30, 2007.

19. David R. Colburn, *Racial Change and Community Crisis: St. Augustine, Florida, 1877–1980* (New York: Columbia University Press, 1985), 159.

20. Andrew Young quoted in Jack [Sisson] to Matt [Ahmann], memorandum, June 9, 1964, NCCIJ Papers, series 33, box 4, St. Augustine folder, Department of Special Collections and University Archives, Marquette University.

21. Colburn, *Racial Change and Community Crisis,* 173.

22. King quoted in ibid., 92.

23. King to Hurley (telegram), June 11, 1964, Hurley Papers, ADSA.

24. Jack P. Sisson to Matthew Ahmann, memorandum, June 17, 1964, NCCIJ Papers, series 33, box 4, St. Augustine folder, Department of Special Collections and University Archives, Marquette University; text of Hurley telegram to King contained in Rev. Irvine Nugent to Rev. John P. Burns, June 18, 1964, Hurley Papers, ADSA.

25. Charles R. Gallagher, "The Catholic Church, Martin Luther King, Jr., and the March in St. Augustine," *Florida Historical Quarterly* 83 (2004): 149–172.

26. Michael J. McNally, *Catholic Parish Life on Florida's West Coast, 1860–1968* (St. Petersburg, Fla.: Catholic Media Ministries, 1996), 399.

27. Hurley diaries, notebook Z8, under heading "Moral Softness," Hurley Papers, ADSA. Yale historian John Lewis Gaddis argues that Pope John Paul II triggered the fall of modern communism when he arrived in Poland on June 2, 1979, and made a universal call for human rights based on a fundamental understanding of innate human dignity. This was one element of what Gaddis calls "the intangibles" of real power. See John Lewis Gaddis, *The Cold War* (London: Allen Lane, 2006), 193–196.

28. Hurley diary, n.d., HAMC, reel 28.

29. "Archbishop Joseph P. Hurley, R.I.P.," *National Review* 19 (November 1967): 1251.

30. "Requiem Mass for Florida's Archbishop Hurley," NCWC News Service, November 6, 1967, NCWC Papers, Obituary Files, American Catholic History Research and University Archives, Catholic University of America.

31. Rev. Frank M. Mouch, e-mail message to author, March 30, 2007.

INDEX

Acheson, Dean, 176–177, 184, 199
addetto, 46, 47
Akkido, Harry, 43
Alerte!, 22
Alexander, Stella, 158, 166, 188
Allen, George V., 189–190, 198–201
Allitt, Patrick, 197
Alter, Karl J., 202
Alvarez, David J., 30
America, 115, 118, 123, 127
American bishops conference. *See* National Catholic Welfare Conference (NCWC)
American Catholic church: and Americanization, 2, 4, 13, 22, 83; and anticommunism, 197; and Bishop's Draft to Pius XII, 137–139; and Coughlin, 52, 59–62; diocesan investment practices of, 214, 215; harmony of spirit between Church and United States, 5, 79, 113, 129–130, 226–227; isolationism of, 101–103, 114–115, 114–123, 135; and Mikoyan's U.S. visit, 210; on patriotism and military combat, 13, 14–15; response to Hurley's interventionist speech, 123–130; response to Jewish persecution, 240n23, 257n36, 257n37; and Stepinac, 189–190, 199–201, 204; Vatican fi-
nances and, 110–111. *See also* Cleveland Diocese; Miami Diocese; National Catholic Welfare Conference (NCWC); St. Augustine Diocese
Americanism, 4, 13, 18, 22, 53, 56, 69–70, 89, 92, 102
Americanization, 2, 4, 13, 22, 83
American Red Cross, 96
antisemitism: Coughlin and, 50–51, 57, 58–62, 69–70; Farinacci and, 62–64; Hurley and, 20–22, 69–70, 146, 149–150, 219, 225, 241n37; Jesuits and, 16–17, 146; *Nostra Aetate* (In Our Times) and, 219; Stepinac and, 167
"Anti-Semitism: Our Problem" (Hurley), 149–150
apostolic delegates, 30
archbishop *ad personam*, 194
Arendt, Hannah, 16
Army Intelligence Corps, 156
Athans, Mary Christine, 56–57
athleticism, 17–18
Atkins, Clyde, 215–216

Barbour, Walworth, 206
Beckman, Francis J. L., 124, 135
Bedell Smith, Walter, 203, 204, 206–207
Bérard, Léon, 147

275

Poland: Catholic refugees in, 95–97; Hitler's invasion of, 77; Hurley's speech about Nazi occupation of, 118–120

Pollard, John, 110–111

Popovic, Vladimir, 203, 204

Powers, John M., 27–28

Protocols of the Elders of Zion, 57

Pucci, Enrico, 67

Putney, Clifford, 17

Quigley, Martin, 85, 154

Radio Priest: Charles Coughlin, the Father of Hate Radio (Warren), 57

Randall, Alec, 30

Ready, Michael J., 120, 137–139, 141–142

Reagan, Ronald, 227

Reams, Robert Borden, 181–182, 183–184

Record, The (Louisville), 117

Reed, Edward L., 107

regency, 155–156

Rerum Novarum (Leo XIII), 14

Ribbentrop, Joachim von, 8–9

Roosevelt, Franklin D.: appointment of Taylor as representative to the Vatican, 9–10, 93–95; and Cardinal Pacelli (Pope Pius XII), 87–88; and Coughlin, 50, 51–52, 53, 65–66, 67–70; and Hurley, 82–83, 114; Neutrality Act speech by, 81–83; plan to use Vatican to keep Italy neutral, 71–73; and proposal to send Hurley to Ireland, 141; and proposal to send Hurley to South America, 134, 135; theology of war argument, 113; and Vatican refugee relief for Poland, 96–97

Rozman, Gregorij, 187–188

Ruddy, T. Michael, 5

Ruzic, John F., 204–206

Ryan, Daniel J., 156–157

Rychlak, Ronald J., 23

Sacred Heart devotion, 100

St. Augustine (Florida): King and Civil Rights movement in, 220–222; World War II economic crisis in, 143–146

St. Augustine Diocese: division of, 215–218; history of, 109–110; Hurley's appointment as bishop of, 105, 109–110, 111–112; and Mikoyan's visit to Florida, 210; real estate investments of, 213–215; Requiem Mass for Hurley in, 224

St. Bernard's Seminary, 19–22

St. Ignatius College, 16–18

St. Mary's Seminary, 22–23

Salic, Ivan, 179

Saltonstall, Leverett, 203

Sánchez, José, 148

Schmitz, Davis, 71

Schrembs, Joseph, 24–25, 26, 43–44, 45

Secretariat of State: and Coughlin, 61–62, 68–70; Hurley's diplomatic style, 30–31, 39, 40–41, 90–91, 160; Hurley's early career at, 44–48

Shantz, Harold, 178

Sheehy, Maurice, 134

Shirer, William, 8

Sigismondi, Pietro, 192

Silvershirts, 57

Sinclair-Loutit, Kenneth, 185

Sisters of Charity crisis, 164–165

Slovene Priests' Association, 187

Smith, Gaddis, 143–144

Smith, Gerald L. K., 57

Social Justice, 51, 57, 64, 69, 127

Society of Jesus (Jesuits), 16–18, 146

Sophia University, 38–39

sostituto, 44–45

Southern Christian Leadership Conference (SCLC), 220–222

Soviet Union: Hurley's protest against Mikoyan's U.S. tour, 209–212; and isolationism, 101; and Japan, 34; Lend-Lease aid to, 132; and Vatican-U.S. diplomacy, 153, 161, 197; and Yugoslavia, 181–183, 186

Spellman, Francis J., 46, 124–125, 189

Stalin, Joseph, 181–183

State Department. *See* U.S. Department of State

Stepinac, Aloysius, 166–174; American Catholic church and, 189–190, 199–201, 204; and antisemitism, 167; "Archbishop's Memorandum" by, 178–181; arrest of, 171–173; and charges of Nazi collaboration, 166–167, 169, 176–181,